SO-BJL-952

Religious Separation
and Political Intolerance
in Bosnia-Herzegovina

RELIGIOUS SEPARATION AND POLITICAL INTOLERANCE IN BOSNIA-HERZEGOVINA

By Mitja Velikonja

*Translated from Slovenian
by Rang'ichi Ng'inja*

TEXAS A&M UNIVERSITY PRESS
College Station

The paper used in this book meets the minimum
requirements of the American National Standard for
Permanence of Paper for Printed Library Materials,
z39.48-1984. Binding materials have been chosen for
durability.
∞

LIBRARY OF CONGRESS
CATALOGING-IN-PUBLICATION DATA

Velikonja, Mitja.
    Religious separation and political intolerance in
Bosnia-Herzegovina / by Mitja Velikonja ; translated
from Slovenian by Rang'ichi Ng'inja. — 1st ed.
        p. cm. — (Eastern European studies ; no. 20)
    Includes bibliographical references (p.   ) and
index.
    ISBN 1-58544-226-7
    1. Religion and state—Bosnia and Herzegovina—
History. 2. Ethnicity—Bosnia and Herzegovina—
History. 3. Ethnicity—Religious aspects—History.
4. Bosnia and Herzegovina—Religion.   I. Title.
II. Series: Eastern European studies (College Station,
Tex.) ; no. 20.
BL980.Y83V45 2003
322'.1'0949742—dc21

2002012709

TO ELENA,
with love, respect, and gratitude

CONTENTS

MAPS

TABLES

ACKNOWLEDGMENTS

This book is based on one that was published in Slovenian, my mother tongue: *Bosanski religijski mozaiki: Religije in nacionalne mitologije v zgodovini Bosne in Hercegovine* (Ljubljana: Znanstveno in publicistično središče, 1998). The present version has been revised and enlarged, and includes new data and references to relevant studies that have been published since it first appeared in print.

I would like to thank my colleagues and friends who contributed in different ways to this book. First among them are Aleš Debeljak and Marjan Smrke of the University of Ljubljana School of Social Sciences, who provided friendly encouragement, expert advice, understanding, and inspiration. I would also like to extend my gratitude to the reviewers of the manuscript, Stjepan Meštrović of Texas A&M University, and Paul Mojzes of Rosemont College, Pennsylvania, for their most careful reading of the text. Equally important were short, though highly important, discussions I had with Ivo Žanić of the University of Zagreb School of Political Sciences, Xavier Bougarel of the Department for Turkish and Ottoman Studies at the Centre National de la Recherche Scientifique in Paris, and Radmila Radić of the Institute for Recent History of Serbia in Belgrade. These scholars helped me gain valuable insights and access to new horizons in regard to the most complicated issues my book seeks to address. My thanks also go to Sandra Bašić-Hrvatin of the University of Ljubljana School of Social Sciences, who read and commented on my first draft of the manuscript. I truly appreciate all of the well-intentioned comments and stimulating remarks I received while writing this book. In addition, I am most grateful to Rang'ichi Ng'inja for his speedy and accurate translation, and the patience he displayed with both the author and the text.

Finally, I wish to thank Douglas Challenger of Franklin Pierce College, New Hampshire, who kindly put me in touch with this publishing house; Jože Pintar for drawing the accompanying maps; and Celia Hawkesworth of the University of London School of Slavonic and East European Studies for translating most of the verses and slogans from Serbian, Croatian, and Bosnian.

Financial assistance from the Republic of Slovenia Ministries of Science and Technology and Culture made possible this book's translation. The Slovenian Scientific Foundation and the University of Ljubljana Dean's Fund and School of Social Sciences provided additional support for research. I am most grateful to all these institutions and the individuals involved. This project could not have been accomplished without their support.

Religious Separation
and Political Intolerance
in Bosnia-Herzegovina

INTRODUCTION
A Land of Dreams and Nightmares

The ominous calm that rests upon Bosnia-Herzegovina, a ravaged land strewn with the embers of war, offers its inhabitants little more than a life of spiri-

> *Weak and fragile is the kingdom where a single language is spoken and a single tradition prevails.*
>
> —STEPHEN I (SAINT STEPHEN), KING OF HUNGARY (CA. 975–1038), CA. 1030

tual and material desolation at best, and a resumption of the carnage at worst. A nostalgia born of bewilderment for that which has been lost is passed on with bitter self-irony and enhanced by a dark premonition of what tomorrow might bring. When, why, and under whose leadership did it all come crumbling down? How fateful is the implication of epic and religious figures, national mythologies, and monotheistic doctrines, and what is the share of their guilt or innocence? Are the answers from the past also a harbinger of the future? These are some of the questions to which I sought answers during my research on the religious and mythological past and present of Bosnia-Herzegovina and South Slavs in general.

Indeed, researchers of the narrative and contemporary dynamics of the religious and national mythology of South Slavs have been shocked by the tragic events taking place in our close vicinity and in the midst of people we have known, by the scenario of their sanguine premiere several decades ago and again, only recently, by "the diabolical synchronization of the pen and the rifle butt, their bloodstained and functional symbiosis," to borrow a poignant expression from Sarajevo historian Dubravko Lovrenović.[1] To me, the incredible expansion of literature on the Balkans, the former Yugoslavia, and Bosnia-Herzegovina over the last few years means that the time has come for the scientific elucidation of issues that in the past were regarded as having been "settled"; the cross-examination of and confrontation with different analyses and discoveries; and associative, synthetic socio-historical discussions that preserve the diversity of opinion regarding the past, present, and future of South Slavic nations. These new revelations are a proper addition to and deepening of the numerous previous publications in Yugoslavia and around the world, which conformed to scientific criteria for impartiality, criticism, and comparison.

This topic has not aroused the interest of the social sciences and humanities—from history and anthropology to psychology and sociology—merely because of the bloodshed in that part of the world. A new necropolis in the body of Europe has fastened us to our television screens and sent social scientists rushing back to their dusty textbooks and to study new ones. There is another reason for this engrossment: the concepts we come across daily that have never been truly and completely elucidated. Concepts such as religious affiliation, national identity, historical myths, religious war, and so forth have again become the subject of heated arguments, disputes, and conflicts.

These loosely defined concepts have been more of a tool for political choice than a subject of scientific contemplation for South Slavs over the last two centuries; more a battle between politicians—where the most cunning, most ruthless, and strongest player reaps the transient victory—than a battle of wits that has no final victor and whose only meaning is dialogue and discussion. The result is that these concepts have been subjected over the last two centuries more to political rather than to scientific elaboration. Moreover, the latter was often replaced by politically apologetic, pseudo-professional instant theories. Perhaps the time has finally come when, in studying the challenging complexities of these delicate social phenomena and processes—religions, national mythologies, national and political histories, and mentalities—we are finally able to distinguish between erstwhile confusing concepts such as myths and history, religion and science, faith and knowledge, poetry and politics; to treat each one individually and, having thus set the stage, investigate and identify their dimensions, interrelationship, and advocates; and to introduce historical dimension into the study of contemporary social phenomena that otherwise often suffer from ahistorical, static explanations.

My research on the history of the religions and national mythologies of Bosnia-Herzegovina repeatedly pointed at the internal diversity of the periods, phenomena, problems, and conflicts under discussion. I came across no single explanations, no unanimity among authors—not only on the interpretation of facts, but also on the facts themselves. Because of the complexity of the events in Bosnia-Herzegovina and their dependence on events beyond its borders, I have had to expound on the religious and national issues of the countries and empires surrounding Bosnia-Herzegovina or of which it was a part, and of its neighboring nations, Serbia and Croatia. To this end, I have discussed the religious circumstances of the medieval Bosnian history, four centuries of Ottoman rule, four decades of Austro-Hungarian rule, the Karađorđević monarchy, the Second World War (when Bosnia-Herzegovina was annexed by Croatia), socialist Yugoslavia (when it became a "Socialist Republic"), and, finally, of the independent, internationally recognized but internally divided country that was established in 1992. The book thus follows the historical sequence of events chronologically, except in chapter 4, which synchronously discusses the evolution of the religio-national mythologies of the Serbs and Croats.

I have also considered sociological dimensions by analyzing quotations, statements, syntax, poems, slogans, messages, obituaries, and speech excerpts of religious dignitaries, politicians, military commanders, writers, and other public figures. I have also used statistical data, censuses, and the estimates and results from accessible and relevant public opinion surveys. Finally, I focused on a number of notorious events, personalities, and far-reaching episodes, comparing their mythical elaboration and transformation in stories that left their indelible imprint on history and today's national and religious communities. I tried to analyze and reach conclusions on the basis of a wide spectrum of sources written by authors from these countries and abroad and also from different historical periods. However, a complete history of the religious dynamics and national mythologies of Bosnia-Herzegovina has yet to be written.

Bosnia-Herzegovina was a stage for encounters, confrontations, symbiosis, transition and/or conflict between different religions, national mythologies, and concepts of statehood. I offer herein some basic views and answers to the questions mentioned earlier, and I try to elucidate some aspects that are less or insufficiently presented in other studies of this specific and controversial field. The most important of these are: relations between the religious and national identities of the peoples of Bosnia-Herzegovina; the gradual formation of national mythologies within and around that country; the religious elements of national mythologies; and, finally, the role of religious communities, institutions, rhetoric, and clergymen in the everyday life of the people as well as in the most fateful events of Bosnian history.

In this book I analyze the history of the religions and mythologies that slowly molded the national identities and political options of Bosnia-Herzegovina. I also explore the processes by which religious-cultural and ethnic identities and borders were gradually transformed into mainly national ones by considering how, why, and when the predominately religious and cultural self-consciousness of the Bosnian peoples was transformed into a national (and political) one;[2] the principal actors in the transformation process; if it was a homegrown or imported initiative; and under what conditions transformation came to pass. An equally important question I shall attempt to answer is that of religious nationalism or national clericalism.

An investigation into the history of the mosaics of religions and national mythologies within and around Bosnia-Herzegovina as a microcosm of the entire Balkan Peninsula cannot overlook several nonreligious factors that continue to mutually permeate, sequester, mold, or deny these religions to the present day. As such, I felt compelled to consider related political dimensions of these events, as much within Bosnia-Herzegovina's borders as beyond them—especially the emergence of religious and national mythologies in both Serbia and Croatia, and the religious and political history, cultural and social development, and territorial and administrative divisions of those neighboring states.

Myths remain very important and persuasive elements in the construction of reality in contemporary complex societies, self-defined as "disenchanted" or "enlightened" in most different fields—from politics to popular culture, from global questions to everyday life, from national and religious identities to cultural ones. As American sociologist Robert Bellah stated, "the separation of church and state has not denied the political realm of religious dimension."[3] If we limit ourselves only to the "profanized" twentieth century, we find mythic constructs, religious rhetoric, and archaic iconography at different times and in different parts of the world. Many nations have perceived themselves as being *Holy, Sacred, Heavenly; as the Christ among nations, as the Most Ancient,* even as the *Elected,* or on a *God-given mission* to fulfill. Other examples include self-declared *warrants of democracy* or *cultured nations;* military campaigns labeled as *crusades;* dictators being glorified as *sent* (or *chosen*) *by God Himself,* or as the *incorporation of the Will of the Nation.* Politicians often refer to religious tradition and values and swear before God at their inauguration. The struggle of the proletariat against the ruling classes was interpreted in terms of a cosmic struggle between *Good and Evil. Holy Wars* were fought in different parts of the world by different religious fundamentalists. The *cleansing* of their different enemies was constitutive for many new states and regimes. An *'Eternal Allies'* versus *Eternal Enemies'* opposition could be found on many of the warring sides, as could the notion of the *Last Bastion* of the religion or *civilization* in question. Borders were perceived as *sacred, historic,* and *untouchable,* and enemies were often demonized, animalized, or bestialized.[4]

I consider mythology as a dynamic, internally cohesive, but continually changing system of individual myths that has some very practical functions and goals to achieve in society.[5] It is "a key element in the creation of closures and in the constitution of collectivities."[6] In some instances it is political discourse, although being told in a poetic way. In other words, "myths are not banal descriptions of the desired society but calls for action."[7] As such, mythology has three main functions, which are evident also in contemporary societies: integrative (it includes inward and excludes outward); cognitive (it explains most important past and present events and foretells future ones); and communicative (it provides specific mythic rhetoric and syntagma).

Myths can, in my opinion, be divided into two large, paradigmatic and ideal-typical groups that are strongly dialectically interacted. "Traditional myths" are those found in premodern forms of constructed social reality: folk traditions, old rituals, sacralized persons, objects and episodes, epics, ancient tales, sets of symbols, legends, beliefs, and so forth. They gaze into the past and try to explain important historical events (the origins and creation of a certain group, great leaders, hardship, "eternal" truths), and are characterized by the fact that they are "incomplete," "unfinished," and are forever characterized by an exegetical deficit. Or, as Claude Lévi-Strauss puts it, "since it has no interest in definite beginnings or endings, mythological thought never develops any theme to completion: there is always something left unfinished." In short, they are "interminable."[8]

On the other hand, "ideological myths" complement the original exegesis of traditional myths: they provide particular conclusions to their "openness." Unlike the former, ideological myths gaze into the future and solicit changes, innovation, and transfiguration—but on ancient foundations. The ideological myth complements and elucidates the deficiency of the traditional myth. The actuality and flexibility of contemporary mythology is guaranteed by the ideological evocations of ancient myths. In other words, the traditional myth lends legitimacy to the ideological myth, whereas ideological myth complements the incompletion of the traditional myth. Mythology is a dynamic and dialectic process in constant motion and encompasses both.

TABLE I-I **Differences between traditional and ideological myths**

Traditional myths	Ideological myths
relative permanence	variability, transience
authority	dictation
static, latent	active, pretentious
reconciliation, justification	attack on the existing order
satisfaction	dissatisfaction
orientation	conduction
spontaneous, unconscious creation	systematic, reflexive, and intentional contemplation
socializing	resocializing

A few of the more typically presented differences between traditional and ideological myths that complement mythology as a whole are listed in table I-1.

Whereas the traditional myth is familiar to all or most of the members of a given society, the ideological myth is the projection of a small interest group that is chained to the past but decisively pointing toward the future. It is important to note that traditional myths do not necessarily anticipate antagonism, conflict, violence, or crime; they can also be used, in conjunction with and complemented by ideological myths, as an excuse for such. So, in terms of exegesis, mobilization, and initiative, the ideological myth is a far more important part of mythology than traditional myth. Another important contradictory, but complementary feature concerns the authorship of myths: whereas it is next to impossible to determine the authorship of ancient, traditional myths, the authors and advocates of ideological myths are usually readily identified (political parties, religious organizations, charismatic leaders). In the past, a period of several decades or centuries was required before a certain myth was accepted or rejected and forgotten. The process is much quicker and more acrimonious today.

Mythology thus synthesizes the inertness of traditional myths and the innovativeness of ideological myths; the conservatism and introversive nature of the former and the aggressiveness, dynamism, and expansionism of the latter. The traditional myth reveals ancient wounds that are nursed by ideological prescriptions. The main characteristics of mythology are an expressive, passionate, and suggestible modification of events; arbitrary interchanging of circumstances and figures; the mobilization of the collective memory and social strengths; a dramatization of events; and substitution of the general with the particular and the particular with the general. Mythological existence knows no temporal constraints: actual historical events or figures were often equated, not merely compared, with examples from the past. Mythologies—in this case national and religious—that seek historical explanation reveal more than the mere fact itself but the conditions, their creators, and promoters, as well as the public and the interests of the mythmakers. From their ahistorical perspective, nations, countries, and religious organizations have always represented stable entities, unchanging through the centuries, existing in some kind of "eternal present."

Italian essayist and writer Claudio Magris notes that the ambivalence of each myth lies in its ability to portray "a bit more and a bit less than is the fact."[9] It furnishes this diminished picture with new elements and dimensions. The comprehension of a historical or actual event can very easily slip into myth. The amorphousness of historical events and political interests presents innumerable possibilities for the mythical comprehension and ideological transformation of the past and present. In other words, the myth "trims" the ramifications and complexity of a historical event and offers in its place a simplified portrayal. I agree with Romanian-American social scientist Vladimir Tismaneanu, who approaches myth not "as a necessarily mendacious vision of reality but as a narrative that is able to inspire collective loyalties, affinities, passions, and actions." For him, "the value of myth is that it mobilizes and energizes the infrarational segments of political behavior."[10]

1

BOSNIA'S RELIGIOUS AND MYTHOLOGICAL WATERSHED

We belong to no-one, always on a frontier, always subject to God-knows whose heritage. . . . We live on the dividing line between worlds, on the frontiers between peoples, exposed to all and sundry, always in someone's way. Our backs are the shoals that break the waves of history.

—MEŠA SELIMOVIĆ, "DERVISH AND THE DEATH"

The perception of national identity in eastern, central, and southern Europe was different from that of western and northern Europe and emerged at a much later date. Whereas a specific historical course of events in the former resulted in the prevalence of the territorial-political concept of the nation-state, the east was more heavily influenced by linguistic, cultural, and religious considerations. There was, however, a very big difference between the way national identity was perceived by individual South Slavic peoples themselves: it emerged first among the Serbs, Croats, and Bulgarians, and developed from medieval traditions of statehood *(translatio imperii).* The identity of the Slovenians that first appeared during the Protestant reformation and later in the late eighteenth century and throughout the nineteenth century was based principally on their linguistic and cultural dissimilarity. The Montenegrins identified themselves as the unconquered nation in the midst of a vastly superior adversary. For the Macedonians and Bosnian Muslims, the evolution of a national identity was—besides some clear linguistic-cultural characteristics for the first and religious-cultural characteristics for the latter—to a large degree a response to the territorial appetites of their neighbors in the late nineteenth century and especially in recent decades.

Religion is generally considered to be one of the earliest and most fundamental forms of collective distinction. Religious dimension also represents one of the most important factors in the creation of national consciousness and politics, especially in the absence of other, more compelling, factors. Indeed, religious dimension is considered one of the most enduring factors, persisting even when other factors weaken and vanish. Churches and religious organizations, as institutionalized manifestations of religions, are social and political entities and, as such, play an important role in the creation and survival of a nation, often providing transcendental goals for the political process. Religious differences play a greater role in the shaping of national identity in those states where religious heterogeneity was and is prevalent.

This book, which examines the history of the religions and national mythologies of Bosnia-Herzegovina, shall focus among other issues on the tension between religious universalism and particularism. An important invariable quantity that must be considered when examining the religious history of South Slavs is the merging of the concept of nation with that of religion. That is, the "nationalization of religions" or the subjection of religious universalisms to tribal or ethnic ideas. In general, religion has always been more of a representation of tradition and collective (national, social, political, even military) action than of individual faith, judgment, choice, and devotion. However, it is important to understand that similar cases exist elsewhere in central and eastern Europe: Polish Catholicism in the midst of Russian Orthodoxy and German Protestantism; during the German diaspora in Hungary and Romania, Lutheranism was considered to be *their* religion; Presbyterianism in Hungary was named the "Hungarian religion" as opposed to Habsburg Catholicism; the emergence of the National Church of Czechoslovakia after the establishment of the country; Romanians and *their* Orthodox religion, and so forth.[1] This logic is quite opposite from the concept of "civil religion," developed by late-eighteenth-century enlighteners or, for example, by the "founding fathers" of the United States, for whom it was not "ever felt to be a substitute for Christianity."[2]

Historian Adrian Hastings points out that "the Bible, moreover, presented in Israel itself a developed model of what it means to be a nation—a unity of people, language, religion, territory and government."[3] In the Balkans, historical and contemporary developments were interpreted in religious terms: analogies were made between contemporaries and episodes and personalities from the Scriptures or the religious history of their own nation. Pedro Ramet cites five crucial reasons for the "marriage" between religion and nationalism: religion represents the historical essence of culture; religion is a symbol of collective identity and distinguishes one people from another; the avant-garde role of religious groups in the development of a national language and literature; the leading role in society assumed by the clergy because of their education, prominence, and political awareness; and the conviction that the religion of a group of people—as opposed to a neighboring people or religion—is theirs alone.[4] National religious messianism strengthens the bond between national identity and religion.

THE INTERMEDIACY OF BOSNIA-HERZEGOVINA

There can be no doubt as to the historical legitimacy of Bosnia-Herzegovina—a land which, more so than any of its neighbors, is characterized by extreme religious changes. Bosnia-Herzegovina constitutes "a historical entity which has its own identity and its own history" that has been shared by people of all its religious denominations.[5] Across the ages, its borders have been more consistent and received wider recognition than those of Serbia or Croatia. These two neighbors have, indeed, occupied parts of its territory, but only for brief periods of time and, as such, cannot make substantial historical claims against Bosnia-Herzegovina. The Serbian and Croatian national identity of the Bosnian Orthodox and Catholic population is more recent than Bosnian, because it only emerged—as will be discussed in subsequent chapters—in the second half of the nineteenth century. Bosnian Serbs and Croats thus have "unique and distinctive features that are not identical to the national cultures of the matrix countries" Serbia and Croatia.[6]

Bosnia-Herzegovina's foremost disposition was and is its universal heterogeneity. This diversity *(šarolikost)* was well represented in Bosnia's prevalent and intricate religious and national structure which—on several occasions in the course of history—proved to be a potential cause of strife. Because individual religious organizations served also as national and political organizations, religious identity usually became synonymous with national and political identity. Starting mainly in the second half of nineteenth century, the behavior and train of thought of the clergy and laity resulted in and reflected the close relationship between the religion and nationality of the three largest communities living in Bosnia-Herzegovina, although the relationships between them were quite different. As a rule, an examination of the association between religion and nationality must always consider the great diametrical differences that characterized the history of these relationships and which have remained to the present day.

Ibrahim Bakić, a Bosnian expert on religio-national relations mentions seven primary reasons for the likening between religion and nationality in that country. First, many pagan aspects acquired a religious and national character. Second is the predominately folkish character of religious life ("ethno-religious" traditions). The third and fourth reasons are the gradual development of secular national institutions and the evolution of social life through religion, and a predominately rural culture in which religious and national institutions were readily interchangeable. The fifth reason is the predominately religious content of cultural output. Sixth, religion is the origin of historical, cultural, and political mythology. Finally, the belated separation of ecclesiastic and national phraseology and the constant interference of religion in society and politics.[7] This immoderate blending of religious and national identity illustrates the impact of religion on the majority of South Slavs, especially in Bosnia-Herzegovina: it has been an important factor in preserving ethnic and cultural identity, and it has obstructed any form of ethnic development independent of religion.[8]

The intermediacy of Bosnia-Herzegovina—lying between great religious and cultural areas of Europe (Western and Eastern Christianity and Islam and their cultures, social organizations, and mentalities)—always exerted an important influence on the internal events of this mountainous country. Over the centuries, territorial divisions in its vicinity invariably resulted in division within the country itself. The Drina River, for example, served as a demarcation line between the Eastern and Western Roman Empires rendered by Theodosius I in the fourth century. Later, the central and eastern Balkans served as the stage of conflicts between the Germanic Ostrogoths (who adopted *Aryan heresis, Arriana Haeresis*) and the "orthodox" Byzantines during the sixth century; after 1054 between Eastern and Western Christendom; between Christian and Ottoman Europe from the fourteenth to the late nineteenth/early twentieth centuries; and between the prevailing Catholic Habsburg Empire and the small aspiring Orthodox Slavic states in the southern Balkans. It also was the stage for the encounter between the nationalist concepts of Greater Serbia and Greater Croatia on one hand, and the aspirations of Muslim Slavs and the Yugoslav idea on the other. Another important factor contributing to the specificity of these events is the remoteness and impenetrability of Bosnia-Herzegovina, which hindered passage through parts of the territory. Consequently, direct interference and external control were greatly limited.

Between the fourteenth and early twentieth centuries, the Balkans became the battlefield on which Christian and Islamic states and civilizations clashed. Bosnia-Herzegovina found itself in the midst of this turmoil. However (with the exception of the twentieth century), despite the high level of religious pluralism and dynamism, frequent changes, and occasional tension, Bosnia was able to avoid the kind of religious antagonism and keen conflicts that were characteristic of other European countries.[9] The religious history of Bosnia is therefore a history of religious division as well as religious coexistence. This Bosnian peculiarity must be given full consideration when examining the history of its religions and national mythologies.

A complex approach and an open mind must be adopted when examining the field of religion: we cannot limit ourselves to doctrine, theology, and dogma but must consider the changing social, cultural, and political ramifications as well. We cannot simply accept the official version; we must also consider specific reception and transformation. We must look beyond inherently universal religious aspirations and examine local and national usurpation, reinterpretation, and "domestication." Both the "true faith" and the "heresies" must be examined. In other words, we must consider both mainstream religions and the alternatives; orthodoxies and heterodoxies, or—in Bellah's words—"various deformations and demonic distorsions."[10] The origins of important aspects of the identity and day-to-day life of the majority of South Slavs can be traced to their religious and mythological tradition: from personal names and surnames to collective symbology; from cultural templates to culinary customs, apparel, and behavior. In short, we are dealing with a mutual, almost indistinguishable conglomerate of religious, cultural, mythical, national, and political attributes blended with characteristics arising from everyday life. The differentiation of all these fields in Bosnia-Herzegovina was—in comparison to neighboring countries—very slow and recent.

The individual religious and national communities in Bosnia-Herzegovina developed in close association and interaction with each other. According to Francine Friedman, "national identification in this area of the world escapes the religious factor only with great difficulty."[11] From the second half of the nineteenth century, the evolution of the three major national groups in Bosnia-Herzegovina was strongly influenced by three major religions—Islam, Orthodoxy, and Roman Catholicism—the first (but not only) lines of division during the evolution and development of the national groups. Religious affiliation and nationalism often proved to be convenient bedfellows and drew strength from each other.

Religious affiliation became the badge of nationalism and nationalism became a "sacred duty." This principle was also adopted by and defined the roles of the religious hierarchies, which more often than not conformed to the prevailing behavioral trends in their national communities.

Another important and common characteristic pertaining to religious practice in Bosnia-Herzegovina was its synthetic and eclectic nature. This resulted in the evolution of heterodoxy rather than religious orthodoxy. Different religious beliefs and features often mixed and merged, new religious elements appeared, customs were borrowed from neighboring religions, on so forth. Another characteristic is religious conversions. Balkanologist Harry Thirlwall Norris discovered several factors connected to this frequent praxis that can be applied also to Bosnia-Herzegovina: for example, a low level of religious (doctrinal) education and the superficiality of conversions.[12]

There were, however, several crucial cultural, economic, political, and other differences between the religious communities. During times of hardship, people of the same faith would combine forces, sometimes with faraway coreligionists with whom they had little in common. Another peculiarity of this region was the endless antagonism between the higher and lower ranks of the clergy, and between different currents within one religion. Furthermore, religious martyrs in the Balkans corresponded to national and political martyrs: the "great men" (politicians, military commanders, religious leaders) were often given religious as well as national eminence for their service to "God and Country."

As a rule, religious institutions pursued an internal policy of integration and assimilation while displaying exclusivity and hostility externally. From the eighteenth century the religious and cultural dissimilarities of South Slavs—in Bosnia-Herzegovina from the mid-nineteenth century—became the most important basis for the development of nationhood, resulting in (forcible) conversions and the slaughter of "enemies and traitors of the faith" and, therefore, of the nation. Due to the identification of the national with the religious-cultural identity, wider or local interreligious tensions and intolerance resulted in the spread of hatred between these nations.

Orthodox churches are, as a rule, autocephalous and are based on a nation-state principle. This autocephalic concept was formed in contrast to the Roman popes' absolutist claims of primacy. According to the Council of Calcedon in 451, the borders of church organization are—ideal-typically—the same as those of the state (a practice that was always difficult to achieve and often led to serious conflicts).[13] Although they cannot change religious Orthodox doctrines, they have jurisdictional and administrative autonomy and their bishops are elected by synods. Despite the existence of "national" elements and connotations in the history of the Orthodox churches, its theology remained as uniform and universalistic as Catholicism or Islam. However, they lack the international organization of the other two mentioned religious communities.

Historical experience has taught Orthodox churches that survival often demands flexibility and political complacence, and they have learned to support the regime even when it is autocratic, non-Orthodox, or atheistic.[14] They are, in other words, wont to the whims and unpredictability of politics and politicians. We need only remember examples from Tsarist or Soviet Russia and from the Ottoman Empire. The Orthodox concept of *ethelodouleia* means voluntary subordination to political power (the sultan's authority for example).[15] This Orthodox tradition of reverence to political leaders dates from the Byzantine period. The state was the domain of God, and the king and the patriarch harmoniously led God's people in fulfilling God's will. In line with the established typology of relationship between the church and the state, the Orthodox Church held the "absolutist sacral" status of the "state church."[16] The principle of "coordinated diarchy" means the "coordination and cooperation of the Church and the state in all vital issues and in mutual respect of authonomy."[17] Thus, the relationship between the Serbian state and the Orthodox Church was interpreted by generations of theologians as analogous to the relationship between body and soul.

Likening religious unity to political unity and later (in the nineteenth century) to national identity became the raison d'être of autocephaly in the Orthodox world.[18] Such reasoning was upheld by patriotic clergy, vernacular (Slavonic) liturgy, and a policy of congruity between the church, the state, and the people. Because of its strong assimilative ability and group orientation, the Serbian Orthodox Church not only preserved, but also strengthened and expanded the Serbian language, culture, customs, political traditions, and, of course, the Orthodox faith under Ottoman rule. The term *Serbian faith* became a familiar expression denoting Serbian Orthodoxy.

This inviolable unity between the church, the nation, and the state is also illustrated in the Serbian national and religious symbol, the four Ss surrounding a cross, with a popular meaning: "Only unity saves the Serbs"[19]—and then, naturally, only if they rally around the cross. In other words, the church rallies the Serb people together as the sole institution that—as is often emphasized—never betrayed them. For the Serbian Orthodox Church, the national issue is not a distinct political problem, it is a form or element of the religion that tries to function as a national and not as an exclusively religious institution.[20] The nationalist bearing of the Serbian Orthodox Church was sometimes, if not often, of greater importance than its liturgical role: It was and is perceived as the Serbian people's last line of defense. It also portrayed itself as the "suffering church," inseparable from its equally "innocently suffering," even "heavenly people." One of the defining attributes of the Serbian Orthodox Church was the sacralization of national phenomena and national heroes, its deep-rooted conservatism, its inability to break with the past, its noncritical and servile relationship with the authorities, and its belief that it was the protector of the Serb people. In short, the influence of religion on the emergence and development of the Serb national group was very important and quite apparent.[21] We must, however, differentiate between the evolution of the Serbian national identity in Serbs living in Serbia and Croatia and Serbs and Croats living in Bosnia-Herzegovina. In the case of the Bosnian Serbs and Croats, the religious and cultural factors in the development of national identity in the nineteenth century were particularly important. First, because of the religious and cultural heterogeneity of the country, and, second, because other nation-building factors such as political or administrative unity and the development of nation-building cultural, intellectual, and educational institutions were missing.

Catholicism and Islam—both of which are universalistic and transnational religions—played significant roles in the development of the national identity of Catholics and Muslims. Croatian historian Ivo Banac believes that "far more than among the other South Slavs, religious affiliation among the Serbs helped to shape national identity."[22] Nevertheless, the influence exerted by Catholicism and Islam on the political and cultural development of their nations was, and remains today, significant. There were specific periods in history when both the Roman Catholic Church and the Muslim religious community played a dominant role in society—receiving privileges from the state, often in the form of ecclesiastic absolutism or religious monopoly (more often the former than the latter).

According to Roman Catholic teaching, the nation is viewed as "a product of the local undertakings of Catholicism and the local church," and the aim of local churches is to "preserve national characteristics and thus strengthen their religious dissimilarity" with the others.[23] In Croatia, the Roman Catholic Church—*Mater et Magistra*—was one of the more important factors influencing the evolution and preservation of Croatian national identity, but it was not the only one. According to Croatian historian Dinko Tomašić, it was "only one of many elements of Croatian national culture and by no means its basic or most important part."[24]

However, some basic Roman Catholic customs and traditions were eventually nationalized and became the basis for the development of national traditions and institutions. Catholicism became the "patron" of national development and evolution. Croatian nationalism thus sought support in Catholicism by nationalizing its essential social functions.[25] However, this is but one aspect of Catholicism in Croatia. If we were to use the labels commonly applied to denote the main branches of Croatian Catholicism, then this nationally exclusive and potentially hegemonic and traditionalist "Stepinac" tendency (after Archbishop and Cardinal Alojzije Stepinac, 1898–1960) is opposed by the more tolerant and ecumenical "Strossmayer" form (after Bishop Josip Juraj Strossmayer, 1815–1905), which was known for its liberal and modernist brand of ecumenism and conciliation.

Islam is a more all-embracing religion than Roman Catholicism and Eastern Orthodoxy and its secular and spiritual spheres are more tightly knit. Islam is not merely a religion; it is a way of life, a legal and political system, and an agglomeration of different cultural practices. As an anthropological and cultural paradigm, Islam does not recognize "the unbridgeable difference between religion and politics or the separation between the church and the state."[26] Because of its universal character, Islam tends to function on a global and more general level, which does not mean that it plays no role in the shaping of national identities. However, advocates of traditional Islam view nationalism (as well as other modernist ideologies) as the greatest danger to their faith.

The Muslim community in Bosnia-Herzegovina became the strong westernmost oasis of this monotheistic religion in what was otherwise a religiously exclusive "Christian" Europe. The evolution of Muslim national identity in Bosnia-Herzegovina shares many similar characteristics with that of the Serbs or Croats, but it is distinguished from them by the significance of the religious factor. There are many different opinions concerning this particular issue. Zachary Irwin and Pedro Ramet, experts on Balkan religions, note that Islam exerted a greater influence on the national identity of Muslims than Orthodoxy did on the Serbs or Catholicism on the Croats.[27] One well-versed assumption is that Islam is the "mother" of the Muslim national group. According to a contemporary leader in the Bosnian Muslim community, the Islamic religious cadre "has always stood by the people, shared with it good and evil, was directly linked to it and sincerely served it within the range of its possibilities."[28]

I believe that a temporal dimension must be added to these views: despite its universal orientation, Islam has indeed exerted influence on the shaping and evolution of the Muslim national identity—but at a much later stage than the Christian religions. The main reasons for this belatedness were that the national identity of Muslim Slavs was categorically and persistently opposed by both Serbian and Croatian ethnoreligious extremists who labeled them "Poturice" or "Turkified" Serbs or Croats, and the national policies of the multiethnic states to which this territory belonged and which did not support their national self-affirmation until Yugoslavian communist authorities did so in the late 1960s. Norwegian anthropologist Tone Bringa states that "Islam is the key to understanding Muslim identity in Bosnia," and yet "Bosnian Muslim identity cannot be fully understood with reference to Islam only, but has to be considered in terms of a specific Bosnian dimension," namely religious heterogeneity.[29]

Islam therefore made a significant contribution to the national acknowledgment of Bosnia-Herzegovina's Muslim Slavs, who since the late 1960s have been referred to simply as Muslims. Over the centuries, Islam in Bosnia-Herzegovina evolved "into a specific and rather independent cultural system, which gradually influenced the ethnic bases of the Muslims" on one hand, and "today performs an important contribution to religious and confessional pluralism and interconfessional relations" on the other.[30] In other words, Islam played a cultural and ethnogenic role in Bosnia despite its general transnational orientation. Bosnia-Herzegovina's Muslim community was more loosely organized than its Christian neighbors and lacked an institutionalized religious hierarchy or clergy. The closest thing they had to clergy were and are the *ulema* ("Ilmija" in the local language): the "learned in Islam." The most senior religious leader in Bosnia-Herzegovina's Muslim community is the chief *ulema* or head of the Muslim religious community (*reis-ul-ulema; reis* is the Arabic word for chief), while *imams* and *hodžas* provide leadership at the local level.

Bosnia-Herzegovina's Muslim religious community has been autonomous since 1882. On the basis of a special document issued by the Porte and approved by the Austro-Hungarian emperor, the Menšura, Bosnian Muslims chose their *reis-ul-ulema*, who exercised certain powers usually reserved for the caliph. The emperor also appointed four of his closest collaborators, a group of elders known as the *ulema-medjlis.*

2

ONE GOD,
THREE RELIGIONS
Bosnia, Croatia, and Serbia
in the Middle Ages

The settlement of South Slavs on the Balkan Peninsula took place in two phases: from the

My brother shall be dear to me, whatever his religion.

—SOUTH SLAV PROVERB

early to the mid-sixth century, and from the late sixth century to the early seventh century. The strongest power in the Balkans at that time— the Byzantines—countered the incursions of the Avars and the Slavs by Christianizing them.[1] The Byzantine emperor, Heraclius (610–40), de- feated the Avars and the Slavs and—according to the later emperor and historian Constantine VII Porphyrogenitus (905–59)—asked Pope Hono- rius I (625–38) for missionaries to Christianize them. The nuclei of me- dieval South Slav states do not correspond to those of their contemporary "successors": the first Serbian state was in Kosovo, the Croatian state was formed along the Adriatic Sea and in the upper Una region, and the Slovenian state emerged north of the Karawanken mountain range. Over the next few centuries (until they were occupied by stronger neighbors) they went through periods of greatness and decline.

The medieval comprehension of independence was quite different from how it is understood today. It was based on *fidelitas*, a vassal's sub- jection and loyalty to a ruler, even when the latter belonged to a different ethnic or religious group. Furthermore, the concept of the state at that time was also very specific: "most of the time it was a lax and territori- ally flexible union of the tribes, whose leader, commander or duke *(dux)* tried to assure himself legitimacy by recognition of his position from Byzantine Emperors or, on the other hand, from . . . Roman Popes."[2]

The very "birth of history," the ethnogenesis and evolution of the first traces of what were later to become South Slav states, is linked to their conversion to Christianity (the Croats in 879, and the Serbs in 891) and the religious homogenization of the states over the following centuries. The struggle between Rome and Constantinople to baptize the Slavs "became the struggle to enlarge spheres of influences."[3] The old Slavic religion consisted of animist as well as polytheist elements; their burial rites still required the cremation of the body. Christianizing—the passage from a tribal to a universal religion—was, for the most part, very superficial and syncretistic: many of the pre-Christian elements have been preserved to the present day.[4]

When they arrived in the Balkans, the Slavs found a firmly established Christian church organization that was under Rome's jurisdiction.[5] The latter went into decline for a few centuries and in some places was destroyed, but it was soon rejuvenated by the Christianizing of the Slavs. The credit for this goes to two Byzantine missionaries and brothers, Cyril (Constantine) and Methodius, and their disciples. They received permission from the Patriarch of Constantinople to conduct missionary activity among Moravians led by Duke Rastislav, who were experiencing strong ecclesiastical and political pressure from the Franks. Well versed in several Slavic languages, from Salonika to Moravia, Cyril translated the most important parts of the Bible and liturgy from Greek to Old Church Slavonic. In 880 the brothers sought and obtained permission from Pope John VIII (872–82) to use the Slavic language for Latin rites (arguing that "He who created the three cardinal languages—Hebrew, Greek, and Latin—created also all other languages for His praise and glory").[6] Slavonic liturgy was fiercely opposed and condemned by the German clergy and the advocates of the "trilingual theory," according to which there existed only three *holy* languages (those listed above) that were appropriate for religious rites. Subsequent popes opposed Slavonic liturgy, and the disciples of Cyril and Methodius were forced to flee persecution. However, they were declared the "Apostles of the Slavs" in the nineteenth century because of the significant role they played in the spiritual development of the Slavic people who were under the influence of Rome or Constantinople.

ROMAN CATHOLIC ADVANCES ON MEDIEVAL BOSNIA AND THE BOSNIAN CHURCH

The first mention of a statelike formation on the territory of present-day Bosnia, named after the Bosnia River, dates from the late eighth century. The territory was still far from the centers of activity in Rome and Byzantium. In his work "De administrando imperio" ("On the Administration of the Empire"), Constantine VII Porphyrogenitus mentions *horion Bosona* (the district of Bosnia). He states that in return for accepting Byzantine authority, the South Slavs received the blessing of Christianity. In the centuries that followed the settlement of Bosnia and Hum (later renamed Herzegovina), there was much mixing between the majority Slavic population and the Romanic, Avar, and non-Romanized Illyrian peoples.[7] In the tenth century, the territory of Bosnia (also called Ramae in Latin) was seized by Mihael Krešimir II of Croatia, Prince Časlav of Rascia, and eventually by King Bodin of Duklja (Diocletian in Latin). The Byzantines and Hungarians also conquered it. A stronger state with a clearly defined Bosnian national identity did not emerge until the late Middle Ages.

The first mention of a bishopric in Bosnia following the settlement of the Slavs can be traced to the "Annals of Pop Dukljanin," an account of an assembly held in Duvno between 879 and 880. Missionaries were sent to Bosnia from Rome, Byzantium, and Dalmatia. Bosnia was first placed under the ecclesiastic jurisdiction of the Roman Catholic archbishopric of Bar, then to the archbishopric of Split and, in the latter half of the twelfth century, to the archbishopric of Dubrovnik (Ragusa). Thus, Bosnia was, at the time, a nominally Roman Catholic country with a long tradition of "Catholic Slavonic-glagolitic liturgy,"[8] even though its bishop—according to one papal letter of 1232—"was illiterate, ignorant even of the formula for baptism and, needless to say, acting in collusion with heretics"[9] wrongly identified as Patarins, Cathars, and such.

Historian John Fine notes that the practical aspect of religion in medieval Bosnia was always more important than the doctrinal or theological. This applied to all religious communities. In the remote, mountainous Bosnian countryside—which was most of Bosnia—a new blend of different religious truths emerged in the specific cults, ritual practices, and magical beliefs of the natives. It was, therefore, the "pragmatic" aspect of religion—an inclination toward immediate goals and effects—that prevailed.[10]

Political awareness in medieval Bosnia also emerged as a result of the religious dissimilarity between the Bosnian Church (Crkva Bosanska) and the Eastern and Western forms of Christianity. Namely, an important element of Bosnia's medieval identity was this national church, which slowly emerged in the twelfth century. The Bosnian Church, that is, the church of the Bosnian and Hum Christians, became autonomous after the Roman Catholic hierarchy left for Slavonia in the thirteenth century. It was, therefore, a heterogeneous church professing to Roman Catholic liturgies.

The "great ruler" magnus banus Kulin, *banus Culinus dominus Bosnae* (1180–1204) ruled during the so-called golden era of Bosnian history. The religiously heterogeneous Bosnian banate was a frontier area under Byzantine domination and faced constant threats from neighboring Hungary. Ban Kulin's political and religious rivals ruled the neighboring lands, so the borders were constantly shifting. King Emeric (Imre) of Hungary-Croatia and Vukan Nemanjić, the sovereign of Duklja, accused him of heresy, and the latter sent a tendentious letter to Pope Innocent III (1198–1216) in 1199 accusing Bosnia and, indeed, Ban Kulin and his family of "considerable heresy." A number of dualists from Dalmatia sought refuge in Bosnia at the time, and Kulin was accused of offering "refuge and protection to a considerable number of Patarins who had recently been expelled from Split and Trogir by Archbishop Bernard of Split." Moreover, "he showed greater respect to these heretics, referring to them simply as Christians, rather than Catholics." Bosnia was accused of harboring many people suspected of professing to the "denounced Cathar heresy." These events took place in an intense atmosphere under which "all heretics, Cathari, and Patarins" were condemned.[11] The Third Lateran Council in 1179 and the Synod of Split in 1185 adopted a similar stance. The pope reacted swiftly, notifying both the archbishop of Split and King Emeric, the pretender to religious and political dominion in Bosnia.

At Ban Kulin's request, papal legate Johannes Casamaris was sent by Pope Innocent III to Bosnia in 1203 to meet with representatives of the "heretics" at Bilino Polje near modern Zenica. In a declaration on April 8, they formally renounced their heresy and declared their loyalty to the Roman Catholic Church, accepting Roman Catholic priests, Roman supremacy, liturgy, benediction, and Roman Catholic rites in general, and reinstating altars and crosses in their temples. The so-called Bilino Polje abjuration was announced and signed by seven abbots. Casamaris, however, found no heresy among the monks, but instead a deep and involuntary ignorance of Roman Catholic doctrine, discipline, and practice. He attempted to correct this by generally condemning any deviation. With the exception of a remark forbidding the monks from offering shelter to Manichaeans, there is no mention of dualism in the document.[12] A similar agreement was later reached between Innocent III and Durand's "indigent Catholics" in southern France (1207) and Bernard Primm's "humiliates" in northern Italy (1210).

Ban Kulin remained a loyal Catholic and supported the construction of Catholic churches. In return, Pope Innocent III recognized him as an "obedient son of the Church." Much to Kulin's dismay, however, the very same pope transferred the bishopric of Bosnia from the jurisdiction of the archbishop of Dubrovnik to the archbishop of Split (Bernard). This was probably a result of machinations at the Hungarian court, which had good relations with Split. Kulin ignored this papal move and continued to nurture relations with Archbishop Leonard of Dubrovnik, whom he even visited. In 1206, Archbishop Leonard consecrated the new bishop of Bosnia, Dragonja, who was eventually succeeded by Bishop Bratoslav (1212–32). In the 1220s, the pope again recognized the archbishop of Dubrovnik's jurisdiction over Bosnia.

After unending accusations about the heresy, heterodoxy, dualism, and even ditheism of the Bosnian Christians, the missionaries of the Catholic order of Dominicans *(Ordo fratrum praedicatorum)*, were sent there as examiners of faith (that is, as inquisitors), arriving in the early thirteenth century under the aegis of Hungary. Bosnian rulers rejected them for political reasons, and the Bosnian people rejected them because they used a foreign language in the liturgy and were generally unappealing. The only Dominican monastery built in Bosnia was founded in 1233 in Vrhbosna (which later became Sarajevo). Hungarian pressure on Bosnia continued. In 1221, papal legate Acontius was sent to Bosnia to investigate claims that "many heretics and subversives *(subversores)* publicly preach and freely express their delusions." Archbishop Ugrin of Kalocsa sent crusaders to deal with them, but without significant success.[13] It is clear that political goals—the subordination of Bosnia by Hungary—were more important than religious ones.

Three years later, Pope Honorius III (1216–27) asked Ugrin to deal with the "Bosnian heretics" but did not specify them. In 1227, Pope Gregory IX (1227–41) began preparing for a new crusade against the "enemies of the cross" *(inimici crucis)*, and a few years later began taking interest in the religious situation in Bosnia by consulting neighboring archbishops. In 1233, the Dominicans were appointed by papal decree to serve as pastors against heresy and as the official "investigators of heretic criminality" (inquisitors), and were sent to Carcassonne in southern France, Lombardy, Bosnia, and Dalmatia. Meanwhile, Croatia became a halfway point for Dominican missionaries on their way to the Eastern Orthodox lands. Many of these Dominicans became the early advocates of conciliarism—reconciliation with the Balkan Orthodox Churches and ecumenism—including Ivan Stojković (1390 or 1395–1443), who participated at the Basle Council, Benjamin Dubrovčan (at the turn of the sixteenth century), and Juraj Križanić (1618–83).[14]

The Vatican and the kings of Hungary sought to remove the bishopric of Bosnia from the ecclesiastic jurisdiction of the Ragusans and place it

under the authority of the Hungarians. In May, 1233, legate Jacob de Pec-
oraria, the titular Cardinal-Bishop of Praeneste, came to the same conclusions as his predecessor, Ivan Casamaris: the clergy were theologically
ignorant, not heretics. He replaced the Bishop of Bosnia, a Slav he accused of being "uneducated and inclined towards heresy and simony,"
with the Hungarian Dominicans' provincial, Johannes Teutonicus of
Wildeshausen, and charged him with Latinizing Bosnian Christianity.[15]
Thus, in October, 1233, Pope Gregory IX placed Ban Matej Ninoslav
(1232–ca. 1249) and the entire territory of Bosnia under the protection of
the Holy See and under a new foreign bishop. Between 1235 and 1241,
crusaders led by Coloman, the governor of Croatia and Dalmatia, were
again sent to deal with "Bosnian heresy" and the "heretic state," as the
pope called it. The latter congratulated Coloman for "cleansing the
heresy and restoration of Catholic purity."[16]

During this period, the Dominicans had the exclusive right to perform
missionary work in Bosnia but, as already mentioned, they were also inquisitors. Many were "conveyed to the Truth of Faith . . . but those who
persistently resisted conversion were taken to the stake by Coloman's
servants."[17] Johannes stepped down after six years and was replaced by
Ponsa, himself a Dominican. Ponsa arrived in Bosnia with a crusader
army intent on reintegrating the territory—under Hungarian control—
into an entity of the Western Church. But his endeavors were in vain: the
seat of the Bosnian Catholic Church was moved from Vrhbosna to
Djakovo between 1246 and 1252, and subordinated to the Metropolitan
in Kalocsa. This further weakened the links between the Bosnians and
Catholicism. Ponsa served as bishop until 1268. In other words, for almost a hundred years—from the mid-thirteenth century to the mid-
fourteenth century—there was no Catholic Church hierarchy in Bosnia.
The end result was the schism between the Bosnian Church and the Roman Catholic Church. The bishopric remained under Hungarian control
until 1878.

There were, therefore, two motives for the 1235–41 war: The religious
motive, re-Catholicization, was the pretext for the political motive, the
subordination of Bosnia to Hungary. This pressure was relieved by two
factors. The first was the two-faced diplomacy and policies of Ban Matej
Ninoslav, who, when circumstances required, declared himself a Catholic (sending an appeal to Pope Innocent IV, who reigned from 1243 to
1254, declaring that he had renounced the "errors of heresy" and had be-
gun persecuting heretics) or a member of the Bosnian Church. The pope
agreed to his request to conduct Roman Catholic rites in Slavonic and to
use the glagolitic alphabet (also called the "Croatian alphabet" or alpha-

betum charwaticum). Documents employing this alphabet were there-fore written in Croatian *(spisani harvacki)*. The second factor was the in-vasion of Hungary and Croatia by the Mongol army in 1241–42, during which both Coloman and Ugrin were killed. In 1247, the pope once again called on King Bela IV of Hungary to march against the heretics, but Matej Ninoslav managed to convince the pope of his loyalty to the Vati-can a year later.

Hence, Bosnia and its leaders survived the first papal and Hungarian campaigns. We can therefore only speak of the schism between the Bos-nian Church and the Roman Catholic archbishoprics of Kalocsa and Dubrovnik, the rising hostility of the people toward the Roman Catho-lic Church, and Bosnian animosity for the Hungarians after the 1230s, when the Roman Catholic Church in Bosnia finally compromised itself by backing Hungary's political appetites. The next few decades remain somewhat nebulous because of the sheer absence of historical material. The next mention of the Bosnian Church as the only ecclesiastic organ-ization within Bosnia does not appear until 1320. However, even during this interim period, the Vatican made a series of appeals for Bosnian heretics to be dealt with either militarily or by Franciscan proselytizing.

THE ORGANIZATION OF THE BOSNIAN CHURCH

There is an express lack of consensus among contemporary historians on the religious doctrines, organization, and way of life of members of the Bosnian Church (Crkva Bosanska or *ecclesia Bosnensis*; also called the "Church of God" or the "Church of Jesus"). This is the result of "sec-ondhand" information provided by sources outside Bosnia that habitu-ally castigated and scorned its "heresy." There was extensive correspon-dence between the Vatican—from Pope Innocent III at the beginning of the thirteenth century to Pope Pius II (1458–64)—and the Hungarian monarchs and high-ranking church officials concerning this matter. All three were characterized by their gross ignorance of the events tak-ing place in Bosnia, their contemptuous arrogance, generalization, and simplistic labeling. All those who in any way deviated from official doc-trine, especially from the Roman Catholic Church's organization, were branded as Manichaeans, Dualists, heretics, and the like. Very few rec-ords can be ascribed to members of the Bosnian Church themselves.

The Bogomil historiographic myth—labeling and dealing with the members of the Bosnian Church as "Bogomils"—dates from the period of Croatian historiographic Romanticism. The name Bogomil was not applied to members of the Bosnian Church in the Middle Ages.[18] The term was not used until the nineteenth century, during the era of enthu-siastic national-revivalist historiography, and then it was applied to Bosnia retroactively. The "Bogomil Church" became a romantic symbol of Bosnia's sovereignty from its covetous neighbors. The founder of mod-ern studies of the Bosnian Church was Franjo Rački (1828–94), the most important nineteenth-century Croatian historian. He saw the Bosnian Church as a neo-Manichaean but moderate variety of the religious dual-ism or *bogomilism* that became popular in the eastern Balkans (Bulgaria, Macedonia, Thrace, and parts of Serbia) after the tenth century. He be-lieved that members of the Bosnian Church were the descendants of Bul-garian Bogomils. From then on, the name *bogomil*, which was unknown to medieval Bosnia, came to be applied to the Bosnian Church and its members in scientific and popular literature. Indeed, the Bogomil or du-alist theory is still advocated (or at least mentioned) by many contempo-rary researchers and publicists.[19]

During the period of national revivalism in the nineteenth and twen-tieth centuries, all three national groups exploited the theory of the Bo-gomil nature and/or the ecclesiastic and religious autonomy of medieval Bosnia. Serbian authors especially (Božidar Petranović in the 1860s, for example) were convinced that the Bosnian Church was actually an Or-thodox entity but with its own (Bosnian) hierarchy. In his book, which was published in 1867 and received an award from the Serbian Royal Sci-entific Society, Petranović argued that members of the Bosnian Church were actually Orthodox Christians who had succumbed to the Bogomil heresy that had been introduced to Bosnia from Macedonia. A similar theory was proposed by Vaso Glušac (1879-1955) at the beginning of twentieth century.[20] Contemporary Serbian historian Dragoljub Drago-jlović argues in his 1987 book that the Bosnian Church was a branch of Eastern Orthodoxy. On the other side, Croatian nationalists believed that the Bosnian Bogomils were ethnic Croats who succumbed to Manichaean heresy and then to Islam.[21] Finally, Muslim historians and sociologists like Handžić and Balić still emphasize the Bogomil origin of present-day Muslims or Bosniaks, and the religious and doctrinal simi-larity between the Bogomil religion and Islam. Hadžijahić, Traljić, and Šukrić write about the old Slavonic Bogomil-Muslim syncretism.[22]

A reconstruction of the religion of the Bosnian Church reveals that it was not the same as that of medieval dualists such as Armenian Pauli-cians, Macedonian and Bulgarian Bogomils, French Cathari and Albi-gensians, and Italian Patarins, who condensed the definition of all cre-ation to a radical battle between good and evil. The dualist theory teaches of the existence of two supreme opposed powers: the good and lucent deity, which creates the spiritual and intangible world, and the evil and dark deity, which substantiates the material and visible world, the Earth, and living beings. The good god came first, whereas the evil god, Satan or Satanael, is a fallen angel who was banished from heaven. In order to save mankind, the good god sends Christ, his second son, to Earth to bring the people back to Him. Christ's crucifixion is the result of the devil's work. Ultimately, the good god is victorious with Christ's second coming. In short, theological dualism.

The Bogomils, for example, believed that the "perfect" (for Cathars, the "perfect" were also known as *perfecti*, the "chosen" were *electi*, the "faithful" were *credentes*, and the "listeners" were *audientes*)—as distinguished from the "laymen"—ascend to heaven immediately after death, whereas the "sinful" are condemned once again to a "life in alienation in the iniquitous" material world. The "impeccable" therefore renounced creature comforts, good food, carnal pleasure, and their families, prayed several times a day, lived on charity, and rejected matrimony, the Old Testament (they believed that the God of the Old Testament was the devil and the Old Testament itself his work), religious rituals, ecclesiastic buildings, baptism by water and icons. They believed that feudal society was Satan's work. They would pray anywhere, in houses, in fields, and in forests, and there was equality between the sexes. The dualists also repudiated the cross, church buildings, and the clergy. They did not consume wine or meat, nor did they glorify saints. They behaved in an ascetic and puritan manner and renounced the wealth and temporal power of the church. They opposed any form of authority and particularly valued the works of the apostles, Saint John's "Revelation," the New Testament, and the Lord's Prayer. They held simple masses at which worshippers blessed each other and ritually broke bread.[23]

Historical studies offer a variety of explanations for the names given to members of the Bosnian Church. Most authors agree that they called themselves Christians: *krstjani* or *krstjanci* (singular *krstjanin*), in Latin *christianus;* also *boni homines* (following the example of a dualist group in Italy), *dobri mužje* (good men), *dobri ljudi* (good people), *dobri Bošnjani* (good Bosnians) or simply Bošnjani (Bosnians, in Latin Bosnenses). They considered themselves Christians "of the holy apostolic faith" *(koi su svete vere apostolske)*, as they are described in Gost Radin's renowned will. Catholic sources refer to them as *patareni* or *patarini* in Latin and *kudugeri* or *kutugeri* in Greek (this term was used to denote the Hum Christians under Duke Stephen Kosača by Orthodox patriarch Gennadios II Scholarios in the mid-fifteenth century). The Serbs called them *babuni* (after Babuna Mountain), the Serb term for Bogomils. The Ottomans referred to them as *kristianlar* (singular *kristian*), while the Orthodox and Catholics were called *gebr* or *kafir*, meaning "unbeliver." Bosnian and Hum Christians differed from eastern Balkan Bogomils and Patarins banished from Dalmatian cities (Zadar, Split, Trogir) in name as well. Fine and Šidak note that the name *krstjanin* (plural *krstjani*) was used only for the clergy and monks of the Bosnian Church, while the nobles who belonged to the Bosnian Church were referred to as "good Bosnians" *(dobri Bošnjani).*[24]

Different historical sources show diametrically opposed images of Bosnian Church doctrine. According to some, *krstjani* retained Catholic theology. This is illustrated in the renowned New Testament codex known as "Zbornik krstjanina Hvala" from 1404. The liturgy in Bosnian and Hum churches was in the Slavic language. They worshipped the cross, accepted sections of the Old Testament, believed in "the almighty God our Lord" *(svemogućega Gospodina Boga),* in the Holy Trinity *(svetu Troicu nerazdelimi,* and *pričista Troica),* and in Jesus Christ *(Gospodin naš Isus edini).* They held mass regularly, learned the Lord's Prayer, erected religious buildings, cultivated vineyards, worshipped saints and the Holy Virgin, and developed their own religious art. They celebrated religious festivals ranging from Christmas to All Saints' Day, and they believed in the resurrection of the soul (but not of the body). They lived an ascetic life, baptized only adults, and so forth.[25]

In any event, the Bosnian Church represented the spiritual dimension of the religious individuality and autonomy of medieval Bosnia. At the top of the church hierarchy was a bishop, the so-called *djed.* Below him were *gost, starac,* and *strojnik.* In a letter dating from the early fifteenth century, the head of the Bosnian Church refers to himself as "Monsignor Bishop of the Bosnian Church." The Latin expression for *djed bosanski* was *diedo Patharenorum Bossine* or *padre spirituale.*[26] We know the names of many *djedi* between the fourteenth century and 1461: Radoslav, Rastudij, Radomer, Mirhona, Miloje, and Ratko, the last of the *djedi.* The *gost* came immediately after the *djed* in the church hierarchy. He was responsible for ministration and, in the absence of the *djed,* conducting liturgical meetings. The *starac* was the head of the local *krstjan* community *(hiža).* The *starci* and *gosti* were collectively referred to as elders *(domini maiores Christianorum),* a title given to them in Dubrovnik.[27] There were few monk-priests in the Bosnian Church. Its structure was fragile, at best, and spiritual life took place almost solely within the walls of abbeys or monastic houses (the so-called *hiža, domus Christianorum).* Also, the Bosnian Church was not a large feudal landowner. Historians have doubts regarding its size because its organization did not include parishes, and its monks *(societas fraternitatis)* had little influence over the general population. It did not seek, and therefore lacked, grass roots support. It was, however, popular among the nobility, and most became members of the Bosnian Church before 1340.[28]

Bosnian Church officials maintained good relations with the Orthodox and Roman Catholic Churches, as illustrated by the meetings held between 1305 and 1307 attended by *djed* Miroslav, Orthodox, and Catholic officials, and local magnates from Bar, Kotor, Hum, and Zeta. The Ragusans might have referred to the Bosnian Church as the "Patarin Church" (and claimed that its members were of Bosnian or Patarin origin), but they maintained good relations with them.

The Bosnian Church might have been schismatic and autonomous, but it was not a dualist or heretic community. In other words, the church followed Roman Catholic theology but rejected Vatican domination. This was the main reason for the flurry of accusations directed at the Bosnia Church by the West. Many of the doctrinal inconsistencies reported by external observers were not "heresies" but deviations—in faith and in custom—from mainstream Catholicism, which was poorly understood and controlled by the local guardians of doctrine. Also of importance is the fact that such deviations were common in other parts of Europe as well. Fine therefore prefers to use the terms *degeneration* and *bastardization* of the religion of the Bosnian *krstjani*.[29] It was not so much a matter of heresy as it was a special "type of piety." Because of the influence of the more ancient "pagan" beliefs, we can speak of a specific, local syncretism; tendencies to advance rudimentary and simpler forms of Christian community could also be noticed. Šidak legitimately compares this distinctive monastic church order to the early medieval Church in Ireland.[30]

The Bosnian Church, therefore, was not a "heretical," deliberately heterodox sect, but rather a Roman Catholic monastic order, severed, abandoned, and alienated from events in Western Christendom. It developed a separate, autonomous, and original Catholic ecclesiastic body under the leadership of a bishop and local abbots. The Bosnian Church preserved the continuity of the Bosnian Roman Catholic bishopric, whose seat the Hungarians officially moved to Slavonia in the 1250s. However, because it did not develop a proper territorial structure of parishes to serve the religious needs of the population, it cannot be referred to as a church in the true sense.[31] Furthermore, it did not seek or encourage social or political changes or the adoption of a less biased social order because it was at the grace of the Bosnian nobility and was once the leading proponent of Bosnian feudalism. In contrast to medieval dualist churches, the Bosnian Church was not an illegal or closet organization.[32] Fine believes that the Bosnian Church was, in fact, some sort of Bosnian "nativistic" reaction.[33] In medieval Bosnia, this political class was composed of the rulers, nobility, and the local monastic hierarchy—all of whom had specific reasons for opposing Hungarian political appetites and Roman Catholic supremacy. In this specific case, the peculiar form of Bosnian Catholicism may be referred to as the "religion of the imperiled."

It is, however, possible that a minority within the Bosnian Church did indeed pick up some of the more popular dualist beliefs, customs, and practices—particularly the rites, abhorrence of the cross, and some sacraments. Dualist beliefs were introduced by Patarins who moved from towns along the Adriatic coast into the interior of the Balkan Peninsula, or by Bogomils fleeing persecution in the east. Papal legates, Franciscans, and external observers labeled them all Patarins, Manichaeans, or dualists from the—as they called it—"Kingdom of Bosnia, the land of very feeble Christians."

The Bosnian Church was tolerated by the state. Although the Bosnian *djedi* were received as guests of honor even outside Bosnia itself, the Bosnian Church did not play a significant role in politics. Only during the reign of King Stephen Ostoja and his son Stephen Tomaš in the early fifteenth century, a period of increasingly apparent threats from Rome, did this church exert considerable political influence. In its heyday, the Bosnian Church forged strong ties with the Bosnian court and through the work of its officials who had been appointed to advisory and diplomatic positions, encouraged the preservation of Bosnian independence.[34]

BOSNIA PROSPERS UNDER THE KOTROMANIĆ DYNASTY

Under the Kotromanić dynasty, Bosnia (Boxina Regno in Italian records) became the last great South Slav medieval state. In 1326, Ban Stephen II Kotromanić (1322–53), son of Stephen Kotroman, seized Hum, which had been ruled by the Serbian Nemanjić dynasty since 1168. Stephen also extended his territory northward and toward the Adriatic Sea. He referred to his subjects as *dobri Bošnjani* (good Bosnians). Stephen maintained good relations with both his neighbors, Hungary (ruled by the Angevins) and Serbia (ruled by the Nemanjićes). His blazon, which was the basis for the first coat of arms of the recently founded state of Bosnia-Herzegovina, was azure with a bend argent charged with gold fleurs-de-lis (the symbol of the Holy Virgin's impeccability), surmounted by a lambrequin and crown. Nominally, his country was still under the Kingdom of Hungary. The influence of the Bosnian Church increased during the reign of Stephen II.[35] This prompted Pope John XXII (1316–34) to make new appeals in 1318 and 1319 for the destruction of this lasting Bosnian heresy. His successor, Benedict XII (1334–42), noted that Bosnian bans and magnates were receiving and protecting the heretics. He instructed Croatian nobles to support the Franciscan inquisitors, whom the Bosnian ruler and nobility were said to be obstructing. Stephen Kotromanić stopped any military advances, among others, Serbian emperor Dušan's incursion into Bosnia in 1350–51.

Stephen's nephew and successor, Ban Stephen Tvrtko I (ban 1353–77; king of Rascia and Bosnia, 1377–91; and king of Croatia and Dalmatia from 1390), was both a politically adept and religiously tolerant ruler. He refused to interfere in the religious affairs of the Orthodox and Catholics in his newly conquered lands. In 1347, he converted (probably from Orthodoxy) to Roman Catholicism ("embracing the unity of the faith," as Roman Catholic chroniclers noted), although he tolerated and even supported the Bosnian Church and its hierarchy. From then on, all Kotromanićes were Roman Catholics, with the possible exception of Stephen Ostoja (1395 or 1398–1404 and 1409–18), who may have been a member of the Bosnian Church. Slovenian historian Vera Kržišnik-Bukić cites the following data: of sixteen medieval Bosnian rulers, six were members of the Bosnian Church, five were Roman Catholics, and four changed religions. The denomination of one ruler could not be established.[36]

Under Tvrtko I, Bosnia reached its peak and became the strongest power in the Balkans. Tvrtko defeated (and then made peace with) the Hungarians and crushed a rebel army led by his brother Vuk. He centralized the state and conquered territories with Orthodox and Roman Catholic populations—parts of Croatia, Dalmatia, and what remained of Hum (Polimje), Kotor, Zeta, and the territory of present-day Sandžak. Tvrtko was crowned in 1377 in Mile (today the village Arnautovići between Visoko and Zenica).[37] The crown was sent to him by Hungarian king Louis of Anjou and the ceremony was conducted by an Orthodox metropolitan. Although Tvrtko was descended from the Nemanjić dynasty and was nominally king of Rascia, he never really ruled Serbia.

Mining (including precious metals) was a particularly well-developed and profitable industry in medieval Bosnia. A Bosnian alphabet, the so-called *bosančica*, was widely used. This Western, stylized form of the Cyrillic alphabet with glagolitic elements was used well into the Ottoman period by both Muslims and Christians. Another cultural peculiarity of medieval Bosnia was the tombstones known as *stećci*, of which

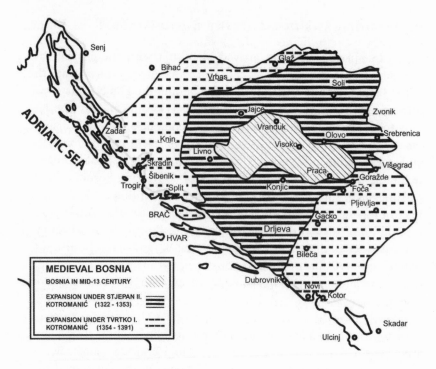

about fifty thousand have been found. These were not Bogomil tomb-stones, as they were commonly believed to be, but were erected by members of all three major religions in medieval Bosnia and Hum, and later by the Muslims.[38] Bosnia also developed a unique form of feudalism, but none of the three major religions were feudal landowners.[39]

In the 1360s and 1370s, the Vatican protested against the situation in Bosnia, accusing its rulers of protecting the heretics and instructing the Hungarian king to take appropriate action against the "Bosnian and Hum heretics and schismatics." Similar accusations regarding the *errores hereticorum Bosensium* and the distinction between the "Bosnian religion" and the "Roman religion" were made in the early fifteenth century. The north, west, and parts of central medieval Bosnia were inhabited by Catholics, the east and parts of the south were inhabited by Orthodox, and parts of eastern, southern, and central Bosnia were inhabited by members of the Bosnian Church. It is important to note that Bosnian bans and kings of this period tried to create "mutual tolerance between the Catholics and the *krstjani*" rather than encourage proselytizing.[40] After Tvrtko's death, Bosnia endured decades of internal conflicts, dynastic wars, weak central authority, and Hungarian interference and pretension. It was also confronted with the rapidly advancing Ottoman Empire.

THE FRANCISCANS IN MEDIEVAL BOSNIA

Franciscan missionaries first arrived in Bosnïa with the papal legate Acontius in 1222. In 1248 they came as inquisitors to investigate the faith of Ban Matej Ninoslav. During this period, the Franciscans *(Ordo fratrum minorum)* worked closely with the Dominicans. By the late 1320s and early 1330s, however, the two orders were already in a dispute over which one should receive the rights to *officium inquisitionis,* the inquisitorial office in Bosnia. In 1245, Pope Innocent IV finally brought the matter to an end by giving the task of converting Bosnian "heretics" or even "traitors" to the Franciscans.[41] According to the Franciscans, they came to Bosnia to "convert the deluded." Their missionary work and inquisitorial tasks in the banate of Bosnia did not begin in full measure until the reign of Pope Nicholas IV (1288–92), who also sent them to Serbia to "bring the Orthodox back to the unity of the faith."[42] The Franciscan inquisition in Bosnia was decreed in the papal bull "Prae cunctis" in March, 1291, and was reconfirmed by Pope Boniface VIII (1294–1303) in April, 1298. In 1327, Pope John XXII used the same bull to prevent Hungarian and Croatian Dominican inquisitors from persecuting "Bosnian heretics" and from calling for a crusade against them.

The rise of the Franciscans in Bosnia began with the Kotromanić dynasty, which offered support to the monastic order. In 1327, Pope John XXII upheld the right of the Franciscans to the inquisitorial office in Bosnia.[43] Ban Stephen consented to the arrival of the Franciscans in Bosnia and earned himself the blessing of Pope Benedict XII. In 1339, Stephen received the general of the Franciscans, Gerard Odinis of Aquitaine (1329–42), who was sent by the pope through the king of Hungary (Charles Robert I of Anjou, 1301–42) to stamp out the Bosnian heresy.

Stephen and Gerard came to an agreement. The "Vicariate of Bosnia" was created in 1340–42 as an administrative province of the Franciscan order. The "Province of Croatia" ("Provincia Sclavoniae") had been established much earlier, in the 1220s. A "vicariate" ranked higher than a "custodia," but lower than a "province," which was directly under the command of the general. The Vicariate of Bosnia extended from Istria to the Black Sea and from Buda to the Adriatic. Its first vicar, the general's lieutenant, was Nicholas Peregrin of Saxony (1340–49). He was also Stephen's most influential adviser. Stephen still refused to pursue a policy of actively persecuting the Bosnian Church, although the pope urged him to do so through his legate, Gerard. In 1372 and 1373, the Franciscans received permission from Pope Gregory XI (1370–78) to conduct all seven sacraments. Pope Eugene IV (1431–47) later reconfirmed this in 1436. The Franciscans were also in favor with Popes Urban V (1362–70) and Urban VI (1378–89), and were permitted to build churches and create parishes.

Ban Stephen built the first Franciscan monastery in Bosnia in 1340 at Visoko. It stood next to a church built in honor of the first Franciscan vicar of Bosnia (Saint Nicholas Peregrinus).[44] Monasteries were later built only in places where the Bosnian Church was strongest. Latin Catholicism began its domination, starting with the immediate vicinities of the Franciscan monasteries. By about 1385 there were twenty Franciscan friars and four monasteries in Bosnia: in Kraljeva Sutjeska, Visoko, Lašva and Olovo; monasteries were later built in Kreševo, Deševica and Fojnica. By the time Bosnia fell to the Ottomans in 1463, twelve more monasteries would be built.[45] The Franciscans actually consisted of two orders: the Observants and the Conventuals. One of the differences between them was the issue of property ownership: the Conventuals believed that monasteries had the right to own property, while the Observants have practiced more strict ideals of Franciscan poverty.

Stephen Kotromanić praised the Franciscans. He asked the pope to send more priests who had been taught to speak the Slavic language to Bosnia. Almost all the Franciscans that had been sent to Bosnia at that time were Italians. Their proselytizing was peaceful and nonviolent. However, because of their increasing influence, the Franciscans came into conflict with the bishop of Djakovo. Bosnian Catholics were becoming more attached to the Franciscans, who lived among them, while their bonds with the "foreign" ecclesiastic hierarchy were weakening. The Franciscans wanted to create their own bishopric in Bosnia but the pope ruled in favor of the bishop of Djakovo, the titular and de jure head of the Roman Catholic hierarchy in Bosnia. Nevertheless, the Franciscans had more success in the field: according to papal records, they were successfully converting the Bosnian *krstjani, infideles et a fide catholica deviantes.*

As soon as the Franciscans established a foothold in Bosnia in the 1340s, the power and influence of the Bosnian Church began to wane. Although the Franciscans were charged with the Bosnians' spiritual upbringing by papal decree (issued in 1444 by Pope Eugene IV), the nobility were still allowed to invite parish priests to their estates. In the decades prior to the arrival of the Ottomans, the Franciscans tried hard to Catholicize the Bosnian people. This was also a period that saw the evolution of Bosnian towns as centers of Roman Catholic restoration. In the last few years before Ottoman rule, Catholicism gained favor with the

Bosnian nobility (*vlastela*) and rulers, but later many members of the Bosnian Church still converted to Islam rather than Catholicism.

THE DECLINE OF MEDIEVAL BOSNIA

Renewed accusations of heresy in the Bosnian Church and the zealous and brutal re-Catholicizing of the Bosnian population began in the 1430s. These continued with new fervor following the arrival of Franciscan missionary Jacob de Marchia, the special visitor to the vicariate and eventually vicar of Bosnia. He introduced reforms intended to increase discipline within the ranks of the order itself and to eradicate heresy. Because of his religious intolerance and his severity toward the Franciscan friars, he soon came into conflict with King Tvrtko II (1404–1409, 1421–43).[46] The mounting Ottoman threat drove the last of Bosnia's kings to seek alliance with Venice, Hungary, and the Vatican. In the mid-1440s, Pope Eugene IV promised the crown to Stephen Tomaš, a *krstjan*, if he would join the war effort against the Ottomans and promise to persecute the local "Manichaeans." Pope Nicholas V (1447–55) made a similar offer. Stephen, a Roman Catholic convert, still tolerated the Bosnian Church and even appointed its officials to his court and the diplomatic service. On the other hand, he assisted the Franciscans in their apostolic work, repaired their monasteries and built new ones.[47] In 1456, Dominican friar Nicholas Barbucci, a papal emissary sent to secure Stephen's assistance for the war effort against the Ottomans, found that Stephen was reluctant to confront the Ottomans because "the Manichaeans, who comprise a near majority in his kingdom, are more inclined towards the Ottomans than the Christians." He was wrong about the "majority" of the Bosnian Church, which he pejoratively referred to as dualist and Manichaean *(manazei).*[48]

The persecution of members of the Bosnian Church began in the 1450s, but neither the Bosnian ruler nor the nobility were involved. Stephen Tomaš finally consented to the direct and brutal persecution of the clergy and members of the Bosnian Church in 1459 when, faced with the imminent threat of Ottoman invasion, he turned to the pope in desperation and agreed to his demands. He gave them a choice: conversion (Roman Catholic baptism), or expulsion from Bosnia. Most chose conversion, but a few, including their leader, fled to Herzegovina, taking refuge with Duke Stephen Kosača.[49] The Bosnian Church practically ceased to exist in its native land. Stephen Tomaš died in 1461 and was buried at the Franciscan monastery in Sutjeska.

Religious dynamics in Hum differed from those in Bosnia. Hum was originally part of the Serbian state ruled by the Nemanjić dynasty and was later conquered by Bosnia but retained a form of semiautonomy. Unlike the troublesome Hungarians, the strong medieval Serbian state did not have territorial appetites toward Bosnia and never sent an army against it. Dušan the Strong was more interested in the south than in the Adriatic coast, selling Ston and Pelješac to the Ragusans (Dubrovnik Republic). The Ragusans immediately began oppressing the Orthodox Church in their newly acquired territories and forcefully converted its members to Catholicism.

In contrast to Bosnia, where the Roman Catholic and Bosnian Church were firmly established, Hum was mostly Orthodox. The Orthodox bishopric of Hum, seated in Ston, was part of the Serbian archbishopric. The Catholic West referred to Orthodox Christians in Hum as "Greeks," "Rascians" *(Graeci, Rasciani)*, or "schismatics," and to Orthodoxy as the "Rascian" religion. The Orthodox Christians of Hum came into conflict with neighboring Catholics, especially during Bosnia's final years as a kingdom. In the 1450s, Gennadios II, the patriarch of Constantinople, noted with great satisfaction the successful Orthodox proselytizing taking place in Bosnia. The same was reported to Pope Calixtus III (1455–58) by Franciscan Johannes Capistranus (1386–1456), who accused the metropolitan of Rascia of obstructing Catholics intent on converting members of the Bosnian Church.[50] The rivalry between the Roman Catholic and Serbian Orthodox Church over Bosnia began during this period.

Herzegovina ("the Herzeg's land"), the modern name for Hum, is named after Stephen Vukčić Kosača (1435–66), who seized the territory from the kingdom of Bosnia. He assumed the title "Duke (Herzeg) of Hum and Primorje" in 1448, and added the title "Herzeg of Saint Sava" a year later because the relics of Saint Sava were in the Mileševo monastery. Although he most likely remained a member of the Bosnian Church, he maintained cordial relations with the Orthodox Church (with the metropolitan of Mileševo, for example) and was benevolent toward the Roman Catholic Church. Italian sources refer to him as *conte Steffano patarino*, and Catholic officials from the Adriatic coast accused him of heresy, sacrilege, destruction of the church, and persecution of Catholics. However, a peace treaty signed in 1454 shows that the religion practiced was Catholicism (Holy Trinity, Virgin Mary, saints, the cross, and so on), not dualism. Duke Stephen appointed *krstjani* to the diplomatic service: *gost* Radin Butković from Seonica was well respected in Dubrovnik. There are no traces of any form of dualism in his will, a consequential document that reveals a great deal about the Bosnian religion. The same may be said of the abovementioned "Hvala manuscript" *(Zbornik krstjanina Hvala).* Both are very close to the "official" doctrine of Roman Catholic Christianity.[51]

Stephen Tomašević, the last Bosnian king, was crowned by the papal legate in Jajce in November, 1461, after he demanded papal assistance in fighting the Ottomans ("Letter of the Bosnian King Stephen Tomašević to Pope Pius II," dated 1461[52]) as well as the Bosnian crown. Pope Pius II responded by proclaiming him the "Defender of Bosnia." When the Ottomans beheaded Tomašević in Jajce in 1463, Bosnia's sudden surrender was blamed on the treason of the "Manichaeans." However, the Bosnian Church, for which this label was intended, had practically vanished by that time, continuing to exist only in Herzegovina under the patronage of Duke Stephen and assisting his anti-Ottoman efforts.

EARLY CROATIAN RELIGIOUS HISTORY

According to Croatian historian Nada Klaić, the early decades of Croatian history are an unfinished chapter. The ancestors of the Croatians were a distinct tribe of Slavs that settled the territory in the late sixth and early seventh centuries, after the Avar and Slav advance.[53] Constantine VII Porphyrogenitus tells us that Byzantine emperor Heraclius, a skilled diplomat with a habit of arousing conflict between the barbarians, incited the Croats, who then lived beyond the Carpathian Mountains, to wage war against the Avars and Slavs and to settle the territory between the Raša and Cetina Rivers. The twelve victorious Croatian tribes were eventually subordinated by the Byzantine Empire. The native population—Illyrian and Celtic tribes and the Romanized population—were pushed into the mountains or fled to coastal towns and islands under Byzantine authority. Though few in number, the Croats reigned over the Slavs, adopted their language, and gave them their name.[54] The first Croatian duchies emerged in the latter half of the eighth century. The territory to the north of the Cetina River was called "White Croatia," and the territory to the south, extending to the Albanian border, was called "Red Croatia."

Ethnogenic myths either "supplement" these historical findings or directly oppose them. I shall relate only those that have met with a wider response. According to the first Croatian ethnogenic myth, the Croats advanced from territory beyond the Carpathian Mountains under the guidance of five brothers and two sisters, namely, Klucas (Klukas), Lovelos (Lobel), Kosences (Kosjenc), Muhlo, Hrovatos (Hrvat), Tuga and Buga (Vuga). In his book *Historia Salonitana,* Archbishop Thomas of Split (ca.

1201–68) declared that the Croats were actually Slavs and cited eight noble Croatian tribes that ruled their lands. Other myths claim that they were of Gothic origin (the Goths arrived in the region between the third and sixth centuries). Benedictine monk and Ragusan chronicler Mauro Orbini proposed a theory on the Gothic origin of many ethnic groups, including all Slavs, in the early seventeenth century (*Il Regno del gli Slavi*, published in 1601). *The Kingdom of the Slavs* was translated into Russian in 1722, after which it was accessible to the Slavs. This theory of the Gothic origin of the Croats was also advocated by Ludwig Gumplowitz (1839–1909), a Polish lawyer and sociologist, and Kerubin Šegvić, a retired theology professor in Zagreb, during the brief period of the Independent State of Croatia (citing similarities between the glagolitic and runic alphabets).

A number of contemporary historians agree that the warrior tribes of Croats and Serbs—supposedly of Persian descent—subjugated the Slavs, who in turn quickly assimilated them. As was the case with the Bulgarians, their only legacy was their name. Croatian historian Vjekoslav Klaić (1849–1929) considered the Croats to be something special: in contrast to other peoples, they were, according to him, a "warring, noble and cavalier nation."[55] On the other hand, according to the myth of Serbian ethnogenesis, the Serbs are the descendants of a powerful and mysterious Hazar tribe that lived between the Caspian and Black Seas.

The Christianizing of the Croats' ancestors took place during the reign of Pope Agatho (678–81) and was completed in the ninth century. This process has been corroborated by archaeological findings and was described by Constantine VII Porphyrogenitus.[56] The first to teach Christianity to the new settlers were Romanic priests from Dalmatia who were trying to renew the church hierarchy in desolated Illyria. The regional center of Christianity prior to the arrival of the Avars and Slavs was in Solin. Ecclesiastic rights over the territory were then sought by neighboring centers of Christianity in Rome, Aquilea, Constantinople, Salzburg, and Split. Split became a new regional center of Christianity. Constantine VII Porphyrogenitus informs us that Croats living in Dalmatia were baptized by Roman missionaries in the seventh and eighth centuries, those living in Istria and the northwest were baptized by missionaries from Aquilea, and those living in the southeast by missionaries from Constantinople. The contributions of two missionaries, Cyril and Methodius, were especially significant: in addition to the comprehensive cultural legacy of the glagolitic alphabet (glagolitic writing, Slavonic liturgy), which they bequeathed to the Slavs, their disciples baptized the Croats and spread Christianity throughout the territory.

Frankish chroniclers in the early ninth century wrote that Prince Ljudevit Posavski of Sisak was "a devoted Christian."[57] Prince Trpimir *(Tripemerus, rex Sclavorum)*, a Frankish vassal and progenitor of the local dynasty, forged ties with the Benedictines, who had started building monasteries and spreading Christian culture in that territory. One Benedictine monk, theologian and Frankish delegate Godescale the Saxon (Godescalus, Gottschalck) of Orbais lived at his court. Trpimir was independent of the bishopric of the Split Church and fought to establish his own church. The only bishopric on Croatian territory was established in Nin during his reign.[58] Disputes arose between Trpimir and the Dalmatian bishoprics, which were in the hands of the local Romanic population.

Following the Frankish political ascendancy, the Byzantines returned to Croatia. However, even though parts of the Croatian territory were under Byzantine rule, the dispute over ecclesiastic jurisdiction was between Rome and Aquilea (in the late ninth century), especially during the reign of Pope Stephen VI (885–91). Prince Branimir (879–92) from Gornji Muć, the first independent Croatian ruler *(Dux Croatorum)*, reversed the foreign policies of his predecessor, Zdeslav (Sedeslav) Trpimirović, who favoured Byzantium. Branimir exchanged letters with Pope John VIII and Bishop Theodosius of Nin. He wrote to the pope as the "beloved son who wishes to be pious in all things and obedient to St. Peter and the Holy Father." In June, 880, the pope addressed his reply to the "noble Branimir, illustrious duke and our beloved son" and acknowledged his "territorial authority" *(principatum terenum)* over all of Croatia. His thirteen-year rule was to have long term and decisive consequences on subsequent Croatian history. During the reign of Mutimir (892–ca. 910), Branimir's son and heir, Bishop Theodosius of Nin unsuccessfully attempted to secure the archbishopric of Split with Aquilean support.[59]

Tomislav (ca. 910–28) was crowned as the first Croatian king in about 925 and claimed Slavonia for Croatia. The pope confirmed his title. The following poem was written for the occasion of his coronation:

> *Glory be to God on high and peace to men on earth,*
> *Glory and praise to God who had mercy on the people*
> *And gave unto them their own crowned king.*
> *Glory and praise to the holy Father, the Roman Pope.*
> *Glory and praise to the good Croatian King [Tomislav].*[60]

Pope John X (914–28) referred to the Croats as *specialissimi filli Sanctae Romanae Ecclesiae*, saying, "they received the spiritual food of the apostolic Church with their mother's milk whilst still in their cribs."[61] He did, however, oppose the glagolitic tradition. Two critical issues emerged at the beginning of the ninth century: the first was which liturgy to use, Latin or Slavonic, and the second concerned ecclesiastic jurisdiction over the territory settled by the Croats. Grgur Ninski, the bishop of Nin at the time and also known as the "Croatian Bishop" *(Episcopus Chroatensis)*, fell into dispute with Bishop John of Split over this second issue.

The synods of Split (assemblies of all the Dalmatian bishops) held in 925 and 928 ruled in favor of the Latin clergy in both cases: the bishopric of Split, referring to the tradition of the ancient bishopric of Solin, became the Metropolitan See; the bishopric of Nin was abolished (it had only been established a few decades earlier, in about 860) and Grgur was appointed bishop of Skradin *(Scradona)*. The use of the Slavonic liturgy was also banned. Pope John X approved the resolutions made at the synods. However, the use of the Slavonic liturgy continued for centuries, as did the use of the glagolitic alphabet. According to Ignacij Voje, a Slovenian expert on medieval southeastern European history, the bishop of Nin's attempt to secure primacy was later misrepresented as being an attempt to create a national church, whereas Tomislav supported the "Latins." The church was a feudal, not a national (and even less a national constitutive) institution during that period: "Grgur obviously challenged the Archbishop of Split over income (from taxes) and land, not the liturgical language." All of Croatia came under the ecclesiastical jurisdiction of the Latin clergy of Dalmatia, with coastal bishoprics extending their authority inland. Croatian rulers therefore "could not rely on the support of the Church to the same degree as if a high-ranking church official had lived in Croatian territory."[62]

The next important Croatian king was Peter Krešimir IV (1059–74), known as *rex Dalmatiae atque Croatiae* because of his annexation of Dalmatia. His coronation took place soon after the final schism between the Western and Eastern Churches (1054). The old dispute concerning the use of the Slavonic liturgy and the glagolitic alphabet remained unsolved. In response to the schism, the pope convened regional ecumenical councils across Europe. Pope Nicholas II (1058–61) sent papal legate Majnard to the Split synod of 1060. The Croatian and Dalmatian bishops accepted all of the resolutions made by the Lateran Council of 1059 and two additional resolutions: that all priests shave their beards and trim their hair (in order to distinguish them from Orthodox priests); and that only those who spoke Latin could be ordained as priests. The synod also condemned the use of the glagolitic alphabet, which was banned the following year by Pope Alexander II (1061–73). These measures were met with disapproval in Croatia and the synod's resolutions were rejected. Consequently, the synod had to be reconvened in 1063.

Dmitar Zvonimir reigned as king of Croatia and Dalmatia between 1075 and 1089. His reign coincided with that of Pope Gregory VII (1073–85), whose energetic reforms swept through the church, signifying an end to such irregularities as simony (the buying or selling of church office), nicolaitism (clerical marriage or concubinage), and laic investiture. During this period, the pope became the official patron of Croatia as well as a political ally. Through his legate Gebizon, the pope sent a crown to the king of Croatia and acknowledged his sovereignty over the region. In return, Zvonimir swore his allegiance and obedience to the Holy See. In order "to raise the prestige of the Croatian bishop," Zvonimir moved the seat of the bishopric to Knin.[63]

The burning issue of the Slavonic liturgy remained unsolved. Some popes tolerated it in spite of numerous protests. Pope Gregory VII sent his personal representative (Girard) to the synod of Croatian and Dalmatian bishops in Split (1075) where, among other issues, there were discussions about the use of the Slavonic liturgy and glagolitic writing. Much later, in 1248, Pope Innocent IV approved Bishop Filip of Senj's request to use the glagolitic alphabet and Slavonic liturgy, "but only in those areas where it is already in use."[64] The fact remains that the Croats were the only people in Western Christendom to conduct the liturgy in their native language: the glagolitic alphabet also remained in use well into the nineteenth century. Monastic orders played a very important role in the religious, cultural, artistic, and political life of the Croats. The Benedictines and Cistercians were followed by the popular Franciscans and Dominicans, and finally the Jesuits as the initiators of the ecclesiastic renewal after the Council of Trent.

The years following Zvonimir's death were marked by internal conflict, which was much to the liking of their powerful neighbors, the Hungarians. In 1094, King Ladislas of the House of Arpad founded the bishopric of Zagreb and placed it under the jurisdiction of the archbishopric of Esztergom in Hungary, although permission to do so had already been granted to King Stephen I (Saint Stephen, ca. 975–1038) by Pope Sylvester II (999–1003). In 1097, Ladislas's successor Coloman (1095–1116) conquered Croatia by defeating the last Croatian king, Petar, who fell in the battle at the foot of Gvozd Mountain (since referred to as "Petar's Mountain"). With the help of the pope, Coloman was crowned as king of Croatia in Biograd in 1102.

Croatia became a part of Hungary, also called the Kingdom of Saint

Stephen (Szent Istvan). This event is described in a document entitled *Pacta conventa* (or *Qualiter*). Coloman ennobled the "bearers of national sovereignty," meaning the representatives of twelve Croatian tribes, and signed a special contract with them.[65] The *"XII nobiles sapientiores de XII tribubus Chroatie"* elected Coloman as their king. He in turn pledged to heed the considerations of the Croatian assembly, conferred special rights on the Croatian nobility and allowed them to keep their possessions, promised them internal autonomy, and decreed separate coronations for the king of Croatia and Dalmatia. It had all the elements of a personal union between Hungary and Croatia. However, recent studies suggest that the document is a forgery and dates from a later period.[66] Croatia did become part of the kingdom of Hungary, but it retained a very high degree of internal autonomy and a powerful nobility.

THE SERBS: SETTLEMENT AND BAPTISM

Constantine VII Porphyrogenitus narrated the early history of the Serbs. Byzantium and Bulgaria scrambled for control over the Serbian principalities of Duklja, Rascia, and Zahumlje. Byzantine missionaries baptized the forefathers of the Serbs. In 891, Prince Mutimir declared Christianity to be the state religion. Kings Mihajlo (1050–82) and Bodin (1082–1101) of Duklja extended the borders of their kingdom inland until it included parts of Bosnia and Rascia as well as Zeta, Travunija, and Zahumlje. King Bodin exploited the schism in the church and persuaded Pope Urban II (1088–99) to confer metropolitan jurisdiction to the bishop of Bar in 1089. Duklja thus achieved ecclesiastic autonomy. The new archbishopric included the bishoprics of Serbia, Bosnia, and Trebinje, as well as those ruled from Kotor, Ulcinj, Drivast, and Pilot in northern Albania.[67] In the twelfth century, the center of gravity of Serbian nationhood moved inland to Rascia. The founder of the Nemanjić dynasty and the strong medieval state, and the first "collector" of Serbian land (to paraphrase a Russian expression), was the grand mayor (župan), Stephen Nemanja (1168–96), who was baptized in the Latin way. He formed a pact with Venice and Hungary in order to rid Serbia of Byzantine advances, but eventually had to accept the predominance of his powerful eastern neighbor. Stephen abdicated in 1196 and became a monk, assuming the name of Simeon; some time after his death in 1200 his remains were moved to the Studenica monastery.

The Bogomils arrived in medieval Serbia in the latter half of the twelfth century, coming from the cradle of this religious movement, Bulgaria and Macedonia. However, the Nemanjić rulers and Orthodox officials strongly opposed what was for them a "diabolical and cursed her-esy" that had even spread to the nobility, and ostracized the Bogomils. The *babuni* were said to be "false Christians" and, as antagonists to the Serbian Orthodox Church, were labeled as pariahs and accursed enemies of Christianity according to the miscellany of anathemas proclaimed in Orthodox churches during Sunday masses. They tried to destroy this "heresy" in two ways. The first was by conversion to Orthodoxy.[68] The second, applied by Stephen Nemanja, was to systematically exterminate the Bogomils, using the army and cruel punishments such as torching, expulsion, seizure, and torture. The result was their eradication. Those who survived fled the country. On the other hand, the Serbian Orthodox Church also "took an explicitly negative stand against the Bosnian *krst-jani* and their Church" by pronouncing anathemas and excommunicat-ing them.[69]

The first Serbian king, Stephen Prvovenčani (the "First Crowned"; 1196–1227) was crowned with a papal crown in 1217. He was benevolent toward Catholicism and Pope Innocent III (to whom he wrote a letter ex-pressing his loyalty), but remained true to Orthodoxy. Medieval Serbia opted for Orthodoxy because of the thirteenth-century balance of power in Balkans, which changed after the schism in the eleventh century and especially after the sacking of Constantinople by crusaders in 1204 and their brutal attitude toward the conquered. Indeed, it was this event and the establishment of the Latin Empire (1204–61) that "intensified the ha-tred of Eastern Christendom for the West."[70] Stephen's authority drew strong support from the versatile activities of his brother Rastko (Saint Sava; 1174–1236), who in 1219 secured autocephaly for Serbian Ortho-doxy and became the first archbishop of the Serbian Orthodox Church. Serbian Orthodoxy had previously been subordinated to the archbish-opric of Ohrid, established in 1018–20. The move received the approval of the emperor and the patriarch of Constantinople, both of whom were in exile in Nicea. Sava, the organizer and administrator of the Serbian Or-thodox Church, thus proved himself to be a proficient diplomat and "for-eign secretary" in what was then a complex international situation, and the political *éminence grise* at the Nemanjić court.

The seat of the archbishopric of Serbia, composed of nine bishoprics, was in the Žiča monastery near Kraljevo (and later in Peć, the "Serbian holy city"). Like his father Stephen Nemanja, Sava spent the last days of his life as a monk at the "holy mountain" of Athos in Greece, the spiri-tual capital of the Orthodox world. He and his father founded the Serbian monastery of Hilandar in this "great and serene refuge of pure Ortho-doxy" (located next to the Bulgarian Orthodox center of Zografon and the

Russian Panteleimon). In the ensuing centuries, Hilandar became the seat of Serbian theology. Sava was buried at the Mileševo monastery.

The Serbian kingdom and church were derived literally "from the same crib": the House of Nemanjić. The church was a highly respected, socially privileged, economically endorsed, and judicially favored institution surrounded and protected by the Serbian state. This resulted in a situation of mutual support between them, a *symphony* of secular and spiritual authority based on the verified Byzantine model, which George V. Tomashevich describes as one of "structural unity and functional harmony."[71] According to this concept, the state and the church are parallel powers that cooperate rather than compete and complement rather than contradict each other. This system is very different from that of the West, which was beset with intrigue, conflict, and even war between the two. As elsewhere in Europe, Serbian literature and painting were under the complete sponsorship and control of the state and the church.

Sava became one of the founders of Serbian ethnic self-awareness and Orthodoxy and remains popular to the present day, not only as an ecclesiastic patron and protector of the Serbs, but as a writer and educator as well. He is a true Serbian "cultural hero," believed to have taught the Serbs every important skill, from farming and crafts to mining and construction.[72] His name is therefore borne by various societies, associations, and religious and cultural institutions. Saint Sava was likened to the apostles (he was even referred to as the "instructor and teacher of the path that leads to life"). His significance to the Serbs is tantamount to that of Moses to the Jews. His organization of the Serbian Orthodox Church and the specific "quintessence" of Serbian Orthodoxy, so-called *svetosavlje*, are his lasting legacy to his successors.

The mid-thirteenth century was marked by conflict between the archbishoprics of Dubrovnik and Bar over jurisdiction in the hinterland. After much intrigue, the latter triumphed. The next great Serbian king was Milutin Uroš II (1282–1321), who extended the borders of his kingdom southward. His contribution to Orthodoxy was the construction of lavish and extravagantly frescoed monasteries. He was succeeded by his son, Stephen Dečanski, who reigned for ten years until finally being deposed and murdered by his son, Dušan (Stephen) the Strong (*Silni*, 1331–55). He increased the territory of Serbia to double its size, for which he will forever be etched in the memory of the Serbs as the king who was responsible for the golden era of Serbian statehood. In an effort to achieve supreme power in the East Balkans, Dušan elevated himself to "Emperor of the Serbs and Greeks" in March, 1346.[73] However, he first had to raise the Serbian archbishopric to the status of patriarchate. Joanikije became the first patriarch of the "Serbs and Greeks" after being elected by the patriarch of Bulgaria, the archbishop of Ohrid, and a representative from Mount Athos.[74] This emancipation provoked a strong reaction from the Greeks: conflict with the patriarch of Constantinople was inevitable. In the early 1350s, Patriarch Callistus proclaimed an anathema and excommunicated the Serbian Orthodox Church, but this had more to do with political than canonical issues. For all his efforts, Dušan was unable to reverse the schism. With the Ottoman threat growing in the east, Dušan sought relations with the papal curia. He sent an emissary to Avignon with a letter acknowledging Pope Innocent III as the father of Christianity. The pope responded by declaring him the "Captain of Christendom" in the battle against the Ottomans.

Dušan's renowned code of laws provided for the support and protection of the Serbian Orthodox Church: its officials were directly involved in discussions and decisions regarding the most important legislative and political issues. Dušan's reign represents the "golden era" of Serbian medieval statehood and is engraved in Serbia's mythical memory. Subsequent historical myths include mutually opposing binary contradictions and simplifications: Dušan "the Strong" is succeeded by Uroš, who is remembered in Serbian mythology as "the Weak." Uroš was not weak, but he personified the downfall of the state.

THE BATTLE OF KOSOVO: OUT OF TIME AND SPACE

It would be prudent at this juncture to focus some attention on the Battle of Kosovo, which became the centerpiece of the mythical self-understanding of the Serbs and Montenegrins, their "myth of all myths." Epic poetry dedicated to the battle formed the mythical foundation for a variety of ideological transformations, rejuvenation and new ideological conclusions in the nineteenth and twentieth centuries.

The Orthodox clergy placed its hopes for the restoration of the Serbian state in the hands of Prince Lazar Hrebeljanović (1329–89), whose ascent began in 1373. They tried to find a genealogical link between the Lazarević (Lazar's) family and the Nemanjić dynasty (and the flourishing medieval kingdom) in order to preserve the continuity that enjoyed divine favor.[75] The second pretender to the Nemanjić legacy—Tvrtko Kotromanić, who was actually from the Nemanjić bloodline (his grandfather was Stephen Dragutin Nemanjić)—was renounced by the Serbian Orthodox Church even though he declared himself king of Serbia and Bosnia. Nevertheless, the two were allies and fought on the same side against the Ottomans.

In the 1370s, Lazar succeeded in allaying the tension that had mounted between the patriarchates of Serbia (Peć) and Constantinople. With the intervention of Isaija, a Serbian monk from Mount Athos, Lazar and Patriarch Philotheus of Constantinople were finally reconciled. Although Philotheus acknowledged the legitimacy and autonomy of the Serbian patriarchate, he demanded that in the event of their ascent, the Serbs would not replace the local metropolitans and would omit any mention of the patriarch of Constantinople in their liturgy.[76] Both the Serbs and their clergy sighed in relief. Lazar built churches and made generous donations to the monasteries at Mount Athos, for which he received the support of the Serbian Orthodox Church and especially of Patriarch Spiridon.

From a wider historical perspective, the Battle of Kosovo was less important than the battle at the Marica River in 1371, at which the Mrnjačević brothers (the despot Uglješa and King Vukašin) were killed. Nevertheless, the Battle of Kosovo is of greater significance to Serbian mythical history and national self-consciousness. Lazar married his daughters to the rulers of neighboring lands in order to secure military support. Following decades of preparations and several minor skirmishes with the advancing Ottomans (at Pločnik in 1386 and Bileća in 1388, for example), he rode into the deciding battle with his two allies, Vuk Branković, his son-in-law and lord of Kosovo, and Duke Vlatko Vuković, the commander of King Tvrtko's Bosnian army. Units made up of Croatian and Albanian Christians also assisted him. The Ottomans were also aware of the importance of the battle: the units—including Ottoman Christian vassals—were under the command of Sultan Murad I (1362–89) and his two sons, Bajazit (who later succeeded him, 1389–1402), and Jakub.

According to the myth, the outcome of the battle had been revealed to the Serbs three years earlier: several omens foretold the future defeat of the Serbs at the hands of the Muslims: "the sun changed to darkness, the stars appeared at noon and the moon was bathed in blood."[77] The fierce battle took place on Vidovdan (Saint Vitus's Day), June 15 (28), 1389. Both sides suffered heavy losses: Prince Lazar and Sultan Murad I were slain, and both armies were exhausted when they finally withdrew. In the long run, however, the consequences were fateful for the Serbian state, which could not recover the loss. In the European West (first Trogir, then Florence), the inconclusive outcome of the battle was mistakenly seen as a victory for Christendom and was attributed to King Tvrtko of Bosnia, who was in Florence and consequently declared the "savior of Christianity."

The Battle of Kosovo became the key event of Serbian national and religious mythology—its "higher criterion" to use Bellah's syntagma[78]—an essential reference that divides time itself into the period *before* and *after* the battle (the "medieval kingdom" before, and "servitude" after). Orthodox officials and theologians explained this event in their own manner. Some sources went so far as to divide world history into two periods: from Creation to the Battle of Kosovo, and from the Battle of Kosovo to the period of the writer. The destruction of the Serbian state at the Battle of Kosovo generated a succession of mythical explanations and other defensive mechanisms intended to redeem the ethnocentric complacency of the Serbs, albeit at the expense of logical consistency and historical accuracy.

The interpretations can be categorized into two types: pessimistic and optimistic. The pessimistic interpretation suggests that the Serbian Empire was destroyed by "sin." The Muslims, the "Ishmaelites" *(Izmailćani)* or "Hagarites" of the Old Testament, were "sent by God to punish our sins." Another source claims that the Ottomans were "abhorred by God." They were, according to Patriarch Danilo, "the satanic enemy." Sultan Murad was portrayed as the bloodthirsty lion sent against the Christian lambs.[79] According to these myths, God was "punishing" the Serbs for the vileness and other sins of their nobility. Their authors seemed to suggest that the defeat was a catastrophe of cosmic proportions, a biblical drama, a Serbian Christology.

The second, more optimistic, interpretation of the battle is based on the theological postulate that death is a precondition for resurrection. Lazar's self-sacrifice was seen as being Christological *(imitatio Christi)* because he dies "as a man and as Christ." He allegedly told his warriors, "It is better to die in heroic deed than to live in shame!" (This became a frequently used phrase in different Serbian resurrections and in preparations for war.) His soldiers thus embraced martyrdom, salvation, and eternal life through suffering (they were summoned to battle with the cry, "Let us die and live forever!"). He armed them with the heroic transcendental belief that they "became martyrs in their heroism."[80] His "blissful death" implied "eternal bliss in the Heavenly Kingdom." Lazar achieved an "ethereal victory," choosing the "Eternal Kingdom" in heaven rather than an "ephemeral" life on Earth (for example, in "The Decline of the Serbian Kingdom"). In the same manner, Jesus Christ died so that his people may survive. In short, Lazar got what he wanted, as illustrated in these verses from the "Eulogy to the Blessed Prince Lazar":

So have you achieved your two desires:
You have indeed slain the serpent
And you received from God the martyr's wreath.

Epic tradition also bequeaths the title of "Tsar" to Prince Lazar. According to legend, this "soldier of Christ," this warrior "for Holy Cross and Sweet Freedom," had already made the decision to give his life and rise to heaven before even going into battle. By making this decision, Lazar is said to have charted the course of his people's destiny, a course that embraces spiritual and immortal values, that remains unchanged by the ordeals of time. Ever since, the Serbs have been experiencing history as though it were a "dramatic stage play, anticipating the final victory of the just and the good," for only thus will fulfill their eschatologically determined destiny[81] Works such as *Žitije kneza Lazara, Slovo o knezu Lazaru*, and *Prološko žitije kneza Lazara* bear witness to this.

Prince Lazar, who was eventually canonized, became a "martyr for God and country," a "decorous successor" to the spiritual, national, and cultural grandeur and magnanimity of the House of Nemanjić. Because of his popularity among the Orthodox clergy and Serbs in general, and because of his efforts to normalize relations between the Serbian and Constantinople patriarchates, the Serbian Orthodox Church embarked on creating his cult immediately after his death. The monks of Mount Athos especially venerated him.

In addition to Prince Lazar's martyrdom, two other topics figure prominently in Serbian myths about Kosovo: betrayal and heroism. Vuk Branković, a historical figure, is accused of the cowardly act of deserting from battle with his army, thus betraying Prince Lazar. The myth of betrayal evolved slowly over the course of two centuries and is, from a historical perspective, pure fabrication: its popularity was increased by, among others, the Ragusan chronicler Mauro Orbini.[82] Branković's first "sin" was that he survived the Kosovo massacre and, hence, did not choose the "Heavenly Kingdom." He did not fit the ideals of the authors of the myths, who viewed the destruction of the Serbian army and the loss of the "Earthly Kingdom" as a victorious choice for the "Heavenly Kingdom."

Branković continued to wage war against the Ottomans after the Battle of Kosovo; he made an alliance with the king of Hungary, thus marring the schemes of Lazar's widow, Princess Milica. Later still, he achieved some military success, seizing Skopje from Marko Kraljević, a Turkish vassal. The Ottomans eventually captured Branković and he died in prison in 1397. Serbian historian Mihaljčić legitimately concludes that Branković did not betray Lazar's cause after Kosovo but more likely "he betrayed the hopes of the Lazarevićs and their loyal supporters." Namely, Princess Milica offered the hand of her youngest daughter, Olivera (with the approval of the Serbian patriarch and the ecclesiastic synod), to the new sultan, Bajazit, in an attempt to protect the Christian population.[83] Still later, the daughter of Đurađ Lazarević, Mara, was married to Murad II (1421–51), who was succeeded by Mehmed the Conqueror. Milica, the patriarch, and the synod were therefore willing to accept Ottoman domination. This was Branković's second "sin," and it proved even more fatal than the first. As an opponent of the official, defeatist line of Serbian authority, he became the antihero of Serbian mythical tradition.

Complementing Vuk's "betrayal" is the "heroism" of the mythical figure of Miloš Obilić (known up to the seventeenth century as Kobilić, Kobilović, or Kobila). Because Lazar wrongfully accused him of disloyalty and treason, Miloš, according to myth, tried to prove his innocence by stealing into the enemy's camp and slaying Murad. As is often the case, the essence of the myth is based on an undisputed historical fact: an unknown Serbian warrior did indeed kill the Ottoman commander at the cost of his own life. Folk tradition mythologized the personality of Obilić. He was said to be a prodigious child, partly because of his mother's magical milk. Other versions say he was a forsaken child, nursed in the mountains by a fairy, or that he was the son of a shepherd girl, Janja, and a dragon. He was said to have a marvelous winged steed (Ždralin). He was given a magical sword by the fairy and was said to possess superhuman strength. His blood brother was a dragon, and he was said to be virtuous, a protector of the poor, and so on. Epic stories and tales about Obilić also often featured the mythical number three. All the characteristics attributed to Obilić generally match those of other Indo-European heroes.

According to Mihaljčić, it took the Serbian Orthodox Church four centuries to begin venerating Obilić because of the nature of his death (by the sword) and his low birth. Instrumental to the popularization of this "holy warrior" were the monks from the monastery at Hilandar. However, his cult spread among the ordinary people much earlier, and he was believed to have been "chosen by God."[84] Miloš Obilić appears as a hero in the folk traditions of Albanians, Herzegovinians, Montenegrins, and Croats as well. The Kosovo myths also panegyrize the deaths of the nine Jugović brothers and their father, Bogdan Jugo, as well as their mother, who died of heartache; the fate of Obilić's brothers, Ivan Kosanić and Milan Toplica; and Strahinja Banović, Srdja Zlopogledja, Pavla Orlović, the Maid of Kosovo and flower *božur* as well as other titles.

Lazar's successor, the despot Stephen Lazarević (1389–1427), acknowledged the dominance of the Ottomans and took part in their battles and conquests (at Rovine and Nikopolje, for example). The vassal Serbian army also took part in the Ottoman siege of Constantinople, the Battle of Angora, and the second Battle of Kosovo in 1448, as well as in the conquest of the central and northern Balkan Peninsula and the infighting between various pretenders to the Ottoman throne. Paradoxically, the Christian army contributed to the external and internal political consolidation of the Ottoman Muslim Empire.

At the same time these events were taking place in the Balkans, the "Turkish terror" was spreading across western Europe. It was considered the greatest danger to Christendom *(Corpus Christianorum)*. Islam became a long-term trauma for Europe: "a symbol of violence, destruction, and demonism for hordes of detested barbarians."[85] It was called the "religion of dogs." Erasmus of Rotterdam said of the Ottomans that they were a "band of barbarians posing the greatest danger to Christendom," and that they were "victoriously advancing towards the heart of Europe solely because of the discord between the Christians." He saw them as monstrous beasts and enemies of the church. His contemporary Thomas More saw "bloodthirsty and ruthless Turks" as an "ignoble, superstitious sect" of Christ's "sworn, deadly enemies." Martin Luther also supported the wars against the Turks, the Turkenkrieg, accusing them of being the servants of Satan, a tool in the hands of the devil, a savage people under whose yoke Christianity would not survive.[86]

Others viewed the Ottomans as "divine retribution." Pope Pius II's main purpose as the Roman pontiff was, in his own words, to "rally Christianity against the Turks and wage war on them." His predecessors Nicholas V (who saw Mohammed as the son of Satan, and the sultan as the harbinger of the Antichrist) and Calixtus III (who also saw Mohammed as the son of Satan) shared those sentiments. Plans were drawn for an anti-Ottoman *(contra Turcos)* alliance or new crusade, but the divisions within the Christian West were far too great for any meaningful action to result. It was, however, on the basis of the mobilization against this external menace, this radical element—Islam, the Turks, and the Orient—that the concept of Europe began to take shape, a concept that, from the early years of the Modern Era, defined and gave form to the self-understanding of Western Christians, who began to see themselves as Europeans.[87] However, the attitude toward Ottomans was ambivalent: Europeans feared them, while at the same time admiring their power, ability, and organization.

Anti-Ottoman sentiments were further fueled by clerics and writers from the still-unconquered parts of the Balkans, such as the aforementioned Dominican monk from Croatia, Ivan Stojković; Andrija Jamometić (ca. 1420–1484, the provincial of the Greek Dominican Province and archbishop of Kruja, Albania), another Dominican; Prince Bernard Frankopan; and, after him, Vuk Frankopan. In the mid-fifteenth century, Franciscan monk Johannes Capistranus zealously argued for a crusade against the Ottomans and even led German, Polish, and Hungarian crusaders into battle against them. After winning a battle against the Ottomans near Belgrade in 1456 with Hungarian regent Janos Hunyadi, he enthusiastically wrote to the pope, saying that the time had come for the liberation not only of Greece and Europe, but of the Holy Land as well.[88] In 1522, Marko Marulić (1450–1524), a Dalmatian humanist from Split and the "Father of Croatian Literature," asked Pope Adrian IV (1522–23) to liberate Christian lands (including parts of Croatia) from Ottoman rule because the "common danger must be driven back with a combined force." The following are two excerpts from his work "Prayers Against the Turks" published in 1522:

> They pursue us, bind us, beat us, flay us,
> They care nought for you, nor for your faith,
> Which they have resolved to trample underfoot;
> As by force of their might they have crushed so many.
>
> Show us, Lord, that, as Your anger can
> Cause us pain for our transgressions,
> So can you also protect us with your mercy,
> And through your power restore to us our freedom,
> Turn back the Turks from their infidel sin,
> Lessen their force, which slays as it flays.[89]

Anti-Ottoman and Islamophobic sentiments were also aroused by exhibiting Ottoman spoils, colors, and seized weapons, by displaying captured Muslim prisoners, and through anti-Ottoman sermons and calls for new crusades. This indirectly promoted the sense of European Christian kinship and encouraged the active defense of Europe.

MEDIEVAL BOSNIA: BETWEEN RELIGIOUS TOLERANCE AND INDIFFERENCE

After this brief look at the medieval religious history of three Slavic Balkan states, we return to Bosnia. One of Bosnia's idiosyncrasies was that its rulers and nobility were largely indifferent to religious issues. As a result, conversions were common, although there were no explicit or sanctioned proselytizing undertakings, such as mass conversions. Despite the political and military turmoil, no widespread or lasting religious intolerance, conflict, or religious wars originated from its territory. The situation was, therefore, very different from that prevailing in other parts of Europe, where conflict and massacres were often motivated by religious differences, and where religious strife was a widely accepted phenomenon.

Religion itself was not the dominating political factor in Bosnian internal history. That happened only when external forces used it as an excuse for their interventions on Bosnian soil. The doctrinally and organizationally different or even mutually exclusive Christian religious communities did not upset the religious symbiosis of the Bosnian population. Nevertheless, there were a few individual exceptions to this—periodic Roman Catholic conversion campaigns, for example—especially immediately before the downfall of the kingdom. The roots of religious heterodoxy, eclecticism, and relative tolerance—important factors in Bosnia-Herzegovina's religious history—were sown during this period.

Despite the dismantling of the Bosnian Church, the concept of the religious seclusion of the Bosnian population from their Orthodox and Roman Catholic neighbors remained alive. There can be no doubt that a specific *Bosnian* political, cultural, and religious identity did indeed exist in medieval Bosnia, a conscious sense of belonging shared by the majority of the population. It was an identity that was constantly being put to the test by Bosnia's trying neighbors, but it endured throughout the Middle Ages. The evolution of this singular Bosnian identity was encouraged by the region's specific judiciary system, currency, alphabet, and customs. The people identified themselves as Bosnians *(Bošnjani)* in a geographic rather than an ethnic or religious sense—"they served the Bosnian state, or identified themselves as subjects of the Bosnian king."[90]

3

PAX OTTOMANICA
Religions in Ottoman Bosnia

The fifteenth-century kingdom of Bosnia found itself in a very difficult situation, caught between the Hungarian anvil and the Ottoman hammer. After decades of clashes, incursions, and the partial Ottoman occupation that followed the battle at Bileća in 1388, Bosnia was conquered in just one month. Bosnia was "quietly subdued" early in the summer of 1463 by Sultan Mehmed II el Fatih the Conqueror (1451–81), whose brilliant military victories included the seizure of Constantinople in 1453.[1] Herzegovina (called *Hersek* by the Ottomans) was taken in 1481. The first *sandžak-beg* of Bosnia was Isa beg Isaković, who had previously governed the neighboring Serbian territories ruled by the Branković dynasty. Resistance to the Ottomans abated the deep-rooted hatred for and mistrust of neighboring Hungary. Some Bosnian rulers had been Ottoman vassals for shorter periods several decades before the occupation, and the Bosnian people had become accustomed to the powerful new neighbors and their religion. There was no organized religious persecution of Christians during the military occupation of Bosnia and the consolidation of the new authority's power.

Between 1463 and 1580, the newly conquered territory fell under the "*sandžak* of Bosnia," with its administrative seat first at Sarajevo (Turkish *Saray-ovasi*, "Court in the Field"; previously Vrhbosna), then at

I am convinced that the heretical past of the people has left them confessionally weak, therefore transferring their allegiance to Islam in order to preserve their liberty upon the arrival of the Turks in Bosnia.

—APOSTOLIC VISITOR PETER MASARECHI, 1624

Banja Luka (Banaluka). In 1580 it was renamed the "Province of Bosnia" *(eyalet,* later *pashaluk),* and was composed of seven military administrative districts *(sandžaks),* namely, Bosnia, Herzegovina, Bihać (Bihke), Zvornik (Izvornik), Pakrac, Krka, Klis (which lay to the east of the Dalmatian city of Split), and (until 1606) Požega as well. In the centuries that followed, it was to undergo further administrative division. Bosnia—administered by the vizier—differed from other Ottoman provinces because of its vulnerable borders, its varied ethnic and religious structure, the extent of its eventual Islamization, its greater autonomy, and lower taxes. It became a strategic base from which the Ottomans launched their armies northward and westward on campaigns of conquest and pillage. The Turks regarded Bosnia as a "bastion of Islam" and its inhabitants served as frontier guards *(serhatlije).*[2]

Slovenian observer Benedikt Kuripečič (also Kuripešić) compiled the first reports on these three major—increasingly crystallized and selfaware—religious communities in the 1530s. It is difficult to estimate the size of the population or the people's religious affiliation. According to records for 1528 and 1529, there were a total of 42,319 Christian and 26,666 Muslim households in the *sandžaks* of Bosnia, Zvornik, and Herzegovina. The population figures for individuals were, of course, several times higher. In a 1624 report on Bosnia (excluding Herzegovina) by apostolic visitor Peter Masarechi, the population figures are given as 450,000 Muslims, 150,000 Catholics, and 75,000 Orthodox.[3]

The theocratic and nonethnically organized Ottoman regime exercised a considerable degree of tolerance toward other monotheistic religious communities. Tomašić ascertained that "religious, social, and ethnic tolerance of Islam made it possible for Christians to develop freely regardless of their ethnicity and faith."[4] This not only ensured that the religious rulers remained in power, it also helped to spread and strengthen their hegemony. The empire gave refuge to thousands of Jews fleeing persecution in Spain and Portugal following the Christian *reconquista* in the late fifteenth century. The exact opposite happened after the Ottomans departed from parts of the Balkans (in southern Hungary and parts of Croatia and Serbia, for example). There was widespread destruction of Islamic cultural achievements, especially buildings, and the Muslim population was persecuted and forced to convert back to Christianity. Today, almost no signs of the Ottoman presence remain in these areas.

When compared to medieval and early Renaissance Europe and Balkan states after the Ottoman retreat, religious freedom and tolerance during this first period of Ottoman rule was at a much higher level. The

rulers tolerated all "people of the Book" (Ahl'el-Kitab) under their jurisdiction because Christians and Jews were considered to have received
God's pre-Islamic revelations. However, this officially recognized toleration was often violated: there was a clear distinction between the positions and possibilities of Muslims and non-Muslims in many vital aspects of political and social promotion. As Bosnian Croat historian
Srećko Džaja emphasizes, it is true that "Islamic Shariat law formed legal and ideological basis for the relations to the Christian subjects," but
its actual employment depended more on political than on legal decisions: in practice, Ottomans sometimes "comported generously and
sometimes violently and cruel."[5] The increasingly patent privileges
awarded to Muslims did not become evident until the Ottoman expansion came to a halt after the golden era of endless conquests.

The partial conversion of Bosnia's Slavic population to Islam corresponded to the development of towns as centers of Ottoman and Muslim
culture and prosperity. In this regard, the situation in Bosnia-
Herzegovina during the Ottoman period was similar to other parts of the
Balkans: whereas the towns were predominately Muslim (for example,
Muslims represented 96.79 percent of Sarajevo's population in 1604), the
surrounding area possessed a preponderance of Christians. Vucinich
states that Turkish immigrants and other foreign citizens—Greeks, Jews,
Armenians, Vlachs, Ragusans, and Germans, for example—populated
towns in Serbia and Bulgaria. The migration of the local Slav population
to urban areas did not begin until the eighteenth century.[6] Thus, in addition to differences in culture and affluence between town dwellers and
country folk, there were religious and ethnic differences as well. These
differences were strongly expressed in anti-Ottoman insurrections and
during the period of national awakening. National renascence and rebellion was instigated in the countryside, where the preservation of ancient
myths, traditions, and ethnic and religious awareness were under the care
of country priests.

Christian people in the Balkans underwent an interesting sociological regression in terms of spiritual creativity and organization: cultural
stagnation and a revival of tribal communities—*zadruge* for Orthodox
communities, *katune* for pastoral communities, and *knežine* for self-
government communities. This regression was evident whether compared to Christian Europe or to the highly stratified pre-Ottoman
medieval states. The return of communities to a primitive and barbaric
state and the reemergence of tribal culture were further hastened by the
departure of the clergy and intelligentsia, who fled to the east (Russia,
southern Hungary, and Romania) and west (Dubrovnik and the Venetian

Republic). However, these basic, primordial social structures ultimately played a crucial role in preserving the traditional, religious, and cultural characteristics of the peoples.[7] The ancestor cult and belief in mythological and historical heroes, militarism, religious messianism, and stubbornness were common within these communities. For lack of any other methods and institutions of recording their collective memory and traditions (public records, nobility, intellectuals, written literal tradition), they developed a rich oral tradition for spreading their knowledge. The Serbian myth thus became a "document of special distinction, which enabled the survival of certain existential forms and established a bridge between generations which preserved and transmitted them."[8] The ancestor cult, which gave rise to the sacralization of rulers, was particularly strong. According to historian Stanford J. Shaw, this cultural underachievement cannot be ascribed solely to the "iron curtain" that separated Christian and Ottoman Europe, but also to the strong influence of the local clergy, which was isolated from ecclesiastical centers and thus intellectually deficient and theologically uninstructed.[9]

The Austrians settled Orthodox Serbs in the so-called Vojna Krajina or Military Frontier (Militärgrenze) in Croatian lands. For three centuries after its inception (1577–1881), the Vojna Krajina was ruled directly by the Habsburg War Council in Vienna. It included the Slavonian (Križevci) and Croatian regions (Senj, Otočac, Ogulin, Karlovac), as well as Žumberak and its vicinity. The fact that the Vojna Krajina was not included in the banate of Croatia is of some significance. The privileges of the *"krajišniks" (krajišnici)*, the inhabitants of the Vojna Krajina, were chartered in the "Statuta Valachorum" or Laws of the Vlachs, which was approved by Habsburg monarch Ferdinand II (1578–1637) personally. The charter entitled them to land and local self-government, and guaranteed them freedom of worship. They were permitted to select their own barons and magistrates, and to trade freely. Confronting the Austrian Vojna Krajina was the Turkish military frontier, which gave rise to a unique class of privileged military aristocracy. Most of the "captains" *(kapudans)*, the administrators of local frontier regions known as "captaincies" *(kapetanije)*, were of Bosnian origin.

THE MILLET SYSTEM

From the sixteenth century, when Western Christendom was in schism, western and central Europe were rapidly approaching the ideal of *cuius regio, eius religio* ("he who governs the territory decides its religion").

The religion in this case is Catholic or Protestant Christianity. On the other hand, the internal organization of the Ottoman Empire was entirely different, based on the principle "your religion is yours, my religion is mine." The most important institution, which not only guaranteed the survival of and provided protection for all religious groups under Ottoman rule but also ensured their augmentation, was the millet system (Arabic *milla*, Turkish *millet*—meaning *religion* or *rite*; it did not come to denote nations until the nineteenth century). People living in the Ottoman Empire were divided according to religious affiliation rather than political association. The millet associated members of individual religions into relatively autonomous and protected assemblages, which had an organized internal hierarchy and was subordinated to the sultan.

The millet system gradually evolved in response to the endeavors of the Ottoman administration to consider the requirements of the organizations and cultures of the different religious and ethnic groups under its suzerainty.[10] In the first instance, it encouraged their religious, cultural, and ethnic continuity. In the second, it facilitated their participation in the Ottoman administrative, economic, and political apparatus.[11] It was, basically, a system that segregated members of different religions in order to prevent contact or even conflict between them. Millets did not correspond to geographic areas or homogenous ethnic or political groups. Individual religious leaders selected by the congregation and approved by the sultan, who was often paid to approve patriarchal appointments, administered them. Needless to say, this practice stimulated corruption within the churches. There existed, therefore, a specific clerical leadership within the Christian communities that showed a remarkable degree of adaptive realism. The autonomy guaranteed by the millet system covered a broad range of subjects—from the observance of local traditions and commerce, to property, the judiciary, weddings, education, tax collection, and so forth.

At first, the millet system was composed of mutually segregated religious communities: Muslim, Orthodox (including the autocephalous Greek Orthodox Church—and for some time the Serbian Orthodox Church as well), the heterogeneous "Armenian" (Georgian or Monophysitic, which also included Roman Catholics, Nestorians, and Jacobites), and Jewish.[12] The emphasis on distinguishing between individual religious (and, to a limited extent, ethnic) groups prevented the mass conversion of the population to Islam. At the same time, it presented an obstacle to the evolution of specific national identities. However, it was on the very basis of millet religious groups that they later sprang out. One result was that the Turkish nationality and "Ottomanism" did not emerge until the nineteenth century—and even then it was primarily because of European influences.[13]

Religious, ethnic, and linguistic pluralism and relative Ottoman tolerance toward Christians and Jews existed not only in Bosnia, but in other parts of the Ottoman Empire as well. Indeed, we may speak of the religious, cultural, and social "pillarization" of Ottoman society, which therefore was not forcibly homogenized but rather was organized in the sense of the adage, "To each race, it's own creed."[14] The extent of Ottoman jurisdiction was limited to criminal, cadastral, and tax law: millets were autonomous in almost every other aspect. The Ottoman society of the time was thus a provocatively complex assemblage of segregated societies, worlds unto themselves, a "mutual life asunder." Muslims, Orthodox, and Catholics living side-by-side in a state of latent repulsion were people who had little knowledge of each other and eyed each other reservedly and even suspiciously. There was an ambivalence that swayed between the extremes of tolerance and hatred at different stages in Ottoman history.

The millet system, based on relative religious tolerance as well as religious exclusivity, had an internal hierarchy: at the top of the ladder was the Muslim millet, *millet-i islamiyye*, which was privileged in all aspects. The Ottoman sultan—beginning with Selim I (1512–20), who conquered Egypt and parts of Arabia (including Mecca and Medina), was also the caliph, or religious leader, of the Muslim world—"Mohammed's successor."

At the head of the second largest millet (*Rum milleti*—the Roman people), the Orthodox millet, was the patriarch of Constantinople—the ecumenical patriarch of the Eastern Orthodox Church—whose election was subject to approval by the sultan and the "porte" (the official title of the imperial government in Istanbul). The patriarchate was established in 1454 under Patriarch Gennadios II Scholarios, and, for the first time since the golden age of the Byzantine Empire, united almost all Orthodox Christians under one roof. However, in contrast to the period when the patriarch of Constantinople was a minion of the emperor, he became a respected counsel at the sultan's court, with full jurisdiction over his congregation, including judicial powers. He ruled with the help of an "oligarchy of patriarchs," namely, the patriarchs of Antioch, Alexandria, and Jerusalem. The Ottomans favored the Orthodox millet over other religious communities because the patriarch of Constantinople and his whole hierarchy lived within the empire, where they could be easily controlled.

The patriarchs of Constantinople exploited the political suzerainty of the Ottomans and tried to recentralize and Hellenize the Orthodox Church. Their aspirations corresponded to Ottoman military victories. They endeavored to abrogate the old Slavic liturgy of the Orthodox Slavs, destroyed Slavic liturgical books, and replaced the Slavic clergy with Greek priests. The Phanariots—high-ranking Greek state officials and Orthodox priests—could still be found in Slavic Orthodox churches in the late-nineteenth century (in Serbia up to 1831). Their name was derived from the Phanar district in Istanbul, and most of them were from aristocratic Greek Orthodox families. They were called the "Christian Turks" and "slaves to tyranny" because of the avarice and ruthlessness with which they asserted their interests.[15] They gradually occupied all the important posts in the Orthodox hierarchy. Their attempts to Hellenize all Balkan Orthodox Christians by forcefully spreading the Greek language continued as late as the eighteenth century.[16]

The case of the Orthodox millet was one of co-option—a stable and cooperative relationship between the church and the state. In return for certain benefits, the church was loyal to the regime and even supported it. Vucinich mentions the privileges enjoyed by the high-ranking Orthodox clergy under the Ottoman regime. Simony, opportunism, avarice, usury and sybaritic behavior were also rife. On the other hand, Orthodox churches preserved not only the religion and customs of the subject peoples, but the cultural tradition and continuity between the past and the future as well. The Orthodox Church gained certain political functions: it represented the Orthodox population at the Ottoman court, it supported and led rebellions, established and developed foreign relations (with Venice, Rome, Austria, Russia), and maintained its central role in society.[17] All this was done at the theological and intellectual expense of the Orthodox faith. It was firmly opposed to Roman Catholic proselytizing, and the issues of tax collection—which was carried out by Orthodox hierarchy—and the ownership of sacral buildings and church property further aggravated relations between the Orthodox and Roman Catholic churches. In those kinds of disputes, "the Ottoman authorities usually favored the Orthodox." Roman Catholic priests in the Balkans had to pay a beard tax, the so-called *bradarina*—permission to shave their beards. All of these factors provoked tension if not hostility among Christians. According to an English traveler who passed through the Balkans in the 1630s, Orthodox and Catholic Christians were "so desperate malitious towards one another, as each loves the Turks better than they doe either of the other."[18]

Catholics in the Ottoman Empire belonged to the Armenian millet (established in 1461), which was presided over by the Armenian patriarch. This millet was also called the "infidel millet." Within the Armenian patriarchate, to which all non-Orthodox Christian churches belonged, each religious group had its own organizational structure. The Ottomans were far less tolerant toward the Roman Catholic Church—the church of their worst enemy, the Habsburg Empire—than toward the Orthodox Church. Although the Roman Catholic Church was acknowledged by the Ottoman regime and was "granted the essential legal status necessary to continue its activities, [it] was regarded with deep suspicion." Catholics were seen as a potential fifth column. In occupied Hungarian territories, the Ottomans even "supported the Protestant and Calvinist movements as a counterweight against the Catholic Church."[19]

The Jewish *(yahudi)* millet, established in the fifteenth century, brought together all four Jewish sects in the Ottoman Empire: the Sephardim, Ashkenazi, Rabbanites, and Karaites. Their head was the rabbi of Erdine (Adrianople), and later the rabbi of Constantinople. He headed the community with the assent of the Ottoman authorities. Jewish communities all over the Ottoman Empire—and in Bosnia as well—had their own administration of justice. In the lower ranks, religious leadership was appointed to local rabbis, who in turn were supported by the most influential individuals in the Jewish political and economic community. Over the centuries, local communities were able to gradually increase their power and autonomy.[20]

The millet system of self-management preserved and encouraged religious tolerance. Nonetheless, it discriminated against the "infidels," who were denied the right to bear arms or ride horses, were required to follow a specific dress code, and whose testimony in court was less substantial than that of their Muslim counterparts. Under the millet system, all privileges—social, economic, and political—were reserved for Muslims.[21] Indeed, a good metaphor for this was that no Christian bell tower was allowed to be higher than a Muslim minaret. Hatred for Ottoman authority also was strong because of some of its discriminatory activities. One of the most painful was known as *devşirme* (the collection), the systematic kidnapping of boys from Christian families, their conversion to Islam and training them to become soldiers (special *janissary* units) or state officials. The practice was not abandoned until the first half of the seventeenth century. Although there were vast differences between Muslims and non-Muslims in terms of status, social standing, and standard of living, they were also substantial within these groups. All of these factors combined to create serious tensions within society. However, it was the very nature of the millet system that caused religion to become one of the most important factors for the survival of ethnic groups and the emergence of the nations that were later liberated from the Ottoman suzerainty and emancipated. Despite all its shortcomings, the millet system was, according to Kemal H. Karpat, a "unique institution" in the annals of social history.

ISLAM'S SUCCESS IN BOSNIA

During the centuries of Ottoman expansion, the opportunity for geographical and vertical social mobility was open to all members of society. Christians and Jews were able to ascend political, social, and military ladders, especially if they converted to Islam. Many Balkan converts to Islam, especially Bosnians, ascended to various high positions. They were appointed to serve as *beglerbegs*, janissary commanders, mullahs, pashas, muftis, writers, and so forth in Istanbul, Jerusalem, and Medina.[22] Serbo-Croat became one of the diplomatic languages of the porte. Guilds *(esaf)* and commerce were another means of climbing the social ladder. At least seven viziers were of Bosnian origin, of which the most renowned was Mehmed-pasha Sokolović. One of the sons of Stephen, the *vojvoda* (duke) of Herzegovina, made a successful career at the royal court in Istanbul. After converting to Islam and assuming the name Ahmed Hercegović (1456–1516), he gained favor with Sultan Mehmed II, who later became his father-in-law. At the beginning of the sixteenth century he became grand vizier *(Hersek-zade Ahmed pasha)* under Sultan Selim I. Ahmed's son became the *sandžak-beg* in southeast Anatolia, and his grandson, Ahmed Čelebi, also became a high official.[23]

An interesting example is furnished by the fate of Osman pasha, whose original family name was Popović. He was of Orthodox peasant stock and converted to Islam as a boy after running away from home and making his way to Sarajevo. There he was raised by a pasha and sent for training and instruction to Istanbul, where his career advanced rapidly. Starting in the 1670s, he was appointed to several high positions, including military representative *(kajmakam)* to the governor of Syria, *beglerbeg* of Anatolia and Bosnia, *sandžak-beg* of Požega, and governor of Egypt, Damascus, and Erlau castle in northern Hungary.[24] He was also one of the commanders during the siege of Vienna in 1683.

Social and religious polarization increased during the centuries that marked the decline of the Ottoman Empire. Whereas feudal estate holders previously could be either Christian or Muslim, all the major landowners in the nineteenth century were Muslim, and the majority of peasants working the land were Christians. The Muslim elite (including ethnic Slavs), more than any other group in Bosnia-Herzegovina, identified themselves with the Ottomans because of the economic and political privileges they received.[25]

The millet system maintained and increased the religious, ethnic, social, and cultural differentiation of the population. It was not Ottoman policy to support the assimilation of conquered peoples into their culture, traditions, or language, or even to convert them to Islam. Nor was it Ottoman policy to support the integration of different cultures or religions. In other words, there was no effort to "Ottomanize" the population. Attempts to convert people to Islam were limited. However, the abrogation of Islam and conversion to Christianity was punishable by death until the nineteenth century, after which apostates were "merely" banished.

The first conversions to Islam (Sunni branch) in Bosnia-Herzegovina took place soon after the arrival of the Ottomans. The process was gradual, but it later became widespread. For different reasons, up to one-fifth of the population had converted to Islam by the end of the fifteenth century, and as much as one-quarter or even one-third had done so by the mid-sixteenth century.[26] The scale of conversion elsewhere in the Balkans was not as high, with the exception of Albania and parts of Bulgaria (Pomaks) and Macedonia (Torbeši).[27] There are several reasons for this Bosnian peculiarity. There was a great deal of confusion and competition in religious circles. Religious anomy and doctrinal ignorance facilitated the conversion of Christians to Islam, which was firmly institutionalized. The Bosnian Church ceased to exist even before the arrival of the Ottomans and was never closely associated with the population.[28] Its remnants were poorly organized and therefore unable to approach the Ottomans with a request for permission to perform its activities, as did the Roman Catholic and Orthodox churches in other parts of the Balkans. Moreover, no other Christian church had developed a strong presence in Bosnia before the arrival of the Ottomans, so there was a distinct lack of influential religious leaders and little sense of affinity toward any religion or religious community.

As elsewhere in rural Europe, the Bosnians practiced a superficial and "nominal" form of folk Christianity infused with all forms of magic and pre-Christian traditions. It was a very loose, inconsistent, and weak faith in regard to the principal Christian dogmas, and lacked any understanding of the main religious rituals. The clergy, who were mostly uneducated and poorly organized, were more interested in temporal matters—such as using magical means to "protect" health, family, and harvests—than in religious doctrine. Some areas were totally void of any form of church organization and had no priests whatsoever. As already mentioned, the Catholic proselytizing "offensive" undertaken against members of the Bosnian Church did not begin until a short time before the arrival of the Ottomans.

The reaction to the vital and well-presented Islamic faith preferred by the new rulers was varied, mainly as a result of the presence of genuine religious pluralism (three competitive but weak rivals) in pre-Ottoman Bosnia. Conversely, most other Balkan countries had well-organized state churches that, because of their previous dominance and strong organization, were preserved under the Ottomans. The reasons for this clearly were not limited to those described above, but were also the result of social and political factors, such as the agony experienced by the kingdom of Bosnia in the final years before the Ottoman conquest. Increasingly independent local nobles resisted the king's authority, and the day-to-day life of the peasants was becoming increasingly onerous. It is not surprising, then, that they saw the Ottomans as liberators. Many converted to Islam for opportunistic reasons, in order to climb the social, political, military, and religious ladders of the Ottoman Empire (Yakub pasha, victor at the Battle of Krbava in 1493, is a good example). Others hoped to escape from *devşirme,* the kidnapping of Christian boys by Ottoman authorities in order to convert them to Islam and train them to become elite military troops or *jannisaries (janičari).*[29]

Frequent contact between the Bosnians and Islam in the final decades of the kingdom's decline familiarized the Bosnians with the new religion. Bosnian *krstjani* and other Bosnian natives did not nurture the same prejudices against Islam as they did against Catholicism for the proselytizing importunities of the hated Hungarians, or against the Orthodox, who were equally indisposed toward the Bosnian Church. The economic reasons for the mass conversion to Islam were misinterpreted in subsequent mythological narratives: the Bosnian nobility did indeed convert to Islam in order to retain their property, privilege, and position; not all, however, chose to do so. Others—primarily peasants—converted to Islam in order to avoid the taxes imposed on Christians. Merchants converted to Islam because of the greater protection and freedom of movement it provided. Prisoners from neighboring territories could avoid slavery by converting to Islam. Moreover, mass Islamization corresponded to the urbanization of the territory. It is also important to know that "the Balkan Christians were never subjected to systematic and sustained proselytism" by the Muslim Ottomans.[30] Forced conversions were rare, and were required by only a few religiously fanatical local Ottoman rulers. Much has been reported on this by apostolic visitors, travelers, and observers (including Jesuit priest Bartol Kašić in 1613–14, Peter Masarechi in 1624, Bosnian bishops Franjo Baličević in 1612, Jeronim Lučić in 1637, and Franciscan provincials Nikola Brajković and Martin Brguljanin).[31]

Finally, conversion to Islam was further encouraged by the resounding Ottoman victories over Christian armies, such as the Battle of Mohač in 1526. On the other hand, the rate of conversion fell whenever the Ottomans suffered defeats, such as those at Lepanta in 1571 and Sisak in 1593. Temporal success was considered a sign of divine benevolence and favor. Islam was also spreading because of the vitality, attractiveness, and dynamism the Bosnians saw in their Muslim conquerors. Generally, historians agree that the Islamization of the Bosnian population was not the result of violent methods of conversion but was, for the most part, peaceful and voluntary.[32] This was also reported on by Kuripečič, a contemporary of the phenomenon.

It is important to note that members of the Roman Catholic and Orthodox churches (and not only members of the Bosnian Church) were also becoming Muslims, and that Catholics were being converted to Orthodoxy, and vice-versa, which only increased the suspicion between the two churches. The conversion of members of the Bosnian Church to Orthodoxy was more common than conversions to Catholicism because they were ethnically and politically closer to the Serbs than to the hated Hungarians. However, the exact opposite was reported by Franciscan Johannes Capistranus in a letter to Pope Calisto III in 1455, in which he states that "the Bosnian Pataren heretics who heed the Word of God are converting to Catholicism . . . rather die without faith than convert to the religion of the Rascians [Orthodox]."[33] Secondly, converts belonged to all social classes of Bosnian society.

Two more points must be added. First, ethnic Turks and other non-Slavic Muslims did not migrate en masse to Bosnia-Herzegovina. Historians agree that their number was low, but they are not certain of its actual share. Namely, the population in Ottoman tax registers (Defters) was classified according to its religious affiliation (and not by ethnicity or language). Džaja rejects Mandić's estimate that they were 2 to 3 percent as "unfounded."[34] Predominately they were employed "at the vizier's office, in army forces, and also in government and administration." According to Hadžijahić, they were predominately in the ruling class (in the families of the *begs*), but they also were civil servants, missionaries, and soldiers.[35] They amounted to at least 10 percent of the *spahijas* (cavalry) in the 1530s.[36]

The second point is that initial conversion to Islam was only superficial and formal (the acceptance of Muslim names, for example), or even fictive. I therefore agree that the term "acceptance of Islam" would be more suitable than "conversion to Islam," because at that time the old traditions and beliefs thrived under the façade of compulsory Muslim practices. The fact that these often contradicted each other did not seem to vex the acceptors at all. As one popular saying puts it: "Until midday Ilija, after midday Ali."[37] According to Džaja, the Ottomans "generously tolerated syncretism—cripto-Christianity." Similarly, Norris notes "syncretism was a major factor in the conversion of Balkan peoples to Islam."[38] It thus is no surprise that many similarities between folk Christianity and folk Islam, which had more in common with magical practices than with religious orthodoxy, can be found throughout history.

Nonetheless, Islamic conversion remained a sensitive and traumatic issue, embedded in the religious-national mythologies, and literature and folk epics of all South Slav Ottoman subjects. Converts to Islam were regarded as Christian apostates (odmetnici) who converted to Islam in order to retain their wealth and status. Romantic historians chose to understand and explain this Bosnian peculiarity by such popular sayings as, "they preferred the Turkish turban to the papal tiara." This peculiarity eventually culminated in the tragic events witnessed in the nineteenth and twentieth centuries. Following such logic, however, it can be said that not only Muslim converts "betrayed their faith." All of the southern Slavs, Christian and Muslim alike, "betrayed" the ancient, pre-Christian beliefs of their Slavic forefathers.

THE MUSLIM SLAVS OF BOSNIA-HERZEGOVINA

According to reports by observers traveling through the territory of Bosnia-Herzegovina during this time, Muslims were the absolute majority in the late sixteenth and early seventeenth centuries. Many Muslims—Slavs and non-Slavs—fled to Bosnia-Herzegovina following the loss of the occupied territories in Hungary, Croatia, Dalmatia, Slavonia, and Lika after the Habsburg-Ottoman war of 1683–99. It was the first example in this area of cleansing the Muslim population that also "enjoyed the benediction of the Catholic Church."[39] At the beginning of the nineteenth century, Muslims comprised half of the entire Bosnian population. This figure dropped to two-fifths by the middle of the century.[40] Because of constant political unrest, peasant and other revolts, impoverishment of the country, fear of Austrian attacks, and so forth, Bosnian

Muslims began to migrate to the central parts of the empire. At the time of the Austro-Hungarian occupation, they represented the second largest religious group in Bosnia-Herzegovina.

The Illyrian-oriented Bosnian Franciscan monk Franjo Jukić (1818–57) applied the common name of Bosniaks (Bošnjaci) to all the inhabitants of Bosnia-Herzegovina, and further distinguished them according to religion as *krstjani* (Catholics), *hristjani* (Orthodox), and Mohamedanci (Muslims, who, he noted, "we erroneously call Turks"). He was convinced that "all were of the same origin, Slavs descended from Illyrian southern-Slavic tribes, all speaking the same language." Indeed, up to the end of the eighteenth century the Ottomans themselves referred to the inhabitants of their Bosnian *eyalet* as "the *Bosnian people*, although they distinguished them by religion." Several other labels were also in use: expressions such as Turkus, Turkuše, Turki Osmanlije and Osmanli were used for ethnic Turks, that is, for Anatolians; Turčin was used for Turks in a cultural sense; and Turki Bosanlije, Potur, Poturica, or Poturčenjak (*poturčiti se* and *isturčiti se* are verbs meaning "to Turkify oneself" or to turn Turk) were used for Bosnian Slavic Muslims.[41] The Christians distinguished between Latinci or Šokci (Catholics) and Vlasi (Orthodox, in Latin also Graeci or Rasciani); or between *hrišćani* (Orthodox) and *krsćani* or *karsteni* (Catholics).[42] The Catholics commonly referred to the Orthodox as *šizmatiki* (schismatics). So important was the Vlach element in the creation of the Bosnian Orthodox population that, by the nineteenth century, the term *Vlach* was used to mean any member of the Orthodox Church.

The Slavic Muslims of Bosnia-Herzegovina were members of the empire's ruling religion. Also because of this, their religion was not linked to national consciousness in the nineteenth century, as were Orthodoxy and Catholicism to Serbian and Croatian consciousness. Islam forged a very close bond between all the Muslims of Bosnia-Herzegovina, regardless of their social standing: it was the principal and most important form of identity. The Bosnian Slavic Muslims only began to develop their ethnic distinction in contrast to Ottomans in the mid-nineteenth century.[43] However, because they belonged to the "religion of the Turks," they called themselves Turci, Turčini, or Bošnjaci. The term *domaći Turci*, meaning "local Turks," was far less common. Because of their language, traditions, and literature, the Ottomans called them Bošnjaci (Bosniaksi) or Potur. They were also known as *Bosnalu takimi* (Bosnian people), Bosnaklar (ethnic Bosnians), *Bosnak taifesi* (the Bosnian class or tribe), and Bošniakati.[44] Physical Slavic features such as fair hair and blue eyes also helped distinguish many of them. Because of the duality of their position—ethnic kinship with the Christians and religious kinship with the Ottomans—neither side fully trusted them. Western Christendom was also well aware of this ethnic diversity within the Ottoman Empire: Italian sources distinguish between *Turchi Asiatici e Constantinopoli-tani* and *Turchi Bossinensi et Albanesi.*[45]

In some cases, Bosnian Muslims still observed ancient pre-Christian and Christian traditions such as the patron cult, Christmas, wedding ceremonies, belief in demons and witches, the worship of family saints such as Saints George and John, superstitions, and belief in miracles. Christians often were godparents to Muslims, and vice-versa. They also exchanged felicitations for religious festivals such as Christmas and 'Id al-Fitr *(bajram)*, and they had the same superstitions and believed in the same magic. Together they celebrated Christian festivals such as Jurjevo (Saint George's Day), Ilinden (Saint Elias's Day, known by the Muslims as Alidjun), Saint Peter's Day, Easter, and the Orthodox *slava* or Feast of Saint John the Baptist. Moreover, the entire population of this central Balkan region, regardless of religion or ethnic origin, believed in the magical powers of the relics of Saint Sava, the Serbian Orthodox personage par excellence. Catholics, Orthodox, Muslims, and Jews alike venerated the cult of Saint Sava and expected great miracles of healing and prosperity from his mortal remains.

Muslims often had their amulets blessed by Franciscan monks, including the cross, the most important Christian symbol. At times, Muslims prayed in Catholic churches, attended Christian masses, kissed Christian icons, venerated the Virgin Mary, and even followed the practice of painting candles (as a substitute for the Christian custom of painting Easter eggs). Conversely, Christians invited Muslim dervishes to read the Koran over them in order to cure a serious illness. Christians sought help from Muslim *khojas (hodže)*, and Muslims sought help from Catholic churches or Orthodox monasteries. There is a recorded example of Muslim, Orthodox, and Catholic worshippers visiting an image of the Holy Virgin that was believed to have miraculous powers of healing. The case of the Bosnian Muslims is, therefore, one of syncretism: a blend of Christian and Muslim elements, rather than crypto-Christianity. But rather than "bitheism,"[46] it is more probably a specific form of religious eclecticism that served to reconcile the isolated groups of people living under the millet system. All of these syncretistic customs and beliefs were practiced until quite recently, and several are still observed today. This religious fusion of Muslim and Christian beliefs, customs, and traditions often bordered on religious confusion.[47]

In stark contrast to these "heretic" practices, most observers regarded

Bosnian Muslims as "orthodox and pious." Muslim fanaticism, long regarded as a permanent feature of Islam, only developed under the social and political circumstances of "the nineteenth century among some of the *begs*, the Muslim clergy and lower-class urban Muslims." As a political movement, the "pan-Islamist trend in Bosnia-Herzegovina goes back only to the 1930s."[48]

As elsewhere in the Balkans, dervish orders played an essential role in the Islamic conversion of Bosnia and the development of Muslim towns. Sarajevo (and Skopje before it) became a center of Islamic mysticism (Sufism) and dervish orders. Dervish lodges, known as *tekkes* (*tekije* in Serbo-Croat), became the centers of religion, culture, and fellowship for local Muslims. According to Balkanologist Norris, the most influential order within the Bosnian Sufi movement was that of the Mevlevi dervishes (*mevlevije* in Serbo-Croat). Known as the "dancing (or whirling) dervishes" because of their ritual prayer *(zikra)* performed by spinning on the right foot to the accompaniment of musical instruments such as tambourines and flutes, the Mevlevi dervishes applied this mystical ritual to achieve a mysterious ecstasy, contact with God, through meditation. They were also known for their internalized spirituality and rapturous devotion—a form of quietism, the quest for absolute perfection and cosmic passion. Mevlevis rejected the public profession of faith: even their charity work was done in secret. This order was renowned for its tolerance, humanism, and kindness to other faiths, especially Christianity. It was especially compassionate toward religious converts and therefore very successful in proselytizing Orthodox Bosnians. Because of such deviations, the Muslim authorities persecuted the order, which opted for a more "orthodox" orientation in the early seventeenth century.[49]

In the sixteenth century, a heretic movement whose followers were known as the "Hamzamites" *(hamzevije)* spread through Bosnia. The movement was founded by Hamza Bali Bošnjak, who was executed for heresy in Istanbul in 1573 on the orders of Grand Vizier Mehmed-pasha Sokolović. Followers of this movement, which was particularly strong in Bosnia and among Muslim Slavs and janissaries across the empire, deviated from orthodox Islam as much in terms of doctrine as in political and social matters. Mohammed, according to the Hamzamites, was merely one of the prophets and no less or more important than those that came before him. They also disputed Judgment Day and were accused of pantheism and of breaking the Muslim creed. They abjured rituals in oratories and nurtured mystic practices (contemplation, for example). The Hamzamites were particularly strong under the leadership of Begtaš in the seventeenth century, and could still be found as late as the mid-eighteenth century. According to the reports of a "pious" observer, the Hamzamites were "tall, short in intellect, apostate, and professed a false doctrine."[50]

Bosnia-Herzegovina's Muslim Slavs underwent a cultural revival during this period, a true renaissance: the Bosnian language was used, albeit in Arabic script (Aljamiado literature). For example, Mehmed Havaji Uskufi Bosnevi, also known as Potur Šahdija (died 1651), who compiled a Bosnian-Turkish dictionary, used them in literary works, and Hasan Efendi Kaimi (or Kaimia, died ca. 1680 or 1690–91), wrote religious poetry and enticed others to join his religion:

O, Croats, hear my words and be forewarned:
Yield to Islam and embrace Allah!
Be not enemies of the Faith and embrace the exalted Qur'an!
Allah shall abet the faithful and vanquish the foes![51]

Hasan Quaimi Baba (ca. 1630–91 or 1692), a native of Sarajevo, described life in the *tekkes* and contemplated the future in his religious treatises. Mula Mustafa Ševki Bašeskija (died 1803) celebrated the rich vocabulary of the Bosnian language and wrote a chronicle of Sarajevo and Bosnia in the second half of the eighteenth century. Bosnian Muslim authors wrote mostly in Turkish, Arabic, and Persian, composing ballads, epics, lyrical poems, and laments. The Bosnian alternative to Cyrillic, the *bosančica* script, continued to be used to a limited extent. The cultural revival extended over a wide range of areas, from architecture to painting and education.

REVIVAL OF THE SERBIAN PATRIARCHATE

After the Battle of Kosovo, and finally after the complete occupation of the Despotate of Serbia in June, 1459, (following the fall of Smederevo), the Ottomans and Serbs made peace. Probably as a result of the Ottoman victory, the Serbian Orthodox Church lost its autonomy and fell under the jurisdiction of the Ohrid archdiocese in 1459 or 1463. The last patriarch of the Serbian Orthodox Church was Arsenije, and the Episcopal diet last convened in 1466. Despite this, the Orthodox Church immediately adjusted to the new, dramatically different socio-political and cultural environment and its non-Christian rulers. Sava's system of state and church hegemony collapsed. Because it enjoyed a certain degree of protection, the church gradually assumed the role previously played by the state: traditions were preserved and fostered in monasteries. It began to present itself as the "widowed mother."

The campaign to restore the Serbian patriarchate began in the 1530s on the initiative of Pavle, the metropolitan of Smederevo, who resisted the abolition of the Serbian Orthodox Church and its complete incorporation into the archdiocese of Ohrid. Grand Vizier Ibrahim Pasha, who was of Greek origin, probably oversaw the subordination of the Serbian Orthodox Church. The Serbian clergy resisted the decision by ignoring the aspirations of Prohor, the archbishop of Ohrid, and electing Pavle as their archbishop. Following complications over the next few years, the Ohrid *sabor* dismissed the rebellious Serbian bishops and Archbishop Pavle: the latter was excommunicated by the *sabor* as well as by the patriarch of Constantinople.[52] Despite its failure, the endeavor managed to arouse the interest of the Ottoman authorities.

Grand Vizier Mehmed-pasha Sokolović (born ca. 1505, and assassinated in 1578 or 1579) revived the patriarchate of Peć in 1557 with the approval of Sultan Süleyman II the Magnificent. Mehmed-pasha, an Islamicized Orthodox Christian (a Catholic, according to Franciscan historian Father Mandić) from Višegrad, who was abducted in his late teens and recruited into Ottoman service, remembered well his original faith and the history of his people. He assumed the position of grand vizier (chief minister)—second only to the sultan in authority—in 1565 and held the highest office continuously from the last months of the reign of Süleyman II, throughout the reign of Selim II, until the early years of Murad III's reign. With the restoration of the patriarchate he brought to an end a long-lasting dispute between the dioceses, the patriarchate of Constantinople, and local Ottoman authorities. It was also seen as a reward from the sultan to the Serbs for their active role in conquering southern Hungary.[53]

Mehmed-pasha appointed a relative (his brother, according to some reports), Makarije Sokolović, to the position of patriarch of Peć. The next two patriarchs, Antonije and Gerasim, are also said to have been his relatives. Banja Luka mosque was named after his brother, Ferhat-pasha Sokolović. The new Orthodox clergy came from the theologically strong monastery area of Mount Athos, and the Serbian Orthodox Church underwent internal reorganization. The new *sabor* thus consisted of church dignitaries as well as laypersons. According to the previously mentioned principle of clerocracy, the patriarchs were also the political leaders of the Orthodox community *(miletbaša)*.

The Serbian Orthodox Church spread its authority and traditions to new territories conquered by the Ottomans. This was the basis for the adage "Whereunto Turkey, thereunto Serbia."[54] In reality, its jurisdiction reached as far as Austria, where Orthodox Christians fleeing the Ottoman assault had found refuge. The Serbian patriarchate of Peć, the ancient spiritual capital, was composed of forty dioceses. Its extent was greater than ever before and included northern Macedonia, eastern Bulgaria, Serbia, Montenegro, Vojvodina, Bosnia, and Herzegovina, as well as Orthodox colonies in Croatia, Dalmatia, and Hungary.[55] The Serbian Orthodox Church rallied together the Orthodox congregation scattered across the Balkans and nurtured in them a common ethnic identity and mythical and historical recollection.

The paradox of Ottoman suzerainty over Serbia is that it provided the Serbs with a means of national expansion: Banac calls the millet system "a great instrument for the spread of Serb national identity in the western Balkans."[56] The Ottoman decree that restored the patriarchate of Peć helped preserve Serbia's political, religious, and ethnic identity by reviving customs and traditions that had been lost. This was an era of social and cultural prosperity for Orthodoxy and the Serbs in the Ottoman Empire. Indeed, it could be said that they "profited from the privileges afforded to them by the Ottoman state."[57] In short, in the millet system established by the Ottomans, the Serbian Orthodox patriarchate functioned as the administrative intercessor between the Serbian people and the Ottoman state, as well as the Serbs's political representative. This may be regarded as proof of the exceptionally adaptive realism and ingenuity of Serbian Orthodoxy on one hand, and the Ottoman Empire's benevolent policy toward Christian religious communities on the other.

The attitude of Balkan Orthodox churches toward the Ottomans can be divided into two periods. In the first period—when the Ottoman wars of conquest brought prosperity and expansion to the empire—the Orthodox clergy cooperated with the authorities, while at the same time safeguarding local traditions and customs. Immediately after the capture of Constantinople in 1453, the sultan vowed to protect the Orthodox Church and preserve its privileges. He appointed a new Greek patriarch and, immediately thereafter, an Armenian patriarch and a chief rabbi. After the seizure of Constantinople, Mehmed the Conqueror was convinced that he would unite Muslim, Ottoman, and Roman traditions into a unique universal suzerainty. He considered the city to be the center of a global empire.[58]

During the period of the patriarchate of Peć, the Serbian Orthodox Church enjoyed strong support from the Ottoman regime, assuming almost all the civil authority—including judiciary powers based on Dušan's law code—of the former Serbian state. It was also given other competencies, such as counseling and endorsing the Orthodox people's trade and craft guilds. The church appointed its own bishops, patriarchs, priests, and abbots—with the sultan's assent. In addition, it was also the largest Christian landowner in that part of the empire. The church's strength and organization were the main reasons for the low rate of conversion of the Orthodox people to Islam.

The most important point, however, was the fact that, under Ottoman rule, the Serbs were able to mythologize their medieval state, their rulers, and other notables without hindrance. Serbian Orthodoxy institutionalized local and national cults and the ancient ancestor cult, and canonized its rulers—those who built Orthodox churches and monasteries or supported the church in other ways. It was a specific political-religious syncretism: rulers' biographies were transformed into saintly *žitije* (written legends about Slavic saints). An example of this may be found in the "sacrosanct lineage" *(svetorodna loza)* of the medieval Nemanjić dynasty (only the fratricidal Dušan the Mighty is denied sainthood because of his connivance of the assassination of his father, Stephen Uroš III), as well as in the Petrović dynasty of Montenegro. From the tenth century onward, five royal and aristocratic families provided forty of the 130 cults known to Serbian Orthodoxy (Nemanjić 21, Branković 9, Lazarević 4, Petrović-Njegoš 4, and Mrnjavčević 2). Of the 130 Christian saint cults, the church initiated only eleven. "They pay homage to their local gods" *(domesticos colunt deos)*, wrote one medieval observer.[59]

Historians are of the opinion that Orthodoxy was already firmly established in Hum (Herzegovina) by the Middle Ages, and that it did not make significant inroads into Bosnia and Croatia until after the Ottoman conquest. The introduction of a large Orthodox population as a direct result of Ottoman policy ensured a significant Orthodox presence by the sixteenth century. The first document mentioning the presence of an Orthodox priest in Sarajevo was dated 1489, while the first Orthodox church in Sarajevo was built between 1520 and 1539. This was followed by the construction of Orthodox monasteries and churches across Bosnia, beginning in northwest Bosnia (near Bihać) in 1515.[60] The Orthodox metropolitan of Bosnia is first mentioned in 1532. He established an official residence in Sarajevo in 1699 and, within a century, had four bishops under him in Mostar, Zvornik, Novi Pazar, and Sarajevo.

The spread of Orthodox Christianity in Bosnia can also be attributed to the influx of Orthodox Vlachs from the eastern Balkans. These nomadic warrior-herdsmen settled in territories evacuated by the Ottoman authorities. The motives of the latter were economic as well as military. The spread of Orthodoxy in Bosnia was further strengthened by the conversion of members of the Bosnian Church. Despite the expansion, theological scholarship remained rudimentary and corruption and ignorance were rife among high-ranking church dignitaries. According to one report from that period, the clergy were unfamiliar with confession, the Ten Commandments, many prayers, and even the significance of the cross.[61]

Conflict between the Ottoman authorities and the Serbian patriarchate began in the late sixteenth century. Patriarch Jovan I. Kantul supported the Saint Sava rebellion in 1593, consecrating the rebels' banner. The patriarchate and insurgents also established relations with Russia, Austria, Spain, Poland, and Venice in hopes of securing funds. As punishment for such disloyalty, the Ottoman authorities brought him to Istanbul and hanged him. In addition, the relics of Saint Sava, the founder of the Serbian Orthodox Church, were—by order of Grand Vizier Sinan Pasha in 1594 or 1595—disinterred and moved from Mileševo to Vračar near Belgrade, where they were publicly incinerated and the ashes scattered. Such retribution, according to George V. Tomashevich, caused deep shock among the Serbs, especially if we consider the period of relative peace, even prosperity, enjoyed by the Orthodox under the Sokolovićes.[62] The relationship with the Ottoman authorities then more or less calmed for a century, albeit with some tragic episodes: The Ottomans executed Gavrilo Rajić (?–1659), patriarch of Peć from 1648–55, for seeking financial support from the pope and tsarist Russia for the liberation of the Serbs.

The first signs of the stagnation and eventual collapse of Ottoman military feudalism appeared in the last quarter of the sixteenth century. One of the milestones in this respect was the Habsburg-Ottoman war, which began with the unsuccessful siege of Vienna in 1683 and ended with the Treaty of Karlowitz (Sremski Karlovci) in 1699, in which the Ottomans were forced to cede Hungary, Srem, and Slavonia, as well as parts of Dalmatia. The western borders of modern Bosnia were drawn during this period. The Serbian Orthodox Church also openly allied itself with the rebels during this period, thus ending the relatively good relations they had enjoyed with the Ottomans up to that time. During this second era of Ottoman suzerainty in the Balkans, the church took upon itself the task of arousing national consciousness, encouraging insurrection against the Ottomans, and searching for allies in neighboring Christian lands—acts for which its priests were habitually persecuted and monastic lands confiscated. The Serbian Orthodox Church began losing the privileges it had secured in the era of the Sokolovićes.[63]

THE GREAT ORTHODOX MIGRATIONS

Large migrations of the Orthodox population began with the deterioration of conditions within the borders of the Ottoman Empire. The first mass migration took place in the decades following the downfall of the despotate of Serbia in the late fifteenth century, when two hundred thousand Serbs fled to southern Hungary and were taken into the service of the Hungarian army. New monastic centers developed in Slavonia. However, truly large Serb migrations, especially to Vojvodina, Slavonia, and Baranja—culminating in 1690 and 1739—took place under the guidance of the Serbian Orthodox clergy. The first took place in 1690 under the leadership of the energetic, capable, and openly anti-Ottoman patriarch Arsenije III Crnojević, who supported the uprising and petitioned the Austrians, Russians, and Albanians for help. He led the migration after Austrian troops withdrew, the Serbian uprising was quelled, and severe Ottoman reprisals were expected. The second migration took place in 1739 under the leadership of Patriarch Arsenije IV Šakabenta for identical reasons. These events led to the Serb evacuation of "Old Serbia"— Kosovo and Metohija. Estimates of the numbers vary. The first migration is said to have involved thirty thousand to eighty thousand numerous families.[64] The Ottoman authorities later encouraged Albanian Muslims to settle in the evacuated territory.

The sultan appointed Kalinik to replace Arsenije III as patriarch. Although initially rejected by Orthodox bishops, they eventually came to accept him. The patriarchate of Peć retained its spiritual primacy over Orthodox Christians living under Austrian rule, and when Arsenije IV fled to Hungary as well, the sultan appointed Joanikij III, a Greek clergyman, as head of the Serbian Orthodox Church. From then on, Serb and Greek patriarchs alternated as head of the Serbian Orthodox Church, which fell into recession. The last patriarch was Vasilij Jovanović-Brkić. The patriarchate of Peć was finally abolished in September, 1766, which can be attributed to the aspirations and intrigues of Samuil, the patriarch of Constantinople, and the Holy Synod. The Serbian patriarchate was subordinated to the patriarchate of Constantinople, as was the patriarchate of Ohrid soon thereafter.

The Serbs themselves bore the loss rather well as the Serbian Orthodox Church enjoyed special privileges in Austria. It represented the Orthodox people of the Vojna Krajina (Krajišnici), who defended the borders from Ottoman incursions. In the nineteenth century, Vojvodina, which had a strong central European cultural character, became the center of modern cultural development for all Serbs, including those living in the rising Serbian state south of the Danube. The church thus reorganized itself north of the Danube and Sava Rivers, in Sremski Karlovci, as the Metropolitan See of Sremski Karlovci. Several other Orthodox dioceses (eparchies) were created in the western Balkans during the course of the eighteenth century, including the diocese of Severina-Lepavina, the Kostajnica-Severina episcopate, the Sremski Karlovci-Senj-Littoral eparchy, the Kostajnica-Zrinjpolje and Gornji Karlovci eparchy, the Dalmatian eparchy (early nineteenth century), and the Metropolitan See of Bukovina-Dalmatia (established 1874). The Metropolitan See of Zagreb was established in 1931.

The departure of the center of Serbian Orthodox authority did, however, result in the further weakening of Serbian religious and intellectual life in the Ottoman Empire, as expressed in the lack of educated persons, the theological ignorance of both the clergy and laymen, the retardation of religious and cultural enlightenment, the spread of corruption and avarice within the church, and the revival of ancient cults (the ancestor cult, for example) and pre-Christian religious customs based on historical figures and events. Priests became local "shamans," closely associated with the population—literally the first among equals. Foreign travelers were surprised by their religious ignorance.[65] Old superstitions were aroused, such as that about the *zduhač*, the man-demon each area or tribe is said to have had. The Montenegrins, for example, believed that Peter II Petrović Njegoš was a *zduhač*, a man with extraordinary powers, and a protector of sorts. The grandson of the despot Đurđe Branković—a soldier in the army of King Matthias I Covinus and implacable foe of the Ottomans—is even said to have been a "dragon," as indicated by his name, Zmaj-Ognjen Vuk (Dragon-fire Wolf). Other heroic and benevolent "dragons" celebrated in verse are Miloš Obilić, Banović Sekula, Relja Bošnjanin, Ljutica Bogdan, and Marko Kraljević.[66]

A unique practice that developed in Serbian Orthodoxy is the so-called *slava*. An old adage says, "Where there is slava, there is a Serb."[67] Slava is a Christianized form of an ancient ritual of worship: each family (as well as other groups, such as schools,[68] churches, villages, guilds, or military units) has and celebrates a saint or protector, and gathers on the saint's feast day for a celebration. Absent family members are expected to celebrate the saint's feast day on their own. Preparations for this event take several days: a priest consecrates the house and family, the family fasts, and family members clean the house and prepare the food. Friends, even strangers, are invited to attend, and a brief ritual is held before dinner. The celebration continues in church on the second day and later at home. The Catholics and Muslims of Bosnia-Herzegovina also observed this custom of celebrating slava, albeit on a much smaller scale.

By institutionalizing religious groups in the millet system, and by legalizing and keeping records of customs and traditions, the Ottomans gave the Orthodox Balkan nations a means of preserving and even augmenting their traditions and institutions under the pretext of fidelity to the state. More specifically, the millet system enabled the spread of Orthodoxy and assimilation into the Serbian national identity of the Orthodox people (including, for example, Orthodox Vlachs or gypsies) both in the Ottoman and Austrian Empires. In the nation-building process, the Orthodox population of the western and central Balkans gradually adopted Serbian national identity. Meanwhile, the Orthodox clergy preserved and spread the old Serbian traditions and kept alive the memory of lost statehood. The emerging Serbian national consciousness thus became entwined with the Orthodox religion.[69]

CATHOLICISM IN OTTOMAN BOSNIA

Bosnia's neighbor Croatia was engaged in a personal union with the more powerful Hungary. The Croats realized that, after Serbia and Bosnia, they were next in line to be conquered by the rapidly advancing Ottomans, and fought fierce battles with them. In 1519, Pope Leo X (1513–21) informed Ban Berislavić and the deputies of the Croatian *sabor* (assembly): "the Holy See shall not allow the defeat of Croatia, the shield of Christendom."[70] In the ensuing centuries, the Croats used this expression, *antemurale Christianitatis*, as the cornerstone of their own religious-national mythology (the Ukrainians and Poles considered themselves the "bastion of Christianity" during this time as well). A turning point for the Croatian kingdom was the disastrous defeat at Mohač in 1526, following which parts of Hungary and Croatia came under the sultan's rule (so-called Turkish Croatia). The once great kingdom shrank to a "remnant of the remnants" *(reliquiae reliquiarum olim incliti regni Croatiae)*, according to one report. To protect the land from the Ottoman onslaught, the *sabor* elected Archduke Ferdinand of Habsburg to the Croatian throne in 1527.

The Protestant Reformation in Europe had also reached Croatia. The more significant figures in the movement included Matija Vlačić Ilirik (Flacius Illyricus), Baldo Lupetina, Antun Dalmatin, and Štefan Konzul. However, Croatia was still firmly allied to Rome: the Croatian *sabor* passed a strongly worded anti-Reformation law in July, 1604 (confirmed by Habsburg emperor Rudolph II in January, 1608), which banned all denominations in Croatia save the Roman Catholic Church. The Catholic clergy—closely tied to the Catholic Habsburg dynasty—opposed the independent ideas of Croatian nobles Petar Zrinski and Capt. Franjo Krsto Frankopan in 1670 because they feared Hungarian Protestantism on one side and Islam on the other.[71]

For centuries, the Franciscans were the only Roman Catholic clergy in Bosnia. They were, therefore, more willingly accepted and commanded greater respect than the priests sent to Bosnia later from outside. In addition to performing their "spiritual" duties, the Franciscans were also physicians and teachers, and they protected the people from the authorities. However, they were loyal to the Ottoman regime. In 1463, Sultan Mehmed II the Conqueror signed a pact with Angel Zvizdović of Vrhbosna, the Franciscan curator of Bosnia. In his edict, the *Ahd-name* (a grant of privilege, similar to the one issued to Orthodox Patriarch Gennadios II), the sultan allowed the Franciscans and Catholics under his rule to retain their originality and guaranteed them freedom of movement, protection of property, and freedom of worship. The document says "the Bosnian priests shall have freedom and protection, and may return to and settle the lands in the [Ottoman] empire in their monasteries without consternation. No-one is to attack them, nor threaten their lives, property or churches." In short, he allowed them to practice their Roman Catholic faith in return for their loyalty and the promise to deal only with spiritual work.[72] These rights were reiterated by all subsequent sultans. Despite this, the Franciscans and Bosnian Catholics in general ran into many problems with Ottoman authorities at the local level: professing the faith of the Ottomans' major enemy—the Habsburg Empire—their activities were constantly restricted and under suspicion.

The pope gave Bosnian Franciscans permission to act as parish priests. Although they were superstitious and rather illiterate in theological terms, they did nourish and advance cultural traditions and translated and wrote several books (for example, the two books by Franciscan priest Matija Divković (1563–1631), written in his native tongue in 1611 and 1616). They were particularly strong in Herzegovina, where the Ottoman rulers guaranteed them the exclusive right to work with the Roman Catholic population. For want of sacral buildings, they wandered across the country with portable altars, improvising their rituals and caring for their Catholic flock.

The Ottoman occupation of Bosnia resulted in the partitioning of the Franciscan vicariate, of which the greater part fell under the vicariate of Croatian Bosnia (*Vicaria Bosnae Croatiae*). The smaller part, which remained under Ottoman rule, was transformed into the province of Bosnia ("Provincialat Bosne Srebreniške," or *Bosna Argentinea*) in 1517. Between 1517 and 1735, the province included Dalmatia (which was under Venetian rule), Bosnia and Serbia (Ottoman Empire), and Slavonia, Hungary, and Banat (Austrian Empire). The Franciscans began spreading Roman Catholicism in all these places and were allowed to collect taxes.[73]

The spiritual life of the Catholics was centered on the monasteries. There was no proper territorial organization, nor were there any parishes or bishops. In contrast to their Orthodox brethren, the Catholic Christians only received permission to repair their sacral buildings with the greatest difficulty. The Franciscans had 39 monasteries in all of Bosnia and Herzegovina before the Ottomans arrived.[74] Several Franciscan monasteries were destroyed, abandoned, or turned into mosques over the next few decades. According to Franciscan historian Mandić, there were 24 monasteries in the vicariate of Bosnia in 1493, some 149 Franciscan monks in 13 monasteries in about 1600, 355 monks in 17 monasteries in 1624, 412 monks fifteen years later, and 375 monks in 18 monasteries in 1674. However, only 29 Franciscan monks remained after 1699. Voje's estimate differs: 14 monasteries by the end of the sixteenth century, 8 monasteries and 300 monks by 1675, and only 3 monasteries remaining by the eighteenth century: Fojnica, Kreševo, and Kraljeva Sutjeska.[75]

The deterioration of the position of the Bosnian Catholics and their exodus from the country was largely during and after the lengthy wars between the Ottomans and their Catholic neighbors: Venetians in the Cretan war (1645–69) and Austrians in the Vienna war (1683–99). Many fled to Croatia and Dalmatia, particularly after the latter conflict. All together, about 22,800 Catholics fled to Austria in 1700. The Catholic flight from the Ottomans took them even farther: to Venetian Istria, Gradiščansko (Burgenland in Austria), and even to the southern Italian region of Molise. At the beginning of the eighteenth century, "the number of Bosnian Catholics was at least halved."[76]

Some Catholics were converted to Orthodoxy by force (as Franciscan Johannes Capistranus reported during the reign of the Serbian despot Đurađ Branković in the mid-fifteenth century, when the pope was Calisto III). The evacuated territory was settled by Muslims and Orthodox Christians with the encouragement of Ottoman authorities. However, there were already twenty-five Franciscan monasteries and 725 monks by 1729.[77] Of all the religious communities in Ottoman Bosnia, the Catholics probably suffered the greatest loss of population and experienced the harshest economic hardship. It was also in a much less privileged position than the two larger religions. But the migration current also went in the opposite direction: The entire Slavonian Muslim population fled south into Bosnia after the Treaty of Karlovac in 1699.

All of this had a negative influence on Catholic religious education. All manner of syncretism and magical beliefs emerged, such as the belief in talismans, black power *(crna moća)*, the omnipresence of evil, and the division of the world into the " Upper Earth" (the Divine Realm),

"Middle Earth" (the stage of the battle between good and evil, God and Satan), and *Poljana* or Earth (the dwelling place of humans). Priests were believed to bring the goodness of God to the people and to have the power to ward off evil and sanctify objects. Because of their supposed magical powers, they came into conflict with women soothsayers (known as *kalajdžija* or *proročnica*), whom the priests accused of being heretics *(gatara)*.[78] Catholics in Herzegovina believed in *slava*, the Orthodox ancestor cult, as late as the 1880s.

After the Habsburg-Ottoman war, the Franciscan province was divided into "Bosna Srebrena" ("Bosna Argentinea") and the "Herzegovinan Province of the Assumption." The "Apostolic Vicariate in Ottoman Bosnia" ("Vicariatus Apostolicus in Bosna Othomana") was established in 1735. Indeed, it was the Franciscans, an order that does not fall within the organizational hierarchy of the Roman Catholic Church, who maintained the presence of Catholicism in Bosnia-Herzegovina, as there were almost no other Roman Catholic priests up to the time of the Austro-Hungarian occupation. They forged bonds with the people—who addressed them as uncle *(ujak)* or *pater*—nurtured their culture, and represented them before the authorities. They also established a foothold on the Bosnian population at this time. Furthermore, Franciscans nurtured cultural and spiritual traditions and the recollection of the medieval Bosnian state, mostly in monasteries. Many Bosnian Franciscan monks were educated in neighboring Croatia, bringing a sense of Croatian national consciousness to the Catholic population of Bosnia-Herzegovina. Some clerics also stood in the frontline of resistance against the Ottomans. For example, a priest named Marko Mesić (1640–1713) in Lika (he started to convert the remaining Turks immediately after the Ottoman retreat) and Luka Ibrišimović, a Franciscan from Slavonia (1620–98). Franciscan Ivan Musić (1848–88) was given the title "Duke *(Vojvoda)* of Herzegovina" by Prince Nikola of Montenegro for his activities during the 1875 and 1878 rebellions. Franciscans Bono Šarić and Stipe Krešo and parish priest Ivan Mišić joined him.

As in all other reconquered territories, the Muslims (who, for example, comprised two-thirds of the population in Lika) in Croatia were either converted to Catholicism or banished. During the Vienna war (1683–99), Catholic Austrian army chaplains in conquered areas of Serbia, Vlachia, and Erdely started proselytizing, which raised concern among the Orthodox population.[79] The Roman Catholic dioceses of Srem (1678) and Bosnia (1703) were resumed and merged in 1773 to form the diocese of Bosnia and Srem, and existing dioceses increased in size.

The policy of neighboring Austria regarding religious issues on its southern border was unambiguous. In the Austrian part of the Balkans, the Roman Catholic Church embarked on a deliberate policy of converting Orthodox Christians into Uniates, and was successful to a limited extent. The goal of this "Uniate program" was the acceptance of the "Faith of the Emperor."[80] In Croatia, a Uniate eparchy was created in the provinces of Karlovac and Varaždin in 1611 under the rule of Simeon Vratonja, whose official title was *svidniško-marčanski vladika* (bishop-prince). Approximately sixty thousand believers accepted the union with Rome. The Croatian Uniates renounced obedience to the patriarch of Peć fifty years later, although they were also worried about the Latinization of their faith and liturgy. Following the mass exodus of Serbs (and therefore Orthodoxy) to Slavonia and southern Hungary, proselytizing and conflicts between the Uniates and the Orthodox became more common.[81] The eparchy became the Greek Catholic diocese of Križevci in 1777.

THE BOSNIAN JEWISH COMMUNITY

The Jews formed a relatively tight religious community in Bosnia-Herzegovina. The community was much smaller than any of the other three religions, but was an important feature of the Bosnian religious, ethnic, and cultural mosaic. During Ottoman times, discrimination against Jews in the Ottoman Empire was significantly less than that in any Christian country. The first ten or fifteen Jewish families moved to Sarajevo from Salonika (Thessaloniki), the "stop-over" for many Sephardic Jews, in 1541 or 1551. The first document proving their presence in Sarajevo is dated 1563 or 1565.[82] The first synagogue was built shortly thereafter, in the 1580s. The Jewish community of Sarajevo was subordinated to Salonika until the 1760s and 1770s, when it became independent.

The Sephardic Jews, whose exodus from the Pyrenean peninsula began in the late fifteenth century, spoke Ladino (a Judeo-Spanish dialect developed from Castilian Spanish in the fourteenth century; the name "Sephard" or "Sepharad" means Spain in medieval Hebrew) and lived a traditional lifestyle in patriarchal, outwardly closed family units. However, they still were able to adapt to the complex environment they found in Bosnia-Herzegovina. In a sense, the fate of the Sephardim in Bosnia symbolizes the journey taken by the renowned illuminated manuscript known as the "Sarajevo Haggadah," which traveled with the expelled Jews from Spain in 1492, via northern Italy in the seventeenth century, through Split or Dubrovnik to Sarajevo, then to a nearby mountain village, where it was hidden from the Nazis in 1941. It has been on display at the Sarajevo Museum since 1945 and was hidden again during the siege of Sarajevo during the most recent war.

A large majority of Jews lived in Sarajevo, where they had their own quarter from the end of the sixteenth century onward. A number of Jews lived in Travnik and Mostar as well. The Jews were, for the most part, traders (dealing mainly in cloth). Many also were tailors, shoemakers, butchers, wood and metalworkers, and glassmakers. There were also several renowned pharmacists and physicians among them. The Jews developed a rich cultural and spiritual life. They had strong commercial and religious ties with other large Jewish communities in Skopje, Salonika, and especially Belgrade.[83] It seems likely that some Ashkenazi Jews from Belgrade came to Sarajevo, but they must have been absorbed by the Sephardic community there. The numbers of Sarajevan Jews grew gradually, from sixty-six families in the 1720s and 1730s, to more than a thousand persons half a century later. The Jewish population in Bosnia-Herzegovina was slightly more than two thousand at the beginning of the nineteenth century, and reached three thousand by 1876.[84]

RELATIONS BETWEEN RELIGIOUS GROUPS DURING THE DECLINE OF THE OTTOMAN EMPIRE

The might of the Ottoman Empire was gradually but irreversibly waning. The expression "Ottomanization" had come to signify the agonizing and irrevocable deterioration of a once powerful state. The Habsburg rulers sent contradictory information to the Muslim Slavs regarding their religious fate should they take up arms against the Ottoman Empire. During the Austro-Ottoman war of 1737–39, they threatened to expel the Muslims unless the latter converted to Christianity. During the 1788–91 war, the more tolerant Emperor Josef II (1765–90) promised them freedom of worship and the inviolability of faith and property in the event of Austrian occupation.[85]

The Ottoman era in Bosnia-Herzegovina knew individual periods of violence, persecution, mutual distrust, and violence. Wars between the Ottoman Empire and European powers such as the Hungarian-Croatian kingdom, the Habsburg Empire, and the Venetian Republic directly or indirectly influenced life in Bosnia-Herzegovina. The Ottoman state progressively exerted pressure on the Bosnian population: economically (tax increases because of military campaigns and corruption), socially (against lower classes regardless of their religious adherence) and also religiously (against non-Muslims). All of this led to unrest, riots, and rebellions. Some were religiously motivated, some socially, while neighboring states incited others. The repression of authorities was brutal which contributed to the formation of "vicious circle" of violence and retribution.

Relations between religious communities and organizations—which varied from official recognition to obstacles in their activities, from resentments to everyday syncretism—were in last two centuries of Ottoman rule increasingly interrupted with obstructions, oppression, competition and (open) hostilities. The empire was losing its previous ability to extend and collapse was manifold: the feeling of distrust, threat and enmity between the religious communities became more and more present. However, these negative aspects and tragic episodes of life in Ottoman Bosnia-Herzegovina cannot be compared with the coincidental religious wars and systematic religious persecutions and ruthless cleansing that affected other parts of Europe, nor with the horrible events of the 1941–45 and 1992–95 wars. Despite the periodic violence and hard times already mentioned, four religious groups remained and consolidated themselves in Ottoman Bosnia-Herzegovina.

At the beginning of the nineteenth century, Bosnia was one of the least developed provinces in the empire. It was also the most autonomous. It was composed of seven sandžaks: Sarajevo, Zvornik, Travnik, Bihać, Novi Pazar, Banja Luka, and Herzegovina. The conservative Bosnian Muslim elite resisted the reformist efforts of Sultans Selim III (1798–1807) and Mehmed II (1808–39).[86] Disputes between Muslims lasted throughout the second quarter of the nineteenth century, and there was discord and even armed conflict between the porte, the vizier and local Bosnian *magnats*, the Muslim aristocracy, and the janissaries as none were willing to relinquish their privileges and submit to the reforms, which were intended to centralize the administration.

The 1831 revolt of the Bosnian Muslim aristocracy against the sultan's attempt at modernization was especially resounding. The rebels demanded a special autonomous status for Bosnia-Herzegovina within the Ottoman Empire. They vowed to remain loyal to the sultan only if the porte were willing to implement both undertakings.[87] With the assistance of their Albanian allies, the rebels defeated the sultan's troops and took Travnik. By the following year, however, their leader, the charismatic captain from Gradačac, the "Dragon of Bosnia" *(Zmaj od Bosne)* Hasan Gradaščević, had been defeated by the sultan's superior army and was forced to flee the land. This episode was deeply etched into the memories of all inhabitants of the *eyalet* of Bosnia (in legends and tales of the Dragon of Bosnia, for example). As a reward for his assistance in quelling the revolt, Ali-pasha Rizvanbegović was appointed to govern Bosnia-Herzegovina in 1833.

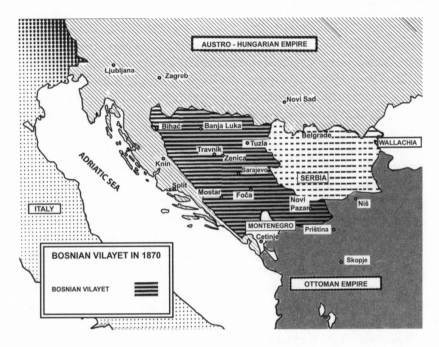

In the 1850s, the administration of Bosnia-Herzegovina was handed over to Omer-pasha Latas, born Mihael Latas, a sergeant in the Austrian army from the Vojna Krajina who converted to Islam and served the Ottoman court. He modernized the land (introducing a unitary administrative division of nine districts governed by *kajmakams*), subdued the disobedient local leaders, and exercised his authority with great severity (including brutal onslaughts), which caused a great deal of indignation among the people. He combed the empire for competent civil servants, who were among the few foreigners to hold high office in Bosnia-Herzegovina. Latas was given the task of implementing the unpopular Tanzimat reforms, intended to effect a fundamental reorganization of the Ottoman system, and attempted to Turkify Bosnia-Herzegovina. The Tanzimat reforms were promulgated by Sultan Abdülmecid in the 1830s and called for the establishment of new institutions that would guarantee security of life, property, and honor for all of the empire's subjects, regardless of their religion or race. They also authorized the development of a standardized system of taxation to eliminate abuses, and established fairer methods of military conscription, a new secular school system, freedom of worship, equality before the law, and participation in provincial, municipal, and judicial advisory bodies.[88]

The reforms introduced by Omer-pasha Latas, which were intended to curtail the political might of the Muslim landowning aristocracy, were met with strong opposition. Also, "many of the conservative leaders of the Christian communities were themselves resistant to change" because they were afraid of losing their foreign connections and feudal privileges.[89] The Bosnian feudal lords' resistance was gradually broken, and Latas also sought to suppress anti-Ottoman notions of liberation or armed revolt by the Bosnian Christians.

During the decline of the Ottoman Empire, the Bosnian Muslims also began taking interest in great events of the past, such as the Battle of Kosovo. They acclaimed the virtue, honor, saintliness, and miraculous powers of Sultan Murad and the moral chastity of his soldiers, who were totally devoted to their faith. Murad also is portrayed as a positive personality in Albanian folk legends: chosen of God, a miracle worker who can part the waters of the sea, brave, righteous, and devout. In Ottoman folk epics, the Battle of Kosovo is the event that opened the way of conquest to Europe. Because Murad's death was voluntary, he is seen as a martyr: his sacrifice became "built in the very basis of future Ottoman Empire and statehood."[90] Another such Muslim hero from the Balkans was Sari Saltik (Mohamed Bohkar), the "holy warrior" who was said to work miracles and—like Saint George—rescue princesses from dragons. His name has been much celebrated in verse, and several places in the Balkans claim to be his final resting place.[91]

Bosnian Muslim legends also featured heroes from other parts of the Islamic world. One such hero is Gazi Sejid Batala, who was killed in a battle with the Byzantines in 740. Sultans were said to be of "divine origin" *(carhalifet)*. Constantinople (Stambol) was said to be a "saint's palace" and a "fountain of power and sanctity." The most renowned and celebrated local Bosnian mythical hero was Gerz Eljas or Gürz Ilyas (Đerzelez Alija), an actual historical figure who distinguished himself in battle against Hungary in the 1479–80 border battles and the Battle of Krbava in 1493. He held estates in Bosnia and in Macedonia. Folk legend has him riding a winged horse, rescuing Ottoman noblemen (the Husrev *beg* from the clutches of a Christian army, for example), and is generally depicted as a great warrior (his name means "the warrior with the mace"). His enemies were Serbian and Croatian noblemen and *hajduk* bandits (the *hajduk* Sava, for example). According to legend, he was slain during prayer. He chose not to interrupt his prayers even though he was aware of his imminent death. His venerated burial place lies in Gerzovo polje near Jajce. His memory is observed on Saint Elias's Day or Ilinden (Alidjun), on August 2. Other Bosnian Muslim heroes were Alija Bojičić, Mustaj-beg Lički, the Hrnjica Brothers (Mujo, Halil, and Omer), and Tale Ličanin.[82]

According to Malcolm, in Bosnia, "the main basis of hostility was not ethnic or religious but economic," between the mainly Christian peasantry and the Muslim landowners.[93] However, this economic, social, religious dichotomy began increasingly to be interpreted predominately in religious terms. The pressure exerted by the Muslim aristocracy, coupled with social frustrations and the influence of folk legends and the traditions of the Christian churches (Orthodox more so than Roman Catholic), resulted in Christians idealizing their ancestors' feudal society and turning toward those early nationalists and movements that promised its restoration. Although pressure on the mainly Christian peasantry was increasing, they were able to preserve their cultural and religious identity and social organization. Corruption, violence, extravagance, and lawlessness were widespread. The sultan's court in Istanbul was quite clearly losing control.

All of this—strengthened by important impulses from aspiring neighbors Serbia, Montenegro, and Austria—prompted peasant revolts in 1852, 1857–58, and 1861–62; discontent over tax policies; hostility between local rulers and the regular army; and economic distress. Rebellious Orthodox peasants, pervaded with new, nationalist designs, were able to count on the support of the clergy. Religious affiliation, however, was not always the most important factor—Muslims are known to have stood by the Orthodox peasantry even though their privileged position gave them less cause to do so. Christians saw the actions of the groups of bandits known as *hajduks* as heroic deeds and religious feats. They were seen as the "scourge of divine justice upon Turks" and "freedom fighters." National and political consciousness became closely associated with the existing and highly developed religious identity of the Christians living under Ottoman rule.

Nationalist agitation and attempts to entice the Muslim Slavs by both neighboring nations—Serbs and Croats—began in the first half of nineteenth century. The Ottoman authorities also began distinguishing among the population according to ethnic affiliation. *Srb-milleti* came to signify the Serbian people, *Bošnjak-kavmi* and *Bošnjak taifesi* were applied to the Bosnian people, and so on.[94] After the rule of "Islamic-Christian coexistence" in past centuries, increasing ethnic differentiation escalated intolerance and the occurrence of incidents between individual religions, especially from the Muslim side against Orthodox and Catholic Christians.[95] Despite this, there was significant development in education, and a greater number of sacral buildings, both Orthodox and Catholic, were being erected with funds from abroad. By the 1860s, there were roughly 380 Catholic priests and more than four hundred Orthodox in the country. It was a time of revival for both Christian churches.

Three important and contradicting novelties appeared during this final period of Ottoman rule in Bosnia. First, the Ottoman sultans encouraged the emergence of pan-Islamic ideologies in the 1870s. They wanted to strengthen their weak empire by mobilizing the Islamic world.[96] The second novelty was the civic concept of "Ottomanism": members of all millets, regardless of creed or race, were to become citizens with equal rights. The Ottoman authorities had first encouraged such a concept in the 1840s, but the issue was legally settled in 1869. Despite this, Muslims demanded a special status and position in society, which inevitably lead to conflict with the non-Muslim population. The first two novelties were of wider significance than the third one, namely the new policy within the province of Bosnia that encouraged members of all religious and ethnic groups to identify themselves as Bosnians. The porte referred to all inhabitants of Bosnia-Herzegovina as Bošnjaci or Bosniaks.[97] Indeed, there was a sense of citizenship in Bosnia. This was particularly true for the Muslims, because of the open discord between Bosnian Muslim landlords and the Ottoman government in Istanbul for several decades, and also because of their aspirations for autonomy.

The approximate figures for the population of Bosnia-Herzegovina (including the *sandžak* of Novi Pazar) in the final years of Ottoman rule (the 1870s) is shown in the table below.[98]

One advocate of the so-called Bošnjak concept was Osman Šerif Topal Pasha, a Bosnian governor (1860–69) of Pomak origin. He embarked on a program in which numerous public buildings, new roads, telegraph lines, and schools were built. He encouraged cultural development and set up a printing press that produced publications in Serbo-Croat and Turkish *(Bosanski vjesnik, Bosna, Neretva, Sarajevski cvetnik)*, and promoted general development. Ottoman Bosnia had developed relatively strong trading relations with the neighboring Habsburg Empire. The new Austrian authorities, especially colonial administrator Benjamin von Kallay, later adopted Topal Pasha's concept of integral, multiethnic citizenship.

In short, Bosnia-Herzegovina had always maintained a certain level of autonomy and a religious and cultural continuity with the bygone era under Ottoman rule. A sense of Bosnian citizenship had also been preserved, although it differed in economic, political, religious, and cultural terms. Most of its rulers during the four centuries of Ottoman rule were of Bosnian origin (Malkoč Karaosmanović, Ferhat Desisalić, Ferhat Sokolović, and Hasan Predojević, for example). In the final years of Ottoman

TABLE 3-1 *Population of Bosnia-Herzegovina, 1870s*

Sandžak	Muslims	Orthodox	Catholics	Jews	Total
Sarajevo	98,921	51,566	24,590	2,696	179,675
Zvornik	178,964	131,471	32,787	354	349,098
Travnik	122,251	70,547	65,110	441	260,199
Bihać	127,027	104,343	5,898	0	238,393
Novi Pazar	147,942	85,952	0	112	236,093
Banja Luka	84,061	126,228	40,554	65	252,623
Herzegovina	110,964	66,041	51,414	0	230,319
Total	870,128	636,208	220,353	3,669	1,746,399

Bosnia, aspirations for autonomy, especially among richer Muslims, grew steadily.[99]

Four distinct religions coexisted in Bosnia, four different cultures and mentalities: Muslim, Roman Catholic, Orthodox, and Jewish. All four were derived from religious, cultural, and political centers outside of Bosnia-Herzegovina. I agree with Vucinich's contention that the Ottoman Empire was weakened by its own policy of preserving the different cultures within its borders, the insistence on social and political distinctions, the encouragement of religious heterogeneity, and a policy directed primarily at conquest. Rather than evolving a strong sense of affiliation to Ottoman society in general, the empire's subjects were more closely linked to their religious communities because of the millet system.[100] The millet system, however, was unable to meet the task of resolving discord and conflict between the supranationally organized multinational empire and the nationalist ideas based primarily on religious differences that surfaced in the second half of the nineteenth century.

4

HONED MINDS
The Origins of Contemporary Serbian and Croatian Religio-National Mythologies

The relationship between religion and national identity is fundamental to understanding the relationship between the South Slavs, and especially between the peoples of Bosnia-Herzegovina. Two mutually infused dimensions are of essential importance: the mythical/historical dimension and the religious/national dimension. It is particularly interesting to note that contemporaries dealing with this question—politicians, religious leaders, historians, writers, military leaders—often express and make utterly contradictory and exclusive assertions, opinions, and conclusions. In this chapter, the only one in the book that does not follow historical chronology, I shall deal with the origin, modification, and consequences of individual Serbian and Croatian religio-national mythologies between the eighteenth and twentieth centuries, especially from the perspective of their usurpation of Bosnia-Herzegovina and the Muslim Slavs.

Blessed is the nation that professes to a single religion. We Greeks share in this blessing— thanks be to God—and accursed be the nation of those who would conspire against the unity of the Greek religion with foreign doctrine, no matter what the pretext, or whatever the means.

—SPYRIDON TRIKOUPIS, NINETEENTH-CENTURY GREEK HISTORIAN

Sarajevo historian Dubravko Lovrenović asserts that the stage for the "real" war in Bosnia-Herzegovina from 1992–95 had been set by the "historiographic war" that was waged on the battlefield of South Slav and Bosnian historiography.[1] The first national historians of nineteenth-century Europe were also the progenitors of myths inspired by romantic and patriotic ideals and national or even religio-national messianism. Likewise, a common argument among national revivalist writers was that there could be no freedom without sacrifice, that their nation was the chosen one, and so forth. New concepts proposed by ideological myths summed up the unexpressed essence of traditional myths: the benign nature of old tales was often the foundation for the malignancy of the new. The myth transformed historical, political, religious, and social incongruity into instructional reproductive harmony.

Michael Sells, an American specializing in the sociology of religion, refers to the religio-national mythology of the Christian South Slavs as "Christoslavism." This mutually related system of myths portrays the Muslim Slavs as traitors to both their Christian faith (even as Christ killers) and their nation. This type of religio-national mythology is based on three interrelated myths that emerged in the nineteenth century: conversion to Islam because of cowardice and greed (the archetype of the "Turkified degenerate"); the perseverance of national-religious groups through the centuries; and the complete depravity of the Ottoman authorities (the archetype of the "evil Turk"). The implied hypotheses behind this train of thought are twofold: "that Slavs are Christian by nature and that any conversion from Christianity is a betrayal of the Slavic race.[2] According to this mythical logic, the converts change not only their religion but their nationality as well.

SERBS: BETWEEN THE "SUMMONING THE ANCESTORS" AND ORTHODOX EXCLUSIVISM

Although they were always present, the motives of the Battle of Kosovo were not preeminent features of Serbian epic poetry until the nineteenth century. Other events and personalities were given more attention before that time. For example, Kraljević (Prince Royal) Marko was "the main Serbian epic hero." Even during the first Serbian uprising in the early nineteenth century the cult of Stephen (known as Prvovenčani, the "First-Crowned") was more important than that of Prince Lazar.[3] Kraljević Marko, although a real historical figure, was very different from the person later portrayed in myth: He was the son of King Vukašin, ruler of a small state near the town of Prilep, and an Ottoman vassal who died in the Battle of Rovine in 1395. The myth portrays him as a chivalrous, sometimes roguish, and even merciless hero, the very personification of the trickster from classical mythologies. In the myths, which are characterized by inconsistencies in time and space, he is said to be the son of a fairy and, as such, to possess superhuman strength ("he fights the three-headed beast"); is accompanied by his fabulous steed, Šarac; is cunning ("he offers his services to the Turks then deceives them"); and is merciless not only to his foes but his relatives as well ("slays both his father and brother").

The motif of a sleeping king is as familiar to Serbs and Montenegrins as it is to Germans, English, Danes, Portuguese, Brazilians, Slovenes, or Czechs. The myth tells us that Kraljević Marko is asleep in Šar Planina Mountain, and that when he awakens he will revive the medieval Serbian kingdom and take revenge for Kosovo. Another myth claims that God placed Marko and his steed Šarac in a cave after a bloody battle and thrust his blade into a rock. When the blade slides out of the rock, Marko will awaken and return to the people. Many simple people believed that the First Balkan War (October, 1912) actually signaled the awakening of Kraljević Marko.[4]

The dictum "the Bugle of Kosovo sounds in our hearts from that day on and every day" can, therefore, be applied to the Serbs and Montenegrins.[5] However, its sound was particularly strong in the early nineteenth century when the Battle of Kosovo became the source of all Serbian religious and national ambitions. The reconstruction of Serbian religio-national mythology—obviously influenced by Herder's *"Sturm und Drang"* literary movement—begins in parallel with the Serbian *reconquista*, with the uprising of the Christian peasantry against the Turks in 1804–13 and 1815, and the creation of the modern Serbian state.

Serbia was granted limited autonomy within the Ottoman Empire when Russia and the Ottomans reached an agreement at the Convention of Akkerman in 1826. The Serbs were granted full independence under the Treaty of Edirne (Adrianople) in 1829, and the first modern Serbian dynasty was established a year later by the leader of the second Serbian uprising, Miloš Obrenović (1789–1860). Both Obrenović and the leader of the first uprising, Karađorđe Petrović (1768–1817), were descended from Montenegrin families that migrated to Serbia.

The nationalist movement had both a religious and rural character from its beginning. Many of the rebel leaders were Orthodox priests and monks who made sure that the peasants did not forget the tragic Battle of Kosovo. An equally powerful source of inspiration was Serbian historiography. However, the concept of a modern Serbian state derived primarily from the higher social and ecclesiastic echelons of the Serbian diaspora in southern Hungary, who were in direct contact with European enlightenment and the emancipating influence of the French Revolution. Nevertheless, we can observe an interesting tendency: The church considered the liberation struggle from the Ottoman Empire not "as part of a modernisation process involving the whole of Europe but as the resurrection of the medieval Serbian kingdom."[6]

The Kosovo myths, now actualized with ideological pretensions, became—as expressed by Serbian historian Rade Mihaljčić—"the driving force in the wars of liberation." The motif of the hero, Miloš Obilić, and the concept of betrayal, which also features in Serbian uprisings, was also preserved.[7] "Serbianhood breeds the memory of Obilićes": The Miloš cult flourished in the mid-nineteenth century when the church officially recognized it, after which time Miloš more frequently appeared in church frescoes.[8] Vuk Branković also became a timeless, albeit negative, figure, the personification of a traitor to the Serbian people.

Likewise, the Lazar cult did not become firmly established until the eighteenth century, when he became a source of inspiration for the struggle for Serbian freedom and statehood.[9] There is yet another important dimension to consider: More often than not, a military hero accompanies the cultural and religious leader—Kraljević Marko (or Tsar Dušan, Miloš Obilić, or Prince Lazar) standing abreast of Saint Sava, for example. These phenomena were labeled "summoning the ancestors" by Serbian ethnologist Veselin Čajkanović (1881–1946).

The antipathy between Muslims and Orthodox and between Muslim Slavs and Serbs was a product of nineteenth- and twentieth-century Serbian nationalism and as such was projected five or six centuries backward. The ruthless persecution of Muslims became a holy quest that also was advocated by militant Orthodox clergymen. At the beginning of the nineteenth century, Serbian nationalist writers, painters, playwrights, poets, and composers began portraying the Kosovo issue—motives of death, sacrifice, heroism, betrayal, and rebirth—in their own way. An enormous number of cultural and artistic events were dedicated to the subject. This ideology was further strengthened through the education system. The implicit goal of all these national liberation efforts and expansionist ambitions is found in the popular maxim: "To avenge Kosovo!"

As Sells shows, the likeness of Prince Lazar was gradually and ultimately transformed to that of Jesus Christ: he was invariably portrayed in the company of a group of acolytes (apostles); the Last Supper corresponds to the eve of the battle; he is betrayed by Vuk Branković (Judas), who, according to the myth, converts to Islam; Miloš Obilić is portrayed as the role model for all Serbs; and Kosovo is referred to as the "Serbian Golgotha," the "Serbian Palestine," and the "Serbian Jerusalem." History was "divided to the period from Adam to the battle Prince Lazar fought at Kosovo and from Kosovo and Prince Lazar to a chronicler's own time."[10] All this is partially drawn from folk tradition, epics, and legends, which served as the basis for such derivation. The local myth thus acquires a global character.

With the help of the tradition of the Orthodox Church and early Serbian historiography, the folk epic poetry portraying the Battle of Kosovo helped bridge the gap between the old and the new Serbian state. The ideological myth of Serbian religious nationalism, now recast with artistic reflection, completes the structural inadequacy of the traditional myth, that is, the familiar unanswered questions of "How was defeat possible?" "When will the glorious Serbian Empire be rebuilt?" "Who will be the new Dušan, Lazar, Miloš, Vuk Branković?" and so on. From such a perspective, Kosovo truly becomes "a Serbian being"[11] or—in the words of contemporary Serbian writer Matija Bećković, "the equator of the Serbian planet." The Montenegrins also identify with the heroes of Kosovo: Each of the Montenegrin tribes eventually traced its origins to one of the Kosovo heroes.[12]

Montenegrin ruler Peter Petrović II Njegoš (1813–51) imputed the downfall of the medieval Serbian kingdom to the iniquity of the people and their estrangement from God. As such, the Serbs were assumed to be responsible for their own defeat and the punishment was the loss of national freedom. Njegoš, who desired that the "everyday life of Montenegrins would be imbued with the symbols of Kosovo myth," called converts to Islam traitors.[13] His epic poem *The Mountain Wreath* (1847), a recital of the massacre of Muslim converts in Montenegro on Christmas Day in 1709, became an ideological upgrade of the traditional myth and license for anti-Muslim pogroms. It epitomized and then elaborated on all that had thus far been said regarding conversion: that Muslim Slavs—"traitors of Serbian blood and Christ's faith"—were as much to blame as the Ottomans, the murderers of Prince Lazar, because they had converted to a "foreign" religion, the "Ottoman" faith.

Djordjević notes that although Njegoš's literary work abounds in historical errors, it still inspired a Montenegrin liberation movement. The significance of the myth therefore overshadows its historical accuracy. Voje comes to a similar conclusion: The massacre of the Turkified Slavs was not a unique event but "a process that was repeated on numerous occasions throughout the liberation struggle in the eighteenth century."[14] This mood is well reflected in a verse from Njegoš's *Mountain Wrath*, where one of the Montenegrin leaders, Duke Batrić, tells local Muslims, "Bairam cannot make peace with Christmas!"[15]

Sells found similar Christoslavic themes and Islamophobic bigotry in the literary works of other nineteenth and twentieth century writers. Much of this literature went through a process of nationalist popularization and militant vulgarization in the late 1980s and early 1990s.[16] An illustrative example of this is the flagrant perversion of the opus of Nobel laureate Ivo Andrić (1892–1975) for this purpose. In honor of this Bosnian Croat, who strongly believed in a united Yugoslavia and whom Serbian nationalists declared the "greatest Serb of non-Serbian descent," the Serbs held a festival in 1995 in the "ethnically cleansed" city of Višegrad.[17]

Vuk Stefanović Karadžić (1787–1864) narrated the Battle of Kosovo and the heroic Serb warriors in that fateful battle. Other writers created the Christologic portrait of Prince Lazar. The martyrdom of the heroes for their faith—choosing death, and therefore the Heavenly Kingdom, over bondage under the yoke of the heathen—was transformed into martyrdom for national liberation. The Kosovo topic was also discussed by such writers as author and pedagogue monk Dositej Obradović (1739–1811) from Vojvodina; historian Ljubomir Kovačević (1848–1918); monk, bishop, author, and historian Lukijan Mušicki (1777–1837); and writer Jovan Sterija Popović (1806–56). Ljudevit Gaj was at the forefront of the Illyrists, who were also sympathetic toward Serbian history and the Kosovo episode.[18]

Lazar's curse was "understood as a call to uprising."[19] His heroic death—his conscious and voluntary sacrifice—also signified the death of the Serbian nation. However, resurrection would come in the nineteenth century, when the Serbs began taking revenge on their enemies. Indeed, the persecution, eviction, and extermination of Muslims, regardless of their ethnicity, began in reconquered territories. According to this logic, the Ottoman victory over the Serbs was temporary. The real victor was Lazar.

In short, the myth of Kosovo became the foundation of Serbian religio-national identity and the driving force for Serbs under foreign dominance, as well as the focal point for their perception of their own history—their main source of national unity, religious identity, and cosmic hope. The history that followed seems like a sequel to the battle. Karađorđe presented himself as the avenger of the defeat at Kosovo. In his celebrated address to the rebels at Topčider, he referred to the Battle of Kosovo and the Orthodox and Nemanjić heritage. He likened his military commanders to Obilić. Njegoš likened Obilić to Spartan and Roman heroes and issued medals bearing his name. Several Serbian military units, from the wars of the early nineteenth century to the recent clashes in Bosnia-Herzegovina, have been named after heroes of the Battle of Kosovo. The Obrenović dynasty was fond of comparing itself to the medieval Nemanjićes. Serbia became a kingdom in 1882 with Miloš Obrenović on the throne. The press perceived this as the realization of the dream that for centuries had lived in history, poetry, the church, and people's assemblies.[20]

Serbian king Peter I Karađorđević (1844–1921), or "Čika Pero" (Uncle Pero) as he was popularly known, was totally devoted to the myth of the Battle of Kosovo and the tradition of Serbian uprisings. Following Kosovo's occupation during the First Balkan War in the autumn of 1912, which for the Serbs was tantamount to a return to Jerusalem, Peter I lit a gigantic candle at Dečani in 1913, which, according to tradition, "was to be set burning only when the Battle of Kosovo was avenged."[21] In 1924, his successor Alexander lit the two candles that had long been saved for the occasion when the Ottomans were finally driven from Serbia.

The *recuperatio* of "ancient Serbia," as Kosovo was known—which was one of the military objectives of the First Balkan War—was an emotional experience for the Serbs. During the First World War, Peter I was perceived as the "new Lazar" and had a bronze crown cast from a piece of Karađorđe's first cannon. Serbian historian Dimitrije Djordjević relates a significant episode from that period. According to his eschatological understanding of national identity, the commander of the Serbian First Army, the brilliant strategist and renowned general and duke Živojin Mišić (1855–1921, victor of the Battles of Cer and Kolubara, also decorated at the Salonika front) demanded that his forces halt their retreat at Kosovo and engage the numerically overwhelming German, Austro-Hungarian, and Bulgarian forces in a final battle at Peć. His alternatives were the as those in 1389: "victory or extinction!" The Supreme Command rejected his suicidal notion and ordered the retreat to continue through Montenegro and Albania.[22] At the same time, Serbian prime minister Nikola Pašić—borrowing a phrase often used in dramatic situations by political or military leaders all over the world—proclaimed, "It is better that we die as free men than live like slaves."[23]

The systematic cleansing or massacre of Slavic and non-Slavic Muslims, who could only save their lives by fleeing or converting to Orthodoxy, accompanied Serbian conquests before the Balkan wars of 1912 and 1913. A similar situation existed throughout the Balkans after the Ottomans left (in Greece, Bulgaria, and parts of Hungary and Croatia). The towns of Užice, Valjevo, Čačak, Požega, and Nikšič, for example, were predominately Muslim before they were occupied by Serbia or Montenegro. At the beginning of the seventeenth century there were 217 mosques, thirteen *mesdžids* (small mosques or prayer rooms, from *masjid*), seventeen *tekkes* and eight *madrasahs* (theological colleges) in Belgrade. Today, only the Bajrakli-džamija mosque remains standing. In 1878, the year that the Congress of Berlin was held, there were six mosques, two *mesdžids*, and ten *tekkes* in Leskovac, none of which have survived to the present day. Between fifteen thousand and twenty thousand Muslims fled or were expelled from Serbia in the 1820s and were replaced by Bosnian Serbs. The cleansing was, as British historian Heywood describes it, "rapid, bloody and effective, leaving no traces of what had been."[24]

Modern Montenegro was created in a similar fashion after it was granted self-government at the Treaty of Požarevac in 1718, but power was assumed by Orthodox metropolitans. The Metropolitan See of Cetinje was "the main unifying force of the discordant clans and *knežine*."[25] These "dual leaders," the Petrović-Njegoš bishop-princes, coerced the tribes into a theocratic state order, transcending mere tribalism. They attempted to suppress the widespread blood feuds and glorified their collective struggle against the Ottomans; they created a myth about Montenegrin merits and celebrated their glorious history (Duklja, Zeta), their resistance, and their covenant with the Serbs and Orthodoxy; and they sought alliances with the Russians and Venetians.

Vladika (bishop-prince) Peter Petrović II Njegoš was acclaimed as the "greatest and most representative Serbian poet, philosopher, and theologian," metaphorically the "Serbian Shakespeare" or the "Serbian Milton."[26] During his reign, churches, schools, and roads were built, printing presses founded, and industry encouraged. Peter introduced a new civil service and pacified the tribes by settling old grievances. He traveled extensively throughout Europe and met European leaders. In his own words, he was a "ruler among barbarians and a barbarian among rulers." In the revolutionary year of 1848, he lent his support to Jelačić's endeavors for greater Croatian independence and offered his military assistance. He also tried to induce the Serbs to liberate Bosnia-Herzegovina.

The Kosovo tradition was also strongly preserved in Montenegro. In Bishop Vasilij's *History of Montenegro*, published in Russia in the mid-eighteenth century, the author repeatedly refers to the Battle of Kosovo and Serbian medieval statehood.[27] After two centuries of territorial expansion, Montenegro became a kingdom in 1910 with Nikola I at the throne. "Direct" links were claimed with the medieval rulers of Zeta, such as Vojislav, Mihajlo, and Bodin. Particularly interesting were popular theories of that time which held that the Montenegrins were not Slavs but of Illyrian descent, or identified Montenegro as the "Serbian Sparta." As was the case in Serbia, Montenegro's Poturs (Muslim or

"Turkified" Slavs) were brutally massacred and ostracized during the re-conquest of ancient lands, all with the connivance of the bishop-princes (for example, Danilo of the first Njegoš dynasty during the first three decades of the eighteenth century). The national mythologies of Mon-tenegro and Greater Serbia overlapped in several aspects.

Serbian Orthodoxy "absorbed almost all Serbian pagan rituals, cus-toms, and festivals, and transferred them to Christian saints and feasts." The evolution of the feast of Vidovdan (Saint Vitus's Day) is idiosyncratic. During the 1860s, Saint Lazar's Day was associated with the feast day of the pre-Christian god Vid (Svatenvid), the supreme deity of light. Serbia's pre-Christian mythology was solar in nature, and Vidovdan was a feast celebrating the battle between the forces of light and darkness. The Vi-dovdan tradition consisted of several interrelated legends—totemic, rit-ual, cult, magical, divinatory, and sacrificial. The narrative framework for the composition of the whole was the myth of the eternal recurrence of the sun. As such, Vidovdan could easily be linked to the Kosovo drama of 1389: cosmogony descended into history.[28]

After the great migration of 1690, the anniversary of the Battle of Kosovo—Vidovdan—became a kind of All Saints' Day for the Serbs dur-ing which commemorations were held in honor of the Kosovo warriors and all who fell "for their faith and fatherland." The fallen warriors, au-tomatically elevated to hero status, become martyrs "for Holy Cross and Sweet Freedom."[29] Vidovdan became a feast day of the Serbian people and the Orthodox Church in the nineteenth century. Although institutional-ized in 1849, and the first public festivities held in 1851, it did not truly become popular until after 1903. The evolution of Vidovdan as a Serbian national and religious holiday took place in concert with the evolution of national and political holidays throughout Europe in the latter half of the nineteenth century and was intended to empower national con-sciousness and nurture patriotism.[30]

General interest for Vidovdan increased even more on the Battle of Kosovo's five hundredth anniversary. All Serbian institutions were repre-sented at the commemoration, and the holiday was celebrated in Serbia, Vojvodina, Srem, Montenegro, Bosnia, and Zagreb, where Rački pre-sented his work about the battle.[31] In 1892, Vidovdan was celebrated as an ecclesiastical holiday for the first time. In the twentieth century, with the emergence of mass nationalism (grand national revivalist rallies, ed-ucational system, celebrations, greater access to the media), it finally be-came the main national holiday. It is perhaps worth noting that the Serbs declared war on the Ottomans on Vivodan in 1876; the Second Balkan War began on or about Vidovdan; Archduke Francis Ferdinand was assassinated in Sarajevo on Vidovdan in 1914; the centralist constitution was passed on Vidovdan in 1921; the six hundredth anniversary of the Battle of Kosovo was celebrated on that day in 1989 in Gazimestan, where Slobodan Milošević delivered his infamous speech foretelling battles to come; and the Serbian opposition organized the "Vidovdan assembly" in 1993.

Albanians suffered treatment similar to that of the Muslim Slavs at the hands of the Serbs. They were considered to be either an inferior people or a race of savages, and those from Kosovo as merely Albanian Serbs (the Arnautuše; the Albanian national hero Skenderbeg is said to have been "semi-Serb").[32] Conflicts heightened after the First World War in Yugoslav areas populated by Albanians (from Montenegro and Kosovo to West Macedonia). Albanian rebels—so-called Kaçaks (Kačaci)—withstood the brutal and assimilatory Serbian policies that were enforced in multiethnic territories for five years.

Mistrust and even the demonization of members of other religions and nationalities became an integral part of the Serbian Orthodox mythology known as *svetosavlje*. This mythology presumes a mythical unity of the collective and the individual, of the holy and the profane, in the Serbian nation. Saint Sava represented and continues to represent "the symbol of unity of the Serbs, with an independent Church and with its own national, cultural and social identity."[33] The history of the Serbs was presented as the history of Serbian Orthodoxy, threatened by all and sundry. That Orthodoxy was the very heart of the Serbian national identity was a belief also held by Nikolaj Velimirović and Justin Popović, the most important Serbian theologians of the twentieth century, and church dignitaries like Atanasije Jevtić, all of whom are religious exclusivists.

Saint Sava's legacy was said to be the "conscience of the Serbian people" and "its guide to the future."[34] All of the Serbs' woes and suffering were said to be the result of a defection from *svetosavlje*. *Svetosavlje*, therefore, "is nothing but Orthodoxy, but Orthodoxy of the 'Serbian style and taste,'" according to Bishop Irinej Bulović of Bačka, one of its latest advocates.[35] The mythology of Saint Sava addresses all classes of people, as can be seen in the following poem by a nineteenth-century Serbian poet:

Servant, peasant, and master,
All are equal before you,
All limbs of the same body,
Inseparable, completely commensurate.

The ancestor cult, the adoration of great historical leaders, is further expressed in Orthodoxy through the practice of reinterring their mortal remains. The Mileševo monastery, where Saint Sava is buried, becomes a place of national pilgrimage. He was declared a martyr in the late sixteenth century, when the Ottomans desecrated his mortal remains as punishment for an uprising. In the nineteenth century, monks moved the remains of Stephen Prvovenčani from Studenica to the safety of the Vraćevšnica monastery on liberated Serbian soil, and during the retreat of 1915 the sarcophagus containing his body was removed to the Ostrog monastery in Montenegro.

Prince Lazar was canonized not only in order to soothe relations with the patriarch of Constantinople, but also because of his martyrdom (beheading). An "exquisite and sweet fragrance" is said to have emanated from his body. He was buried in Priština after the battle and his remains were moved to the Ravanica monastery between 1390 and 1391, where he remained buried until 1690. The "martyr of Kosovo," Lazar was little revered until the great Serbian migration.[36] During the retreat of 1690, he was disinterred and moved to Szent Endre near Budapest in Hungary. Seven years later, his remains were transferred to the monastery of Nova Ravanica (Vrdnik) in Srem, where his cult was revived after Vrdnik became a place of Serbian pilgrimage in the eighteenth century. During the Second World War, Lazar's remains were moved from the territory of the Independent State of Croatia to Belgrade, and in 1988 back to Ravanica via Gračanica.

Ivo Banac notes that "the process of steady equation between Orthodoxy and Serbdom was completed after the Serbian uprisings and the establishment of an autonomous Serbian principality," that is, in the first three decades of the nineteenth century.[37] Influenced by the rise of newly autonomous Serbia, the Serbian Orthodox seminary in Prizren became an important center of Serbian national revivalist activity after 1871. Students, future teachers and priests, came from neighboring countries with Orthodox populations (Montenegro, Sandžak, Bosnia-Herzegovina, Serbia). They were instructed in the urgency of liberating and unifying all of the Orthodox, who were automatically recognized as Serbs, into one state.[38] Similar activities were promoted by Serbian lay teachers.

Following the abrogation of the patriarchate of Peć, jurisdiction over Serbian Orthodoxy was assumed by the patriarch of Constantinople, who was thus able to directly collect taxes in Bosnia-Herzegovina, appoint Greek bishops, and so forth. The gradual political emancipation of the Serbian state from Ottoman domination, which began in the early nineteenth century, was followed by the emancipation of the Serbian

Orthodox community from Greek domination—that is, the attempts of the Phanariots to Hellenize the Serbian Orthodox Church. Indeed, the entire process was a much wider one: Nineteenth-century Balkan Orthodox groups showed greater concern for their future as national groups than for the cohesion of the Orthodox population in the Ottoman Empire as a whole.

The bond between the state and the Orthodox Church in the Serbian principality (and later kingdom) was a strong one. The church regained its autonomy in 1830, became autocephalous in 1879, and became a patriarchate in 1920. Many Orthodox priests actively participated in Serbian party politics. In 1881, the state assumed control over the functioning of the church, practically changing it into a state agency. Thus, from the primacy of Metropolitan Mihajlo, the government was able to influence the synod through its lay delegates and even interfered in the church's organization. Moreover, Orthodoxy was declared the state religion in the 1903 constitution, religious rites were conducted during national holidays, and the state gave financial support to the clergy.

Early Serbian nationalism was strongly tied to Orthodoxy and the heritage of the church. Namely, prior to the two celebrated uprisings, the identification of the population was first of all religious—Orthodox.[39] The process of national liberation from Ottoman rule had strong religious connotations; the struggle for freedom and independence was tantamount to the struggle for faith. As was often the case in other South Slav nations, ecclesiastical, intellectual, and cultural leaders became the heralds of national expansion. Because of their devotion to Orthodoxy they opposed Illyrism, as did the first Serbian contemporary historian and monk, Jovan Rajić (1726–1801), and publicist and national revivalist Teodor (Todor) Pavlović (1804–54), for example.

Foreign politics was another important factor. In 1768, Russian empress Catherine the Great pressured the Ottoman sultan to make *Matushka* (Mother) Russia the protector of and ally of all Orthodox Christians in the Ottoman Empire. This allowed Russia to make a strategic thrust for the "warm" Mediterranean Sea. The end of the eighteenth and beginning of the nineteenth century was particularly intense in this regard: high-ranking Serbian Orthodox dignitaries (Archimandrites Jovanović and Gagović) sent proposals for the creation of a Slavic-Serbian Empire to the Russian tsar.[40] Other proposals anticipated a Russian protectorate over Serbia. Vojvodina politician and cultural patron Sava Tekelija (1761–1842) proposed the restoration of the Serbian state to Napoleon and Austrian emperor Francis I. In 1804, Metropolitan Stefan Stratimirović amended Tekelija's map and sent it to Tsar Alexander I.

The hegemonic concepts of a Greater Serbia first appeared in plans drawn during the period of the consolidation of the Serbian state. In 1844, in what was then known as the "Autonomous Principality of Serbia" ruled by Alexander Karađorđević, Ilija Garašanin (1812–74), later dubbed by foreign observers as the "Bismarck of the Balkans," drafted the first Serbian program for national emancipation, a secret memorandum known as the "Draft Plan" *(Načertanije)*. The Polish leader in exile, Prince Adam Czartoryski, and his ambassador to Belgrade, Franjo Zach, inspired the plan. The latter went as far as to propose that the entire state of Serbia should be given military character. In the Draft Plan, Garašanin appealed for Serbian historical rights (on the basis of "holy historical rights") and advocated the reunification of all of the lands that had been under Dušan's authority into an independent and strong Serbian state. He regarded Croats and Slavic Muslims "as Serbs of the Catholic and Islamic faiths."[41]

The goal is unambiguous: The unification of all Serbs living under the Ottomans and their "salvation" from the foreign yoke. Being sure of the imminent defeat of the Ottoman Empire and of the liberation mission of his country, Serbia was for Garašanin the "natural protector of all Turkish Slavs" and he believed "a new state must grow on the steady foundations of the ancient Serbian state."[42] Garašanin's criterion for national identity consisted of a combination of ethnic lineage, language, customs, and religion. In contrast to such ambitions, Serbian liberals preferred a united struggle by Balkans Slavs aimed at creating a federation.

Other elements slowly joined the Orthodoxy in defining Serbian nationality: historical episodes, folk tradition, and the presence of an Orthodox population in the central and western Balkans.[43] According to Great Serbian ideologues, Serbia lies wherever there are "Serbian homes" or even "Serbian graves." Vuk S. Karadžić chose another criterion for determining Serbian nationality among the southern Slavs: language. Under the influence of the literary nationalism represented by German philosopher, historian, and poet Johann Gottfried von Herder, Karadžić determined in 1814 that Croatians and Muslim Slavs ("these are Serbian Muslims") were Serbs as well, using the Shtokavian dialect as the basis for his argument. His renowned statement that "All are Serbs and everywhere" dates from 1849.[44] Karadžić's theories were sharply criticized. Croatian clerics accused him of attempting to "Serbianize" the Croats and convert them to Orthodoxy. Serbian conservatives—who accused him of being in league with the pope, of trying to "Catholicize" Orthodox Serbs, of being in the service of "demonic forces," and so forth—criticized his liberal, reform-oriented thinking.

National consciousness evolved among the Serbs much more rapidly than it did among the Croats or the Muslim Slavs of Bosnia-Herzegovina. Revenge for Kosovo, the revival of Dušan's medieval empire, and the expansion of Serbia to wherever there were Serbs became the goals of the national struggle and the instruments of its legitimization. These goals can be found in various publications by different authors, such as the first published history of the Serbs by Jovan Rajić, printed in Vienna in 1794, a similar publication by Dimitrij Davidović in 1821, and the history textbook about the kingdom of Serbia by Milan Vikičević. Serbian anthropologist-geographer Jovan Cvijić (1865–1927) was convinced that Serbia was predestined "to link and unite the western and eastern South Slav territories and tribes." According to Cvijić, the Muslims of Bosnia-Herzegovina were "Muslim Serbs" or "Mohammedan Serbs with Dinaric characteristics," and therefore, "the oldest Serbian population in these dominions" (i.e., in Bosnia, Herzegovina, and the Novi Pazar Sandžak).[45]

Among the authors of the myth of Bosnia-Herzegovina's Serbian origin were prominent nineteenth and twentieth century Serbian historians, all of whom diffused politically motivated historical falsehoods: that Bosnia-Herzegovina had been Serbian from the time of its settling in the seventh century, that Tvrtko Kotromanić professed only the Orthodox faith, that the Catholics and Muslims of Bosnia-Herzegovina are "Serbs of Catholic and Muslim denomination," and so on.[46] The period of Ottoman domination was exhibited in the most negative possible way. Even Czech historian Konstantin Josef Jireček (1854–1918), a student of medieval and modern Balkan history, claimed that the era of Ottoman rule was the darkest period in the history of the local peoples.

This contributed to the fact that all Serbian political parties in Serbia proper considered Bosnia-Herzegovina as Serbian territory in the years prior to the First World War. There was talk of the "unification of the Serbs" and the "great solution." Insofar as Jovan Cvijić was concerned, "the Serbian problem must be resolved by force of arms." A military solution was also favored by, among others, the Radical Party and a secret society of officers with political ambitions known as *Ujedinjenje ili smrt* (Union or Death), which also believed that all South Slav territory in Austria-Hungary should be annexed to Serbia. The organization was also known as *Crna ruka* (Black Hand), and its members were initiated into the organization by taking an oath over a dagger, a revolver, and a cross lying on a table covered with a black tablecloth.[47] Its members rallied around the periodical bearing the loquacious title of *Pijemont*. Another nationalistic and militant organization was the Serbian National Defense *(Srpska narodna odbrana)*, which had revolutionary cells in

Bosnia-Herzegovina. Kosovo rhetoric and the goal of unifying "all the Serbs of the ancient empire" were also present in the programs of the Serbian youth organization United Serbian Youth *(Ujedinjena omladina srpska)* and the Society for Serbian Unification *(Družina za ujedinjenje srpsko).*

In addition to the concept of Greater Serbia, the Serbs entertained other ideas as well: the Illyrian concept, the unification of Serbia and Bulgaria, and the belief that Serbs and Croats are two tribes from the same national group (a notion also held by historian Stojan Novaković). Writer and translator Jovan Jovanović Zmaj (1833–1904) was of the same opinion. Referring to the Serbs and Croats, he wrote: "We are one, not two!" and "One body, one endeavour, one conviction, one hope."[48] Early concepts of a Yugoslav state can also be detected in the writings of Teodor Pavlović, an otherwise staunch opponent of Illyrism. In 1839, Pavlović described South Slavs as "Yugoslavs" (Jugoslavljani) and proclaimed, "Yugoslavs: let the Carniolans be Carniolans, and the Croats be Croats, and let the Serbs be Serbs, but when we speak of them all, we must be called that which by nature is our name: born of one tribe, dear brother Yugoslavs, Yugoslav!"[49]

If we summarize the methods used to achieve Serbian national interests and goals, we find that four different currents in the last two centuries have been advocating different ideas and exerting varying influence. The strongest was undoubtedly the last of these four. "Federalist Yugoslavism" was nonassimilatory and adhered to the notion that a multinational state would protect the people from foreign interests. This view was held by Svetozar Marković and later by the Yugoslav communists. "Integrated Yugoslavism" recognized only one "South Slav" nation, a philosophy that was held by the ideologues of the kingdom of Yugoslavia. "Lesser Serbia" accentuated the dissimilarity between the Serbs of Serbia proper and those from other parts of the Balkans. "Greater Serbia" denies any form of Yugoslavism or Illyrism, its only goal being the unification of all Serbs (or, better, areas inhabited by the Serbs) into one state.[50] Religio-national mythology has been most strongly associated with this last concept, which was also the strongest.

CROATS: BETWEEN CATHOLIC EXCLUSIVISM, ILLYRISM, AND YUGOSLAVISM

Croatia's national resurrection also began in the late eighteenth century and was, in a way, a response to the pressures of Hungarian nationalism and Habsburg centralism. It was, however, very different from that of the

Serbs. Although Croatia's Roman Catholic clergy exerted a strong influence on culture, politics, and the economy in the nineteenth and part of the twentieth centuries, its influence was not conclusive. The high-ranking clergy were of local descent and rekindled the memories of the historical tradition of Croatian statehood, actively participated in forging modern Croatia's national consciousness, and directed political action.[51] For this reason, it could play an important role in the resistance to Hungarian predominance. An example is Franciscan priest Andrija Dorotić (1761–1837), who led the movement for the unification of Dalmatia and Croatia after the collapse of the Venetian Republic.

Croatia's Catholic clergy eventually participated in the creation of a Croatian national consciousness, but to a lesser degree than the Orthodox clergy in Serbia, and later in the process. This was also a consequence of the policies of the Roman Catholic Church in the Habsburg Empire, which sought to adapt to the heterogeneity of the empire while desisting from any involvement in the name of the people. In June, 1849, a conference of Austrian bishops drafted a pastoral letter in which the church established that the division of mankind into different nations was indeed the work of God, but that national and political activity were not justifiable.[52]

However, the Roman Catholic Church in Croatia eventually did expand to local and later national dimensions. The cult of the Virgin Mary, *Majka Kroatica* ("Croatian Mother"), became firmly established, and the Virgin of Marija Bistrica became the "protector of the Croats" in 1684. Also powerful were the cults of regional and local patron saints, such as Saint Jerome, Saint Martin, Saint Vlah, Saint Duja, and others. Croatian Catholic priests, especially those in Istria and Dalmatia, also used the glagolitic alphabet and held mass in the vernacular, thereby resisting attempts to denationalize the population.

Two major options of national mythology emerged in nineteenth century Croatia: the integrational option, the aim of which was to unite the various South Slav peoples, and the exclusivist option, which fostered Croatian religio-national mythology. The first group included Illyrism and Yugoslavism. Early attempts to provoke a national consciousness were based on Illyrism: the indigenous Illyrians were said to belong to the Slav ethnic body.

However, its roots were older. A sixteenth-century Dominican theologian, Vinko Pribojević, defended the existence of a distinct Illyrian race, arguing that the Slavs were descended from Illyrians, Thracians, and Macedonians, and from such famous personalities as Aristotle, Alexander the Great and Saint Jerome. On the other hand, the book *Origin and*

Achievements of the Slavs, published in 1525, claimed that the Czechs, Poles, and Russians were descended from the Croats. Chevalier Bernadini of Dalmatia believed that all Slavs were descended from the Illyrians.

Similarly, Juraj Križanić (Crisanius), a Dominican theologian, priest, and writer from Karlovac in Croatia, believed that the Croats, Serbs, and Bulgarians belonged to an Illyrian branch of a "wider Slav race." He advocated an open and tolerant dialogue with the Orthodox Church and had ecumenical ambitions and ideas of uniting the Russian Orthodox Church with Roman Catholicism. He wrote to Rome in 1641: "I do not think of the Muscovites as heretics or as schismatics (for their schism was not the result of conceit, which is the true root of schism, but of ignorance), rather, I think of them as Christians who were seduced into fallacy." He added that he would go among them and speak to them, but not "preach" to them. He believed that it was the Greeks who deceived them into apostasy, which, he maintained, was "more a matter of jurisdiction than of faith." He also entertained the notion of creating a uniform Slavic language. Križanić is considered to be one of the founders—indeed, an "apostle"—of Pan-Slavism and Yugoslavism. It was he who formulated the view of national, linguistic, religious, and political "unification of all Slavs under the leadership of Russia."[53] This concept of a "union of Slavs" and the emancipatory mission of Russia, especially during the reign of Peter the Great, took root among many Slavic peoples, from Poland to Dubrovnik.

Illyrism became one of the political aspects of activity of the Roman Catholic Church in late-eighteenth-century Croatia. One pioneer of Illyrism was Maksimilijan Vrhovac (1752–1827), an enlightened national revivalist and bishop of Zagreb. He endeavored to make the church the custodian of Croatian national culture and was known for his national-romantic efforts to compile Croatian traditions. He struggled to establish the public use of the Croat language, to raise the general level of education of the people, and he supported writers who published in the native language. He strove to abolish serfdom, supported the press, and encouraged the building of libraries. He also corresponded frequently with the great thinkers in neighboring Slavic nations. In the name of liberalism and Emperor Joseph's reforms, he advocated freethinking and religious tolerance. He was also in charge of the spiritual revival of his bishopric, which he traversed frequently. Because of his efforts, motivated by his "zealous love for his beloved homeland," he can legitimately be regarded as the driving force behind the enlightenment of the Croatian people. Like many of his laic and ecclesiastic contemporaries, he was a freemason, for which his opponents repeatedly condemned him.

Starting in the seventeenth century, Croatian theologians (citing Saint Cyril and Saint Methodius as examples) began expounding the responsibility of the Greeks for the schism of 1054 and called on the Slavs to transcend it. The so-called Cyril-Methodius Idea emerged as a specific religious dimension of the concept of Illyrism in the nineteenth century. Its adherents advocated Slavic solidarity in the face of foreign domination and the unification of Serbian Orthodoxy and Roman Catholicism. The ecumenical and tolerant alignment of this concept is illustrated in the acceptance of the theological authenticity of the Orthodox religion by Catholic priest Franjo Rački (a Croatian politician and historian, and a personal friend of Bishop Josip Juraj Strossmayer), for which he was severely criticized. It must be added, however, that such ideas were viewed with great suspicion by the Orthodox side as well, which was afraid of possible hidden Uniate tendencies.[54]

Franciscan monk Ivan Franjo Jukić, who in the mid-nineteenth century adopted the familiar and rather widespread theory that Bosnia-Herzegovina's Muslim aristocrats were descendants of apostate Christians who had accepted Islam in order to preserve their property, position, and privileges. Jukić was an Illyrist and published a history of Bosnia under the pseudonym Slavoljub Bošnjak (Slavophile Bosniak). He publicly advocated a collective spirit of Bosnian nationhood based on the three religious groups. In the early 1850s he published the Zagreb newspaper *Bosanski prijatelj (Friend of Bosnia),* through which he spread his ideas on Bosnia.[55] Illyrism was common among the Bosnian Franciscans, who were accustomed to a multiethnic and multireligious environment. An important representative of these was Grga Martić (1822–1905), a poet and educator, and before him Peter Katanić (1750–1825) and Toma Mikloušić (1767–1833), both of whom were Franciscans as well.

The most important representative of Illyrism was Croatian national revivalist, publicist, and linguistic reformer Ljudevit Gaj (1809–72). He too used lingual similarity as the criterion for determining Illyrian ethnicity and sought to bridle the mistrust and hatred between Catholic and Orthodox Christianity. His ultimate goal was to unite the South Slavs. Other Croatian Illyrians—such as politician Andrija Torkvat Brkić (1826–68), and writer and politician Imbro Ignatijević Tkalac (1826–1912)—believed that the Croats and Serbs were one people. According to Tkalac, both banks of the Sava and Danube Rivers were settled by "one nation, speaking one language, sharing the same customs, one worldly orientation, and one future, which we must accomplish together, else fall into ruin for all time." The Illyrist movement "even promoted tolerance of the domestic Muslims in the Ottoman Empire."[56]

The movement reached its peak in the 1830s and 1860s and was popular among the enlightened and nationally conscious bourgeoisie, intellectuals, youth, and clergymen. The Illyrists published the newspaper *Novine Horvatske (Croatian News)*. Beginning in 1833, in his poem *Croatian Unity and Unification (Horvatov sloga i zedinjenje)* Ljudevit Gaj uses syntax similar to that found in the Polish national anthem.

Croatia has not fallen, while yet we live
And she will rise up high, when we arouse her.

Other important Illyrists included the liberal humanist Count Janko Drašković (1770–1856); writer and later *ban* (governor) Ivan Mažuranić (1814–91); writer, historian, and politician Ivan Kukuljević Sakcinski (1816–89); composer Ferdo Livadić (1799–1878); and writer Antun Mihanović (1796–1861). Indeed, the latter wrote a poem published in March, 1835, in the literary supplement of the Illyrist newspaper *Danica (Danicza—Horvatzka, Slavonzka y Dalmatinzka)* entitled "Croatian Homeland" *(Horvatska domovina)*, of which the opening stanza is:

Lovely homeland of ours,
Oh, beloved heroic land,
Birthplace of our ancient glory,
May you always live in honor!

Following the publication of this poem, the expression *"Lijepa naša"* (Our Beauty) came to denote Croatia. It is interesting to note that the adjective used in the original, Lepa, is in the Ekavski dialect.

Another author, Vjekoslav Babukić (1812–75), published the following poem in the same newspaper, expressing the Illyrist idea in a unique manner:

Lovely is the Danica's face,
Still lovelier is her good heart,
Which loves all the old Croatians,
Serbs, Bosnians, Herzegovinians,
Steierians, Krajnzians, Carinthias;
For these are all brothers from of old,
The sons of our one dear homeland.[57]

The Illyrist movement achieved greatest popularity in the Croatian provinces, Dalmatia, and the Catholic part of Bosnia-Herzegovina, although its ambitions were to unite all South Slavs from Carinthia and Carniola to Bulgaria. In January, 1843, the government in Vienna yielded to the demands of the Hungarian aristocracy and banned the use of the name Illyrian in any context.

In the 1860s the idea of integration gained new impetus in Croatia. Yugoslavism, the concept of the political, cultural, and religious unification of all South Slavs, and the struggle for Croatian national rights were strongly supported by a group of liberal intellectuals gathered around the energetic Catholic bishop of Djakovo, Josip Juraj Strossmayer, a cultural and scientific pioneer, politician and patron, and an advocate of cooperation with the Serbian Orthodox Church. A great humanist and aficionado of practical ecumenism, Strossmayer (reportedly a freemason) strove to make Zagreb the center of South Slav cultural, scientific, and artistic activity, to which end he founded the South Slav Academy of Sciences and Arts (JAZU, *"Academia scientiarum et artium Slavorum meridionalium,"* 1866), and a "Croatian University" (1874). In his speech at the opening of the latter, he emphasized that "'faith, verity, and unity' must be cultivated in the Croatian people."[58]

There had been contacts pertaining to ecumenical matters between the Balkan Roman Catholic and Orthodox Churches in previous decades. Strossmayer maintained correspondence with Mihajlo, the metropolitan of Belgrade, whom he met personally in 1868. They drew attention to the harm caused by the religious division of the South Slav peoples. The neighboring Serbian state was under Strossmayer's ecclesiastic jurisdiction. He was even hoping to heal up the split between the two churches.[59] According to him, religion should not divide the "sons of the same nation," and "Religion which sows dissension between brothers is not religion but superstition." His primary goal can be summarized in the adage "from the manifold emerges one," which represented a promising answer to the familiar and successful Habsburg policy of "divide and rule." It is thus understandable that Strossmayer consecrated the magnificent Neoromantic cathedral in Djakovo to the "unity of the Churches."[60]

On the other hand, he entertained the thought of Orthodox Christians reconverting to Catholicism, albeit as Uniates. Like Križanić, he blamed the Greeks for the schism and not the Orthodox Slavs. At the first Vatican Council (1869–70), the freethinking Strossmayer was a leading opponent of (but ultimately had to concede to) the doctrine of papal infallibility, realizing fully that his concession would deeply injure the

Orthodox. Indeed, his opposition to papal infallibility might very well have been the reason he was never appointed archbishop of Zagreb. Strossmayer—whose motto was "For Faith and the Homeland!"—openly opposed Hungarian and German predominance. His and Rački's political goals were twofold: first, the unification of all Habsburg South Slav territories in a federalized Habsburg Empire; then the creation of a South Slav federal state that would embrace Habsburg South Slavs with Serbia and Montenegro.[61] He met with Serbian prime minister Garašanin in 1867 and discussed plans to liberate the Christians from Ottoman rule and to create a joint state. The priests of the Catholic hierarchy spread his ideas throughout Croatia.

Strossmayer's efforts represent an integrative aspect of Croatian national mythology. Yugoslavism, neo-Slavism (the acknowledgment of the leading role of Russia in the Slav world), even the idea of unification between the Croatian and Serbian people were advocated by many prominent Croatian politicians during the final years of the Austro-Hungarian Empire. These included Ante Trumbić (1864–1938), Stjepan Radić, Franjo Supilo (1870–1917), and sculptor Ivan Meštrović (1883–1962). The latter, a politically oriented artist, "spoke of the new *Marko's people*, the new brave South Slav nation, born on ethos of heroism and sensitive soul of Kraljević Marko."[62]

Among Catholic clergy, Dalmatian Mihovil Pavlinović and Rački also supported Yugoslavism. The latter became the first president of the "South Slav Academy of Sciences and Arts." His works demonstrate several contradictory concepts: he writes of the Serbs and Slovenes as part of the Croatian "political" national group; he uses the term *Yugoslavs* as a collective denomination; and he states that the Serbs and Croats are tribes of the same race. The young Croatian politician Stjepan Radić held a similar opinion. In 1902 he declared, "Croats and Serbs are today no longer two tribes, but one inseparable body, two nationalities of one and the same nation."[63]

Ancient mythical tales and historical figures helped in the struggle against denationalizing tendencies. One of these figures was Grgur Ninski, portrayed as the very embodiment of the aspiration for ecclesiastic and national independence. Other mythical figures dating from the period of anti-Ottoman conflict and that were deeply etched in the collective memory of the Croats included Ban Nikola Šubić Zrinjski (ca. 1508–66; the tercentenary of his heroic death at Siget was marked with particular pomp); Duke Peter Zrinjski (1621–71), a conspirator against the Habsburgs; and Ogulin nobleman Franjo Krsto Frankopan (1643–71), who was also beheaded by the Austrian authorities.

The second, more exclusivist, option of Croatian national mythology, emerged in the early eighteenth century. In his book *Croatia Revived (Croatia rediviva)*, published in 1700, Pavao Ritter Vitezović (1652–1713) declared his belief that all South Slavs were Croats and tried to find proof for his theory in Croatian history and national law. However, such ideas did not gain popularity until the late nineteenth century and were based also on ambitions for an independent Roman Catholic Croatia or for its autonomy within Austria-Hungary. The so-called *pravaši,* members of the "Croatian Party of Rights" *(Hrvatska stranka prava),* alluded to the historical continuity of the Croatian state and its historical jurisprudence. They were led by Ante Starčević (1823–96), a disgruntled Illyrist (known for his paroles *Croatia to the Croats!* and *God and the Croats)* and the first Croat to publicly oppose Karadžić's linguistic reforms. His followers called him "Old Man" *(Stari)* or "Father of the Homeland." Together with Eugen Kvaternik (1825–71), he yearned for a Greater Croatia, which was in direct contrast to the ideals of Illyrism.

Their maxim was: "Neither under Vienna nor under Budapest, but for a free and independent Croatia!" The only South Slavs they acknowledged were the Croats and the Bulgars. They claimed that the Nemanjić's were a Croatian dynasty and that the Serbs and Muslim Slavs of Bosnia-Herzegovina were actually Croats. Slovenes, according to them, were "alpine" or "Nordic" Croats. Kvaternik even advocated the establishment of an autocephalous Croatian Orthodox Church for "Orthodox Croats." Other Starčević supporters had a more unionist stance, advocating a Croatian state under Habsburg rule in which "Slovenes and Croats and Serbs would be entitled to equal rights."[64]

The political goal of the *pravaši* later became the unification of all Croats in one independent state. They wanted to shake off Hungarian predominance and unite all Croatian lands ("from the Soča River to the Foča, from the Alps to the Drina, from Albania to the Danube and to Timok"). Their aim, therefore, was the restoration and enlargement of the medieval Croatian state, which would include Bosnia-Herzegovina as a "historical part" of the Croatian state. As was the case with the Serbs, such ideas enjoyed the support of a number of Croatian historians. According to them, Bosnia-Herzegovina was an inseparable part of Croatia, and the Muslim Slavs were descendants of Bosnian *Patarins,* who were originally Roman Catholics. These were assumed to be "the purest Croats." Historian Tomašić stated that Croats partly accepted Muslim culture, too, and that "Islam as well as Catholicism became an integral element of contemporary Croatian national culture."[65] Bosnia thus was considered Croatian, both ethnically and legally. This obsession with abstract legalism—in Banac's words, "the mentality of struggle for the violated rights" *(pravdaštvo)*—is considered by Schöpflin to be one of the most important characteristics of Croatian nationalism.[66]

The first indications of a modern Croatian national consciousness can be traced to 1848 and Croatian resistance against their centuries-old rulers, the neighboring Hungarians. To the delight of the Croats, Josip Bužimski Jelačić (1801–59) was appointed ban of Croatia on March 23, 1848. Jelačić terminated the union with Hungary and appealed for the unification of all Croatian lands (Dalmatia, the banate of Croatia, and Slavonia), pledged to establish a *sabor* (assembly), convened a government, and abolished serfdom. Orthodox patriarch Josif Rajačić, the metropolitan of Karlovac, conducted the religious ceremony at his inauguration.

The Hungarians soon withdrew Jelačić's title of *ban*, to which he responded by sending his forces against them and (with the aid of the Imperial Russian army) helping the Austrians crush the Hungarian nationalist revolution. This earned him a strong mandate and his near-dictatorial powers were strongly criticized and opposed by many. As a result of Jelačić's persistent ambitions and determination, Pope Pius IX (1846–78) issued the bull "Ubi primum placuit" by which the archbishopric of Zagreb (with bishoprics in Djakovo and Križevci) was established. Its first archbishop, Juraj de Varallya Haulik (1788–1869), who was of Slovak descent and had been the bishop of Zagreb since 1837, became a cardinal in 1856. Jelačić, a controversial figure in Croatian history, was later depicted in mythical and historical narratives as only a national revivalist and freedom fighter.

The so-called *Nagodba* of 1868, an agreement between the Croats and Hungarians, who the year before had gained equal status in the Austro-Hungarian Empire, finally buried Jelačić's dreams. With Slavonia and Croatia (less Dalmatia) now as Hungarian dominions within the empire, a large part of Croatia again became subject to the government and assembly in Budapest. Finance and banking, insurance, communications, industry, and trade were centralized. Croatia, however, retained its assembly and internal autonomy in legislation, administration, the judiciary, education, and religious affairs. An independent government in Zagreb was headed by a *ban*, who was appointed by the king of Hungary on the recommendation of the Hungarian prime minister, and who was only formally responsible to the Croatian assembly.

According to Serbian historian Milorad Ekmečić, after the Catholic congress held in Vienna in 1877, and the first Croatian Catholic congress held in 1900, "the history of withdrawing the Catholic movement from the Balkans and its opposition to the South Slav ambitions" began.[67] The "Croatian Catholic Movement" was also founded during this period, on the initiative of the Slovenian-born bishop of Krk, Anton Mahnič. The movement was a response to the liberal and secular tendencies of society. Its goal was the religious, social, and political rejuvenation of the Croatian nation. The establishment and function of this movement must be understood in the wider context of the Christian-social tendencies of the time—in the encyclical *"Rerum novarum"* of 1891, and similar movements throughout Europe.[68]

The *pravaši* closely linked the exclusivist Croatian national idea to Roman Catholicism, which they saw as the bastion of Croatian national identity. In Bosnia-Herzegovina, the integristic tendency of Croatian nationalism and Catholicism—Tomašić called it "exclusivist Catholicism"—did not prevail until after 1900, primarily because of the activities of Archbishop Josip Stadler of Sarajevo (1843–1918).[69] Stadler, a Slavonian, denied the primacy of national over religious sentiments and attempted to build Croatian nationality on firm Roman Catholic foundations. Some historians therefore correctly regard him as a representative of Croatian clericalism in Bosnia-Herzegovina, which, among other factors, was also a consequence of his non-Bosnian origin.

There was a significant lack of harmony even within the *pravaši* movement. Whereas Starčević bore an anti-Habsburg disposition and advocated an independent Croatia, the nationalist circle around Josip Frank (1844–1911) accepted the concept of Croatia as a part of the Dual Monarchy. Even Ban Jelačić advocated Austrian federalism during the turbulent episodes of 1848 and 1849. After 1895, the *frankovci*—now associated with the "Pure Party of Right"—expressed their loyalty to Austria and saw the Hungarians and Serbs as their enemies. They harshly criticized the political alliance between the main Croatian and Croatian Serb parties, especially during the First World War. Their goal was the creation of a kingdom of Croatia within Austria-Hungary that would "comprise Croatia proper, Slavonia, Dalmatia, Bosnia-Herzegovina, Istria, and the provinces of the Alpine Croats [Slovenes]."[70] A third group, the liberal Starčević supporters (Trumbić, Supilo, and S. Radić), supported the idea of Croats, Serbs, and Montenegrins joining forces, but on an equal footing.

One of the methods the Hungarian authorities used to counter such ambitions was supporting Croatian Serbs against the Croatian majority. It guaranteed the Serbs a high degree of protection, special laws, their own schools, alphabet, and freedom of worship even after the military frontier (Vojna krajina) was formally reunified with Croatia in 1881. Because of this, Serbian politicians in Croatia (and some Pro-Hungarian Croatian aristocracy as well) were loyal to the Hungarian authorities and supported the absolutist Hungarian *ban*, Karoly Khuen Hedervary (1849–1918), also known as *ban huzar*, who upheld the rationale of "divide and rule." The Croats therefore referred to them as "Hungarian Serbs" or "Khuen's Serbs" *(madžaroni/Magyarones, Kuenovi Srbi)*. It was only after Hedervary's departure that "national unity," cooperation between the majority parties of both ethnic groups in Croatia, began. After the 1906 elections, the Croatian-Serbian coalition (the so-called HSK), which indulged in South Slav rhetoric but remained loyal to the monarchy, gained a majority in the assembly. During the final years of the monarchy, the Croats, as a national grouping, began to lose faith in the notion of a tripartite reconstruction of the Habsburg Empire.

Finally, it should be mentioned that the Serbian and Croatian grand nationalist movements were also inspired by other pan-national movements in Europe—Pan-German, and, of course, Pan-Slavic (Slavs from the Adriatic to Japan). There were also various Pan-Slavic and pro-Yugoslav (mass) organizations, such as the *Sokol* (Hawk) gymnastic society. Nevertheless, Croatian and Serbian national concepts differed. Whereas, Croatian exclusivity notwithstanding, the former was based on reciprocity and the integration of the South Slavs (that is, unionism), the latter was based more on assimilation and unitarianism.[71]

According to Friedman, "the idea of Yugoslavism thus almost disappeared between 1878 and 1903, as relations between the Serbs and the Croats became increasingly marred by contradictory nationalist and territorial aspirations."[72] This entire period was marked by a specific contradiction: Most Serbian and Croatian politicians indulged in a loose and unbalanced pro-Yugoslav persuasion during the period before the First World War. However, a continual rise of religious nationalism, intolerance, and hatred toward other religious communities (and consequently—because of religio-national affinity—toward other national groups as well) could be observed.

5

BENEATH THE TWO-HEADED EAGLE
Religio-National Issues in Bosnia-Herzegovina, 1878–1918

This period is cru-
cial to the analysis
of the issue men-
tioned in the in-
troduction, namely,
when, why, and un-

From Trebinje to the gates of Brod not a Serb was there nor a Croat.

—SLOGAN OF THE WEEKLY JOURNAL *BOŠNJAK* (1891–1910)

der whose direction did the three major groups in Bosnia-Herzegovina begin to substitute their preponderantly religio-cultural identity for a national one? Until the beginning of the nineteenth century, the religious affiliation was understood as the definition of nationhood throughout the Ottoman Empire. For example, Alexander Gilferding, the Russian consul to Sarajevo and traveler through Bosnia-Herzegovina and Serbia in the mid-nineteenth century, reported that for "Turkish Slavs the national affiliation is not the matter of the nation but of the religion."[1]

Austria had been inciting rebellion against Ottoman rule in the Balkans over the last few centuries and was later to support Pan-Slavism among Slav peoples living under the Ottomans. Further changes in Austro-Hungarian foreign policy and the decision to play a more active role in the Balkans are associated with the Dual Monarchy's foreign minister, Count Julius (Gyula) Andrassy (1823–90), who was in office until 1871 and was a great admirer of German chancellor Otto von Bismarck. Tsarist Russia, which had considered itself the protector of all Slavs since the reign of Peter the Great, also began to display increased interest in events in the Balkans. The rivalry between these super powers came to a dramatic conclusion in the mid-1870s.

After 1850, the Ottomans had to deal with several peasant uprisings by Herzegovina's Christians. The so-called Nevesinje Rebellion in July,

1875, directed against the land reforms of 1859 that favored landowners, proved to be decisive for the future of the land. Pro-Serbian political demands, namely the unification of Serbia and Montenegro, also came to the fore: a number of rebel leaders spoke of Herzegovina as the land of the "purest Serbian blood." Recollections of the Battle of Kosovo and their heroes were rekindled. As rebellion spread across the land, the rebels were faced not only with Ottoman regulars but irregular troops as well, the so-called *bashi-bazouks* commanded by local *begs*. There was much violence; villages were torched and waves of refugees fled Bosnia-Herzegovina to neighboring provinces. Some Muslims fled even farther, to the heart of the empire. Estimates of the number of refugees range between one hundred thousand and 250,000.[2]

In July, 1876, Serbia and Montenegro tried to take advantage of the chaos and declared war on the Ottoman Empire. They had agreed that the former would annex Bosnia and the latter Herzegovina. They found justification for the war in their "Kosovo mission," and Montenegro's Prince Nikola announced that it was time for them to avenge Kosovo.[3] Both states were soon defeated, however, leaving Bosnia-Herzegovina's Orthodox population particularly vulnerable to violence. Russia intervened in April, 1877, and the Ottomans were forced to sign the Treaty of San Stefano in March, 1878. This Russian dictate resulted in the expansion of Bulgaria, which became an important Russian ally in the Balkans. The West viewed these events with great aversion, prompting Andrassy to seek and effect changes to the treaty at the Congress of Berlin in June and July of the same year.

Article 25 of the treaty—which caused much anxiety among the Hungarians, who were afraid of the Slavs within their borders becoming too powerful—gave Austria the right to "occupy and administer" Bosnia-Herzegovina. Part of Herzegovina was given to Montenegro, the *sandžak* of Novi Pazar to Serbia, and Bulgaria was reduced in size. The previously vassal principalities of Serbia and Montenegro were granted full sovereignty. The eastern border of present-day Bosnia-Herzegovina was thus created. Later, observers and diplomats described the Congress of Berlin as the "source of all instability in Europe for the next several decades and the root of the cause for the First World War." This was true for the Balkans more than for any other part of Europe.

A Bosnian force composed of Muslims and Orthodox Christians led by their high priests resisted the Austrian occupation troops in the summer of 1878. It took the Austrians four months to quell the rebellion at a cost of five thousand dead, wounded, or missing. The initial seventy-two thousand Austrian troops were increased to a total of two hundred thou-

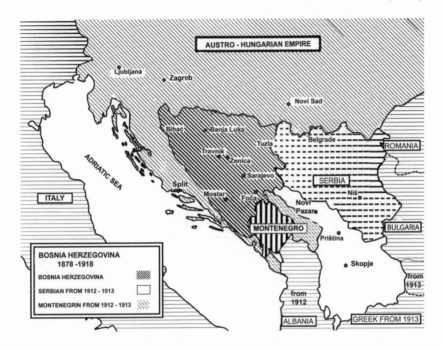

sand. A guerrilla hero emerged: one of the most popular commanders was Hafiz Hadži Lojo, who the Austrians eventually hunted down and incarcerated. Nevertheless, the Bosnian forces were poorly organized and quickly defeated. The commanding general of the imperial force, Croatian-born Baron Josip Filipović von Philippsberg, received orders from Vienna instructing him to be particularly tolerant not only toward the Catholics but the Muslims as well. The latter were considered to be "the relatively most progressive and most enlightened part of the population." He was further instructed to "encourage alliance between the Catholics and the Muslims, and to isolate the Orthodox at any cost."[4] In spite of this, the Muslims and Orthodox in eastern Herzegovina again joined forces against the Austrians between 1879 and 1881, and again between January and March, 1882.

As a result, Bosnia-Herzegovina became the first and only colony of the "black-yellow monarchy": it did not belong either to Austria or Hungary, but instead served as a kind of *corpus separatum*. The Congress of Berlin anticipated the settlement of Bosnia-Herzegovina's legal status in negotiations between the Austro-Hungarians and the Ottoman Empire, which was then ruled by the despotic Sultan Abdul Hamid II (1842–1918). Hamid was known as the "Bloody Sultan" because of his persecution of democratic and independence movements within the empire. The negotiations were held at Novi Pazar (Yenipazar) in Sandžak, which, in addition to Nikšič, was a historical part of Bosnia-Herzegovina: both Sandžak and Nikšič had a majority Muslim population of 83 percent.

In April, 1879, the two sides reached a compromise. The province was to remain *de iure* (until formal annexation in 1908, the time of the revolution of the Young Turks) under the jurisdiction of the sultan, although it would be a de facto protectorate of Austria-Hungary; Ottoman civil servants were to keep their positions; the Ottoman currency was to remain in circulation; Muslims were to be allowed to maintain contacts with religious leaders in the Ottoman Empire; the new authorities were to respect the traditions and customs of the Muslims, including that of hanging out Muslim banners; and the previous administrative division of six *sandžaks*—which were renamed *kresije* (*Kreisamt* in German)—with centers in Sarajevo, Travnik, Bihać, Donja Tuzla, Banja Luka, and Mostar, was also to remain unchanged. The Austro-Hungarian side did not honor most of these promises.

The most important Austro-Hungarian political influence on events in Bosnia-Herzegovina was Finance Minister Benjamin Kallay von Nagy-Kallay (1839–1903), who was also the colonial administrator between 1882 and 1903. Von Kallay, a Hungarian diplomat and historian with extensive knowledge of South Slav history, was also the author of a history of the Serbs. His predecessors were Leopold Friedrich von Hoffman (1879–80) and Joszef von Szlavy (1880–82). He was succeeded by Istvan Freiherr Burian von Rajecz (1903–12 and 1916–18) and Leon Ritter von Bilinski (1912–15).

Von Kallay explained his own mission and that of Austria-Hungary in an interview for the London *Daily Chronicle* in 1895, saying that the Austro-Hungarian Empire had been given the task of bringing civilization to the peoples of the East. This "cultural mission" would be achieved through rational administration. He aspired to build a new from the old, so the colonial administration would introduce novelties while preserving the country's traditions.[5] Von Kallay saw both his own and the Austro-Hungarian Empire's missions in the entirely mythical binary categories of transition from chaos to cosmos. Before the occupation, according to his views, Bosnia-Herzegovina was a totally chaotic country engulfed in complete confusion, corruption, and anarchy. The new authorities would solve these problems, restore order, and ensure the equality of all religions.

The fact remains that "Bosnia-Herzegovina" (as it was officially renamed after the Austro-Hungarian occupation—as a "Crown land"

(*Reichland*), a special territory within the Dual Monarchy under the leadership of a diligent and "progressive" colonial administration (according to the administrators themselves)—achieved in only four decades exceptional economic progress and ambitious general modernization. The centuries-long isolation from its neighboring European states had been broken. Modern administration was introduced, roads, railways (some fifteen hundred kilometers), factories and hotels, schools (about two hundred), and cultural institutions were built, mineral wealth and lumber was more efficiently exploited, and farming was modernized. Tens of thousands of serfs who had been dependent on the landowners were set free. The basic level of education began rising, albeit at a very slow rate: according to 1910 statistics, only 5.64 percent of Muslims, 11.21 percent of Orthodox, and 29.11 percent of Catholics were literate.[6] The four Bosnian army regiments (whose uniform included a blood-red fez) were staffed with chaplains from all three religions. The new administration consisted of mainly foreign, non-Bosnian employees. In 1907, only a third of the civil servants were native Bosnians. Of that number, 61.56 percent were Catholics, 29.29 percent were Orthodox, and only 8.63 percent were Muslims.[7]

The development of towns with a majority Muslim population also accelerated. Sarajevo, one of the most important cities in Ottoman Europe, ranked alongside Salonika and Edirne. Its rise began in the early sixteenth century, when it was an almost exclusively Muslim town (1,024 Muslim families), while the surrounding countryside remained Christian. Beg Gazi Husrev encouraged its rapid development: new mosques, *madrasahs*, bazaars, and roads were built. In the 1520s, Sarajevo's population was estimated at 5,500. Fifty years later that figure had risen to 23,500. It was the most rapidly developing city in the Balkans. Before Prince Eugene of Savoy torched it in October, 1697, Sarajevo had a population of about 80,000. In 1807, its population had shrunk to 60,000, although it was still quite large when compared to the populations of Belgrade in 1838 (12,963) or Zagreb in 1851 (14,000).[8]

Following a few decades of decline, the population of Sarajevo again began to increase, as shown in table 5-1.[9] Other sources estimate Sarajevo's population shortly before the departure of the Ottomans at slightly more than thirty thousand, and that it had thirty *hans* and more than sixteen hundred shops. The city's Muslim population had 101 mosques and *mesdžids*, seven religious schools (*madrasahs*), and nine *tekkes*.[10]

By 1931, Sarajevo's population had reached 78,173. The population growth rate for Mostar was equally explosive, as shown in table 5-2.[11] On

TABLE 5-1 **Population of Sarajevo by religious affiliation, 1879–1921**

Year	Muslim	Orthodox	Catholic	Jewish	Total
1879	14,848	3,743	698	2,077	21,377
1885	15,787	4,431	3,326	2,618	26,268
1895	17,158	5,858	10,672	4,058	38,083
1910	18,640	8,450	17,922	6,397	51,919
1921	22,474	16,468	19,242	7,458	66,317

TABLE 5-2 **Population of Mostar by religious affiliation, 1879–1910**

Year	Muslim	Orthodox	Catholic	Total
1879	6,421	3,026	1,366	10,848
1895	6,946	3,877	3,353	14,370
1910	7,212	4,518	4,307	16,392

the other hand, McCarthy notes that the populations of Mostar and Banja Luka stood at fifteen thousand immediately before the Austrian occupation.[12]

THE NATIONALIZATION OF RELIGIOUS COMMUNITIES

The more or less forcible transplantation of the religio-national ideological myths from the neighboring nations manifested a new dimension in the multinational and interreligious relations of what was a heterogeneous Bosnia-Herzegovina. These myths encouraged division, intolerance, and usurpation from the start. The primary intellectual forces in all three emerging national groups were drawn from religious circles at the beginning of this period. These were the sources of not only cultural and economic progress, but of political and national development as well. The secular intelligentsia did not emerge and begin to make an impact until the turn of the century.

One result of the millet system was that religion became the main identifying factor for the individual ethnic groups. However, it was only during the Austro-Hungarian occupation that the religio-cultural identity of the inhabitants of Bosnia-Herzegovina (Orthodox, Roman Catholic, Muslim) was substituted for a national one (Serbian, Croatian, and eventually, albeit to a decisively lesser degree, Muslim). This process—if

I may paraphrase, *Cuius religio eius natio*—did not begin until the mid-nineteenth century, and the population was still nationally undifferentiated by the 1860s.[13] In the years preceding the Austro-Hungarian occupation, the population began to nationally differentiate. However, in the absence of nationalist programs and political parties, these differences had not yet been politicized.

The process of nationalization in this heterogeneous community reached its peak in the last decade of the nineteenth century. According to some authors, the grand-national ideas were imported into Bosnia from abroad.[14] However, they found additional support from local, "home-grown" advocates of national identification and the politicization of religious groups. The religio-cultural consciousness gradually transformed into a nationalistic one, although this nationalism was, for the most part, oriented against the ruling Ottoman and Habsburg regimes. Bosnian Orthodox and Catholics began to gaze across the border to the neighboring states, toward "their own" Serbian and Croatian national groups, and so began progressively to recognize themselves as Bosnian Serbs and Croats. Only the Muslim Slavs failed to develop a specific and separate national identity, thus preserving their primarily religio-cultural identity far into the twentieth century. In other words, they remained largely uninterested in any kind of national affiliation during that period.

Bosnia-Herzegovina was a colorful mosaic of different ethnoreligious groups and social classes during this period of its history. Among them were three main ethnic groups.[15] The Serbs were primarily agrarian with only a handful of landowners. The clergy was, for the most part, uneducated; a middle class gradually emerged in the towns and cities; and schools and Serbian cultural institutions were eventually built. The Croats, too, were primarily agrarian with few landowners. The Franciscans, who were politically and nationally minded, heavily influenced them. Although few lived in towns or cities, they were the most homogenous group in 1878.

Muslim Slavs made up the third group. The millet system ensured their segregation from other Slavs, and it is for this reason that I find it important to study the development of the collective Muslim consciousness during the four decades of Austro-Hungarian occupation of Bosnia-Herzegovina. The Muslims were divided into three groups. The most numerous were the peasants, who lived close to the Christians. Their spiritual guidance was provided by relatively uneducated *hodžas*. Despite the social and economic gap between them and the Muslim elite, they were aware of the privileges they enjoyed under the Ottoman system. Middle-class Muslims lived mainly in towns and cities and were primarily craftsmen and traders. The elite—composed of religious leaders, wealthy merchants, and the landed gentry—were concerned primarily with preserving the privileges and status they had acquired under the Ottoman Empire. Indeed, the new authorities enabled them to do so.

Data show that in 1910 there were 267 Croatian, 633 Serbian, and 9,567 Muslim landowners with serfs in Bosnia-Herzegovina, although the estates were relatively small. Most of the serfs *(kmets)* were Orthodox (73.92 percent) or Catholics (21.49 percent). The figures for landowners without serfs are different: of 4,281 such landowners, 70.6 percent were Muslims, 17.8 percent were Orthodox, and 10.7 percent were Catholics. Of the 136,854 peasants, 57 percent were Muslims, 26 percent were Orthodox, and 17 percent were Catholics.[16]

The Austro-Hungarian authorities in Bosnia-Herzegovina pursued a policy of "continuity and graduality" that avoided conflict and introduced moderate reforms in all areas. It did not attempt to solve many urgent issues, such as land reform, the property of the *vakufs* (this important issue was centralized in 1883 and entrusted to the "Provincial Committee for Vakufs," which was headed by Muslims), or the *shariat*.[17] Although they lost their administrative and judicial functions, most of the Muslim elite pledged their loyalty to the emperor and Austria-Hungary in general. On one particular occasion, the Muslims were declared the "last bastion of the Kaisertreue" (loyalty to the emperor).

The new authorities' policies surprised many European observers and disappointed Bosnian Christians. The agrarian question remained a central source of contention and conflict under Austrian rule. It is worth noting, however, that when agrarian reforms were finally introduced in 1906, they undermined the multiethnic "coalition" of Muslim landowners, rich Serbian farmers, and the Roman Catholic middle class.[18]

RELIGIOUS COMMUNITIES IN HABSBURG-RULED BOSNIA-HERZEGOVINA

In the early 1880s, religion was still the prevailing element in the lives of Orthodox, Muslim, and Roman Catholic Slavs in Bosnia-Herzegovina. There was no major interreligious contradistinction of which to speak. The environment they lived in was one of relative tolerance. The new authorities thus were extremely cautious in their attempts to reorganize the three major communities. Their goal was to weaken the bonds between the communities and religious centers abroad, and gain control of their hierarchies by imposing religious functionaries loyal to Austria-

Hungary.[19] The authorities quickly realized the importance of the various religious and ecclesiastic organizations in Bosnia-Herzegovina, and the relationship between the state and these organizations always had a political significance. Nevertheless, education, for example, was entrusted to the religious hierarchies of the three major communities.

The Ottoman sultan was both the political and spiritual head— the caliph or *sheikh al-Islam (seyhülislâm)*—of the Muslim community. The Austro-Hungarian government strove to sever Bosnia-Herzegovina's Muslims from the political and religious predominance of Istanbul. It therefore ruled in favor of a petition submitted by a group of leading Muslims from Sarajevo, who in 1878 and 1881 demanded a religious hierarchy in Bosnia-Herzegovina independent of Ottoman control. In order to secure the loyalty of the Muslims, the *ulema-medžlis*, the highest religious body, was established as by Imperial decree in October, 1882. The *ulema-medžlis* had four members and was the office of the *reis-ul-ulema*, the leader and spiritual head of the Muslims in Bosnia-Herzegovina. Autonomy from the Ottoman caliphate was thus achieved.[20] As mentioned earlier, this arrangement was unique to the Muslim world. Because the position of *reis-ul-ulema* was awarded to a pro-Austrian Bosnian mufti, Mustafa Hilmi Omerović, many Muslims refused to acknowledge his spiritual authority.

The *reis-ul-ulema* was appointed in Vienna and confirmed with a so-called *Menšura* issued by the *sheikh al-ulema,* the supreme head of the Muslim community in Istanbul. His task was to handle those sections of Islamic law that were incompatible with Austro-Hungarian administrative procedures. Pressure from Muslims compelled Emperor Franz Joseph to sign the "Statute for the Autonomous Administration of Muslim Religious Institutions and Vakufs" in May, 1909. Hence, although there was major reorganization, the *vakufs* continued to be independently run by Muslim administrators. Muslim religious and cultural institutions received support from the state and the issue of schooling was finally settled. The supreme and independent supervisory body of all *vakuf* holdings became the "Vakuf-Mearif Sabor."

Religion in Austrian-ruled Bosnia-Herzegovina became a very critical issue, especially the question of Muslims being converted to Catholicism, which provoked several incidents (the Ćokić incident in 1881, the Delahmetović incident in 1890, the Omanović incident in 1899, the Sivrić incident in 1903, and others in 1893 and 1897). Hidden or evident Roman Catholic proselytizing provoked protests, petitions, and unrest in the Muslim community. Indeed, proselytizing was the primary cause of the disruptive public conflict in Bosnia-Herzegovina during the Austro-

TABLE 5-3 *Population of Bosnia-Herzegovina by religious affiliation, 1879–1910*

Year	Muslim	Orthodox	Catholic	Jewish	Total
1879	448,613	496,485	209,391	3,426	1,158,164
	38.7%	42.9%	18.1%	0.3%	
1885	492,710	571,250	265,788	5,805	1,336,091
	36.9%	42.8%	19.9%	0.4%	
1895	548,632	673,246	334,142	8,213	1,568,092
	35%	42.9%	21.3%	0.5%	
1910	612,137	825,418	434,061	11,868	1,898,044
	32.2%	43.5%	22.9%	0.6%	

Hungarian occupation.[21] Conflict continued despite the enactment of a "Conversion Statute" in 1891 because the state and the Roman Catholic Church were secretly undermining it.

The Muslims were indeed confused and opportunistic in a national sense, but they remained steadfast when it came to religious and even wider cultural interests. In other words, the common perception was built on religious and cultural as well as economic and political foundations (the establishment of companies and banks, petitions, the first Muslim political parties, demands for the autonomy of Bosnia-Herzegovina).[22] In 1900, a group of distinguished Muslims petitioned von Kallay for religious autonomy. Their concern for their interests and their active opposition to some of the measures introduced by the new authorities characterized the profile of their national dissimilarity to neighboring ethnic groups. The path to national identity, however, was still a long one.

Austro-Hungarian estimates and population censuses show that the percentage of Muslims in Bosnia-Herzegovina dropped steadily over the course of a few decades. According to the official Ottoman census of 1850–51, there were 424,000 Muslims, 486,000 Orthodox, and 171,000 Catholics. By 1870, there were approximately 694,000 Muslims, 534,000 Orthodox, and 208,000 Catholics. Table 5-3 shows how the percentage of Muslims declined, primarily due to emigration and persecution, after the Austro-Hungarian occupation.[23]

Immigrants from other parts of Austria-Hungary increased Bosnia-Herzegovina's Catholic population. There were also changes to the geographic pattern of settlement because the Muslims (especially between 1895 and 1910) moved from areas where they were in the minority to areas where they were in the majority.

No less than 100,000 Bosnian Muslims emigrated from the country between the beginning of the occupation and the First World War.[24] Others estimate their number at about 60,000 between 1882 and 1911. According to official records, 28,000 emigrated between 1883 and 1905, and 24,000 emigrated between 1906 and 1918. Hadžijahić estimates a total of approximately 160,000 left, whereas Pinson says there were only 140,000 emigrants.[25] Although there were many reasons for emigration, the doctrinal excuse was that Muslim worshippers would not be allowed to live under Christian authority.

In 1840, the Bosnian Catholics came under the patronage of the Habsburg court: thirty-eight years later they hailed the annexation of Bosnia-Herzegovina by a nominally and predominately Roman Catholic empire.[26] The new authorities wanted loyal and manageable clergymen at all levels of the church's hierarchy, and the emperor himself gave final approval to the appointment of bishops and archbishops. Talks between Austria-Hungary and the Vatican on the new hierarchy and the position of the Roman Catholic Church in Bosnia-Herzegovina began in 1880 and ended in 1881. A papal bull—*Ex hac Augusta,* issued by Pope Leo XIII (1878–1903)—confirmed the creation of the archbishopric and Metropolitan See of Vrhbosna and the bishoprics of Mostar and Banja Luka. Sarajevo bishop Josip Stadler, a Jesuit, was elevated to the position of archbishop of Vrhbosna and remained there until his death in 1918. Franciscans were appointed to the bishoprics. The Austro-Hungarian authorities encouraged the construction of Catholic churches (including the Sarajevo Cathedral) and monasteries, and invited Jesuits to Bosnia-Herzegovina.

Pope Leo XIII hoped to establish the normal church structure in which Franciscans concentrated on missionary work rather than dealing with the parishes, which would be run by ordinary parish priests. There were also political differences between the two. Whereas the Franciscans displayed a higher level of religious tolerance and were more inclined toward the Illyrian idea, the parish clergy favored the clerical pro-Croatian option. This further separated them, and they soon considered each other to be rivals. The dispute was finally settled by the Holy See, which allocated one-third of the parishes to the parish clergy and the remainder to the Franciscans. The parish hierarchy was more widespread in Bosnia than in Herzegovina. Stadler and the church hierarchy reproached the Franciscans several times for being insubordinate, unenlightened, semiliterate, incompetent, and impatient. Nevertheless, the Franciscan organization in Bosnia-Herzegovina remained strong and influential, and in 1892 the "Herzegovina Franciscan Province" was established.

The parish clergy found it particularly difficult to undermine the popular Franciscans in Herzegovina. This was primarily because of the small number of parish clergy, but also because some non-Catholic traditions in the province were threatened. The veneration of the *slava* continued well into the nineteenth century, when Catholic authorities finally and permanently banned it. The ancestor cult sharply contradicts Roman Catholic doctrine. Furthermore, Catholics in Herzegovina were almost totally ignorant of one of the most important elements of the Roman Catholic mass, the Holy Communion (Eucharist).[27] For these and other reasons, they boycotted the new parish priests, and there was an atmosphere of hushed resistance to the decisions and decrees "from above." Nevertheless, the Catholic authorities encouraged the enlightenment of the Franciscans and greater doctrinal discipline.

In the first two decades of Austro-Hungarian rule in Bosnia (until the emergence of the first political parties) the church was the only institution to "systematically build Croatian national consciousness among the population."[28] Catholic priests applied new concepts for solving the Croatian national issue, abandoning the ideas of Illyrism and Bosnian nationhood (Franciscan Jukić), and progressing to Croatian nationhood. On the other hand, the Franciscans also displayed much sympathy toward the neighboring Serbian state in the years leading to the First World War. They gradually became more active in their attempts to convert Bosnia-Herzegovina's Muslims, "often under the aegis of Ante Starčević's Croatian Party of Right."[29] However, they did not express the extreme anti-Muslim sentiments characteristic of the Greater Serbia extremists.

Roman Catholic priests—including Archbishop Stadler—paid much attention to the social problems of their flock, in the spirit of the pope's 1891 social encyclical entitled *Rerum novarum.* They supported cooperatives, provided reciprocal help, and established banks such as the Croatian Cooperative Bank of Bosnia-Herzegovina, which was chartered in 1910. New orders of monks (Trappists, Jesuits, Carmelites) and nuns (Ursuline and Dominican sisters) also arrived in Bosnia-Herzegovina during this period.

Likewise, the Orthodox clergy encouraged Serbian national self-identification among the Orthodox population. Serbia had been supporting the Orthodox Church in Bosnia-Herzegovina during the final years of Ottoman rule and continued to do so during Austro-Hungarian occupation. Orthodox monk Teofil Pertanović, a teacher at the Orthodox school in Sarajevo in the 1860s, formed a special group of activists whose job was to persuade the Orthodox country folk to identify themselves as Serbs rather than *hrišćani*. His colleague Vaso Pelagić, from the Orthodox school in Banja Luka, also advocated Serbian nationalist options. One of the centers of pro-Serbian propaganda was the Orthodox monastery of Žitomislić in Herzegovina.[30]

The new rulers of Bosnia-Herzegovina also wanted to solve Orthodox religious issues. A year after Bosnia-Herzegovina's occupation, Austria-Hungary began discussions with the ecumenical patriarch of Constantinople. An agreement was reached in March, 1880, by which the Habsburg monarch could appoint or dismiss Orthodox bishops, in return for which the Serbian Orthodox Church would receive financial support from the state. Despite this, the Orthodox established parallel organizations known as "Church Communities" that united the Orthodox people. An outcome of likening Orthodoxy to Serbian ethnicity was that Orthodox Vlachs—who were the descendants of Romanized Illyrian natives—also were assimilated into the Serbian body.[31] We can therefore speak of an important Vlach contribution to the creation of the Serbian ethnic community in Bosnia-Herzegovina and Croatia. Like the Orthodox Church, the Catholic Church and Islam also assimilated foreign-born peoples and achieved national homogenization on religious grounds.[32]

Despite their small numbers, the Jews represented a fourth important religious group in the religious mosaic of Bosnia-Herzegovina. After the Austro-Hungarian occupation, Ashkenazi Jews began arriving from other parts of Europe. However, the Sephardic community did not accept them, so there was little contact between the two groups.[33] As was the case with the other religious communities in Bosnia-Herzegovina, fundamental differences led to division within the Jewish community. In 1882, the Sephardic Jewish community's internal structure was reorganized in accordance with the "Provisional Regulations of the Sephardic Israelite Religious Community in Sarajevo," which was ratified by the regional government. This placed the community in the same position as other Jewish communities in central Europe: under state control.

The Ashkenazi, who had peculiar prayers and spoke German, Hungarian, and Yiddish, arrived in Sarajevo three years earlier, in September, 1879 (and after that in Tuzla and Banja Luka). They built their own synagogue, religious school, cemetery and other cultural institutions.[34] Unlike the Sephardim, who led a communal life in close proximity, the Ashkenazi were more dispersed.

Whereas the Ashkenazi were more compliant and better represented in the professional middle class (civil servants, lawyers, physicians, engineers, and the like), which was partly because they spoke German and were familiar with the Austro-Hungarian administrative system, the

TABLE 5-4 *Jewish population of Sarajevo by Sephardic and Ashkenazi origins, 1878–1913*

Year	Sephardim	Ashkenazi	Total	% in Bosnia-Herzegovina
1878	3,000	30	3,030	No data
1879	No data	No data	3,426	0.29%
1885	No data	No data	5,805	0.43%
1895	5,729	2,484	8,213	0.52%
1910	8,219	3,649	11,868	0.62%
1913	No data	No data	12,735	No data

Sephardim were more comfortable in wholesale trade, banking, and industry. Many Sephardim were in the lower income bracket. Commerce was particularly lucrative (especially with Adriatic ports and the interior of the Balkan Peninsula), as were banking and cottage industries. They took advantage of their commercial contacts with other Jews across Europe, in Istanbul, Salonika, Skopje, Belgrade, Dubrovnik, and Split, as well as Trieste, Venice, and Vienna. After 1894, Serbo-Croat was taught in Jewish schools. Over the next few decades, Jews represented 10–12 percent of Sarajevo's population. Their numbers trebled, primarily because of the immigration of the Ashkenazi, although the Sephardim remained in the majority, as shown in the table 5-4.[35]

BOŠNJAŠTVO: THE NATIONHOOD
OF THE BOSNIAN PEOPLE?

Religions and their organizations became the most important constituent element of the three nations in Bosnia-Herzegovina. At the close of the nineteenth century, Catholics finally identified themselves as Croats and the Orthodox identified themselves as Serbs.[36] However, the evolution of this new national identity did not follow the same formula in all three ethnic groups, emerging somewhat later with the Muslims, who at the time were less nationally conscious. Because of their historical links with the Ottoman Empire and their attachment to Islam, they did not develop a separate national identity until much later. But it was "Austro-Hungarian occupation itself which more directly sparked a new consciousness" in the Bosnian Muslims.[37]

There are several reasons for this. Enver Redžić cites the following reasons. The Muslim bourgeoisie and working class were few in number.

Cohesiveness of Muslim religious organizations was very high, and their religious, cultural, and spiritual identification was closely associated with the Ottomans. The transnational characteristics of Islam were always of greater importance, and the national "ignorance" of Muslim Slavs was further encouraged by the evident ethnic similarities between themselves and the Catholic Croats and Orthodox Serbs. Finally, their intellectuals were divided among all three national movements.[38]

Regarding this last issue, the dispersion of Muslim intellectuals until the end of the nineteenth century, a greater number identified themselves as ethnic Croats than as ethnic Serbs, although they maintained their Muslim religious identity throughout and continued to participate in Muslim political organizations. Banac estimates that in the first half of the twentieth century, the ratio was perhaps ten to one in favor of the Croats but "at least a third of Muslim intellectuals and the overwhelming majority of ordinary Muslims shunned any process of 'nationalization.'"[39]

Other scholars find different explanations for the late emergence of Bosnian Muslim national consciousness. For Irwin, the reasons lie in the millet system (which discouraged political activity), Islam's nonnational orientation, and the lack of Muslim identification with the secularized national state, which was no longer under a Muslim suzerain. For Donia, the most common reasons are the anomie resulting from the departure of the Ottomans, political opportunism (which was characteristic of all three national groups), the religious peculiarities of Islam (nonnational orientation) and the interests of the upper class (especially landowners). Pinson points out that Muslims also lacked a historical reference because the medieval Bosnian kingdom was Christian.[40]

Among the factors present during the earlier stages of Muslim national identity in Bosnia-Herzegovina are the loss of some of the privileges and social status they enjoyed under the Ottomans, political and cultural dissimilarity with the new authorities, and the fact that they became a religious minority in a predominately Roman Catholic empire. The struggle for the national identification of the Muslim Slavs began under the influence of Serbian and Croatian exclusivity: the latter mostly utilized "patronizing" methods (like "these are our countrymen of a different faith"), while the former employed more aggressive tactics (persecution and annihilation). The fact remains that neither of them "could advance majority claims to Bosnia-Herzegovina without winning the Muslims."[41]

Three main theories about the national origin of Bosnia-Herzegovina's Muslims are based on the fate of the medieval Bosnian population that converted to Islam. According to the pro-Croatian theory that emerged in the late nineteenth century (although there were earlier advocates of the theory, such as eighteenth-century Franciscan monk and writer Filip Lastrić), the medieval Bosnians were Croats (and the Bosnian Church was essentially a branch of the Catholic Church, probably a monastic order). Bosnia-Herzegovina's Croatian right was upheld by, among others, Ante Starčević ("Bosnia is the heart of Croatia" and "Bosnian Muslims are the best Croats"),[42] Munir Šahinović-Ekremov in 1938 ("Bosnia is the heart and the paunch of Croatia"),[43] Martin Tomičić in 1940 ("Bosnia is the cleanest, most beautiful and most interesting Croatian province"), and Abdulatif Dizdarević, who in 1936 wrote about the "Croatian character" of Bosnia-Herzegovina and its Muslims. Ivo Pilar (1874–1933), a Croatian geopolitician and social scientist, believed that in history Bosnia-Herzegovina was "part of Croatian state" and that the Bosnian Muslims were "undoubtedly of Croat origins."[44] The Croats cajoled the Muslim Slavs, whose techniques differed from those of the Serbs: Croatian writers and other artists glorified the history of the Bosnian Muslims (for example, the story of the "Dragon of Bosnia").

The pro-Serbian theory relies on the advocates of Greater Serbia. They, too, considered Bosnia-Herzegovina and the Muslim Slavs to be inherently Serbian. They believed the medieval Bosnians to be of Serbian origin: the Muslims (and indeed the Catholics) of Bosnia-Herzegovina were said to be converted Orthodox Christians, schismatics from the Serbian Orthodox Church. The Serbian origin of the Muslim Slavs was emphasized by, among others, Ilija Garašanin and social democrat Svetozar Marković (1846–75), a critic of Greater Serbia and an advocate of a South Slav socialist federation, who wrote "the Serbs in Bosnia-Herzegovina are divided into three religions" (as explained in his book *Serbia on the East*). Also Dimitrije Tucović (1881–1914), who believed the people of Bosnia-Herzegovina were the "greatest, purest, and most ingenious segment of the Serbian nation." A common practice was the distortion of historical facts about Bosnia-Herzegovina, for example, that the Bosnian Church was actually just an Eastern Orthodox Church, that Tvrtko I Kotromanić was a Serbian king, and so on.[45] Also common was the demonization of the Ottoman period, which was said to be the most dismal era in the history of the Balkan Slavs and which was supposed to be devoid of any cultural input. Although such convictions, infused with anti-Ottoman and anti-Muslim notions, were repulsive to the Muslim Slavs, some Muslim intellectuals, such as Dervišberg Ljubović in the 1890s, adhered to the pro-Serbian theory.

In contrast to the previous two, the third theory proffered a dynamic rather than a static national formative process. The Muslim Slavs of Bosnia-Herzegovina were said to possess their own specific national identity, which differed from that of the Croats and Serbs. This was also the opinion of one of the early advocates of Muslim national identity, Hussein Husaga Čisić, in 1929.[46] The majority of Muslim Slavs displayed some form of local patriotism that distinguished them from their Ottoman coreligionists. They were interested in neither national self-definition nor Serbian or Croatian national movements. A few identified themselves as Muslim Croats or Muslim Serbs, mostly for practical or political reasons. Indeed, it was their very affiliation to a community based on religious identity that enabled them to withstand the nationalist pressures applied by the other two national groups.

Austro-Hungarian national policies in Bosnia-Herzegovina can be divided into two periods: before and after 1903. The first period was almost entirely influenced by colonial administrator Benjamin von Kallay. The goal of his policies of integral "Bosnianism" *(bošnjaštvo)* was to isolate Bosnia-Herzegovina's population from its irredentist neighbors (the Orthodox in Serbia, the Catholics in Croatia, and the Muslims of the Ottoman Empire) and to develop the idea of Bosnian nationhood as a separate and unifying factor. He tried to prevent the disruption of existing relations within Bosnia-Herzegovina and, indeed, within the monarchy itself. At the same time, diplomacy and threats would coerce neighboring governments and religious leaders into cooperation and neutrality. The Austrian authorities also wanted to prevent the emergence of national consciousness among the Muslims.

Of great importance was the agreement signed by Serbian prince Miloš Obrenović in June, 1881, by which his government agreed to abandon anti-Austro-Hungarian propaganda and conspiracy, and redirect its foreign interests toward Macedonia (for them, "Southern Serbia"). This move caused a wave of indignation among Greater Serbia nationalists because Bosnia-Herzegovina was considered to lie within the Serbian sphere of interest. The "Kingdom of Serbia" was declared the following year. Following the 1903 putsch in which King Alexander Obrenović was murdered, Peter I Karađorđević, who was known to harbor anti-Austrian and pro-Russian sentiments, assumed the throne. Ruling Serbian radicals were also known to share his sentiments. Serbia successfully endured Austrian economic pressure in 1906 (the so-called Pig War involving punitive duties on the export of Serbian pork to Austria-Hungary) and almost doubled its territory in the 1912–13 Balkan Wars.

Back in Bosnia-Herzegovina, von Kallay was strenuously trying to develop a specific Bosnian identity, *bošnjaštvo*, or Bosnian nationhood. According to his theory—actively supported by some Bosnian Muslim intellectuals—all of Bosnia-Herzegovina's inhabitants, regardless of their religious affiliation, belonged to a distinct "Bosnian nation": the *Bošnjaci* (Bosniaks). The last two decades of the nineteenth century were thus characterized by a centralist "administrative absolutism" that von Kallay hoped would depoliticize Bosnia's people. On one hand, he banned political organizations and the use of national names for public institutions, while on the other he authorized the operation of religious and cultural organizations, encouraged education, and so on. He supported the study and romanticizing of Bosnian medieval history and traditions, and introduced a Bosnian flag and coat-of-arms. The only common language was "Bosnian." Von Kallay was convinced that the Bosnian Muslims would be the first to accept this concept.

Both the Serbs and the Croats criticized von Kallay's Bosnian nationhood. Their media and public figures claimed it was a trick and invention of the new administration designed to enable it to govern more efficiently. They denied any collective Bosnian tradition. Von Kallay's concept of integration never really caught on because the religious and national identities of the Orthodox Serbs and Catholic Croats were already too strong. Nevertheless, "multireligious" Bosnian nationhood was not exclusively von Kallay's invention; it had some historical and social bases. A certain provincial and territorial identity was indeed discernible: originally, all the inhabitants were "Bosnians," but of different faiths because national self-definitions were a relative novelty. The sense of Bosnian nationhood was established firmly only among the Bosnian Muslims, especially among the feudal and aristocratic class, which was the subject of Serbo-Croatian rivalry.[47]

The second period in question came after von Kallay's death. His policies, which were recognized as being unsuccessful, were abandoned. The new colonial administrator, Istvan Burian, took a more realistic approach to the situation. Serbian and Croatian national self-confidence had become indisputable facts, the first invigorated by visions of a greater Serbian kingdom, and the second by the *pravaši*. Political circumstances became more liberal following annexation: national and political options were permitted, as were parties and cultural associations that carried national and religious propositions. In conclusion, the fateful differences between the peoples of Bosnia-Herzegovina emerged mainly as a consequence of external nationalist influences and existing internal religious distinctions. In contrast to this, the Austro-Hungarian authorities attempted to halt or at least minimize these processes. The new Habsburg possession, according to them, was inhabited only by "Bosnians, speaking the Bosnian language and divided into three religions with equal rights."[48]

POLITICAL ACTIVITY IN RELIGIO-NATIONAL COMMUNITIES

Following the von Kallay era, religio-cultural movements "matured" into politico-national ones. Peter Sugar, an expert on Bosnia-Herzegovina's history, notes that the Bosnian Muslim Slavs did not begin to awaken politically until after the emergence of Serbian and Croatian political movements and parties. Muslim politicians were secular rather than clerical. Secular (preserving the privileges of the landed gentry), rather than religious, interests dictated Muslim politics at the time. They felt no inclination to adopt religious fundamentalism.[49] On the other hand, their nascent national consciousness was so strongly anchored in Islam that it remained unassailable to both Serbian and Croatian nationalists. For example, the most important conservative Muslim politician of the time, the charismatic mufti of Mostar, Ali Fehmi efendi Džabić, devoted much more of his time to theological enlightenment than to the creation of political programs.[50] This second current within the Muslim political stream was more religiously oriented.

The Muslim movement for cultural and religious autonomy originated in Mostar. In the early years of Austro-Hungarian domination, they addressed many petitions to the government demanding autonomy for Bosnia-Herzegovina and respect for religious and economic interests. A landowner, Alibeg Firdus, headed one such movement. Hence, the first Bosnian organization to articulate the religious, political, and economic demands of Muslims did not emerge until the Austro-Hungarian period. This was the Muslim Movement for Cultural and Religious Autonomy, established in 1899. The Muslim political elite held several meetings during this time: in August, 1899, in Kiseljak; between May and August, 1900, in Budapest; in August, 1900, in Mostar; and in September of that year in Sarajevo.

Although it already existed by 1900, the Muslim National Organization (MNO) was not formally established until 1906. It enjoyed the support of Muslim landowners (according to some sources there were about seven thousand *begs* and *agas* in Bosnia-Herzegovina at the time), but received no support from outside Bosnia's borders, as did its Serbian and Croatian rivals. Two years later, Ademaga Mešić founded the pro-Croatian Muslim Progressive Party, which in 1910—after being renamed the Muslim Independent Party—distanced itself from Croatian and Serbian attempts to encroach on the Muslim Slavs.[51]

The first decade of the twentieth century therefore witnessed the evolution of Muslim party politics in Bosnia-Herzegovina and the emergence Muslim national consciousness despite the fact that a small number of Muslims proclaimed themselves ethnic Serbs or Croats—as some still do today. Several "national conversions" have been recorded, such as those of landowner Šerif Arnautović (from promoting Croatian national identity to Serbian), Suljaga Salihagić (Serbian to Bosnian Muslim), writer Musa Ćazim Ćatić (Serbian to Bosnian and eventually Croatian), and Avdo Hasanbegović, Hasan Rebac, and Hamid Kukić (all from Croatian to Serbian).[52]

This Muslim political awakening did not evolve in the same manner as those in other central and eastern European nations in the great European empires of the time. At the core of Muslim political demands were cultural, religious, and economic interests—not national ones.[53] In May, 1909, the Muslims successfully concluded two years of negotiations with the Austro-Hungarian government concerning cultural and religious autonomy. The Muslims were politically "courted" by both the Serbs and the Croats, who needed their support to secure a parliamentary majority and form a government. Frantic attempts to create long-lasting political alliances, pragmatic coalitions, and cooperation with or accommodation of the central authorities became permanent features of Muslim politics, for which reason many saw them as cynical opportunists.

In 1907, the Bosnian Serbs formed the Serbian National Organization (*Srpska narodna organizacija*), headed by Petar Kočić, whose platform claimed Bosnia-Herzegovina for the Serbs and a Serbian national identity for Muslims. Serbia's political influence on the party was apparent: it was this party that provided the final link between Orthodox and Serbian national identities.

In Bosnia, "the Croatian nationalist movement had a weaker social base than Serbian" for two reasons.[54] First was the absence of institutions such as the Serbian Orthodox Church and school communities. The second was the low number of Catholics in Bosnia's middle class. The Bosnian Croats had two political options from which to choose: the clerical option, which rallied around Archbishop Josip Stadler; and the liberal-bourgeois option, which united Croatia's secular intelligentsia, Franciscan monks, and Muslims who identified themselves as Croats. In February, 1908, the latter became the Croatian National Community (*Hrvatska narodna zajednica* [HNZ]), headed by politicians Džamonja, Jelavić, and Čabrajić.

Their political program included the annexation of Bosnia-Herzegovina by Croatia, the expansion of Croatian national consciousness, and improvement of the economic and education situation. They viewed the Muslim Slavs as ethnic Croats. The Stadler group also used the *pravaši* program. In October, 1910, they founded the clerical and exclusivist Croatian Catholic Union (*Hrvatska katolička udruga* [HKU]). This party advocated Catholicism as the national perspective because it was viewed as the basis of Croatian national identity. Stadler even argued for the conversion of Bosnian Muslims.[55] The conflict between the parish clergy and the Franciscans thus moved into the arena of party politics. Both parties were represented in parliament, but the HNZ had more seats.

The two parties reconciled and merged in 1911 on the basis of the *pravaši* program, and the HKU was dissolved the following year. Both parties accepted the Starčević vision, which held that Bosnia-Herzegovina was historically, ethnographically, and demographically a Croatian territory. Like their compatriots in Croatia proper, Bosnian Croats favored the idea of "trialism": reorganizing Austria-Hungary into a monarchy made up of Austria, Hungary, and the South Slavs. Among its advocates were Stadler, a close friend of heir apparent Franz Ferdinand, who also favored the idea, and Ivan Šarić, who later succeeded Stadler as archbishop of Sarajevo.

The first Bosnian parliament, the *sabor*, convened in 1910, was a bicameral assembly: an upper chamber of twenty notables (including the *reis-ul-ulema*) and a lower chamber of seventy-two representatives (thirty-one Orthodox, twenty-four Muslims, sixteen Catholics, and one Jew). Among the parties that failed to be seated in parliament were the Social Democratic Party (*Socialdemokratska stranka*) and the pro-West party of intellectuals, the Independent Muslim Party (*Muslimanska samostalna stranka*). The Social Democrats, founded in 1909, advocated equal rights for all national groups, although they considered the Slavic majority to be one people with two names: the "Serbo-Croats" and the "Croato-Serbs." They also published a party paper, *Glas slobode (Voice of Freedom)*. The Sarajevo city council had an interesting composition: it consisted of six Orthodox, five Muslim, four Jewish, and three Catholic councilmen.

In Bosnia, the Serbs and Muslims began to find common political ground: both were concerned about Roman Catholic proselytizing. The new Austrian authorities treated both with suspicion, which eventually resulted in demands for Bosnian autonomy. But each had their own perspectives: the Serbs wanted union with Serbia or Montenegro, whereas the Muslims—especially the landed gentry—were concerned for their estates and wanted to maintain their link to the Ottoman Empire.

Among the reputable Muslim politicians to express pro-Serbian sentiments were Dervišbeg Miralem and Šerif Arnautović. The latter went as far as to aid "Serbian agitators who were touring Bosnia to advance the goal of Serbian annexation."[56] The Muslim-Serbian political alliance disintegrated after the crisis resulting from Bosnia's de jure annexation by Austria-Hungary and the recognition of this act by the European superpowers. This prompted the Serbs to intensify their efforts to achieve union with Serbia, while the Muslims still insisted on autonomy for Bosnia-Herzegovina—either under Istanbul or Vienna. The period between 1911 and the outbreak of the First World War was one of Muslim-Croatian parliamentary coalition.

The highly motivated, pro-Yugoslav underground liberation movement called Young Bosnia (Mlada Bosna) adopted an explicitly anti-Habsburg stance and consisted mainly of students. Among them was Gavrilo Princip who, for example, knew Njegoš's epic poem *The Mountain Wreath* by heart. In addition to their revolutionary activity (assassinations, demonstrations, propaganda), Malcolm writes of their anticlericalism, anarchism, Yugoslav nationalism, desire for social revolution, and also of their youthful heroism and martyrdom.[57] A number of them, including Vladimir Gaćinović, harbored strong pro-Serbian sentiments. As far as they were concerned, Bosnia-Herzegovina was Serbian territory.

THE CULTURAL ACTIVITY OF RELIGIO-NATIONAL COMMUNITIES

In the 1890s especially, "the Serbian and Croatian nationalist movements both endeavored to woo Muslim intellectuals and to absorb the Muslim community."[58] The Muslims resisted this in various ways. These included the establishment of the reading club Kiraethana (founded by the reformist Mujaga Komadina), the publication of textbooks in the Bosnian language (from 1890), demands for the autonomy of religious schools *(mearif)*, and the encouragement of the use of Arabic script for the Bosnian language.[59]

Von Kallay, Austria's colonial administrator in Bosnia-Herzegovina, encouraged the pro-Austrian concept of Bosnian nationhood in all fields, including culture. The weekly *Bošnjak*, published between 1891 and 1910, was printed in the "Bosnian language." Its first editor was the former Ottoman administrator (Kajmakam) and pro-Austrian mayor of Sarajevo before and after the occupation, Mehmedbeg Kapetanović

Ljubušak (1839–1902), an advocate of Bosnian nationhood and collector of folklore. Ljubušak worked hard to instill a sense of ethnic conscious-ness in Muslim youth. He gave new impetus to the Muslim community, which was going through a period of identity loss, illiteracy, and cultural stagnation (reading societies, writing in the native language, and so forth)

Ljubušak was an eager adherent to von Kallay's theory of *bošnjaštvo.* For him, Bosniak was a common name for all the inhabitants of Bosnia-Herzegovina, regardless of their ethnic or religious affiliation. His pri-mary goals were to protect Muslim interests from Serbian and Croatian nationalist appetites (that is, to gain acknowledgment for the Muslim national identity and preserve the privileges of the Muslim elite), and to articulate the values and objectives that the Austro-Hungarian regime wished to propagate among Muslims.[60] Articles published in *Bošnjak* were written mainly by authors who supported the government's poli-tics, including Hilmi Muhibić, Edhem Mulabdić, S. Bašagić, Jusuf-beg Filipović and Mehmed's son, Rizabeg Kapetanović (1863–1931, noted for his statement that "Bosnia is not the western part of the East but the eastern part of the West, a part of Europe"), all of whom demonstrated their Slavic and Bosnian origins.

Three cultural options coexisted among the Muslims: pro-Turkish, pro-Serbian, and pro-Croatian. The pro-Serbian option was associated with the cultural society *Gajret* (Endeavor), established in 1903. It did not take an openly pro-Serbian stance until six years later, and was renamed the Serbian Muslim Cultural Association in 1929. In January, 1911, a newspaper bearing the same name went into circulation. Both the soci-ety and the publication tried to instill a sense of Serbian national con-sciousness in Muslim Slavs, who were seen as being "Serbs who lacked ethnic consciousness, and thus even 'anational' Serbs." Osman Đikić, who advocated "the unity of the Muslim and Orthodox Serbs," edited a second pro-Serbian Muslim newspaper, *Samouprava (Self-Government).* It was known for its hostility toward the feudal order and sentiments against Croatian national movement that were becoming more and more apparent.[61]

The pro-Croatian (and pro-Austrian) cultural option was associated with the newspaper *Behar (Blossom,* 1900–11). The Narodna Uzadnica Society was founded in 1924 and renamed the Croatian Muslim Natio-nal Society in 1941 under the new Croatian state. Pro-Croatian Bosnian Muslims promulgated their religious specificity in publications such as *Muslimanska svijest (Muslim Consciousness)* and saw themselves as the descendants of Croats who converted to Islam. They saw their future as being inseparable from that of the Croats, and considered Serbs to be their most dangerous adversaries.[62] The paper of the Muslim National Organization was the weekly *Musavat,* which initially supported the Muslim-Serb political alliance. The goal of this modernist cultural movement, headed by Mehmed Šaćit Kurtćehajić, was the fusion of Muslim oriental tradition and Western culture.[63]

The Bosnian Franciscans played an important role in the development of Catholic cultural and national self-awareness. During the last decades of Ottoman rule and throughout the Austro-Hungarian period, they were involved in education and publishing, encouraged literature (in the *Matica Hrvatska* Society and the Society of Saint Hieronimus), opened primary and secondary schools, and established cultural societies. In 1884, the Franciscans in Mostar began circulating the newspaper *Glas Hercegovine (Voice of Herzegovina),* and publicly advocated religious plurality in Bosnia-Herzegovina through the magazine *Osvit (Dawn),* which was in direct opposition to Stadler's own plans. Among the more important Franciscans in this respect are Grgo Martić, Paškal Buconjić and Didak Buntić. They were among the first to support both Catholicism and Croatian nationalism in their schools. Their spiritual center became Široki Brijeg.

Eminent Bosnian Serbs demanded special cultural autonomy for their people and succeeded in getting it during the governorship of Istvan Burian, who granted them religious and educational autonomy. They issued their own newspaper, *Srpska riječ (The Serbian Word)* and applied pressure on the government with various petitions. Their political goal was to weaken Austria-Hungary's role in Bosnia-Herzegovina. In 1910, there were 170 Serbian cultural societies, 183 Croatian, and only nineteen Muslim. There were six Serbian and six Croatian newspapers, and four Muslim publications.[64]

WORLD WAR I: THE ESCALATION OF RELIGIO-NATIONAL TENSION IN BOSNIA-HERZEGOVINA

The Habsburg monarchy took advantage of internal strife within the Ottoman Empire (the Young Turk Revolution) and announced the full annexation of Bosnia-Herzegovina in October, 1908. Although this step was preceded by talks between Austro-Hungarian foreign minister Alois Aehrenthal and Russia, the annexation was met with disapproval by other European powers, especially Serbia and Montenegro. The Bosnian Serbs and Muslims were also alarmed. Bosnia was hit by a wave of rebellions such as the one in 1910 over agrarian reform issues, while the main cause of unrest in eastern Herzegovina was the people's desire to unite with the kingdom of Serbia. The anti-Serb policy and mood that emerged in the months leading up to the First World War were the result of the machinations of Gen. Oskar von Potiorek (1853–1933), Bosnia-Herzegovina's heavy-handed military governor. It was a period of severely strained relations between the Dual Monarchy and Bosnia's neighbors Serbia and Montenegro. On the other hand, the Montenegrin armies dealt harshly with the Muslims of Sandžak during the Balkan Wars, killing many, burning villages, and forcing religious conversions.[65]

During the First World War, the Muslim-Croatian parliamentary coalition remained loyal to the crown while Bosnian Serbs took sides with their compatriots on the other side of the Drina River. Both pro- and anti-Serbian options emerged among the Croats. In 1917, a number of leading Muslim politicians (including Šerif Arnautović) petitioned the Habsburg emperor for Bosnian autonomy within the Hungarian part of the empire. The second option—supported by Speaker of the Assembly S. Basagić, among others—was for closer union with Croatia in a future trialist arrangement. *Reis-ul-ulema* Džemaludin Čaušević supported both autonomy and stronger union with other South Slavs. In 1917, Archbishop Stadler spoke of the urgency of creating a Croatian state that would extend to the Drina River and thus protect Catholics. He was opposed to the May Declaration of 1917, which was supported by the Roman Catholic clergy, especially the Bosnian Franciscans, as expressed in their statements of December, 1917, and January, 1918.[66]

There were frequent battles during the First World War between the *Schutzkorps*, an auxiliary militia composed mainly of Muslims, and Serbian units (the *Četnici* [Chetniks] and *komiti*). Unfortunately, the main victims were civilians. Muslims were also drafted into special counter-insurgency units known as the *Steifkorps*. In neighboring Srem, the authorities defaced frescoes of Kosovo heroes in the Vrdnik monastery because of their "patriotic message."[67] The Austro-Hungarian authorities terrorized Serbian nationalists and the Serbian population through trials, massacres, internment, and ostracism. They interned between 3,300 and 5,500 suspected Bosnian Serbs: of these, 700–2,200 died in camps and 460 were executed. Some fifty-two hundred families were driven across the border into Serbia because they were regarded as a potential fifth column.[68] For the first time in their history, a significant number of Bosnia-Herzegovina's inhabitants were persecuted and liquidated because of their national affiliation. It was an ominous harbinger of things to come.

BETWEEN THE SERBS
AND THE CROATS
Religious and National Issues in Bosnia-Herzegovina during Karađorđević's Reign in Yugoslavia

Immediately after the First World War, Bosnia-Herzegovina joined a short-lived "State of the Slovenes, Croats, and Serbs" consisting of South Slav nations that were, until then, part of Austro-Hungary, and on December 1, 1918, became part of the "Kingdom of Serbs, Croats, and Slovenes" (Kingdom SHS). The next few lines are therefore dedicated to this new state that was from the beginning shaken by strong internal contradictions. The fundamental political conflict that existed in the first Yugoslavia (and later in the second) revolved around the choice between a unitary or federalist option. This was evident in the first Yugoslavia because of the antagonism between the Yugoslav centralist alternative, which was often a mere disguise for Serb hegemony, and the autonomist—some would say separatist—alternative, which was supported by the main Croatian party, the Croatian Peasant Party (*Hrvatska seljačka stranka* [HSS], and for a time also as the Croatian Republican Peasant Party [HSRS]), and the main Slovenian and Bosnian Muslim parties—the Slovenian People's Party (*Slovenska ljudska stranka* [SLS]), and the Yugoslav Muslim Organization (*Jugoslovenska muslimanska organizacija* [JMO]). However, for strategic and pragmatic reasons, these antagonists often sought compromises that were sometimes in direct conflict with their principles.

Fear God and respect your King.

—ALOJZIJ STEPINAC, AT AN AUDIENCE WITH THE KING AND HIS GOVERNMENT IN BELGRADE, SUMMER, 1934

The political, economical, national, cultural, religious, and other diversities of the newborn state often resulted in contradictions and even armed conflicts. Montenegrin separatists, Albanian insurgents, Croatian federalists or separatists, Macedonian nationalist guerillas, Slovenian advocates of autonomy, and other malcontents had a common adversary: Serbian nationalism and its protagonists' clear wish to secure for themselves the ruling position in the state. Belgrade responded to such challenges in many different ways: one of them was the newly emerging myth of "one Yugoslav nation comprising three tribes." It was meant to preclude the individual national characteristics of the South Slavs: "the denial of the national individuality of each South Slavic nation, a position inherent in the precepts of unitaristic Yugoslavism, greatly facilitated the introduction of centralism."[1]

"Integral Yugoslavism" adopted the slogan "One King, One Country, One Nation, One Language" and phrases such as "linguistic conjunction" and "national unification," and encompassed both the political and scientific spheres. The universities of Belgrade and Zagreb in particular attempted to "scientifically prove the ethnic sameness of the South Slavs."[2] Yugoslav integration was further bolstered by King Alexander's declaration of personal dictatorship in January, 1929. Throughout the kingdom's existence, these conflicts did not fade away. They simply took different forms and ways of articulation, ultimately contributed to the kingdom's ignominious end, and announced the forthcoming tragedy of the Second World War.

Charged with hegemonic visions of a Greater Serbia, the nationalists considered themselves to be saviors, the "Piedmont," of the other Yugoslav nations. In December, 1914, Serbia's parliament declared that the nation's primary military objective was the liberation of "our oppressed Serb, Croat, and Slovene brothers."[3] The end of the war was celebrated in an atmosphere of Serbian triumphalism, and the heroism of Serb soldiers began to acquire mythical dimensions. The Serbs developed the myth that they were the "principal driving force in the country and the architects of Yugoslavia," that they were "more advanced than their brethren," and of the "pan-Yugoslav significance of the unification of the Serbs."

The new authorities tried to build a cult based on the Karađorđević dynasty as the "people's monarchs." Peter I became the "Great Liberator," and Alexander I became the "Chivalrous King," the "Unifier," and the "Martyr." The cults of the Battle of Kosovo and of the early-nineteenth-century Serb uprisings were consolidated into the new cults of the victorious wars of 1912–18.[4] Indeed, the Kingdom of Serbs, Croats, and Slovenes solved the timeworn "Serb question" because all Serbs at last lived in one country. Success was complete. Commenting on the adoption of the new constitution on Vidovdan, June 28, 1921, *Samouprava*, the journal of the Serbian Radical Party, wrote: "this year's Vidovdan returned to us our Empire."

As during the Balkan Wars, triumphant Serbian and Montenegrin troops acted violently against the Slavic Muslims. In 1917, the leader of the Radical Party, Stojan Protić (1857–1923), announced that they would give the Bosnia-Herzegovina's Muslims, whom he regarded as "Turks," twenty-four or at the most forty-eight hours to convert to Orthodoxy, "their ancestral religion," or they would "be cut down, as we did in Serbia earlier." Serbian soldiers ransacked Muslim property and killed many Muslims immediately after the war. Local Radical Party officials encouraged violence in Bosnia-Herzegovina. According to one Muslim religious official, about a thousand people were killed, seventy-six women were burned to death, and 270 villages were pillaged and laid to waste. Bosniak historian Imamović reported that two thousand Muslims were killed before September, 1920. Serb extremists conducted several pogroms against them in the mid-1920s, especially in the eastern Sandžak villages of Šahovići and Pavino Polje.[5] The Muslims were tauntingly referred to as "Asiatics" and were told to "Go to Asia!" They also were accused of being "turncoats, parasites, liars, pretentious, lazy," and so forth. There was talk of "social de-Islamization" and "nationalization," and of "Serbianizing the Muslims."[6]

The king's reforms brought a redistribution of land and an end to serfdom. By July, 1919, more than four hundred thousand hectares of land had been taken from 4,281 Muslim landowners. Sometimes land was taken without any refund. In other cases, the compensation offered by the state—some of which was paid immediately and the rest in installments—was well below the land's fair-market value. All of this had a catastrophic economic and social effect on the Muslim community as many landowning Muslim families were reduced to poverty. One result was a new exodus of Bosnian Muslims to Turkey. The Muslims were also generally uneducated. In the 1930s, the level of illiteracy for Yugoslavia as a whole was 88 percent, while the figures for Muslims were even more dismal: 95 percent (99.68 percent for women).[7]

Bosnia-Herzegovina preserved its territorial integrity, guaranteed in the so-called Turkish Paragraph of the 1921 constitution, until 1929 because of the loyal policies and skillful maneuvering of the leaders of the most influential Muslim organization. Whereas Bosnia-Herzegovina kept its historic borders, this was not the case with the remaining twenty-three provinces in the new state (except the two Slovenian). The new Bosnian *oblasts*—whose headquarters were in Bihać, Banja Luka, Tuzla, Travnik, Sarajevo, and Mostar—corresponded to the Austro-Hungarian and Ottoman administrative divisions. Although there was not a single Muslim among the "grand mayors" (administrators) of the

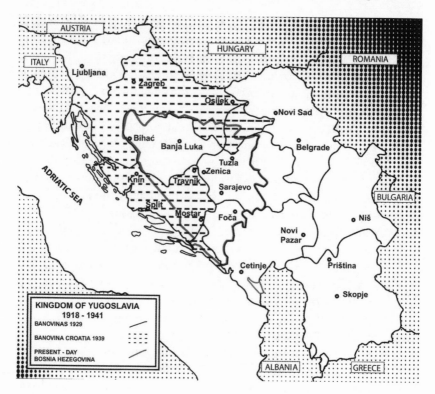

KINGDOM OF YUGOSLAVIA
1918 - 1941
BANOVINAS 1929
BANOVINA CROATIA 1939
PRESENT - DAY
BOSNIA HEZEGOVINA

oblasts, Serb radicals were very vocal in their tirades on the dangers of appointing "Turks" to positions of power.[8] In 1929, Bosnia's territorial integrity was violated for the first time since the Middle Ages as the territory was partitioned and divided into four banates in which Muslims were a minority: Vrbaska, Primorska, Drinska, and Zetska.

In August, 1939, Bosnia was again subdivided when the large *banovina* of Croatia was created. This subdivision took into account Serb and Croat ethnic majorities at the expense of the Muslims. Its creation and the appointment of Ivan Šubašić (1892–1955) as *ban* was intended to finally bring an end to the pressing Croatian issue that had been smoldering for two decades. Of a population of 4,299,430, three-quarters were Catholics, one-fifth was Orthodox, and only 4 percent were Muslims. Of the 116 districts *(kotari),* ninety-five had an absolute and five a relative Catholic majority.[9] The *banovina* of Croatia included the "Croatian" parts of Bosnia-Herzegovina, namely Derventa, Gradačac, Brčko, Travnik, Bugojno, Fojnica, Prozor, Tomislavgrad, Livno, Konjic, Ljubiški, Mostar, and Stolac. What remained of Bosnia-Herzegovina fell under the projected Serbian portion of Yugoslavia and had a Serb majority.

The notion of creating a special *banovina* consisting of parts of Bosnia-Herzegovina and Sandžak with an autonomous status similar to that of the *banovina* of Croatia was proposed in 1940 by Džafer *beg* Kulenović, a pro-Croat and the last leader of the JMO, but it was largely ignored. Kulenović suggested that Yugoslavia be divided into four provinces: Serbian, Croatian, Slovenian, and Bosnian. His rejection of the division of Bosnia-Herzegovina between the Serbs and Croats "was seconded by most Muslims, whether of Croat or Serb orientation."[10]

THE BATTLE FOR THE NATIONAL ASSIMILATION OF MUSLIMS CONTINUES

The Muslim population in the Kingdom of Serbs, Croats, and Slovenes and later in Yugoslavia was composed of the following ethnic groups: Bosnian Muslim Slavs, Muslim Albanians, Turks, Macedonian Muslim Slavs, Muslim Slavs from Sandžak and Montenegro, and Muslim Roma. The 1921 census did not have a special designation for national groups. Of a total of 1.3 million Muslims living in the kingdom, there were between 727,650 and 750,000 Muslim Slavs.[11]

The influential JMO was founded in 1919. In 1921, Mehmed Spaho (1883–1939), replaced its pro-Serb leader, Hadži Hafiz Ibrahim efendi Maglajlić, a mufti from Tuzla. Another influential party figure was Sakib Korkut. Although the JMO's leaders considered Muslims to be a separate ethnic category, they acknowledged the religious nature of their party. Its supporters also considered it a religious party and voted for it out of religious loyalty.[12] More than a third of the eligible voters in Bosnia-Herzegovina voted for the party in 1920. It represented the cultural and religious interests of Bosnian Muslims, especially the hereditary rights of the landed Muslim gentry.

Muslims from other parts of the monarchy, especially the south, voted for the Džemijet Party, whose statutory and organizational lines were similar to those of the JMO in that it represented the interests of Muslim landowners and advocated religious autonomy. Later, certain individuals associated with Maglajlić formed a new pro-Serb party, the Yugoslav Muslim National Organization (JMNO), although it never exerted as much influence as the JMO. On the other hand, the JMO reacted to centralist Serbian parties and initiatives in a very opportunistic manner and in contrast to its established autonomist policies. In order to achieve its goal—the integrity of Bosnia-Herzegovina—the JMO backed Pašić's centralist government in the constitutional debate, thus facilitating the adoption of the centralist Vidovdan constitution of 1921. This helped alleviate the effect of the agrarian reforms and secured the autonomy of Muslim religious and educational institutions and sharia courts.

By 1923, however, resistance to Serb domination had pushed the party closer to the HSS and other federalist and antiunitarist options in the country. Later still, it abandoned the opposition and once again backed the government. The JMO retained its pro-Yugoslav outlook throughout this period. In 1936, it merged with Serb radicals and Slovene clericals to form the Yugoslav Radical Union *(Jugoslovenska radikalna zajednica* [JRZ], ironically referred to as "Jereza," which sounds like "hereza" or heresy) and thus lent legitimacy to Stojadinović's regime. Many historians therefore view the JMO as a conservative, opportunistic, defensive, and outwardly shortsighted party that was content with the crumbs others had left behind and constantly swaying between risky political options. One thing was clear to both Serb and Croat nationalist politicians: Whoever ruled Bosnia-Herzegovina, either by acquisition, annexation, subjugation, or assimilation of Bosnian Muslims, would gain decisive advantage in the political struggle between them.

Yugoslavia's Muslims were considered exclusively as a religious category, regardless of ethnic affiliation—whether it was Turkish, Albanian, Gypsy, or Slav. Although Bosnian Slavic Muslims were under increasing political, economic, and administrative pressure to identify themselves nationally—that is, to choose between the existing national options, which most of them vehemently rejected—they "only lacked a national name." In their defense, the Muslims emphasized their autochthonous nature, pure Slavic origin, and the autonomy of the medieval kingdom by declaring that they were the descendants of "Bosnian Patarins," thus evoking the memory of King Tvrtko and others.[13] Many Muslim Slavs believed that any form of national identification was in direct contradiction with their faith. One such person was the Muslim writer Osman Nuribeg Firdus, who reportedly said, "Islam transcends nationality."

By that time, some circles within the Muslim elite were already aware of the urgency of winning recognition for the distinct national identity of Bosnia-Herzegovina's Muslims. Husag Čisić, one of the advocates of this during the interwar years, believed that the national basis of the Muslim population was Islam. According to Čisić, religious affiliation corresponded to national identity, as was the case with the Orthodox Serbs and the Roman Catholic Croats. Irwin notes that the move to create a distinct Muslim Slav national identity that would have been independent of religion came too late: Muslim religious and cultural institutions lacked the political experience of their Serb and Croat counterparts.[14] In March, 1941, a pan-Islamic organization known as the Young Muslims *(Mladi muslimani)* was established, uniting radical Muslim intelligentsia. Founding groups from Sarajevo, Mostar, and Zagreb "developed a network which, little by little, covered most of the towns of Bosnia-Herzegovina."[15]

The Muslims were also hesitant to declare themselves to be Serbs or Croats because of the conflict-riddled relationship between these two national groups and their territorial appetites for Bosnia-Herzegovina. Nevertheless, a number of Muslims did identify themselves with one or the other national group as a "religious minority within the national group"—sometimes as Serbs, but more often as Croats (because of their opposition to Serb hegemony). One indicative example is that of the Spaho brothers. Under Austria-Hungary, Mehmed favored the Serbs but later refused to identify himself with either national group; his brother, Fehim Efendija, was the *reis-ul-ulema* between 1938 and 1942 and identified himself as a Croat. A third brother, Mustafa, an engineer by profession, identified himself as a Serb. Of the JMO's twenty-four deputies—members of the first constituent assembly of the monarchy in 1920—the majority nationally identified themselves as Croats. In 1923, seventeen of the eighteen Muslim deputies declared themselves to be ethnic Croats (the sole exception being Spaho).

Croatian politicians emphasized the Croat origin of Bosnia's Muslims: Starčević's theories that the Muslim Slavs of Bosnia-Herzegovina were the "best Croats" and that Bosnia-Herzegovina was actually a "Croat land" continued. Stjepan Radić believed that they were *ethnic Croats,* whilst Vladko Maček declared that they were "by descent, history, and dialect the purest segment of the Croat race." Before the war, the Ustasha also asserted that Bosnia-Herzegovina was merely a part of Croatia and that the Muslims were ethnic Croats. They stated that Muslims could not be distinguished from the Croat nation "because Bosnia is the heart of the Croatian state, and the Muslim tribes are part of the Croatian nation."[16]

Percentage wise, the ratio between the two major religious communities in Bosnia-Herzegovina did not change. The data for 1921 and 1931 are taken from a population census, while those for 1939 are only estimates.[17]

Communists in interwar Yugoslavia—who considered Karađorđević's kingdom to be an "artificial creation of the Treaty of Versailles"—initially recognized Bosnia-Herzegovina's Muslim Slavs only as a religious group. Politician and theoretician Sima Marković, one of the leading members of Yugoslavia's Communist Party, is quoted as saying in 1923 that, in regard to the Muslim Slavs, "religion is the only criterion for na-

TABLE 6-1 **Percentages of major religious communities in Bosnia-Herzegovina, 1921–39**

	1921 Census		1931 Census		1939 (Estimated)	
Muslim	588,173	31.1%	717,562	30.1%	848,140	31.2%
Orthodox	829,360	43.9%	1,028,723	44.3%	1,226,991	44.6%
Catholic	443,309	23.5%	557,836	24%	595,974	21.7%

tionality." In his 1938 book titled *The Evolution of the Slovenian National Question,* Slovenian Marxist Edvard Kardelj wrote about the "Catholic, Orthodox, and Muslim population of Bosnia." However, in several other parts of the same book he mentions only four "indigenous" national groups in Yugoslavia: the Slovenes, Serbs, Croats, and Macedonians.[18]

This view was later changed. At the Fifth Conference of the Communist Party of Yugoslavia, held in Zagreb in October, 1940, Bosnia-Herzegovina's Muslim Slavs were given special recognition as a "separate ethnic group." The motion was proposed by a Muslim Communist from Bosnia-Herzegovina, Mustafa Pašić, but opposed by Milovan Djilas. On this occasion, Josip Broz Tito is quoted as saying: "Bosnia is one, because of centuries-old common life, regardless of confession." This recognition of the Muslims as an ethnic group and not as a nationality was repeated by Rodoljub Čolaković during the Second World War. On the other hand, Veselin Masleša recognized them "neither as an ethnic group nor as a nationality," and emphasized that they were of Serb descent.[19]

THE ORTHODOX AND ROMAN CATHOLIC CHURCHES DECLARE THEIR LOYALTY TO THE NEW STATE

The Serbian Orthodox and Roman Catholic Churches had a long tradition of resisting the territorial appetites of their neighbors on one hand, and of loyalty toward the state bordering on servility on the other. The most populous group in the new state, which was finally "their own," were the Orthodox. The 1931 census listed 6,785,501 Orthodox compared to 5,217,847 Roman Catholics, 1,561,166 Muslims, and 44,608 Greek Catholics.[20] The 1921 and 1931 constitutions made no mention of official state churches, but merely of "recognized" ones. These performed certain functions for the state, such as the registration of births, weddings, and deaths, and exercised jurisdiction over these matters. Religious education was compulsory in all schools.

The authorities' attempt to place all religious groups under their control resulted in conflict, especially with the Muslim community and the Roman Catholic Church. For example, religious education in schools was to be taught by teachers "chosen by the government, without the approval of the bishop."[21] Supporters of South Slav unity proposed a common, anticlerical Yugoslav idea that did not succeed because of Roman Catholic resistance. Those in favor of a united Yugoslavia and advocates of a Greater Serbia condemned Catholicism as "anti-Slavic" but viewed Orthodoxy—the faith of the royal dynasty—as "native and national."[22] The compliant Serbian Orthodox Church played an important role in the Yugoslav centralist scheme. The authorities were able to count on the support of its highest representatives whenever it confronted the Roman Catholic Church.

In the months following the birth of the new kingdom, the Serbian Orthodox Church merged the Metropolitan Sees of Serbia, Sremski Karlovci (Vojvodina), Bosnia-Herzegovina, Montenegro, Macedonia, and two Dalmatian dioceses (Zadar and Kotor) into a uniform structure. The revival, or "resurrection," of the Serbian patriarchate with seventeen dioceses headed by Patriarch Dimitrij Pavlović, the metropolite of Belgrade, was announced in September, 1920. The new patriarchate was proclaimed the direct successor to the medieval Serbian church founded by Saint Sava. It also received the blessing of the ecumenical patriarchate.

In 1926, the Ministry of Religious Affairs, representing the government, and the Episcopal Synod of the Serbian Orthodox Church reached an agreement that was essentially the equivalent of a concordat. The agreement secured a better position for the Orthodox Church in its relationship with the state and provided for financial assistance. A bill enacted in 1929 ultimately defined relations between the state and the Orthodox Church. It was at this time that Serbian theologians began the intensive revival of the Saint Sava cult *(svetosavlje).*[23]

The Serbian Orthodox Church began to actively proselytize in ethnically heterogeneous areas. Catholic extremists claimed that the number of Catholics converted to Orthodoxy exceeded two hundred thousand, which is an exaggeration. Although there were numerous cases of Catholic women converting to Orthodoxy after marrying Orthodox men, and many converted to Orthodoxy in order to promote their careers in the civil service or military, the actual number of conversions can no longer be accurately determined.

Slovenian historian Jože Pirjevec notes that while the Roman Catholic Church enjoyed the respect of the authorities, it "was unpopular because of its one-time open sympathies for the Habsburg monarchy." Anton Bauer, the archbishop of Zagreb, welcomed the new state and hoped for good relations with the nine religious communities recognized by it, especially the Serbian Orthodox Church. The church in Croatia hoped for reconciliation with the Serbian Orthodox Church and sought the pope's permission to use the glagolitic liturgy. The Catholic clergy in Slovenia were equally enthusiastic about the new state: The bishop of Ljubljana, Anton Bonaventura Jeglič, had labored for the unification of the South Slavs but later rejected the Vidovdan constitution, while Anton Mahnič welcomed the Kingdom of Serbs, Croats, and Slovenes as a "work of God," created by the "Prudence of God."[24]

The Catholic Church in Bosnia-Herzegovina also declared its loyalty to the new state, although there were many who opposed the appointment of Ivan Šarić to the position of archbishop of Bosnia, replacing Stadler, who died in 1918. There were 151 parish priests and 328 monks in Bosnia-Herzegovina in 1937. However, disputes between the powerful Franciscan *provincialate* and the archdiocese regarding the division of parishes and funds provided by the state continued. In an agreement signed in 1923 and ratified by the Vatican, the Franciscans were allocated all the areas they would have acquired through missionary work among the Orthodox and Muslims. In addition to the sixty-three (of seventy-nine) parishes in Herzegovina, the Franciscans also had twenty-nine monasteries, five seminaries, and several other institutions.[25] Despite opposition from the authorities of the Independent State of Croatia, the Vatican appointed Peter Čule as the new bishop of Mostar in 1942, a position traditionally held by the Franciscans.

The organizational structure of the Roman Catholic religious community in the new state changed considerably. New appointments were made to dioceses and archdioceses, while parts of Slovenian and Croatian Catholics (the Primorska region, Istria, and other parts of the Adriatic coast) were placed under the ecclesiastic jurisdiction of Italian archdioceses. Immediately after the war, a group of Roman Catholic priests in Croatia sought organizational reforms, including the abolition of celibacy, the introduction of Slavonic liturgy, and the rectification of social injustices against the lower clergy. A trio of priests—Stjepan Menzinger, Rikard Korytnik, and Stjepan Zagorac—headed the group, known as the Yellow Movement *(Žuti pokret)* because of the yellow covers of the members' booklets.

Following unsuccessful discussions with Archbishop Bauer of Zagreb, and with the support of HSS leaders Stjepan Radić and Vladko Maček, these "apostate" priests founded the Croatian Catholic Church. Radić believed that this Old Catholic Church would preserve the unity between the various national groups within the kingdom and forge stronger ties with the Serbian Orthodox Church. His views were strongly criticized by the Roman Catholic press. Members of the new church (which, incidentally, sanctioned divorce) considered themselves the successors to Saints Cyril and Methodius, Grgur Ninski, Andrija Jamometić, and Josip Juraj Strossmayer. On Christmas Day, 1921, Archbishop Bauer excommunicated them from the Roman Catholic Church. After being accepted into the "Utrecht Union of Old Catholic Churches," the Croatian Catholic Church was renamed the "Old Catholic Church of Croatia" and recognized by the state in December, 1923. Its first bishop was Marko Kalodjera.[26]

CROATIAN RESISTANCE TO SERBIAN CENTRALISM AND THE UPROAR OVER THE CONCORDAT

There was passive as well as active resistance to what the Croats justifiably believed was Serb discrimination: Serbs were an absolute majority in the state apparatus and armed forces.[27] There were demonstrations against the monarchy in Croatia as early as December 5, 1918; local peasant uprisings in 1920 and 1932 were quelled with much bloodshed; and there was more bloodshed in Senj and Sibinj following pro-Croat demonstrations in 1935. Certain political circles within Croatia were growing weary of Serbian patronage. They regarded the Serbs as the new oppressors and Yugoslavia as the instrument of the hegemony of what some of them called "Serbian Asia," the "Mameluk hordes," the "Serbian Bastille," or "Belgrade bandits and militants." According to Stjepan Radić, the Croats represented the *antemurale Christianitatis* in the Kingdom SHS, whose wish was to "Europeanize the Balkans and not be Balkanized themselves, as was the intent of the Serbs."[28]

Unlike Slovenia, the most influential party in Croatia, the Croatian People's Party, was not particularly sympathetic to the clergy. Stjepan Radić (1871–1928) was cautious of Catholic clerics with political aspirations in Croatia.[29] Nevertheless, his populist slogan was: "Faith in God and Peasant Unity!" Radić may, indeed, be reproached for his inconsistency, frequent changes of opinion, and opportunism as he swayed between radicalism and conservatism, Yugoslavism and Croatian secessionism, centralism and federalism. He initially rejected the Vidovdan constitution but eventually accepted it. It thus should come as no surprise that the regime first imprisoned him and then appointed him minister for education. The tragic culmination of this Serbian-Croatian confrontation was a shooting in Parliament that resulted in Radić's death in the summer of 1928. At his funeral, about a hundred thousand people took part in a solemn procession through the streets of Zagreb. Following his "martyrly death," a strong cult (which has reemerged in recent years) developed around the personality of this popular, albeit not very proficient, politician. The heirs of his political legacy kept the cult alive.[30]

One of the reactions to Serbian hegemony and later King Alexander's dictatorship in 1929 was the emergence of the terrorist Ustasha (Insurgent) movement.[31] It had strongholds in its irredentist neighboring states, Italy and Hungary, which felt that the peace treaties at the end of the First World War had favored Yugoslavia at their expense. The Ustasha were an anti-Semitic, anti-Serbian fascist movement. For Ante Pavelić (1889–1959)—the leader and ideologue of both the Croatian Party of the Right and the Ustasha, born in Bradina near Konjic in central Bosnia to parents from Lika—the HRO's enemies were Serbia's state authority, international freemasonry, Jewry, and communism.[32]

It is interesting to note that Pavelić made no mention of the Roman Catholic Church in his exclusivist and separatist program entitled "Principles," published in 1933, which envisaged the creation of an ethnically pure Greater Croatia—by any means necessary. Of the seventeen principles in his program, only the sixteenth mentions "orderly and religious family life." Instead, the future *Poglavnik* (Leader) seduced the peasants, whom he considered an essential part of the Croatian nation. The twelfth principle reads: "The peasantry are the foundation and source of all life and are, as such, the prime bearers of state authority in the Croatian state."[33]

Despite their dissatisfaction with the ruling regime, the Roman Catholic hierarchy in Croatia bid a decorous and loyal farewell to King Alexander (the "gallant king," the "unifier," according to the *Catholic List* publication) in the autumn of 1934 when he became the second protagonist of the era to be felled by an assassin's bullet. In the summer of 1934, Alojzije Stepinac was appointed to succeed Bauer as archbishop of Zagreb ("with the prerogative to succession," *ad nutum Sanctae sedis*). Stepinac, a young and inexperienced priest with a doctorate in philosophy and theology, was ordained not long before his appointment in 1930. He worked as a parish priest on only two occasions: in Samobor and Saint Ivan Zelina. He succeeded Bauer following the latter's death in 1937 and had good relations with the royal court in Belgrade, receiving King Alexander's blessing. He also took "an oath of allegiance to the monarchy when he was consecrated."[34] His pro-Yugoslav sentiments were well documented: As an Austro-Hungarian officer he was captured by the Italians at the Isonzo front and left from there to join the "Yugoslav Legion" on the Salonika front.

However, Stepinac began entertaining notions about re-Catholicizing the Serbs (and the Orthodox in general), hoping to secure "their return to the embrace of the only true Church." In 1934, he declared that Serbia could become a Roman Catholic country within twenty years "if there was sufficient freedom and more workers." He strongly believed in freemason and Communist conspiracies and repeatedly spoke publicly about them.[35] He wrote a pastoral letter in 1937 in which he advocated both the anti-Communist encyclical *Divini redemptoris* and the anti-racist encyclical *Mit brennender Sorge,* issued by Pope Pius XI (1922–39). Stepinac, who was renowned for his rigid and conservative principles, intended to re-Christianize all of society and infuse it with a Christian ethos, with a special emphasis on the family (he fiercely opposed civil marriages), the destitute, and the homeless.

He undertook a number of ambitious projects, including the reorganization of the parish network (especially in Zagreb), reinforcing religious discipline among the clergy and the congregation, and creating a more uniform Croatian Catholic "pillar." He was very strict regarding the use of profanity in everyday speech (calling it "an insult to the Almighty God"). A zealous adorer of the Holy Virgin, he tried to create a Croatian version of Lourdes in Marija Bistrica, a renowned pilgrimage town. He expected the patriotic and apolitical religious press, which he supported, to encourage a comprehensive and widespread religious revival. The only Catholic daily of the time, the *Croatian Guard (Hrvatska straža)* which had a rather low circulation, was replaced by the *Voice of Croatia (Hrvatski glas)* just before the start of the Second World War. Stepinac was extremely moderate and restrained in his private life. He deplored extravagance, and his apostolic frugality earned him the epithet "Bolshevik Archbishop" among the higher clergy. In a sense, Stepinac represented the institution he headed: The Roman Catholic Church in Croatia was "traditionalist, authoritarian, and even at that time old-fashioned."[36]

Interecclesiastic relations in Yugoslavia (and, consequently, interethnic relations as well) deteriorated because of the dispute over the concordat with the Holy See. The concordat was expected to resolve many pressing issues: defining diocese borders and conforming them to national borders, determining the procedure for appointing bishops, addressing the questions of religious education and Slavonic liturgy, facilitating the functioning of "Catholic Action," and determining the state's financial obligation to the Roman Catholic Church. Specifically, it was expected to address the share of state aid to the Roman Catholic Church, the appointment of bishops by the Vatican with Belgrade's assent, permission to use the glagolitic alphabet and liturgy, Roman Catholic baptism for children of mixed marriages, and the ban on clergy engaging in political activity.[37]

The laws and concordats that were being used in Yugoslavia at that time were inherited from its predecessors. The former Habsburg territories still used the 1855 concordat (Croatia and Slavonia) and the 1874 act (Slovenia and Dalmatia). Vojvodina solved the problem by enacting new legislation. Bosnia-Herzegovina was bound by the convention of 1881, and Montenegro by the concordat of 1886. The kingdom of Serbia signed a concordat on June 24, 1914, the eve of the war. In 1921, Pope Benedict XV (1914–22) declared all previous concordats null and void as a result of the creation of the new state. Discussions on the new concordat began in the early 1920s and were held between Yugoslav authorities (and later by King Alexander in person) and the Vatican, thus encroaching on the authority of the Yugoslav Roman Catholic hierarchy. The king expected the concordat to guarantee a higher degree of Catholic allegiance to the state, mitigation of the Croatian issue, and a closer working relationship in fighting communism. The concordat was signed in July, 1935, by Yugoslav prime minister Milan Stojadinović, but the indignation of the Orthodox population prevented him from tabling it in parliament until November, 1936.[38]

News of the concordat provoked an unexpected storm of protests from the Orthodox part of the state. Despite his previous concurrence with the concordat, Patriarch Varnava (Barnabas) now fiercely opposed it, as did certain Serbian opposition and nationalist circles that were envious of the relations between Yugoslavia and the Vatican. They "exposed" a conspiracy by the pope (the "black leader of the black internationale") against the Yugoslav state and the Orthodox. The Serbian Orthodox Church's leadership saw four flaws in the concordat: they believed that it would facilitate Catholic proselytizing; they saw the share of state aid allocated to the Catholic Church as too high (although other data suggest quite the opposite: the Orthodox Church claimed the lion's share— between almost two-thirds and three-quarters—of budgetary funds intended for all recognized religious communities);[39] they found the solution to the issue of religious education and religious textbooks unacceptable; and they opposed the ban on political activity by the clergy (some clerics from the Orthodox Church were members of parliament). In November, 1936, Patriarch Varnava proscribed all Serb members of parliament, senators, and cabinet ministers, under threat of excommunication, from voting for the concordat.

Parliament debated the concordat and passed it on July 23, 1937, with a majority of 166 votes to 129. Varnava's death that same evening provoked demonstrations and violent clashes with the police. Rumors began to spread that Varnava had been poisoned. The Holy Synod of the Serbian Orthodox Church (the permanent body of the assembly of Orthodox bishops; in addition to the patriarch, it consisted of four members serving one-year mandates) and the new patriarch, Metropolite Gavrilo (Mihajlo Dozić) of Montenegro, saw the concordat as an attempt to privilege the Roman Catholic Church.

The Serbian Orthodox Church—which made a similar agreement with the government in 1926—went through with its threat and excommunicated all Orthodox parliamentarians involved in the matter. A raging propaganda war ensued, and violent demonstrations continued (the so-called Bloody Procession in Belgrade). Orthodox bishops from across the nation participated in the demonstrations, including Dositej from Zagreb, Simeon from Šabac, Platon from Banja Luka, Sava from Karlovac, and Irinej from Dalmatia. Side-by-side with the predominately oppositional and pro-Orthodox Serbian political parties, national and cultural associations, and clubs, several hundred Communists led by student Milovan Djilas also participated in the demonstrations, seizing the opportunity to launch an attack on the regent and his government. All this and other pressure prevented the Senate from ratifying the concordat. In 1937, Stojadinović informed ecclesiastical authorities that there would be no agreement regarding the concordat.

Three months later, the government declared that it had no intention of proposing a new concordat. Stella Alexander notes that the Roman Catholic Church in the country played an insignificant role in the dispute between the Serbian Orthodox Church and the central government in Belgrade and was more of an observer than a participant.[40] The Catholic side—the Vatican and the Yugoslav Conference of Bishops—did not react until after the concordat was withdrawn. They complained bitterly but remained unheeded. The Yugoslav bishops issued a pastoral letter announcing their deep regret over the refusal of the concordat and the intolerance of the Orthodox Church. They also released a series of vocal attacks against the government, accusing it of violating the basic human rights of the non-Orthodox (especially Roman Catholic) population.

Both archbishops of Zagreb followed the instructions of Pope Pius XI to the letter during this period, fiercely opposing any attempts by the clergy to participate in politics. They believed that the Church must stay away from party politics by all means: Stepinac's motto during this period was: "Neither left nor right, only by the path of Jesus Christ."[41] The

Church responded to pressure from the government by organizing mass Eucharistic congresses, all with the presence of archbishops. The slogan of the congresses was: "Christ, O King of the Eucharist, protect the Croatian nation!"[42] Their criticism of the authorities increased in other ways as well: in 1935 Archbishop Bauer proscribed the participation of Roman Catholic pupils at the seven hundredth anniversary celebration of the death of Saint Sava. The bishops also issued a pastoral letter denouncing the Sokol movement and accusing it of centralism and nationalism. This deepened the suspicion of the Belgrade authorities and generally impaired relations between the Vatican and Yugoslavia.

The Roman Catholic Church continued to play an active role in culture and education and in the community. It founded "Catholic Action" (CA) on Christmas Day, 1934, in response to society's increasing secularization and atheism. Pope Pius XI defined this new form of laic Catholic fraternization in the *Urbi arcano dei* encyclical of 1922. Its purpose was to secure the participation of the laic segment of society in the work of the ecclesiastic organization. Catholic Action was intended to deal primarily with religious and moral issues, not politics. Although Stepinac founded the Croatian chapter of CA in order to bring the different segments of the Croatian Roman Catholic movement under one roof, he explicitly emphasized its apolitical character. Other Roman Catholic organizations were accused of political pettifoggery.

The Roman Catholic camp was very disunited. In addition to CA, it included the Croatian Catholic Movement (HKP, founded in Austria-Hungary by Bishop Anton Mahnič of Krk; a fiercely patriotic and anti-secularist movement), Domagoj (a Catholic students' movement founded in 1906) and the Croatian Eagle Union (the so-called Orli or Eagles, founded in 1923). The latter was a Roman Catholic youth organization created in response to the liberal Sokol movement, and was headed by the charismatic Ivan Protulipac (1889–1946), known as the "Pope of the Crusaders," and Ivan Merc (1896–1928).

The Domagoj movement was supported by theologians, Franciscans, Dominicans, and the Sisters of Charity in Zagreb and Split, while the Eagles found support in Sarajevo, from some parish priests, Franciscan Conventuals, and Jesuits. After the declaration of the January 6 dictatorship, the Domagoj movement was renamed the "Apostolate of Saints Cyril and Methodius" and the Eagles became known as the "Brotherhood of the Crusaders" (or simply the "Crusaders"; they were also known as the "Protulipac Guard"). The slogan of the former was "God—the Croat Nation—Social Justice." The latter's slogan was "Sacrifice—Eucharist—Apostolate."[43]

THE MUSLIM RELIGIOUS COMMUNITY

The monarchy acknowledged and supported the Muslim religious community as an authentic and powerful organization. Nevertheless, Belgrade's attempts to control the Muslim community, which began immediately after the creation of the Kingdom SHS was proclaimed, were fiercely resisted by the Muslims, who opposed moving the seat of the *reis-ul-ulema* to the capital. The Muslim community lived in three separate regions whose centers were in Sarajevo (for Bosnia-Herzegovina, Croatia, and Slovenia), Belgrade (for Serbia and Macedonia) and Stari Bar (for Montenegro). After the declaration of the dictatorship in 1929, the Muslim community was centralized by royal decree and placed under the control of a central authority, the "Supreme Council of the Muslim Religious Community" in Belgrade, with two regional chapters in Sarajevo and Skopje. The Skopje chapter was composed of five muftiships, while the Sarajevo chapter (the *ulema-medžlis*) was composed of the muftiships of Mostar, Sarajevo, Banja Luka, and Tuzla (two were abrogated).

The council's views were published in the "Gazette of the Supreme Council of the Muslim Religious Community in the Kingdom of Yugoslavia." A new constitution and bill was passed for the Muslim community in 1930. Relations with the community were regulated by the "Muslim Religious Community in the Kingdom of Yugoslavia Act" and the "Constitution of the Muslim Religious Community" of 1936. That same year the Supreme Council was moved to Sarajevo. *Reis-ul-ulema* Mehmed Džemaludin efendi Čaušević was renowned for his relatively broadminded and modernist views.[44] These were strongly opposed by conservative Muslim clergymen and worshippers. When Čaušević stepped down, his place was taken by Ibrahim Maglajlić, a Serb sympathizer.[45] Islamic mysticism (Sufism) was also a major consideration.

Although the level of education of the Muslim Slavs in Bosnia-Herzegovina was improving, they were still poorly represented in the civil service. Only 732 Muslims had a university education at the start of the Second World War.[46] The Muslim educated class were predominately lawyers, professors, and doctors. Only a handful opted for more technical professions. Muslim religious press, education, and culture were gaining ground, and ties had been established with Muslims abroad.

THE "GOLDEN AGE" OF THE YUGOSLAV JEWISH COMMUNITY

There was a well-organized Jewish community in Sarajevo before the Second World War. Indeed, Sarajevo came to be known as "Little Jerusalem" or "New Jerusalem" *(Yerušalayim ketana* or *Yerušalayim chico)*. Its Jewish population numbered around 11,400, mostly Sephardim (only about 13 percent were Ashkenazi), with forty rabbis. There were 13,142 Jews in Bosnia-Herzegovina in 1921, 13,643 in 1926, and 14,710 at the beginning of the Second World War. They lived in Sarajevo, Travnik, Višegrad, Banja Luka, Visoko, Zenica, Zvornik, Žepča, Brčko, Bihać, Bijelina, Bugojno, Jajce, Prijedor, Zvornik, and a number of other towns, and they developed a remarkable artistic, cultural, and intellectual life.[47]

The Federation of Jewish Communities in the Kingdom SHS was founded in 1919 and the "Jewish Religious Community in the Kingdom of Yugoslavia Act" was passed ten years later. This was the religious, cultural, and social "golden age" of the Yugoslav Jews, and a period during which their population was greatest: 64,746 in 1921 and 68,405 ten years later. The chief rabbi between 1923 and 1940 was Isaak Alcalay. In October, 1940, the Cvetković-Maček government followed the example of neighboring and central European countries and passed a series of anti-Semitic laws whose purpose it was to curb Jewish influence on the economy (especially food processing and retailing) and preventing Jews from enrolling in secondary and high schools *(numerus clausus)*.[48] Anti-Semitic publications appeared, strongly attacking the activities of Jewish communities.

COMMON CHARACTERISTICS OF RELIGIOUS COMMUNITIES IN INTERWAR YUGOSLAVIA

Ecclesiastic organizations in the kingdom of Yugoslavia were conflict-ridden, undemocratic, and infused with religious intolerance and animosity. In addition, they had very strong nationalistic ties. This, however, was only strongly expressed in the final years of the monarchy. In stark contrast to this general attitude, Western observers reported having witnessed a high level of mutual tolerance in the relationships between individuals of different religious backgrounds in Bosnia-Herzegovina.[49]

One of the disturbing characteristics of the churches as institutions with national-political ambitions was their preclusive and militant nationalistic clericalism and political conservativism. Anti-Semitism, anticommunism, antiliberalism, antimasonry, and negative stands against other "dangers for the Faith and Nation" on one hand, and an inclination toward fascist, "church-friendly" integration and national exclusivism on the other were common. Patriarch Varnava said in 1937 that "Communism is the worst poison of the World" and that "Adolf Hitler's struggle benefits all the humanity."[50] Ivan Šarić, the Roman Catholic archbishop of Sarajevo and a noted Croat nationalist who emigrated in 1945, is quoted as saying in 1936 that "God is on the side of the Croats," and "how foolish and unworthy of Christians it is to believe that the battle against evil can be fought in a noble and chivalrous manner." Nikolaj Velimirović, a notable Serb theologian and bishop, wrote: "when Welkin sends the war on Earth it is only to raise the look of the Earth to Welkin" and that "war—as all other calamities—invigorates religious consciousness of the men." Thus, war also achieved a "certain eschatological dimension."[51]

7

BELLUM OMNIUM IN OMNES
Politics, National Groups, and Religions in Bosnia-Herzegovina during the Second World War

Long before the 1992–95 war in Bosnia-Herzegovina, the Second World War represented a period of extreme

There can be no turning back!

—A SLOGAN OF THE PARTISAN LIBERATION AND SOCIALIST REVOLUTION IN YUGOSLAVIA

mutual hatred and bloodletting between all three religious groups in Bosnia-Herzegovina, and between Serbs, Croats, and Muslim Slavs in general. The humiliating defeat of the kingdom of Yugoslavia and its total capitulation in a mere eleven days was a disgrace. The country was totally unprepared for war, the armed forces were in a state of decay, there was an effective fifth column in the country, and so forth. The catastrophic rout of the Yugoslav armed forces by the blitzkrieg of the Germans and their allies was not the result of "Croatian treachery," as certain Serb circles alleged, but of several factors. The falsehood of this condemnation is illustrated by the fact that the Serbs dominated the Yugoslav officer corps and that there were no special Croatian units in the army. One of the first people to refute this contention (on May 18, 1941, in the *New York Times*) was the renowned Croatian historian Tomašić, who was known to have political links with Maček and the HSS. The kingdom of Yugoslavia was carved-up by its neighbors—Italy, Germany, Hungary, Bulgaria, and "Italian" Albania—who simply annexed or occupied various parts of the country.

The Independent State of Croatia was created in Zagreb under the patronage of Germany and Italy on April 10, 1941—even before Yugoslavia capitulated—with, in the words of Ustasha general Slavko Kvaternik, "Divine Providence and the will of our allies." The state included the territory of the former Croatian *banovina* (excluding central Dalmatia and

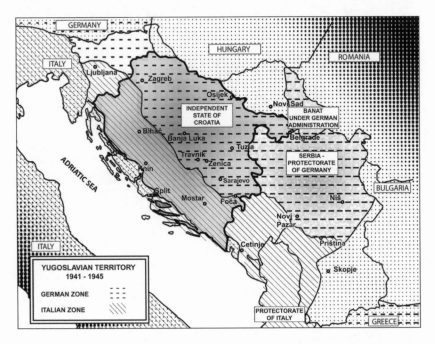

a few islands), the former Vrbaska *banovina*, and the Bosnian and Herze-govinian parts of the Drinska and Zetska *banovinas*, and extended all the way to Zemun to the east. A "border" separating the German and Italian zones ran through the middle of the territory. Its leader was *Poglavnik* Ante Pavelić, who emigrated to Italy after the 1929 coup and organized the Ustasha movement there.

Because of their frustrations with Yugoslavia, the Croats mostly ac-cepted or even welcomed the new independent state; they regarded it as being liberated from "Serb hegemony." However, the criminal preten-sions of the Pavelić regime and the fact that it was a mere stalking-horse soon became apparent. The Croats also found it difficult to accept the Hungarian occupation of Medjimurje and the Italian occupation of large parts of Dalmatia, which the Poglavnik had conceded to Mussolini according to the Rome agreement of May 18, 1941. Like the Croatian *banovina* that preceded it, the Independent State of Croatia was a na-tionally heterogeneous state: of a population of 6.3 million, only 51 per-cent were Croats. The Serbs—including Ante Pavelić's Vlachs and Croats who had converted to Serbian Orthodoxy—comprised 30 percent and the Muslim Slavs 12 percent of the population.[1]

The Ustasha began the mass persecution and slaughter of members of different national and religious groups (Serbs, Jews, and Gypsies) and antifascist Croats soon after the birth of the "independent" state of Croatia. In a speech delivered in Gospić on June 22, 1941, Mile Budak (once a writer), the minister for religious issues and education, made an ominous announcement that he later repeated on several occasions and which his thugs attempted to implement: "one-third of the Serbs in NDH would be expelled, one-third killed, and one-third converted to Catholicism."[2] Such violent policies and murderous actions provoked strong reactions of self-preservation and unprecedented violence on the side of the Serbs and Muslim Slavs, making this by far the most tragic period in Bosnia-Herzegovina's history. The Ustasha's genocidal policy and extremely brutal methods were so shocking that soldiers in the occupying German and Italian armies, which included some of the infamous German SS units, found them nauseating.

The Ustasha authorities tried to create a strong historical foundation for their Croat identity. The name of the currency, the *kuna* (means *marten*; it later became a synonym for worthless money) dated from the Middle Ages. They adopted a medieval coat of arms, the so-called chessboard that has been used as a Croatian symbol for centuries. The new Croatian state also had its ancient "historical borders" restored. The Ustasha leadership formally declared a monarchy and invited King Tomislav II—Prince Aimon d'Aosta of the House of Savoy, duke of Spoleto, and nephew of King Emmanuel III of Italy—to assume the throne. The new "paper" king, who was offered the "Crown of Zvonimir," never actually set foot on Croatian soil. The Ustasha also claimed that the Croats were "pure Aryans" of Gothic or Persian descent, as distinguished from the Slavs and the "Semitic and Indid peoples." Clergyman Kerubin Šegvić, for example, proposed a theory on the Gothic origin of the Croat nation, and Pavelić himself stated that Croats were not Slavs but racially appertained to Germanism.[3]

Fascist tendencies emerged among Serb extremists as well. Some were well developed in Serbian political life already in 1930s.[4] Historian Vladimir Dedijer notes that they also used Hitler's annihilating methods against Muslims and Croats. A German protectorate was created in the diminished territory of Serbia and was governed first by ex-Belgrade police chief Milan Aćimović and then from August, 1941, until October, 1944, by former general and defense minister Milan Nedić. The regime, which was ideologically Nazi-oriented, collaborated with the Germans: its gendarmes and other armed forces were involved in active antipartisan activities, ethnic cleansing, and the annihilation of Serbian Jews and anti-Fascists of all nationalities in Serbian concentration camps (for example, Banjica and Sajmište). In August, 1941, many prominent Serbs and high dignitaries of the church openly called for loyalty to the Nazi occupiers. During the war, Nedić advocated the creation of Greater Serbia, which would include—besides Serbia proper—the Dalmatian coast, almost all of Bosnia-Herzegovina and Vojvodina, Eastern Slavonia, Macedonia, Montenegro, and part of Albania.[5] However, the Germans never fully trusted Nedić's regime.

The Chetnik movement had a long history of waging guerrilla wars against foreign rulers and violent campaigns against ethnic and religious "enemies," from the first Serbian uprising in 1804 on. It can rightly be considered as continuity with Great Serbian politics—as Philip J. Cohen puts it—"in both its goals (the expansion of Serbia and assimilation or elimination of non-Serb population) and its methods (terror and genocide)."[6] But compared to the well-organized and coordinated Ustasha, the Chetnik movement and its forces were much more amorphous, crumbled into territorial units that disabled their more efficient actions and also left to the self-will of local commanders.[7] In the first months of the war—until November, 1941—some Chetnik units fought together with partisan forces against the Germans. From that time on, however, they decided in favor of hidden or open collaboration with the occupation forces. Their activities varied from antipartisan, anti-Croat, and anti-Muslim politics and propaganda to military actions and ethnic-cleansing operations.

On the other hand, they received moral support and material aid from Western allies as fighters against fascist forces until early 1944. However, all Chetnik groups had a common Great Serbian and royalist goal. Dragoljub (Draža) Mihajlović (1893–1946), the most important Chetnik royalist leader and minister of war in the royal government from January, 1942, made no effort to conceal his intention of preserving Yugoslavia's prewar social order. "Serbian lands," however, would be cleansed of all non-Serbs. The Chetnik directive of December 20, 1941, foresaw the creation of "an 'ethnically pure' Greater Serbia, consisting of Serbia, Macedonia, Montenegro, Bosnia-Herzegovina, and Vojvodina, 'cleansed of all national minorities.'" The notion of cleansing "Bosnia of everything that is not Serb" was discussed at the Chetnik conference held near Kotor Varoš in June, 1942.[8]

The Chetnik attitude toward the Muslim Slavs in Bosnia-Herzegovina during the war was a fanatically nationalistic one: They believed the country should be annexed by Serbia and that all non-Serbs should be cleansed from the area. Indeed, this was the ideology advocated by the two leading intellectuals of the Chetnik movement, Dragiša Vasić (killed at Jasenovac in 1945) and Stevan Moljević, who published their ideas in the memorandum of June, 1941, entitled "Homogeneous Serbia," which would include "Bosnia-Herzegovina, Montenegro, Macedonia, Kosovo, Vojvodina, most of Croatia, northern (and possibly all of) Albania, and parts of Bulgaria, Romania, and Hungary as well as Serbia proper." In achieving it, the plan of "cleansing the lands of all non-Serb elements" was proposed.[9]

The first mass atrocities against non-Serbs in Bosnia-Herzegovina and other ethnically heterogeneous territories were committed late in the spring of 1941. The Muslims, especially in eastern Bosnia, were branded as "Turks" and "Ustasha cronies." The result was that few Muslims joined Chetnik initiatives, organizations, or military units. The most notable exception were Ismet Pupovac, Fuad Musakadić, and Mustafa Mulagić, a member of the "National Council." By December, 1943, up to 8 percent of Mihailović's Chetniks were Muslims.[10]

A number of important Chetnik commanders operated in the Independent State of Croatia, including Duke *(vojvoda)* Ilija Trifunović-Birčanin (Mihajlović appointed him commander of Dalmatia, Herzegovina, western Bosnia, and southwestern Croatia; he was replaced by Lt. Col. Mladen Žujović following his death in February, 1943), self-proclaimed Duke Dobroslav Jevdjević, Maj. Boško Todorović (the Chetnik delegate for Bosnia-Herzegovina), the self-proclaimed duke of northern Dalmatia and Orthodox priest Momčilo Đujić, Lt. Col. Ilija Mihić, Maj. Slavko Bjelajac, and Lt. Col. Petar Baćović (Herzegovina, southeastern Bosnia).[11] The Chetniks in the Italian zone of influence were actively supported by Italian troops, who considered them a useful force against partisan resistance. Despite their anti-Croat attitude, Chetnik politicians and commanders continued to endorse pragmatic agreements concerning coordinated actions against the common enemy with both the Croatian state and the Nedić regime in Serbia.

In the autumn of 1942 the Chetniks embarked on a plan known as the "March on Bosnia," the aim of which was to surround and conquer the territory taken by the partisans in order to secure control of the interior of the country in the event the Allies invaded Dalmatia. The Chetniks did not begin openly collaborating with the Germans until after Italy, which had provided them with arms and equipment, capitulated. A special phrase was invented for this kind of collaboration: "the use of the enemy." German general Alexander Löhr described this unpleasant cooperation between German troops and the Chetniks (which, however, was exclusive of any political negotiation) as a "necessary evil."[12]

The Chetniks believed that the internal ideological enemy, the partisan movement and neighboring nations, Croats, and Muslims, posed a much greater threat than the occupying army. In February, 1943, Mihailović openly admitted to a British colonel that the Chetniks' principal enemies were—in order—"the partisans, Ustashas, the Muslims, the Croats, and last the Germans and Italians." Despite German support, the Chetniks' opportunistic attention and internal divisions contributed to their inefficiency and eventual defeat. This situation, according to Jozo Tomashevich, an expert on the Chetnik movement, was the result of its Greater Serbia orientation (making it of no interest to any other southern Slavs except Montenegrins) and its increasingly apparent collaboration with the occupiers throughout the country.[13]

ROMAN CATHOLIC CLERGY IN THE INDEPENDENT STATE OF CROATIA

Archbishop Stepinac met Gen. Slavko Kvaternik on April 12, 1941, and "congratulated him for the formation of NDH" even before Yugoslavia formally capitulated (on April 17). On April 16, he met with Pavelić, but "never took an oath of allegiance either to the NDH or to Pavelić personally, unlike some of the other bishops."[14] In the beginning, the Roman Catholic Church in Croatia embraced the new regime without reservation. In a circular issued on April 28, 1941, Stepinac cautioned that "in building the foundations for the new State of Croatia, pious zeal and noble enthusiasm must be inspired by the fear of and love for God's Laws and His Commandments." In the *Catholic Gazette (Katolički list)* of April 21, it was written that the NDH was created through "God's providence." Stepinac and most of the clergy did not show "the caution which the Holy See always exercises towards changes in jurisdiction brought about the war."[15] In this respect they often acted hastily, carelessly, and in a politically shortsighted manner.

The creation of the Independent State of Croatia on April 10, 1941, co-incided with two religious feasts, adding to the singularity of the ongoing events in Croatia. Firstly, the pope declared in May, 1940, that the "Holy Year of the Croat Nation" would begin on June 29 and last for one year. The festivities were expected to take place in Split and Solin and end with a Eucharistic congress and a mass pilgrimage to Rome. Secondly, the thirteen-hundredth anniversary of the first contact between Croats and the Holy See was commemorated in March, 1941. The Catholic press covered both religious events and concluded that it was, in fact, the Roman Catholic Church that had been the spiritual guide of the Croat nation through the centuries: Croatia had "remained loyal," *Croatia semper fidelis*, throughout this period, and the Croat nation was a "godly nation, devoted to the Saviour Jesus Christ and His Church, which is built on Peter's rock." Indeed, many people regarded the creation of the new Croatian state as having taken place within the context of these events: "This is the Lord's doing; it is marvelous in our eyes," wrote Stepinac to the clergy on April, 28.[16] In the editorial of the May, 1941, issue of the journal *Katolički tjednik (Catholic Weekly)*, Bishop Šarić wrote that the Holy Virgin appeared to the Croats as a sign *(signum in cielo)*: "Our Lady came to visit Her Croatia."[17]

Religious issues became part of the Ustasha regime's policy. Although there are some clear indications that Pavelić was anticlerical and that he was not particularly tied either to the church or the Holy See, he and other leaders emphasized Croatia's Roman Catholic propensity: the Poglavnik and his ministers took an oath to "God the Almighty and Omniscient."[18] In July, 1941, Budak announced that "our whole work is based on our fidelity to the Church and the Catholic faith, for history teaches us that if we had not been Catholic, we should soon have ceased to exist." The old Catholic Church of Croatia was abrogated, the Jewish community was decimated, and the Serbian Orthodox Church was declared a political and national organization that had no business being in Croatia. Orthodoxy was officially referred to as the "eastern and Greek religion," and the Cyrillic alphabet was banned. Special legal prohibitions and restrictions were introduced for the Serbian and Jewish populations.[19]

The state commenced a moral campaign in which mendicancy, vagrancy, and prostitution were banned; profanity was punishable by imprisonment (one month for the first offence and two months for the next), as was working on Sundays or public holidays; mixed marriages and certain authors were banned; and abortion was punishable by death. The state embarked on an ambitious plan to convert all non-Catholics in Croatia. All of these, however, were state policies and had nothing officially to do with the Roman Catholic hierarchy, although a number of clergymen were actively involved in the project and its dignitaries were constantly informed what was going on.

The Ustasha regime found three solutions to the "problem" of Orthodox living on their territory: slaughter, persecution, or expulsion; conversion to Catholicism; and the creation of a Croatian Orthodox Church. Because Orthodoxy was considered a threat to Catholicism and Islam, the Ustasha dealt with it first (together with the annihilation of Jews and Gypsies). In line with the policy of "Croatizing" and "Catholicizing" the country, the vast majority of Serbian Orthodox clergymen in Croatia were brutally murdered or expelled; property belonging to the Orthodox

Church was confiscated, and 299 churches were torched. All told, a quarter of all churches and monasteries were destroyed and half were damaged during a four-year period in the territory of the former Yugoslavia. The worst recorded cases were in the Karlovac diocese, where 175 of 237 churches and chapels were destroyed and only fourteen remained functional.[20]

The Serbian Orthodox Church in Croatia—nine dioceses in all—practically ceased to exist. There were 577 Orthodox priests, monks, and other religious dignitaries in Croatia in April, 1941. By the end of the year there were none left: 214 (or 217) were murdered, 334 were exiled to Serbia (by the autumn of 1941), eighteen fled there of their own accord, three were detained, and five died of natural causes. Three bishops who refused to leave were murdered: Sava Trljajić (1884–1941) from Sremski Karlovci, Platon Jovanović (1874–1941) from Banja Luka and Petar Zimonjić (1866–1941) from the diocese of Dabar-Bosna (Sarajevo); in Serbia, bishops Nikolaj Jovanović from Zahum-Herzegovina and Nektarije Krulj from Zvornik-Tuzla were ostracized; Bishop Irinej Djordjević went into exile in Italy. Dositej Vasić, the metropolite of Zagreb, died in 1945 in a Belgrade hospital as a result of wounds inflicted during torture in a Ustasha dungeon before he was banished to Serbia.[21]

In mid-May, 1941, the Ustasha regime introduced a new and simpler procedure for conversion to Roman Catholicism (without consulting the church). Mass conversion was entrusted to the religious affairs department of the "Ministry of Justice and Religious Affairs," under Minister Radoslav Glavaš, a Franciscan monk. The auxiliary bishop of Zagreb, Josip Lach, immediately condemned the move but was largely ignored by the Croatian government, which announced the introduction of the new regulations in July and began recruiting individual priests to carry out the conversions without the official permission of their bishops (which were, however, well informed about the course of events).

By 1943 between two hundred thousand and three hundred thousand Serb and Gypsy "schismatics" had been converted, thus escaping certain death or banishment. There were, however, some cases in which even converted Serbs were massacred after the ritual. The Ustasha authorities considered the conversion of the Serbs a "priceless gift to the Holy See." Nikola Rusinović, the unofficial representative of the Independent State of Croatia to the Vatican (eventually succeeded by Duke Lobkowicz), used the same expression. It was described as the "rectification of past errors, the return to the only true Church, the return of the schismatics to the true faith," and sometimes simply as "evangelization." The Ustasha regime openly supported the theory proposed by clergyman Krunoslav

Draganović that many Catholics converted to Orthodoxy under Otto-man rule and their reconversion to Catholicism was simply a "return to the faith of their fathers."

The conversion of Orthodox Serbs followed three basic rules. First was acceptance of Roman (Latin) Catholicism, not the eastern Uniate ver-sion. Church representatives and Stepinac himself suggested to Pavelić that converts might feel more at home as Uniates, but the idea was re-jected.[22] Second was the annihilation of the Orthodox intelligentsia. The third was conversion of only the uneducated masses. Sarajevo became the center of the Ustasha Catholic conversion campaign. Priests and mainly Bosnian and Herzegovinian Franciscan monks recruited by the Ustasha conducted the rites. However, they were still members of the church hierarchy.[23]

The Episcopal conference led by Archbishop Stepinac had a specific opinion about it. First, he sent a circular letter—which the state obvi-ously ignored—on May 8, 1941, in which he imposed a series of condi-tions for the possible conversions to Catholicism.[24] Second, on Novem-ber 20, 1941, he wrote a letter to Pavelić sanctioning nonviolent proselytizing: the voluntary and humane religious conversion to the Ro-man Catholic faith in accordance with a precise and complicated set of rules based on canonical law and under the supervision of bishops and others in the Catholic hierarchy. These procedures were applied, but in far lesser numbers than the "statal" mass conversions. Converts from the Orthodox faith to the Roman Catholic Church officially became Croats. Stepinac did not protest the conversions per se, but the brutal methods ("acts of irresponsible elements," "brutality of some individu-als," "excesses of young non-expers," and the "cruelty of Ustasha offi-cers") with which the state carried them out. As he wrote in the above-mentioned letter, it was because of those methods that "the conversions of the Orthodox could not develop in such measure and with such suc-cess which would be achieved if they would be avoided."[25]

The third method of "solving the problem" of the Orthodox living in Croatia was the creation of the "Croatian Orthodox Church" of April 7, 1942, by Ustasha authorities. It would be—according to the auto-cephalous principle of Orthodox churches—the organization of "Ortho-dox Croats" living in NDH. Hermogen (or Germogen) Maksimov (1861–1945), a former bishop of the Russian Orthodox Church from Yekateri-noslav who had lived in exile in Sremski Karlovci since the Bolshevik Revolution, was appointed by Pavelić—"by the Grace of God"—to head the new church at the age of eighty-one.[26] He made an oath of allegiance to Pavelić after he was enthroned. The Croatian Orthodox Church included the Metropolitan See and eparchy of Zagreb and the eparchies of Sarajevo (for eastern Bosnia and Herzegovina), Petrovac (for Lika, Istria, and northern and central Dalmatia), and Brod (for Slavonia).

Its symbol consisted of the Orthodox cross on Croatia's red and white "chessboard" shield. In August, 1944, Pavelić appointed Spiridon Mifka, a disgraced and already suspended Orthodox clergyman, as bishop of Sarajevo. Although the Serbian Orthodox Church denounced the Croatian Orthodox Church, a handful of surviving Serbian Orthodox priests (about seventy, including also some Russian priests) joined the church in order to survive and protect the remaining Orthodox living in the Independent State of Croatia.[27]

Support for the Ustasha regime came mainly from the lower ranks of the church and mainly from young clergymen. Senior Catholic clergymen were mostly more pro-Yugoslav oriented. Pavelić admitted this to the German and Italian foreign ministers, Joachim von Ribbentrop and Count Galeazzo Ciano, adding that although the lower clergy were cooperating, certain bishops, including Stepinac himself, were "openly hostile" to his regime. Indeed, canon Josip Lončar, a senior church official known for his anti-Ustasha stand, was sentenced to death by the regime for protesting the persecution and forced conversions of Serbs in the summer of 1941; the sentence was later commuted to 20 years imprisonment.[28]

However, criticism of the Ustasha crimes by senior Catholic clergymen was, at best, cautious and tepid. It rarely went beyond a feeble grumbling about the methods used by the Ustasha regime and not the mass persecution itself. Here are a few examples: Bishop Alojzije Mišić of Mostar, a Franciscan, shocked by the atrocities committed by the Ustasha (including the mass murder of the Orthodox population living in and around Žitomislići and the monks from the nearby monastery), reported the matter to Stepinac in the summer and autumn of 1941. Mišić preferred the "re-Catholicization of the schismatics" to their extermination. For him, "Thanks to God today we have a chance like never before to help the Croatian cause, to save great number of souls, men of goodwill, peaceful peasants who live among the Catholics. . . . The conversion is easy and acceptable."[29] He issued a circular to his clergy explicitly instructing them that there was to be no absolution for the murderers and looters. The persecution of the Serbs was also criticized by Josip Ujčić, the Roman Catholic bishop of Belgrade (from 1936–64). Bishop Antun Akšamović of Djakovo publicly appealed to the Serbs "to convert to Catholicism in order to save their lives," adding that they could "re-convert to Orthodoxy after the war was over."[30]

On the other hand, much of the Ustasha clero-fascist rhetoric (such as "God and the Croats!" or "For Croatia and Christ against the Communists," or "Faith in God and peasants' unity") and symbolism (a cross within the capital U, the sign of the Ustasha) were connected with militant and nationalistic elements of Croatian Catholicism. Ustasha oaths were made over the same items employed in the Serbian "Black Hand" extremist group's initiation: a crucifix, dagger (sometimes also a hand grenade), and pistol.[31] Many Croat priests and monks were members of or sympathized with the Ustasha movement even before the war. They imported Ustasha ideology to Croatia from Italy and other foreign countries that welcomed and even supported the Ustasha. For example, Ivo Guberina, a priest, stated that Ustasha's "revolutionary activity is in maximal harmony with the Catholic morality."[32] Archbishop Šarić of Sarajevo joined the Ustasha movement as early as in 1934 and made trip to Ustasha bases in South America. On Christmas Day 1941 he dedicated a panegyric in praise of the Poglavnik in the *Katolićki list*, glorifying him as a "wondrous Ustasha" *(ustaša divni)* and likening him to "Zrinjski." The following verses are from his exaltation:

> Dr. Ante Pavelić, dear is his name,
> He is Croatia's heavenly treasure,
> May He, the King of Heaven, always watch over you,
> Our dear leader![33]

One of the Ustasha's main goals, announced even before the war began, was cleansing "greater Croatia" of Orthodox Serbs. Several leading Ustasha officials were educated at Franciscan parochial schools (mostly in Široki Brijeg), including Andrija Artuković (a Herzegovinian), Jozo Dumandžić, and Glavaš.[34]

A number of pro-Ustasha priests and Franciscan monks serving as chaplains to Ustasha units participated in atrocities against non-Croats. The most infamous of these was Miroslav Filipović (he also used the name Majstorović), a mass-murderer from Jasenovac nicknamed the "Evil Monk" and "Satanic Friar." A former Franciscan monk, he had been banished from the order in May, 1942. Other Franciscans and clergymen who were Ustasha officers or members of Ustasha military units included Vjekoslav Šimić, Zvonimir Brekalo, Josip Vukelić, Ivan Miletić, Dionizije Juričev, Stjepan Naletilić, Petar Berković, Jerko Eterović, Božidar Bralo and Djuro Marić. The Franciscans expelled two other monks, Justin Medić and Hinko Prlić, who worked as chaplains for the Ustasha.[35] Partisan, British, Vatican, and Italian sources confirm that the members of Catholic clergy in Croatia and Bosnia-Herzegovina were involved not only in military operations some of them also in atrocities against non-Catholic population.

Other clergymen who actively supported the Ustasha regime were Stipe Vucetić and Vilim Cecelja, both military chaplains, and Ivo Guberina, one of the leading Ustasha ideologues and a member of the movement until 1940. Stepinac dismissed him from the priesthood in 1943. Some journals and editions of the Catholic press of the day were ardently pro-Ustasha. The *Katolički list* was particularly zealous in its support for the NDH, applauding it as "Zvonimir's Croatia restored" and adding, "our Poglavnik with his government walks in Zvonimir's footsteps."[36] Archbishop Šarić openly approved the Ustasha conversion program. Zealous anti-Communist church dignitaries (in addition to Stepinac) were Franciscan Bishop Josip Stjepan Garić of Banja Luka (from 1913–45); Antun Akšamović, a bishop from Djakovo; and Janko Šimrak, a Uniate bishop from Križevci.

Archbishop Stepinac maintained ties with the Ustasha regime throughout the war, holding services on the anniversary of the founding of the state and on Pavelić's birthday. Nevertheless, he did not hesitate to criticize the Ustasha's crimes, and he offered help to the victims and refugees on several occasions. Stepinac condemned the persecution of Jews and the massacres in Glina and in Herzegovina beginning in the spring 1941, but his initial protests were faint, personal, and ineffective.[37] In 1942 he more forcefully and precisely condemned the atrocities and pogroms against the Serbs and others, the systematic demolition of Orthodox churches, and denounced "the injustices and false ideology of the NDH."[38] In February, 1943, after seven Catholic priests had been killed in Jasenovac, Stepinac wrote to Pavelić, calling the extermination camp a "shameful stain for the Independent State of Croatia."[39]

In a letter dated May 22, 1941, Stepinac told the authorities: "anti-Semitic legislation and similar measures against the Serbs etc. are carried out in such a way that the human personality and dignity are respected." However, appalled by the regime's criminal policies, he publicly rejected racist doctrine on March 14, 1943. He made a similar statement at the feast of Christ the King on October 25, 1943: "all men and all races are children of God. One cannot exterminate Gypsies or Jews because one considers them of an inferior race." On October 31, 1943, he declared, "We have always asserted in public life the principles of the eternal Divine order, irrespective if it was for Croats, Serbs, Jews, Gypsies, Catholics, Muslims, Orthodox or any other."[40]

Instead of looking for the real culprits, Stepinac sought to lay the blame elsewhere. In June, 1943, he declared that the war and evil are a "righteous punishment from God" for amassed sins, including fornication, a non-Christian codex, abortion, contraception, alcoholism, falsehood, deception, and for dishonoring Sundays and feast days. All these sins apparently "called upon Heaven for revenge." He found himself more and more disappointed with Pavelić's regime, as did the large majority of the people.[41]

In the spring of 1942 Stepinac told Stanislav Rapotec, a Slovenian captain who worked for British intelligence, that he believed in a renewed, federalist postwar Yugoslavia, and that he was collaborating with the Ustasha regime only in order to save people's lives and prevent matters from deteriorating. The Germans murdered Stepinac's brother in November, 1943, for engaging in partisan activities, and his mother supplied food to the partisan forces. Stepinac intervened on behalf of the victims through Interior Minister Andrija Artuković, regardless of their national, religious, or political affiliation. His intervention on behalf of Serbs, Gypsies, antifascist Croats, Polish and Slovenian refugees, and the children and orphans of Communists and partisans, Orthodox, and Jews are well documented. His efforts saved many thousands of lives.[42]

Ustasha leaders were unhappy with Stepinac because of his anti-Nazi stands (his rejection of racist theories and his persistent criticism, for example) and threatened to arrest him. He told sculptor Ivan Meštrović that he would be murdered either by the Ustasha or the Communists, and that "our Fascists [the Ustasha]" had threatened his life. O'Brien notes that the Germans and Ustasha considered him an "Anglophile Archbishop" and a "partisanophile." According to Ustasha general Slavko Kvaternik, Pavelić and the Ustasha regime disliked the archbishop. They even tried three times to persuade the Holy See to recall Stepinac from his position. The auxiliary bishop of Zagreb, Franjo Salis Sewis, confirmed that relations between Stepinac and Pavelić were "tense" from the beginning. A rumor spread that Ustasha leaders had already decided to arrest Stepinac but then later reversed their decision.[43]

Being an important and influential institution in Croatian and Bosnian society at the time, it could be said that the church deserves some of the blame because of its mostly passive and indifferent attitude and its failure to do more to prevent the atrocities, persecution, and mass slaughter committed in the NDH, and because of its active or passive support of the regime. The church reacted vigorously against it on only a few occasions. Stepinac and the Catholic press declared that the Croats were suffering disproportionately and that they were, once again, the *antemurale Christianitatis.*

The Vatican also acted in an ambiguous way. On one hand, Pope Pius XII (1939–58) granted a private audience to Pavelić, who was a renowned criminal and terrorist even before the war, and the Croatian king, the Duke of Spoleto, on May 18, 1941.[44] Stepinac declined an invitation to attend. But on the other hand, despite the efforts of the Croatian authorities, the Vatican did not *de iure* officially recognize the NDH, as it had Jozef Tiso's allied state of Slovakia. Instead, the Vatican maintained contact with the exiled Yugoslav government. Only the Axis countries and their puppet states (Germany, Italy, Japan, Slovakia, Bulgaria, Rumania, and Spain) officially recognized Croatia. Diplomatic efforts by Pavelić, the king, and a special emissary, Kerubin Šegvić, to gain Vatican recognition for the NDH were in vain. The only Vatican representative in Croatia was Abbot Ramiro Marcone of Monte Cassino, accompanied by his secretary, Don Giuseppe Carmelo Masucci. Marcone, who was not in the Vatican's diplomatic service, was an Apostolic Visitor to the church in Croatia and had no official contact with the state.

An Episcopal conference (more precisely, a meeting between Catholic bishops from Croatia) was held in late March, 1945—the first since November, 1941. In a pastoral letter issued by the conference, the bishops denied allegations that the Catholic Church was responsible for atrocities committed during the war; they promised to bring clergymen involved in any of the crimes to justice; they announced that they were against "materialistic communism"; they expressed Croatian aspirations for freedom and independence; and they protested against the use of violence. Shortly before the collapse of his regime, Pavelić begged Stepinac to head an interim government, but the latter refused, saying he had no intention of getting involved in politics and that he was determined to remain at his station in Zagreb. The Poglavnik fled to Austria, then Italy, and from there, with the help of emigrant Croatian clergymen, to Argentina and Chile. He tried to establish an Ustasha organization among the Croatian diaspora but found it difficult to do so. On April 10, 1957—the sixteenth anniversary of the establishment of the NDH—he left Argentina after a failed assassination attempt in Buenos Aires. He died in Madrid on December 28, 1959.[45]

THE TRIBULATIONS OF THE SERBIAN ORTHODOX CHURCH

Patriarch Gavrilo complained bitterly to the regent, Prince Paul, about the pact with the Axis powers and broadcast an appeal to Serbs to remain true to the ideals and traditions of their nation and church. A few days later, the Serbian Orthodox Church welcomed the coup d'état, and the patriarch broadcast an enthusiastic statement for Belgrade radio.[46] Before the outbreak of war in April, the patriarch had instructed his bishops to remain at their stations in the event of war; after it began, he gave his blessing to the fleeing king. The Germans imprisoned the patriarch and subjected him to mistreatment, which caused his health to deteriorate and required his removal to Rakovica and the Vojlovica monastery near Belgrade. He refused to collaborate with them to the very end. In August, 1944, at the age of sixty-seven—after being moved from one German concentration camp to another—he was sent to Dachau together with Bishop Nikolaj Velimirović, a notable Serb theologian and writer from Žiča.

In the patriarch's absence, a holy synod composed of Bishops Emilijan Piperković of Timok, Jovan Ilić of Niš, Nektarije Krulj of Zvornik-Tuzla, and Irinej Čirić of Bačka headed the church. The acting patriarch, Metropolite Josif Cvijović, was not a member of the synod, although the church constitution required that the synod's most senior member assume the position. The synod met with the patriarch on July 7, 1941, and issued a statement calling for—among other urgent issues—the public to obey German laws and cooperate with the occupiers, and to remain calm and submissive. The postwar Socialist authorities used this message as proof that the Serbian Orthodox Church collaborated with the Germans.[47]

In addition to the persecution of Serbs in the NDH, the Serbian Orthodox Church was persecuted elsewhere in the Balkans and in central Europe as well. Its clergymen and both bishops in Macedonia were banished to Serbia, as was Bishop Vladimir Rajić of Mukašev-Prjašev (in what was formerly Czechoslovakia). Albania banished Bishop Serafim of Raška-Prizren to Tirana, where he died in January, 1945. Hungarian army forces also murdered many Serbs, including seven Orthodox priests. The Orthodox Church reacted immediately to these losses and appointed new bishops and priests to the vacancies. Bishop Vikentije went to Žiča, and Bishop Krulj was placed in charge of four dioceses in Croatia and elsewhere. However, the appointments, especially those in Croatia, were often only titular. The new appointees reported atrocities committed by Croatian, Hungarian, Albanian, and Bulgarian authorities to the German military administration in Belgrade. In July and August, 1941, they asked the Germans to put an end to the persecution of Serbs in those territories. They also kept the international public informed about events through their ties with the exiled Yugoslav government and the Western allies.

The Orthodox Church was antifascist and nationalist in nature, but it was more inclined to the Chetniks than to the partisans. According to some estimates, "roughly three quarters of Yugoslavia's Serbian Ortho-dox priests supported the Chetniks throughout the war."[48] Some, like Savo Božić, even fought on their side. The most renowned of them was Duke Momčilo Đujić, the Orthodox priest and Chetnik who served as commandant of the Dinaric Division, which was formed in Croatia in the spring of 1942.

High-ranking church representatives adopted historical slogans such as "Only harmony saves the Serbs," or "We are all Serbs, parts of one body, united by one faith, Orthodoxy, by one language, by blood, by our cele-brated past, that we are descendants of the celebrated saints, St Sava, St Simeon, St Prince Lazar and the two heroes Miloš and Marko." The Nedić regime and German occupiers were unhappy with, as they put it, the church's "two-faces," especially their lack of cooperation. Like Patriarch Gavrilo before him, Metropolite Josif refused to cooperate with either. This upright wartime posture of Gavrilo and Nikola Velimirović gained them the respect of the Serbs and turned them into symbols of patriotism and courage, although the close personal friendship between Velimirović and the militant Serbian fascist leader Ljotić compromised him.[49]

MUSLIM DISCORD

During the interwar period, Bosnian Muslims had been more inclined toward Zagreb than Belgrade, and it came as no surprise that some Mus-lim civic and religious leaders welcomed the creation of the Independent State of Croatia. Others were more skeptical and "counted on Bosnia and Herzegovina becoming a German protectorate."[50] In April, 1941, Pavelić promised the Muslims full civil rights, including religious rights and the right to education. The Ustasha coaxed Bosnian Muslims, calling them "Muslim Croats" or the "blossom of Croatia." Mile Budak, a writer and minister for culture and education, referred to the Muslims as the "purest of Croats." The Poglavnik referred to them as "brothers of the purest Croat blood." He was also convinced that the "Croat national con-sciousness never was extinguished in the Muslim element of Bosnia, and after the departure of the Turks has resurfaced."[51] NDH became a coun-try of two religions: on the country's first anniversary, Pavelić posed for a photograph wearing a Muslim fez, "symbolic of Croatian unity with the Muslims."[52]

Some Muslims from the religious ranks, members of the JMO leader-ship, part of the Young Muslims group, and part of the general population collaborated with the Ustasha regime by accepting appointments to dif-ferent levels of the state government. For example, Spaho's successor,

Džafer *beg* Kulenović, replaced his brother, Osman Kulenović, as vice president of the NDH even though he did not believe in the Ustasha ideology. Mehmed Alajbegović was appointed foreign minister, and Muslims took several seats in the national assembly in Zagreb. Among the prewar JMO politicians, Ademaga Mešić became the *Ustasha Doglavnik*, and Hakija Hadžić was appointed "commissioner" for Bosnia. Some Muslim clerics served as imams (so-called *tabor imami)* in the NDH armed forces. The most important was the "Ustasha Mufti," Col. Akif Handžić. The Muslims comprised approximately 12 percent of the civil service and NDH armed forces.[53] Muslim collaborators were responsible for a number of atrocities against Serbs in eastern Herzegovina and southeastern Bosnia.

Džafer beg Kulenović publicly declared (as did some other Muslims) that Bosnia-Herzegovina's Muslim Slavs were Croats as, indeed, was he. Atif Hadžikadić in 1942 labeled them to be "descendants of the old Croatian nobility." That same year, Kasim Gajić wrote that they were Croats by their "feeling, language, traditions, and origins." To flatter Bosnian Muslims, Pavelić ordered that three minarets be added to the Meštrović pavilion in Zagreb, which was converted into a mosque during the war. It came to be referred to as the "Poglavnik's Mosque."[54] However, the Ustasha regime's generosity toward Muslims was purely coincidental. Bosnia-Herzegovina was an integral part of the NDH; it had no autonomy whatsoever. The new Croatian state was divided into twenty-two provinces or "Great *župas*" *(Velike župe),* of which six were in Bosnia-Herzegovina (centered in Sarajevo, Tuzla, Travnik, Banja Luka, Bihać, and Mostar). But some parts of the country were simply added to neighboring *župas.* They were administered by Muslim Great *župans.* In general, though, the share of Muslim civil servants and state officials was very low.[55]

The persecution of Muslims and Croats by Serbian nationalists in Bosnia-Herzegovina compelled many Muslims to join the Ustasha army, independent militias such as the "Muslim Volunteer Legion" (1942), "Huska's Army" (1943), "Hadžiefendić's Legion" (until October, 1943), and the partisan movement, and to seek the patronage of the occupying armies. Yet, collaboration with the Germans was not only a response to persecutions, but also a result of the pro-Nazi orientation of some Muslims, who also believed that Bosnia-Herzegovina should be given internal autonomy under direct German rule.

Initiatives were followed by concrete actions. At Heinrich Himmler's command—and with assistance from the Grand Mufti of Jerusalem, Hajj Amin Al-Husseini, an Anglophobe and Nazi sympathizer who likened pan-Islamism to Ustasha ideological myths—the special 13th SS Division, known as the Handžar (Dagger) Division, was formed in the spring of 1943. Its ranks were filled with pro-Nazi Muslims (and also some Croats) from Bosnia-Herzegovina, mostly volunteers. Himmler, encouraged by the grand mufti, was attempting to find a link between Islam and Nazism. The division numbered thirteen thousand men in 1943 and was under direct German command: almost all of the officers were German. Some muftis and imams helped with recruiting efforts; there were also imams in the division's units. The division, which was viewed with great suspicion by the Ustasha military command, was responsible for several atrocities against Serbian and Jewish civilians.[56]

Most Bosnian Muslims, however, rejected the Croatian annexation of their country. None of the Poglavnik's promises were fulfilled. The Muslims were suspicious of attempts to "Croatize Islam," the creation of a homogeneous state, and the enforcement of Croat national identity. They also feared conversion to Catholicism. By the summer and autumn of 1941, Muslim clergymen from all of the major towns in Bosnia-Herzegovina were publicly protesting against the violence being committed against Orthodox Serbs and others. They distanced themselves from and condemned Muslims involved in criminal acts, and collected and published data about the violence being committed against Muslims. Several resolutions (the Banja Luka, Sarajevo, Prijedor, Mostar, Tuzla, and Bijeljina Resolutions) were signed by religious leaders and representatives of the major Bosnian Muslim associations: El Hidaje, Narodna Uzadnica, the Hurijet craft organization, and various Muslim societies such as Merhamet, El Kamer, Bratstvo, and others.[57]

In the winter of 1942–43, a group of leading Bosnian Muslim politicians, religious dignitaries, and businessmen (the most important among them was Uzeir Hadžihasanović) addressed a memorandum directly to Hitler in which they expressed their dissatisfaction with the Ustasha regime and their aspiration for an autonomous Bosnia-Herzegovina. They also objected to the persecution of Serbs and Muslims in Croatia. The group's representatives denied that Bosnian Muslims were Slavs, claiming that they were actually a tribe of Goths known as the Bosni that came to the region when the Balkans were part of the Roman province of Illyria in the third century.[58] Muhamed Pandža, a senior clergyman from Sarajevo who was in favor of an independent Bosnia-Herzegovina "with equal rights for all citizens, regardless of their religion," made a similar proposal in November, 1943.[59]

Some of the most vicious battles and bloodiest episodes of the Second World War in occupied Yugoslavia took place in Bosnia-Herzegovina. It thus is not surprising that the number of war victims was higher there than in any other of the postwar Yugoslav republics: 316,000 dead (compared to 273,000 in Serbia and 271,000 in Croatia).[60] The death toll in Bosnia was 164,000 Serbs, 75,000 Muslims, and 64,000 Croats.

THE ANNIHILATION OF THE JEWS

Of all the religious communities in Bosnia-Herzegovina (and in the entire territory of prewar Yugoslavia), the Jews suffered the most. German Nazis, other foreign occupiers, and local anti-Semites—Croat and Muslim in Croatia, and Serb in Nedić's Serbia—tackled the "Jewish problem" as systematically as in other parts of occupied Europe. By March, 1942, they had eradicated most of the Macedonian Jews, by August of the same year the Serbian Jews, and by 1944 the Jews in Zagreb and Vojvodina. About four-fifths of Yugoslavia's Jews (57,000 persons) were killed during the war.[61]

In Bosnia-Herzegovina, nearly 12,000 out of 14,000 had been killed,[62] and 30,500 out of 39,500 perished in the NDH.[63] Persecution, the confiscation of property, the destruction of documentation and archives, and the profanation of sacred objects began immediately after the occupation. Anti-Semitic laws were adopted from April 30 on.[64] Jews had to wear special signs. The first Jews were shot on August 1, 1941, and the level of violence grew steadily. In mid-November 1941, 3,000 Sarajevo Jews were deported to the Jasenovac concentration camp; more than 8,500 by August, 1942. A small number of Jews in the NDH survived the war by hiding; others were saved because of mixed marriages or by adopting the Christian faith before the war. Some Jews joined the partisan forces—seventy in 1941, and at least 4,556 throughout the war—and four were awarded the highest partisan decoration, that of National Hero.[65]

THE PARTISAN POSITION ON RELIGIO-NATIONAL ISSUES

The partisans welcomed members of all South Slav nations, regardless of nationality or religion, because their primary goal was to defeat the foreign invaders. Partisan units therefore included members of all four national groups in Bosnia-Herzegovina, fighting side-by-side against the Chetniks, the Ustasha, and their Muslim henchmen. During the war, the Communists stopped their atheist propaganda and purges within partisan ranks, or at least they did so inconsistently. The religious composition of the units was heterogeneous. Partisans in liberated territory were permitted to attend religious rites and ceremonies. Several clergymen went into battle under partisan banners and even more supported the struggle for liberation. The partisans also spared religious buildings and property, except when they served as enemy military strongholds.

Most Orthodox clergymen kept away from the heavy fighting between partisan and Chetnik forces, preferring to wait for the final outcome, although some were involved on both sides. Some patriotic Orthodox priests, especially from Croatia, Montenegro, and Bosnia-Herzegovina, joined the partisans, including Ilija Ćuk from Lika, Jevstatije Karamatijević from Sandžak, Blažo Marković from Cetinje, Jovo Miodragović from Žagrović, and Jagoš Simonović from Kolašin, to mention but a few.[66] A number of clergymen were also present at the AVNOJ (the Anti-Fascist Council for the National Liberation of Yugoslavia) meetings and were members of the ZAVNOH (Territorial Anti-Fascist Council for the National Liberation of Croatia). Miloš Smiljanić became the chief Orthodox chaplain of the partisan army and was appointed minister for agriculture and deputy prime minister of the Serbian government after the war. Like many other Orthodox priests, Vlada Zečević left the Chetniks because of their passive attitude; he renounced his priesthood after the war, joined the Communist Party and became the minister for communications.[67]

Many Roman Catholic priests and monks also joined or actively supported the partisan movement.[68] They wore regular partisan uniforms with a cross above a red star adorning their caps. The partisan struggle was also supported by Franciscan monks Bosiljko Ljevar and Viktor Sakić, Franjo Pos, Bishop Nikola Dobrečić of Bar, and Svetozar Rittig, the pastor of the Church of Saint Mark in Zagreb and an advocate of Strossmayer's ideas. In his youth, Rittig served as Strossmayer's secretary and, despite his advanced age, joined the partisan movement at the age of seventy after Italy's capitulation. Other priests who joined the partisans or cooperated or supported them were Andjelko Buratović from Krk, Franjo Didović from Djakovo, Ferdo Šenk from Kršan and Srećko Stifanić.[69] Bishops and lower clergymen, especially from Dalmatia, lent their support to the advancing partisans and the ZAVNOH meeting held in Split in April, 1945. Among them were Pušić from Hvar, Mileta from Šibenik, and Vicar Fulgosi of Split.[70]

Many South Slav Muslims fought in partisan units. The first Muslim partisan unit was organized in May, 1942, on liberated territory in Herzegovina. Later, the 8th and 16th Muslim Brigades were activated. Propartisan Muslim clergymen in Bosnia-Herzegovina were Mehmed Mujkić, Halil Sarajlić, Omer Maksumić, Sujleman Topić, Ibrahim Begić, Hussein Mujić, Smajl Buljubašić, and others.[71] Remaining active throughout the occupation, most of the Young Muslims were incorporated, "by fair means or foul, in the units of Tito's partisans."[72]

The founding session of the Territorial Antifascist Council for the National Liberation of Bosnia-Herzegovina (ZAVNOBIH) was held November 26–27, 1943, in Mrkonjić Grad, and included Serbian, Croatian and Muslim representatives. During its first session in November, 1942, the Department for Religious Affairs was created as a section of the AVNOJ executive committee. Bosnia-Herzegovina's Muslim Slavs still had not been recognized as a nation by the time of the second AVNOJ session in November, 1943. On the other hand, Bosnia-Herzegovina was expected to have a separate status within Yugoslavia. The AVNOJ resolutions included equal rights for all Yugoslav citizens, regardless of nationality, race, or religion. A similar guarantee was made in the so-called Foča Document of February, 1942, which declared all citizens as equal, regardless of political, national, or religious background. The separation of church and state was also mentioned.

At its second session, held June 30–July 2, 1944, ZAVNOBIH became the highest legislative and executive body in Bosnia-Herzegovina. It was renamed the National Assembly at the third meeting, held in Sarajevo April 26–28, 1945, on which occasion Bosnia-Herzegovina was declared a country of Serbs, Croats, and Muslims—"their common and indivisible homeland," over which no single national group had exclusive rights.[73] Different variants of the status of Bosnia-Herzegovina in postwar Yugoslavia were heatedly discussed by exiled Yugoslav politicians in London, who believed that their country would remain a monarchy.

The Yugoslav partisans were making rapid progress in the diplomatic field as well. After protracted negotiations with the Anglo-American Allies (who wanted to preserve Yugoslavia's political plurality), the Tito-Šubašić compromise was reached. The first provisional government of the Democratic Federal Yugoslavia was formed on March 7, 1945. The government included a number of Royalist ministers (Milan Grol as deputy prime minister, Ivan Šubašić as foreign minister, and Josip Šutej). A "Vice Regency" was also formally established, which guaranteed international recognition. The AVNOJ, which had been enlarged to include 118 deputies from the prewar parties, was transformed into the Provisional National Assembly in August, 1945. The National Front won a landslide victory in the general elections, and on November 29 the newly elected assembly abolished the monarchy and declared the new nation to be the "Federal People's Republic of Yugoslavia."

8

M OR m?
Political vs. Religio-National Myths in Postwar Bosnia-Herzegovina

After the Second World War, Bosnia-Herzegovina became a republic and administrative partner of equal rank in the Yugoslav federation, and its Austro-Hungarian borders were reinstated. This

The fear of God is the best fear for your citizens. If they fear God, they shall fear you, too.

—ROMAN CATHOLIC BISHOP NIKOLA DOBREČIĆ OF BAR TO MARSHAL JOSIP BROZ TITO, 1945

chapter examines some of the common characteristics of the new Yugoslav state, the "second attempt" at cohabitation by these nations, and on the fundamental religious changes that took place during this period. Especially important are the processes taking place within Bosnia-Herzegovina, which can only be fully comprehended if they are portrayed within a wider Yugoslav and Socialist context. Although all the events described in this chapter are closely related, I shall begin with an examination of some of the more palpable Yugoslav Socialist political myths, continue with the Roman Catholic and Serbian Orthodox Churches, the smaller Jewish community, the Muslim religious and national community, and conclude with a review of empirical data concerning the relationship between religious and national identity in Bosnia-Herzegovina before the outbreak of the last war.

The Yugoslav Socialist regime's rise to power interrupted the prevalent religious continuity and momentum and caused much commotion in ecclesiastic circles. The 1946 constitution provided for the separation church and state, freedom of worship, religious equality, and the seclusion of religion to the private sphere, and banned the exploitation of religion or religious institutions for political ends or the creation of political religious organizations. Marriage became a predominately secular affair;

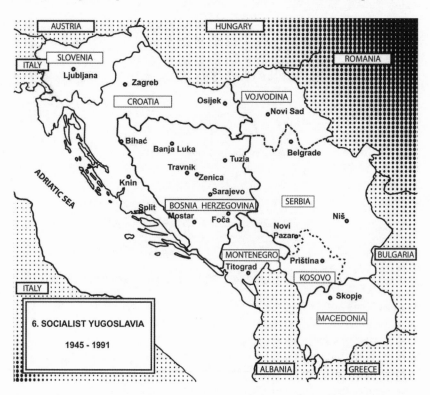

only in the second instance did it have a religious connotation. The separation of the secular sphere from religion set a precedent in the religious history of the South Slavs (and a majority of the eastern and central European nations as well), who had hitherto nurtured close relations with their "native" religious organizations. The legal regulation concerning religious issues in the 1963 constitution was similar to that in the 1946 document.

Religious institutions—because of the interwar collaboration of some clergymen with the occupiers and their inciting nationalistic and exclusivist policy—lost much of their prestige, reputation, and legitimacy among the people. They were further discredited by the new authorities' antireligious attitude and systematic activities. The nationalization of religious assets began immediately after the war, and religious education in public schools was banned a few years later. Many clergymen were sentenced to protracted prison terms or were summarily executed for their wartime activities. Among the most prominent clergymen sentenced to death for collaboration were—among others—the already mentioned Ivo Guberina and Filipović-Majstorović, Bishop Popp of the German Evangelical Church, both bishops of the Croatian Orthodox Church, and Mufti Ismet Muftić of Zagreb, who was accused of inciting anti-Serb hatred. Kerubin Šegvić was also sentenced to death.[1]

The Communist authorities intended to make a clear distinction between the religious and national identity of South Slav nations (in a symbolical sense as well, for example, by removing the cross from the Serbian coat of arms but keeping the four stylized esses), and to socially curtail and politically marginalize religious communities and religion in general. They were well aware of the destructive power of religious nationalism and attempted to find a new basis for national identity that would be beyond the traditionally long reach of religion and the church. Communists advocated the separation of church and state and officially promised religious freedom and tolerance.[2] Alexander notes that the Socialist authorities sought adaptation and not confrontation with religious communities. However, "they were determined to punish any priest who had collaborated with their enemies during the war."[3] The new authorities prevented churches from interfering in politics or influencing the relations between nationalities in any way, but with some important differences. This policy was applied only to the "stronger" religious communities, such as the Roman Catholic and Orthodox. They encouraged national and religious awareness among Bosnia-Herzegovina's Muslim Slavs, especially after the collapse of the concept of integral Yugoslavism.

A similar policy was adopted in Macedonia with the creation of the autocephalous Macedonian Orthodox Church, headed by Archbishop Dositej, in Ohrid in 1967. This investiture coincided with the bicentennial anniversary of the abrogation of the diocese of Ohrid (in 1767), which was founded by Tsar Samuel at the turn of the tenth century. This move was made in order to distinguish the Macedonians as a religious and national entity and to curb the appetites of their neighbors: the Serbs and Serbian Orthodox Church, and the Bulgarians and Bulgarian Orthodox Church. The fact that the University of Cyril and Methodius in Skopje was named after religious figures rather than Socialist heroes, as was otherwise the rule, is also significant.

Agrarian reform also had a devastating impact on religious organizations. The reform was based on the Agrarian Reform and Colonization Act of 1945, the Nationalization and Expropriation Act of 1946, and a number of other laws, the last of which was enacted in 1958. The Serbian Orthodox and Roman Catholic Churches lost a total of 173,000 hectares or 85 percent of their land (seventy thousand hectares belonged to the Orthodox and the remainder to the Catholics) as well as most of their printing presses, hospitals, and other property.[4] The Islamic community lost some 270 buildings (religious schools and others) and about twenty-one hundred hectares of land. Religious education was finally stricken from the school curriculum in 1952. A turning point in the relations between religion and the state came in April, 1953, with the enactment of the Legal Status of Religious Communities Act, which transformed religious organizations into legal entities. The new legislation guaranteed freedom of worship, the inviolability of religion as a personal freedom, freedom of religious choice, and the equality of all religions. Moreover, religious organizations were permitted to run printing presses, religious education was allowed outside of public schools, the creation of different ecclesiastical organizations was authorized, financial support for religious communities was assured, and the exploitation of religion for political ends was banned. The new legislation reflected the interests of the state rather than those of the religious organizations: before it was enacted, the bill was discussed with the Orthodox and Muslim religious communities but not with the Roman Catholic Church (which boycotted the discussions because of the Stepinac affair).

On November 11, 1950, the *New York Times* reported that 300 priests were in jail. The number had fallen to 161 clergymen from all denominations by February, 1953, and a year later 124 Roman Catholic, 32 Orthodox, and 2 Protestant priests remained in prison, most of them for alleged wartime crimes.[5] Many of the sentences were commuted when the state changed its approach to religion in the mid-1950s. In a famous speech delivered in September, 1953, in the town of Ruma in Srem, Marshal Tito condemned the violence against the clergy. A new calm followed these events, however, it was habitually broken. For example, a number of clergymen received heavy sentences for allegedly spreading "hostile propaganda," engaging in "pro-terrorist activities and espionage," and "for spreading religious and ethnic hatred."

Relations between the state and religious organizations thawed in the mid-1950s. It was a period during which Yugoslavia underwent accelerated modernization resulting in a modified population structure. The flight of people from the countryside weakened the influence exerted by tradition and religion. Secularization—authoritarian because of the regime and "spontaneous" because of the global process of modernization—was having an increasingly palpable impact on all vital aspects of society. However, religious affiliation remained an important aspect of social and spiritual life in Yugoslavia, as is illustrated in a census dating from that period. The 1953 census reported that only 2,127,875 Yugoslavs out of a total of 16,936,573 declared they did not belong to any religion. Of those who expressed religious beliefs, 6,984,686 were Orthodox,

TABLE 8-1 *Secularization of Yugoslav society by percent of the entire population, 1953–90*

	1953[a]	1964[b]	1968[c]	1990[d]
Religious/Believers	88.6%	70.3%	39%	43%
Nonreligious/Atheists	12.6%	29.2%	51%	48%
Indifferent/Undecided/"Mixed Type"	0.8%	0.2%	10%	9%

[a] Census results/general affiliation with confession.
[b] Survey question: "What is your relation to religion?"
[c] Survey question: "Do you believe in God?"
[d] Self-definition by respondents.

5,370,760 Catholic, 2,080,380 Muslim, and 362,872 claimed other religious affiliations. In Bosnia-Herzegovina, 88.9 percent of the population claimed to be religious. Of those, 99.5 percent of the Orthodox declared they were Serbs, 98.1 percent of Catholics said they were Croats, and 93.7 percent of Muslim believers identified themselves as "Yugoslavs undeclared."[6]

A result of the rapid rate of modernization (which included industrialization, urbanization, a higher level of education and purchasing power, and so on), the compromised position of religious organizations, and the atheistic inclination of the regime was the gradual secularization of the population. This process had a greater impact on Orthodoxy and Islam than on Catholicism, and was more pronounced among the youth. Findings by Esad Ćimić, a Yugoslav sociologist specializing in the study of religion's impact on society, indicate that 90 percent of Croats and only 7–20 percent of Serbs received the sacrament of baptism in the mid-1960s. The secularization of Yugoslav society is documented in table 8-1, which, despite using different methodological procedures, clearly indicates the predominate trend.[7] We must, however, exercise caution in interpreting this data; we must also consider what was, in my opinion, the relatively common practice of fictional secularization, that is, compliance with the regime and the ruling ideology.

Following a period of relative calm and pragmatism, relations between the Socialist authorities and religious communities again began to deteriorate in the mid-1970s. There were accusations from both sides. On one hand, the state claimed that churches supported nationalism and clericalism, that they were becoming belligerent, and that churches, religious organizations, and religion in general were having a negative effect on relations between different nationalities. On the other hand, the state was accused of discriminating against believers, obstructing the normal functioning of religious organizations, violating human rights, and transforming the education system into an atheist and pro-Communist tool. The 1974 constitution repealed the existing twenty-one-year-old Religious Communities Act (a federal law) and delegated the legislative powers in this field to individual republics. The first to enact the legislation was Slovenia in May, 1976, and the last was Croatia in April, 1978.

With the exception of individual sporadic conflicts, relations between religion and the state were again liberalized in the 1980s and the dialogue between Marxist scholars and theologians continued with new vigor. Owen Chadwick notes that the Socialist regimes in Yugoslavia and East Germany (GDR) exerted relatively little pressure and intervention on churches. The ecumenical dialogue between the Orthodox and Catholic Churches also improved, partly because of the *aggiornamento* initiated at the Second Vatican Council. It was against the background of this modified social environment of the 1980s (the collapse of Yugoslav political myths, the economic crisis and lagging economy, the growth of nationalism, détente, and so on) that religious sociologists in Yugoslavia recorded an appreciable revitalization of religion.[8]

"INTEGRAL" AND "ORGANIC" YUGOSLAVISM

Throughout the Second World War and immediately thereafter, the triumphant Communists believed that the burning ethnic issues plaguing Yugoslavia would be solved as soon as the patent economic gaps existing between individual parts of the country could be bridged. They believed that proletarian interests were more important than individual nationalistic ones. During the second period (from the adoption of the new constitution in 1952 to the mid-1960s) the renamed Communist Party, the "League of Communists of Yugoslavia" (LCY), introduced "integral Yugoslavism" as a new transnational force and basis for loyalty. In 1958, the Seventh Congress of the League of Communists symbolized the peak of a campaign for a new type of Socialist patriotism that was expected to transcend national consciousness and create an impending Yugoslav culture. The campaign, however, was not aimed at substituting the existing nationalities with a specific "Yugoslav nation."[9]

The state undertook to achieve this goal by mobilizing all spheres of society—from politics (emphasizing federal centralism over federalism), culture (the attempt to create a distinctive Yugoslav culture), society in general (emphasizing the "working class" or "working people" over the "nation"), and academia (interpreting all national aspirations of the past as a desire to create a common Yugoslav historical present) to ideology (Yugoslavism as a progressive Socialist concept). This policy was eventually abandoned during a period of dramatic changes on the Yugoslav political scene following the adoption of the 1963 constitution. "Centralist" and "exclusivist" nationalists were ostracized at the Eighth Congress of the League of Communists in 1964, and Aleksander Ranković, Yugoslavia's security chief, was dismissed at the Brioni meeting in 1966.

Two types of Yugoslavism—"organic" and "integral"—were imposed and often simultaneously applied in Socialist Yugoslavia. Both were carried out in the spirit of "brotherhood and unity,"[10] one of the preferred catchphrases of postwar Yugoslavia. Organic Yugoslavism (an expression borrowed from Pedro Ramet) was Kardelj's brainchild and conformed to the policies of decentralization—that is, the creation of a collective, nationally and culturally heterogeneous, community based on the principle of "brotherhood." A harmonious symbiosis was expected to prevail between sentiments for one's nation and for the federal Yugoslav community.

Integral Yugoslavism, was exemplified by the unitarian and hard-line option advocated by Ranković, which—in my opinion—was manifested more in practice than in theory. Aleksander Ranković-Leka (1909–83), one of Yugoslavia's highest-ranking state and party officials and among Tito's most likely inherent successors, head of the Directorate for State Security (UDBa), and the iron hand of the Yugoslav regime, headed a discreet campaign of discrimination against non-Serbs in Kosovo, Vojvodina, Bosnia-Herzegovina, and Croatia. Integral Yugoslavism represented political and administrative centralization, a strengthening of collective Yugoslav awareness, and favoritism for the Serbs. Individual national awareness was deemed incompatible with a collective Yugoslav awareness. On the other hand, according to Friedman, Ranković "may have viewed the indigenous Bosnian Muslims as a potential core around which a hypothesized 'Yugoslav' nation could evolve."[11]

Integral Yugoslavism failed to take root as an explicit and nonnational state mythology that transcended national bigotry, and soon sank into oblivion. However, the sense of belonging and loyalty to Yugoslavia that it had instilled in the population remained a strong sentiment until the country collapsed. Integral Yugoslavism was gradually and in different parts of the state differently replaced by organic Yugoslavism. Slovenian sociologist Mitja Hafner-Fink notes that data analysis of a study conducted in the mid-1980s indicates that Yugoslavism was largely determined by republican awareness in the final years before the country's collapse. Respondents from Montenegro, Bosnia-Herzegovina, Serbia proper, Macedonia, and Vojvodina most readily identified with Yugoslavism, those from Croatia less so, and those from Slovenia and Kosovo mostly rejected it.[12]

An essential ingredient of the Yugoslav mythological construct was the cult of Pres. Josip Broz Tito (1892–1980) who, from a mythical perspective, personified the unity of Yugoslavs and the state's socio-cultural diversity. In articles written during the war he is described as "unwavering, wise and far-sighted"; as the personification of "the invincible strength of our peoples and our Party"; and "the greatest son of our Party and our peoples. . . . The finest expression not only of the perseverance, combative spirit and resolve of our Party, but of the perseverance and determination of our nations as well." Yugoslavia was dubbed "Titolandia" (by Winston Churchill) or "Titoslavia." Tito himself was referred to as the "Last Habsburg" (by historian Arnold Toynbee) or the "Communist Luther." Following Yugoslavia's defection from the Cominform in 1948, the Communists zealously began building Tito's personality cult, using the time-tested method of "cult against cult" to fill the vacuum left by Stalin's cult.[13] During the war, Tito was awarded the country's highest honors: he was promoted to the rank of marshal, appointed president for life, and received the Order of the National Hero three times. He was declared the "greatest son of the Yugoslav people" in a fervent "myth of all myths" campaign. The campaign's success is reflected in this ode written in Tito's honor:

> *Comrade Tito, pride of our race,*
> *Image and likeness of Obilić!*
> *Your glory casts into the shade*
> *Karadjordje, Zrinski, and Gubec.*[14]

Even before the end of the war, Milovan Djilas "contended" that, for the first time in their history, the peoples of Yugoslavia found in Tito a man "who is equally loved and exalted by all—Serbs, Croats, Slovenes, Macedonians and Montenegrins." Historian Franjo Tudjman, a former general in the Yugoslav army, paid him similar homage: "Tito's personality came to symbolize all the peoples of Yugoslavia and more: it came to symbolize liberation and revolutionary movements throughout Europe." Tito's cult was adopted in Slovenia with equal zeal and was elevated above that of the mythical King Matsaž with slogans such as "No, you did not sleep under the mountain with your army."[15] The mythologizing of Tito's personality began during the war. Radovan Zogović dedicated a poem to him, and Croatian poet Vladimir Nazor (1876–1949) wrote the following verses, which portray Tito as the herald of a new age:

That which timidly was concealed
under the embers in our hearts
was kindled into a raging bonfire
by our Comrade Tito, Tito.

The media portrayed him as the "leader and mentor of the peoples of Yugoslavia, the great deliverer, the unifier of the peoples of Yugoslavia, the architect of the new Yugoslavia, the ingenious generalissimo," and so on. Tito "belongs to us, Tito is wise, beloved and heroic; he emerged from the masses; he devotes his life and work to the people; he is a magnet that draws the hearts and affection of all; he is the light of our life; he mirrors the bliss and harmony of the peoples of Yugoslavia." He is the raison d'être of national heroes who "carry him in their hearts."[16] The myth achieved cosmological proportions. The mythical transition between darkness and light, action and inaction, latency and manifestation, is illustrated in Pavle Šegula's prose, a popular propaganda form of the time. It begins with a narration of the dismal plight of the Yugoslav peoples and the tempest brought about by the "mechanized fascist beasts," then continues: "And then there was a stirring. It emerged from the depths of the enslaved and downtrodden masses and brought light to the darkness of the night. A sole utterance: TITO."[17] Tito's death, from a mythological perspective, symbolized eternal life, as media headlines and slogans were apt to point out: "Tito lives and will continue to live with us forever; Tito will live in the hearts of those who cherish freedom; You shall always remain with us; After Tito—Tito; Yugoslavia is and remains Tito; Death cannot kill Tito; Tito was, Tito is, Tito will be"; and so forth.

It is interesting to note that Tito still enjoys a high level of esteem among his former subjects, despite the general demonizing of his personality over the last decade. Unfortunately, the only relevant empirical data I was able to acquire was for Bosnia-Herzegovina's neighbors—the Federal Republic of Yugoslavia and Croatia. In response to the question, "Who is the greatest Yugoslav politician of the twentieth century?" asked in a Mark Plan opinion poll conducted in July, 1998, among 1,403 respondents from throughout the FRY, the old marshal came first with 32.4 percent, followed by Nikola Pašić with 21.1 percent, and Slobodan Milošević with 9.2 percent. Tito's strongest support came from Vojvodina (50 percent) and Montenegro (38.5 percent). In a survey conducted in June and July, 1998, by the *Jutarnji list,* a Croatian opposition daily, Tito was picked as the most important Croat of the millennium, followed by Franjo Tudjman and Nikola Tesla. Ante Starčević was fourth, Ban Jelačić was sixth, Stepinac was seventh, Stjepan Radić was eighth, Strossmayer was thirteenth, Ljudevit Gaj was fifteenth, and Ante Pavelić was sixteenth.

The political mythology of Socialist Yugoslavia relied heavily on a number of different myths: the "National Liberation Struggle" and the partisan movement (the "incessant, unbalanced, and bitter battle against an enemy one-hundred-fold stronger," in Tito's own words); the defection from the Cominform (making it necessary to replace the Soviet allusion with a "local" one); the "brotherhood and unity" of the Yugoslav nations; and Yugoslavia's "unique" internal political system (based on "Self-managing Socialism") and nonaligned foreign policy. Tito and Kardelj were praised as leading the nations of Yugoslavia "along the path that leads to the blissful shore of Marx's empire of freedom."[18] The new authorities symbolically perpetuated the rapid rate of development—the industrialization and modernization of society. Symbolically, a smokestack adorned the coat of arms of the Socialist Republic of Bosnia-Herzegovina, and a cogwheel that of Serbia.

Despite the Socialist authorities' efforts to maintain a national balance in all fields, one of the major problems faced by postwar Yugoslavia (and Bosnia-Herzegovina as well) was the unequal representation of Yugoslav national groups in individual segments of society: the League of Communists, civil service, judiciary, media, armed forces, police, intelligence services, diplomacy, and others. The Serbs, especially those from Croatia and Bosnia-Herzegovina, and the Montenegrins were overrepresented, which occasionally provoked acrimonious protests from other national groups and republics. In Croatia, for example, the Serbs comprised around 12 percent of the population but represented 30–40 percent of the membership of the League of Communists, and 60 percent or two-thirds of the police force.[19] In 1970, 46.7 percent of the generals and 57.4 percent of officers were Serbs (Montenegrins comprised 19.3 and 10.3 percent, respectively).[20] Similarly, in the early 1970s, although Croats made up roughly 20 percent of the Bosnian population, only 12 percent were members of the Bosnian League of Communists, whereas the ratio for Bosnian Serbs was 37 percent of the population and 60 percent of league membership.[21] On the other hand, five of the nine Yugoslav prime ministers from 1946–91 were Croats.

Despite living in different Yugoslav republics and two autonomous provinces, Serbian nationalists often portrayed themselves as being a threatened and deceived nation (especially after the adoption of the decentralizing 1974 constitution). Indeed, some Croatian Serbs declared in the 1970s that they "would not become the Palestinians of Europe." Dobrica Ćosić stated that the Serbs made the greatest sacrifice for Yugoslavia and received the least in return. Some even accused the more developed northern republics of economically exploiting Serbia. On the other hand, during the Croatian Spring of the early 1970s, Croatian leaders pointed out—among other critical issues like Croatia's socioeconomic position and the relation between Croats and Serbs in Croatia—the underrepresentation of Croats in Bosnia-Herzegovina's main political bodies. The most vocal Croatian nationalists "proposed that Croat-dominated territories be detached from the republic of Bosnia Herzegovina and annexed to Croatia."[22]

THE STEPINAC AFFAIR

The following discussion deals with events relating to Archbishop Alojzije Stepinac, the senior Roman Catholic official in all of Croatia and Yugoslavia. There are two reasons for this. First, these events had a consequential impact on the relationship between the Socialist regime, the Catholic Church in Yugoslavia, and the Vatican. The dynamics of the relationship between these three entities were closely related to the fate of the archbishop (later cardinal). Second, Stepinac became one of the key figures in the contemporary Croatian religio-national mythology. The magnitude of his importance was recently corroborated when Pope John Paul II canonized him.

After assuming power in much of eastern and central Europe, the increasingly self-confident Communist authorities began coercing the local Catholic hierarchies to sever their relationships with the Vatican. Tito met with Catholic bishops—in Stepinac's absence—on June 2, 1945. He introduced himself as a "Croat and a Catholic," although the religious affiliation was omitted by the press.[23] He accused the church of placing Italian interests above those of South Slavs and insisted that it become more sensitive to the local population, more "nationally" oriented, and more dedicated to the Yugoslav cause (adding, "as is case with the Serbian Orthodox Church"). The marshal added that he longed to see Strossmayer's spirit of cooperation between the Orthodox and the Catholics. The bishops expressed their desire for a cordial mutual relationship with the authorities and said they would seek God's blessings for Tito's undertakings. However, they also defended the church's role and the record of Archbishop Stepinac ("the greatest living Croat and a first-rate national and social worker") during the war.

A meeting was held on June 4, 1945, between Tito and Vladimir Bakarić (1912–1983), a Croatian Communist leader and prime minister of the Socialist Republic of Croatia, and Alojzij Stepinac, who was placed under house arrest for a brief period after the war for "his own protection." Stepinac complained bitterly about the killing of clergymen, the violence and requisitioning, the nationalization of schools and other buildings, the exclusion of religious education from the secondary school curriculum and its relegation to an optional subject, the ban on religious publications, and agrarian reform. He also complained about civil marriages replacing church weddings. The archbishop contended that only the Vatican could decide on ecclesiastic matters.

Over the next few months, Stepinac made several public protests against the measures taken by the new authorities and met with Bakarić again. A unique manifestation of the power of the Catholic Church that year was the huge turnout at the traditional pilgrimage to Marija Bistrica (between forty thousand and fifty thousand believers), where Stepinac repeated his conviction that God was punishing his people. He was particularly vocal in a lengthy pastoral letter issued by the Episcopal Conference in September, 1945. In it, he condemned the assassination and persecution of clergymen (although acknowledging that some of them were guilty of war crimes), the ideology of atheistic materialism, the new regime's hostile attitude toward the church, the separation of church and state, and the nationalization of church property. Among other things, he demanded the immediate release of all detainees, religious freedom, the restoration of confiscated property (including the press), and the recognition of Christian weddings.[24] His pastoral letter was read in almost every Catholic parish in the country.

The authorities were unsatisfied with Stepinac's lack of cooperation and his headstrong anti-Communist stance. He was unwilling to participate in the creation of a "nationally aware" Croatian Catholic Church that would operate independently of the Vatican. He remained loyal to the Roman Catholic Church and the pope, as well as to the "Croatian nation, which he equated with the Catholic Church." Ramet notes that the Socialist authorities tried to convince the Vatican to replace Stepinac, but their efforts were in vain. The Communists intended to neutralize the only institution that could serve as a basis for real opposition.[25] In late October, Tito responded harshly to what authorities viewed as a frontal assault by the church: the pastoral letter issued in September. He censured them for not being as vocal against the NDH, for not protecting the Orthodox being persecuted in Croatia, for supporting the Ustasha regime, and for not resisting forced proselytizing. He also accused several members of the Catholic hierarchy of being Ustasha butchers. Finally, Tito denied that the Catholic Church in Yugoslavia was being persecuted, adding that only a few individuals known to have committed crimes had been targeted.

In September, 1946, criminal proceedings (actually a political trial) were instigated against Stepinac as the head of the Catholic Church in Croatia. The authorities set the stage for the trial by launching an anti-Catholic propaganda campaign in the media and with the help of graffiti and demonstrations. Stepinac was even assaulted physically (in early November, 1945, at Zaprešić). Stepinac's wartime role was targeted and subjected to particularly caustic criticism (he was branded a "clero-fascist, war criminal, reactionary," and collaborator with "foreign imperialists," among other things). Senior clergymen from the Serbian Orthodox Church, including Bishop Irinej Djordjević of Dalmatia, also accused Stepinac, in archetypal anti-Catholic jargon, of persecuting the Serbs. It was against this background that the authorities proceeded to indict Stepinac on charges of open collaboration with the Ustasha regime, accepting the position of military chaplain, exploiting traditional religious feasts as political manifestations in support of the Ustasha regime, supporting the proselytizing of Orthodox Serbs, supporting the enemies of the Yugoslav state after the war, being in possession of Ustasha archives and the archives of the NDH Ministry of Foreign Affairs, and calling for foreign intervention near the end of the war in order to preserve the NDH.

In order to compromise him even further, Stepinac and other Roman Catholic clergymen were tried together with Erih Lisak, the highest-ranking civil servant in the Ministry of Internal Affairs of the Independent State of Croatia, and a number of other Ustasha functionaries. Two of the accused clergymen turned state's evidence against Stepinac. Stepinac denied all charges and condemned the new authorities for ostracizing his church. "I have a clear conscience before God, the Holy See, the Catholics of this nation, and the Croatian people," he declared. He also insisted that he was "persona non grata neither to the Germans nor to the Ustasha"[26] The following month, Stepinac was sentenced to sixteen years' imprisonment at hard labor and lost his civil rights for an additional five years.

Lisak was sentenced to death and the other clergymen received varying sentences: Ivan Šalić, Stepinac's personal secretary, was sentenced to twelve years' imprisonment (of which he served six), and Modest Martinčić, the Croatian Franciscan provincial, was sentenced to six years (of which he served three). Franciscan monk Lambert Margetić was also imprisoned. Two important figures testified on Stepinac's behalf. The first was Metropolite Ante Šumanović of the Orthodox Church, who recorded a statement noting that only Stepinac's intervention stopped the Ustasha from demolishing the Orthodox Church in Zagreb. The second was sculptor Ivan Meštrović, who wrote a letter in Stepinac's defense. But both were ignored. Other evidence in Stepinac's favor included statements recorded by Orthodox bishop Emilije and numerous Serbs, Jews, and other refugees, but it failed to deter the court. Stepinac's trial was similar to other political trials taking place throughout eastern and central Europe at the time as the authorities sought to neutralize senior Catholic officials. Jozef Tiso in Slovakia, Polish cardinal Stefan Wyszinski, Hungarian cardinal Jozef Mindszenty, and Archbishop Josef Beran from Czechoslovakia (who was first imprisoned by the Nazis and then by the Communists) shared his fate.

Thirty-eight years after the trial, public prosecutor Jakov Blažević publicly admitted that the proceedings against Stepinac had more to do with his refusal to cooperate with Tito's regime than with his wartime activities.[27] Milovan Djilas made a similar statement. Stepinac's real problem was not his relationship with the Ustasha, but his opposition to the new Communist regime, and especially his loyalty to Rome. Had he agreed to establish a Croatian Catholic Church independent of the Vatican, his life might have taken a very different course.

The Vatican reacted strongly to the sentence, condemning it as a "crime against religion," and in October, 1946, Pope Pius XII excommunicated all Catholics involved in the affair. The trial, which he dubbed *"tristissimo processo,"* provoked a strong response in other parts of the world as well. Stepinac was likened to Belgian cardinal Désiré-Joseph Mercier, whose heroic stand against the Germans during the First World War brought him international acclaim, and to German Protestant pastor Martin Niemöller, who was imprisoned in a concentration camp by the Nazis for his anti-Nazi activities. He was depicted as "intrepid under the régime of Pavelić, heroic under that of Tito."[28] London's Foreign Office alone received some 550 petitions with 216,000 signatures calling for Stepinac's release. Several celebrities from public life also supported Stepinac.

In 1951, after five years at the Lepoglava Prison (where, unlike many political prisoners in Yugoslavia and behind the Iron Curtain, he was treated with dignity), Stepinac was transferred to Krašić, in the immediate vicinity of his birthplace, the hamlet of Brezarići. There he continued his modest and ascetic life, never asking the authorities for any favor.

Tito and Bakarić offered to place him in a monastery for the remainder of his sentence or allow him to leave the country, but Stepinac rejected the offers and insisted on a new trial with an independent court. By the autumn of 1950, Socialist authorities were trying to improve relations with the Vatican, which was the result of a complete turnaround in Yugoslav foreign policy. They offered to release imprisoned clergymen, including Stepinac (with the proviso that he leave Yugoslavia), to preserve religious instruction in schools, to restore the religious press, to financially support the building of new churches, and the normalization of relations between the Catholic hierarchy in Yugoslavia and the Holy See in return for which they expected the Vatican to stop its anti-Yugoslav propaganda and provide support for pro-Yugoslav clerical associations and clergymen attempting to create a new society.[29]

Stella Alexander, an authority on the life of Alojzije Stepinac and the religious history of that period, correctly notes that Stepinac became a "triple myth" during his lifetime. Religious nationalists in Croatia saw him as "strong, persevering, invincible, an untainted saint, a suffering martyr." He also became a countermyth for the Yugoslav Communist regime and Serb nationalists. She considers Stepinac's conviction to have been a kind of "historical necessity" for the new regime, which outweighed the equally infamous conviction of Serb general Draža Mihajlović, who was sentenced to death and executed in 1946.[30]

Stepinac died "a martyr's death" on February 10, 1960. Pope John XXIII (1959–63) declared him the "defender of the Croatian people and a truly genuine and pious example of the Good Shepherd." The Serbian Orthodox Church interpreted his pompous funeral at the Zagreb Cathedral to be a "posthumous amnesty." Others viewed the authorities' decision to permit a public obsequy for Stepinac at the Zagreb Cathedral as a first step toward normalizing relations with the Catholic Church. Tanner saw the funeral as Tito's "belated gesture of reconciliation" with Stepinac and also with the Croats. In his three wills, Stepinac issued a series of direct condemnations of the "godless" Socialist regime, saying that "any attempt to pursue culture, civilization, and happiness in a nation devoid of God is to seal the ruin of that nation for posterity," and that "without God there can be only decay." He appealed to his parishioners to "remain true at any cost, even under threat of life and limb, to the Church of Christ, headed by Peter and the Pope as its leader," and to "preserve the traditions of their fathers."[31] The first proposals for his beatification emerged not long after his death. On December 4, 1981, the Vatican began the process for his canonization, which ended with his beatification in October, 1998.

THE ROMAN CATHOLIC CHURCH
IN SOCIALIST YUGOSLAVIA

Because of its ambiguous wartime role, the Catholic Church was singled out and targeted by the new authorities during the first postwar years. This situation was further exacerbated by its openly negative attitude toward the Communists and their ideals. Several bishops and lower clergymen from the "Catholic" parts of Yugoslavia were imprisoned or murdered, including Uniate bishop Šimrak (imprisoned for collaboration), and Catholic bishops Čule of Mostar (sentenced to eleven-and-a-half years' imprisonment, served seven), Josip Srebrnić of Krk (jailed for two months immediately after the war), Ivan Stjepčević, Stjepan Bauerlein of Djakovo (house arrest for three months), and Monsignor Stjepavac from Kotor (sentenced to six years). Catholic bishop Carević of Dubrovnik was declared missing.

According to data provided by the Catholic side, the casualties among the clergy numbered 501: 243 priests and monks were killed, 169 were imprisoned, and 89 are missing. In addition, nineteen theology students, three lay brothers, and four nuns were executed. It must be pointed out that Yugoslavia was not an exception in this respect: clergymen accused of collaborating with the enemy were executed immediately before or after the end of the war in other parts of Europe as well, including Italy.[32] O'Brien notes that only 401 of the 1,916 Catholic clergymen in Yugoslavia remained after the war: 369 were murdered or executed, 175 were imprisoned, 409 fled abroad, and 562 were missing; twelve nuns were executed and fifty were imprisoned. Of the seventeen dioceses, only six had serving bishops and four had assistant bishops.[33]

A large number of clergymen, especially those who openly collaborated with the enemy, sought refuge with the Anglo-American Allies, including Bishops Garić and Šarić from Banja Luka and Sarajevo, and Gregorij Rožman of Ljubljana. None had been authorized to do so by the Vatican. The total number of Catholic clergymen thought to have fled to the West is estimated at between four hundred and five hundred. How many were eventually repatriated and murdered is still unknown. Furthermore, many senior clergymen were physically assaulted or otherwise mistreated by the new authorities, including Assistant Bishop Franić of Split, Dragutin Čelik, the apostolic administrator of Banja Luka from 1951–58, and Ludvik Budanović, the apostolic administrator of Bačka from 1923–58. The number of Catholic publications was reduced from a prewar figure of one hundred to three. The church also lost hospitals, orphanages, and homes for the elderly. Some schools and seminaries were nationalized, various funds were confiscated, and the theology faculty was separated from the university.

The Metropolitan See of Sarajevo (consisting of the archdiocese of Sarajevo and the dioceses of Banja Luka, Mostar, and Trebinje) entered this new age numerically weakened and still reeling from the aftermath of the war. According to some estimates, 127 Catholic clerics were murdered during the 1940s, including fifty-eight Franciscan monks in Herzegovina's Franciscan province.[34] Most were killed by partisans at the end of the war. Bosnia remained without an archbishop for a full fifteen years after the war. Marko Alaupović (1960–68), Smiljan Čekada (1968–77), Marko Jozinović (1977–91), and Vinko Puljić (from 1991 until he was appointed cardinal in 1995) eventually filled the position.

The Catholic Church in Croatia and Bosnia-Herzegovina never fully accepted responsibility for the violence committed by the Ustasha regime during the war. The only important cleric ever to come close to an apology was Catholic bishop Alfred Pichler of Banja Luka. In his 1963 Christmas address he publicly sought forgiveness for crimes committed during the Second World War by Croatian religious nationalists against the Serbs merely because they were not Croats or Catholics. His exact words were: "we beg our Orthodox brothers for forgiveness, as Christ forgave mankind while He was on the Cross." The statement provoked a strong response within and outside his diocese and from the ranks of the Roman Catholic Church itself: some agreed with the statement, while others believed it to be superfluous and even offensive. A number of priests in his diocese refused to read the letter to their parishioners. As an advocate of practical ecumenism, Pichler nurtured cordial relations with his Orthodox counterpart, Bishop Andrej. The first "summit" meeting between Cardinal Šeper of Zagreb and Patriarch German of the Serbian Orthodox Church took place in 1967.

Nevertheless, it is necessary to point out that the Socialist authorities, especially the Serbs among them, and the Serbian Orthodox Church greatly exaggerated the number of casualties inflicted by the Ustasha. The figures for the number of people killed at Jasenovac, the most notorious concentration camp in Croatia and the incontestable symbol of Serbian sufferings in NDH, are conflicting: data released immediately after the war suggest that the number of victims was between 50,000 and 70,000 (the figures officially accepted in Croatia today are Tudjman's estimates of 40,000 killed at Jasenovac and 60,000 in total), but this number was later corrected to between 800,000 and 1 million. The most probable figure for Serb casualties in Croatia is 300,000–350,000. On the other hand, Cardinal Franjo Kuharić's assertion that "only a handful of Serbs" were killed by the Ustasha regime is equally shocking.[35]

The Socialist regime accused the clergy, especially the bishops, of a "dual loyalty"—to the state and to the Vatican. In some of the most aggressive Communist circles, Catholic clergymen were branded as "clero-nationalists," "chauvinists," "reactionaries," and "opponents of the state" because many clergymen had collaborated with the occupiers during the war, some of them supported the so-called Crusaders immediately after it, and because of their stubborn attitude toward the Communists. Although much of its wealth, land, and other property was nationalized, and its public and political role diminished, the church regained much prestige during the Stepinac affair. One of the unexpected consequences of the trial—for the authorities—was that "the Church came to symbolize the entire nation, despite the fact that it had never wielded real political power in Croatia before."[36] Socialist authorities never interfered with or attempted to control the church hierarchy but, rather, tried to reach an agreement with it. The church, however, was initially convinced "that the Communist régime would not last and that the best way of hastening its fall was to press it as hard as possible."[37] Svetozar Rittig—known for his conviction that the Serbs and Croats would eventually live in harmony—was appointed secretary of the Committee for Religious Affairs in Croatia (established in August, 1945).

The Roman Catholic Church in Yugoslavia was shaken by internal discord that often developed into open conflict. One such incident took place between the bishops and the various clerical associations that were beyond the bishops' control. These associations of "patriotic" clergymen were not a Yugoslav peculiarity and were common in other Socialist countries. They went under different names: the Catholic Clergymen for Peace movement in Hungary, the Clergymen for Peace—renamed Pacem in Terris after 1970—in Czechoslovakia, and the Pax movement in Poland, which was headed by the controversial Bolesław Piasecki.

Such associations emerged spontaneously in Slovenia, Istria, and Dalmatia in the late 1940s, while the authorities began encouraging them in 1950 as a way to exercise control over the "progressive" clergy within the church. An association known as *Dobri pastir* (Good Shepherd), established in Bosnia-Herzegovina in 1950, became particularly popular among the Franciscans, who represented three-quarters of its fellowship. The Franciscans used the association, under the guidance of Franciscan Bono Ostojić, as a weapon against the parish clergy, with whom they were in constant conflict, thus earning them such taunting epithets as the "Red Priests." By 1953, similar associations had emerged in Serbia, Montenegro, and in Croatia. But unlike the Good Shepherd and the Association of Orthodox Clergymen in Yugoslavia, the Croatian chapter known as the Association of Catholic Priests failed to take root. The associations had large followings elsewhere, however, recruiting virtually all the clergymen in Istria, four-fifths of the clergymen in Bosnia-Herzegovina, and three-fifths in Slovenia.[38]

These associations of priests (which were, in effect, clerical labor unions that appealed mainly to the lower clergy) were part and parcel of the Socialist regime. They operated under the auspices of the regime's umbrella organization known as the Socialist Alliance of the Working People, and received various forms of assistance (social security status, financial support, access to the press, and such). Officially, the function of the associations was to protect and fulfill the clergy's "professional interests." Another important function of the associations was to promote ecumenical dialogue, especially between the Catholics and the Orthodox. Membership in the associations did not begin to decline until the late 1970s.[39]

An encyclical issued by Pope Pius XII in July, 1949, (although he had come to this decision at the very beginning of his pontificate), prohibited Catholics from joining Communist parties or advocating communism. After the war ended he cautioned Catholics not to succumb to the intellectual trends of the modern age. Because of this interdiction, and because of his conspicuous fear of communism, Owen Chadwick refers to him as the "political Pope" and the "Pope of the political Right." Following his predecessor's footsteps, he signed advantageous agreements with fascist dictators Antonio de Oliviero Salazar of Portugal (1940) and Francisco Franco of Spain (1953).[40] His intolerance of communism was particularly counterproductive in the new Socialist states, where his policies contributed to the exclusion of Roman Catholic parishioners and clergymen from politics and society in general, which was undoubtedly to their disadvantage.

In a letter dated April, 1950, the conference of bishops (chaired by Archbishop Ujčić in the absence of Stepinac) labeled the clerical associations "inappropriate." A confidential encyclical issued by the Vatican in the autumn of 1952 prohibited *(non licet)* clergymen from joining clerical associations, and a number of priests were suspended. Members of the priest association in Croatia were severely punished, especially by Bishops Franić and Čule, Monsignor Majić, and Archbishop Čekada: they lost their pastoral status (which meant they were prohibited from conducting mass, hearing confessions, and preaching) as soon as they joined the association. Even the imprisoned Stepinac secretly wrote letters proclaiming his opposition to the associations. Catholic priests and monks in Bosnia-Herzegovina, however, were under no such pressure or sanctions. Similar associations were allowed to operate freely, without ecclesiastic interdiction, in other countries. The Yugoslav authorities accused the church of persecuting clergymen who were prepared to cooperate with the state.

The question of clerical associations cast a bone of contention between the authorities and the church. When the imprisoned Archbishop Stepinac's appointment to cardinal was scheduled for November 29, 1952, the most important Yugoslav public holiday—"Republic Day"—the dispute developed into open conflict. It could not have happened at a more inopportune moment: Yugoslavia was in an extremely ambiguous diplomatic situation—its relations with other Socialist regimes had been severed, the issue of Trieste remained unanswered, and it was desperately seeking ties to the West. The Vatican's decision caused a bitter reaction in Yugoslavia. Marshal Tito delivered an acrimonious speech in Smederevska Palanka in mid-December, and Kardelj accused the Vatican of being a tool in the hands of Italian irredentist politicians, interfering in Yugoslavia's internal affairs, refusing to participate in solving mutual problems, and denigrating Yugoslavia. On December 17, 1952, Yugoslavia severed its relations with the Vatican. The Vatican's reply, published in *L'Osservatore Romano* the following month, denounced the conditions being imposed on the Roman Catholic Church in Yugoslavia. Tito held another meeting with the bishops at about the same time, but failed to make any progress; the bishops remained staunchly loyal to the Vatican. The position of assistant archbishop of Zagreb was filled by the liberal Franjo Šeper, previously the rector of a seminary, in 1954. He became a cardinal in 1965.

The frosty relations between the Vatican and the Socialist regime in Yugoslavia began thawing in the late 1950s. The "period of conflict" was replaced by a "period of compromise." Both sides pursued rapprochement. The Socialist authorities, finally realizing that they would be unable to use the clerical associations in their negotiations with the church, initiated direct dialogue with the bishops. In 1962, informal talks (formalized in 1964) began between the government and the Vatican, circumventing the Yugoslav bishops. These talks were concluded on June 25, 1966, with the ratification of a special protocol (not a concordat). The state promised to allow the church to freely conduct its religious affairs and rites, recognized the Vatican's authority over the Roman Catholic Church in regard to religious matters, and assured the bishops that they would be permitted to maintain their links with the Holy See. In return, the Vatican promised that its priests in Yugoslavia would uphold the laws and not misuse religious and ecclesiastic functions for political ends.[41] Bishop Franić of Split is quoted as saying on this occasion that the protocol promised a new era for the Catholic Church.

In 1970, Franjo Kuharić was appointed bishop of Zagreb and the church in Croatia was reorganized into three metropolitan sees: Zagreb, Split, and Rijeka. There were also some changes on the diplomatic scene: full diplomatic relations were established between Yugoslavia and the Vatican on August 14, 1970, and the Vatican ambassador replaced the apostolic delegate in Belgrade. The latter had been responsible for maintaining links between the two sides. In March, 1971, Tito became the first Socialist leader to be granted an audience with Pope Paul VI (1963–78), which the international media proclaimed to be an "unprecedented event."[42] The pope hailed Tito's efforts and success in preserving and strengthening peace, saying, "Your Excellency is aware of the keen interest with which the Holy See and I personally have been following the activities that your government has undertaken in the field of world reconciliation." During a visit to the Vatican in December, 1980, Cvijetin Mijatović, president of the Yugoslav Presidium, invited Pope John Paul II (1978–) to visit Yugoslavia.

There were two turning points in the popularity of the Roman Catholic Church in postwar Croatia. The first was the trial of Alojzije Stepinac, while the second was the "Croatian Spring" of 1969–71 (which the Catholic Church in Croatia applauded), and its traumatic quelling. More than ever before, this event transformed the church into an important national Croat institution and the symbol of the "suffering" Croatian people.[43] Many religious manifestations and pilgrimages that had hitherto been well established suddenly became mass events, for example in Solin (1976, the celebration of the thirteen hundredth anniversary of the arrival of Christianity among the Croats), Nin (1979, "Branimir's Year"), and Marija Bistrica (1984, the National Eucharistic Congress). In June, 1970, Franciscan Nikola Tavelić (1340–92) of Šibenik, a martyr who died in the Middle East, was canonized as the first Croatian saint. Leopold Bogdan Mandić (1866–1942) was canonized in October, 1983, and martyr Marko Križevčanin (1589–1619) in 1995.

In 1977, a new dispute developed within the ranks of the Catholic Church in Croatia, between the Episcopal Conference and the Association of Contemporary Christian Theologians *(Teološko društvo Kršćanska sadašnjost* [TDKS]). The association, founded by Cardinal Šeper, himself a liberal and advocate of the Second Vatican Council, had been uniting theologically progressive and ecumenically minded clergymen since 1968. The association published newspapers, brochures, and books that spread the council's ideas. In May, 1977, it changed its legal status to a "self-managing interest community." This move was condemned by several bishops (including Franić) and Jesuits, who viewed the association as the regime's "Trojan horse."[44] Consequently, several clerics who were members of the society were suspended.

Throughout the 1980s, the church was particularly emphatic about granting amnesty to political prisoners and rehabilitating Cardinal Stepinac. In particular, it wanted the cardinal's name cleared of the accusations of collaboration and participating in the brutality against the Serbs. The church participated in discussions on human rights and the development of democracy. For example, forty-three prominent members of the Catholic clergy from Croatia demanded amnesty for political prisoners in 1980. Cardinal Kuharić demanded greater respect for human rights, political equality for Christians, and access to prisons, hospitals, and the armed forces for Catholic priests. He also rejected the accusation that Stepinac was a fascist.[45] In the late 1980s, the church supported the political pluralization of Croatian society and openly displayed its preference for the main party, the Croatian Democratic Community *(Hrvatska demokratska zajednica* [HDZ]). However, it was more cautious than it had been a few decades earlier, and it maintained an independent and critical position that enabled it to distance itself from the outbursts of extreme Croat nationalism and prevent it from leaning too heavily on a single-party option.

The ancient myth that Bosnia-Herzegovina's Muslim Slavs were actually part of the Croat nation (Croats of two denominations) had not been altogether abandoned in some Croatian circles. Cardinal Kuharić demonstrated this in a statement he made in Australia in 1981, in which he hailed "my Croat brothers, both Catholic and Muslim." Similar theses of the common Croat origin and unity of Croatia and Bosnia-Herzegovina were published by the Croatian emigrant press. Catholic historian Dominik Mandić argued in 1963 that Bosnian Muslims are 95–97 percent Croatian and thus are "the purest Croats." In his 1981 book entitled *Nationalism in Contemporary Europe*, Franjo Tudjman, a former general in the Yugoslav People's Army and later a dissident historian, wrote that the two republics are in "geoeconomic connection; their union would be in the interest of Croatia, Bosnia Herzegovina, and all of Yugoslavia" and that "the objective examination of the numerical composition of the population of the Bosnia-Herzegovina cannot ignore that the majority of the Muslims is in its ethnic character and speech incontrovertibly of Croatian origin."[46]

The Communists' fear of a recurrence of the Polish debacle of the 1980s and their commitment to the gradual liberalization of politics in Yugoslavia led them to enter into polemical discussions with the Catholic Church. However, they continued to repress those within the ecclesiastic body who dared speak too vocally, accusing them of "political pettifoggery" and of being "profascist." In the late 1970s and early 1980s, the authorities criticized the wartime role of the Catholic Church, and especially Archbishop Stepinac, on one hand, and the current activities of senior church dignitaries, including Cardinal Kuharić, on the other.

MEDJUGORJE: "MESSAGES FROM HEAVEN"

Events in Medjugorje, a remote region of Herzegovina, first caught the attention of the local public then, at breathtaking speed, of the international (Roman Catholic) public as well. The Holy Virgin, the "Lady" or "Queen of Peace" as she is said to have described herself, was revealed to six local children (originally eight) several times, beginning on June 24, 1981. The apparition once again focused public attention on the intricate conflict between the church hierarchy (more precisely, Bishop Pavao Žanić of Mostar and the parish priests) and the Franciscans, who were not under the direct jurisdiction of the bishop, and between the Socialist authorities and the Roman Catholic Church.

The long-lasting discord within the church remained an open wound even under Socialist rule and began growing in the 1960s, when the Vatican instructed the Franciscans to relinquish jurisdiction over their parishes in the Mostar diocese to the parish priests and concentrate on missionary work instead. Many Franciscans from Herzegovina joined the Good Shepherd Association in protest. Although he had been imprisoned for a brief period after the war, Bishop Petar Čule of Mostar maintained cordial relations with the authorities, inviting the antipathy of the Catholic population whose relations with the state were, at best, somewhat restrained. While in Rome in 1965, Bishop Čule convinced the Vatican to revise the 1923 agreement. As a result, a further twenty-one of the sixty-three Franciscan parishes came under his jurisdiction immediately and the fate of the remaining forty-two was to be discussed. Two years later, the bishop managed to acquire, with the pope's assistance, twelve more parishes, and five more in 1975. The Franciscans reacted strongly to this incursion and, in an open letter, accused the bishop of arbitrari-

ness. They also wrote to the Vatican to protest the injustices they believed were being done to them. Nevertheless, the Holy See remained
firmly on the bishop's side and enabled him to gradually assume control.
In 1976, the Vatican abrogated Franciscan provincial dominion over
Herzegovina and placed the Franciscans under the direct jurisdiction of
the papal Franciscan superior.[47]

When Žanić was appointed bishop of Mostar in 1980 he immediately
fell out with the Franciscans over the new allocation of parishes. The
parishioners, accustomed to the Franciscans, gave the new parish priests
a cold welcome. Franciscan monks were affectionately addressed as *ujak*
(uncle), while priests were addressed with the more stoical title of
gospodin (Sir). Sometimes they ignored priests entirely or physically
prevented them from entering churches. Consequently, some parishes
remained without clergymen of any kind. The Franciscans, however,
continued to covertly conduct masses and offer sacraments in unconse-
crated buildings. Two young Franciscan monks, Ivica Vego and Ivan
Prusina, openly resisted some of the bishop's rulings. Žanić arranged for
their suspension in April, 1981, and their expulsion from the order a year
later. Both remained at a Franciscan monastery in Mostar.

Dutch anthropologist Mart Bax refers to the two-year period before
the first apparition as the period of "mystical preparation," which, needless to say, would not have succeeded had it not been for the rich and long
religious tradition of the region.[48] Even before the Franciscans arrived
centuries ago, the locals revered the spirits and anthropomorphic power
believed to reside in the mountain on which the Holy Virgin is later said
to have revealed herself, and they ritually sacrificed lambs to appease the
spirits they believed dwelt there. The Franciscans added the mountain to
their calendar of religious festivities, organizing processions there in
praise of Jesus and the Holy Virgin in the hope of securing their protection. The Turks built a fortress on Mount Šipovac, also known as Grml-
javinac, and several Serb families moved to the area when it was under
Austro-Hungarian rule. This gave rise to religious tension and reciprocal
violence, especially during the interwar period.

At the pope's request (according to the official version, Pius XI had a
vision instructing him to erect a cross on the "highest Herzegovinian
Golgotha") a huge cross was erected on the mountain, which had been
renamed Križevac in 1933 to commemorate the nineteen hundredth anniversary of the Crucifixion. Brno Smoljan, a Franciscan monk who was
also charged with accomplishing the task, brought the news to Medjugorje.[49] According to oral tradition, the natural disasters that had regularly devastated vineyards and tobacco plantations and destroyed har-

vests never occurred again. The region was, however, overwhelmed by a catastrophe of a different kind: it was afflicted by a series of horrifying war crimes. The Ustasha "cleansed" the area of Serbs by hurling them en masse from a precipice. Needless to say, the Chetniks retaliated with atrocities of their own. The blood-drenched region was finally "pacified"—through brute force, persecution, and appropriation—by the partisans. One of their many accomplishments was the summary execution of twenty-eight Franciscans from the nearby monastery at Široki Brijeg.

In the late 1970s, a Franciscan monk from Medjugorje reported the ongoing dispute between his order and the parish clergy to a number of senior members of a mystical Catholic group known as the Charismatic Revival Movement, who reassured the monk of the Holy Virgin's help. Enthused by this revelation, the monk returned to his monastery and embarked on a vigorous campaign of religious enlightenment, prayer, and confession, and publicly announced that God would reveal a "special mercy" to the local children. It was in this electrified and expectant atmosphere that the Holy Virgin "actually" began revealing herself, and it was none other than Franciscans (including Ljudevit Rupčić) who relayed her messages to the witnesses to the public. Bax notes that an apparition of the Holy Virgin allegedly appeared in another parish within the Mostar diocese at almost the same time. The Franciscans distanced themselves from this second apparition, however, and it fell into oblivion.[50]

It is worth noting that more than 100 apparitions were reported throughout the world from 1930–80, including over 60 in Italy, 11 in France, and 7 in Spain. However, none were ever reported in a country ruled by a Socialist government.[51] The message delivered by the Holy Virgin when she appeared to the three children in Fátima, Portugal, was laced with anti-Communist sentiment.[52] The alleged ability of an individual to channel communication between the earthly world and a world of spirits is an ancient and time-tested instrument for achieving specific goals. People with such an "ability," the exclusive intercessors between the ethereal world and our own—in this case the Franciscans—use their exclusivity to manufacture a legitimacy and authority of their own that they can then use against their rivals or adversaries.

The suspended Franciscan monks, Vego and Prusina, provided support to the witnesses. The Holy Virgin is said to have spoken to some of them about the bishop's wrongful condemnation of the insubordinate monks, adding that the bishop's acrimony was based on a personal grudge, that the two monks should remain in Mostar, that the congregation should pray for them, and that the bishop should publicly reconcile with the "two sons of the Church." Bishop Žanić's reaction was restrained and

occasionally openly skeptical. He advised caution about officially acknowledging such miracles. After an unsuccessful attempt to silence the
Franciscan "truth," a direct conflict developed between them. He issued
a pastoral letter and circulated pamphlets through his parish priests banning parishioners from making pilgrimages to Medjugorje or from participating in the "theatrics" and "religious decadence" taking place
there. He denounced the whole thing as a "farce" and a "lie," and called
the apparitions a "Franciscan miracle." Anyone defying his orders was to
be denied the sacraments.

The Medjugorje "cult," according to Bishop Žanić, did not comply
with ecclesiastic canons and was a threat to the church's normal functioning. The bishop was not alone in this belief. In 1991, the Yugoslav
Episcopal Conference issued the so-called Zadar Statement in which it
officially declared that "it was not possible to state with any certainty
that the apparitions and messages were of supernatural origin." Žanić
managed to convince the bishops at the 1982 Episcopal Conference to
publicly oppose "official" pilgrimages to Medjugorje organized by the
church, although "unofficial" pilgrimages were tolerated. On the other
hand, Žanić defended the witnesses ("these children tell no lies" he said),
the apparitions, and even the Franciscan monks from the "inappropriate
and offensive" press reports by the regime (which labeled the events
"clerical," "fascist," and "nationalist") or other critical and skeptical
media.

The Franciscans were by far the most numerous order in the territory
of Yugoslavia: data from 1978 place their number at 1,094. As explained
earlier, the Franciscans were a highly cohesive order that took a pragmatic and compliant approach toward authority. Needless to say, Herzegovina's Franciscans confirmed the authenticity of the Medjugorje apparitions and saw in this "special mercy" a unique opportunity to
reestablish and secure their foothold in a territory they believed was traditionally "theirs." They skillfully exploited the apparitions to settle
matters within the church in Herzegovina, calling the viewpoint of the
bishop and his priests a "humiliation to God and the people." The
bishop's furious responses worked to the advantage of the monks, who
portrayed themselves as victims of his tyranny. It was a time-tested
method: monastic orders had successfully defended themselves from the
expansionist tendencies of the parish clergy with the "help" of the apparitions of holy figures on several occasions throughout the Catholic
world, including seventeenth-century Ireland and New Spain, seven-
teenth- and eighteenth-century Peru, and nineteenth-century Holland.[53]

The intense popularity of the local Franciscans easily overwhelmed the accusations of the Communist authorities and the skepticism of the Catholic hierarchy. Indeed, the first to support the witnesses and the Franciscans were the local population. The latter were also compelled by the prospect of making a profit and their tacit disappointment in the Socialist regime. The local authorities were evidently pro-Serb: Serb officials in the Croatian section of Herzegovina were referred to as "bureau Chetniks." The Croatian diaspora (which hoped to cause a rift within the Socialist ranks) and a number of prominent Catholic officials endorsed the Medjugorje apparitions. For example, in December, 1983, Bishop Frane Franić of Split declared that the events in Medjugorje had achieved in two years more than their missionary work had in forty. Nevertheless, of the forty-two Catholic bishops in Yugoslavia, he alone publicly "supported" the apparition. Finally, some of the world's most eminent Mariologists, including Hans Urs von Balthasar (the pope's most cherished theologian), Michael Carroll, and René Laurentin, also endorsed the apparitions.

News of the "messages from heaven" traveled to the four corners of the world, changing the karstic backwater that was Medjugorje into a global pilgrimage center and attracting millions of believers and other visitors (70,000 in 1982 and 100,000 by the following year, between 8 million and 10 million by 1987, and a total of 18 million by 1991). The "Lady's voice" *(Gospin glas)* reached out to non-Catholics as well: the "holy site" was also visited by local Muslim and Orthodox believers, which is quite consistent with Bosnia-Herzegovina's syncretistic religious tradition.[54] There were reports of miraculous healing and unusual sightings: new apparitions, sudden illuminations, writing in the sky, revolving crosses, revolving sun, and omens. The witness were said to be able to heal by touch and were asked to bless pilgrims' crosses and rosaries. Today, masses and confessions are still held in six different languages, and dozens of Franciscan monks of different nationalities still live and perform their religious duties in the newly erected buildings. Some of the witnesses—now adults—continue to report apparitions.

The Vatican found itself in a dilemma: it was unable to withdraw its support for the local bishop on one hand, and unable to ignore the exceptional interest Medjugorje generated among Catholic believers throughout the world on the other. It therefore chose to wait and advised the bishop to exercise a "high degree of caution." Žanić convened a commission to look into the phenomenon, but it failed to find any incongruity with the teachings of the church. It was consequently dissolved and replaced by another. The second commission was interdisciplinary and included a lay member. In 1985, Žanić reversed tactics and tried instead to prove that the activities of the Franciscans and the witnesses were indeed in accord with the traditions and teachings of the church.

The Socialist authorities' initial reaction to the events in this remote part of Herzegovina was nervous and repressive. Police blocked the route to the mountain, interrogated witnesses, conducted a search of the Medjugorje presbytery, and sent informers to infiltrate the ranks of the pilgrims. Pressure was applied on both the monks and the pilgrims. Several members of the local Čitluk League of Communists were expelled from the party for making the pilgrimage and even more were chastised. In 1981, Branko Mikulić, a Croatian member of the Presidium of the Central Committee of the League of Communists, accused the "clero-nationalists" of exploiting the "Holy Virgin" to "mislead the unschooled people and for political manipulation." A second Croat politician from Bosnia-Herzegovina, Franjo Herljević, also condemned the events. A local Čitluk politician, Milenko Bernarda, dubbed the apparition the "Ustasha Lady."[55] The press dismissed the entire matter as superstition and accused the Franciscans of being skilled manipulators.

The authorities eventually arrested three Franciscans. Ferdo Vlašić and Jozo Križić, the editor and secretary of the religious publication *Naša ognjišta* (which was particularly popular with the Croatian diaspora), were jailed for eight years and five and one-half years, respectively, for "hostile activities, contacts with Croatian nationalist circles in the West, preaching to Croatian emigrants," and for "being in possession of seditious literature" about Stepinac.[56] Also imprisoned was Jozo Zovko, the charismatic parish priest of Medjugorje, who was accused of preaching against the state in two sermons delivered in 1981 (in which he mentioned "forty years of slavery and discrimination against believers") and sentenced to four and one-half years in prison. The persecution of these clergymen was soon likened to that in Vendée during the mutiny against the French republican authorities in 1793–94. Less severely punished Franciscans were also seen as "political martyrs."

A media campaign against the defendants was launched as soon as the trials began. Zovko was accused of being pro-Ustasha, which provoked reactions from abroad: some forty thousand letters of support were sent from Italy alone. As a result, Zovko's sentence was commuted twice and he was released after serving only eighteen months. The exceptional interest the Medjugorje phenomenon generated worldwide eventually prodded authorities to relax their stance and, seeing an opportunity to profit from religious tourism, they granted permission in 1989 for the construction of hotels in Medjugorje).

Despite the ongoing war in Bosnia-Herzegovina, and contrary to common practice, Pope John Paul II—known for his interest in the Holy Virgin and the Medjugorje apparition—immediately accepted Bishop Žanić's resignation when the latter turned seventy-five in June, 1993.[57] Many saw this as a "reproof" for his opposition to the apparition. However, Ratko Perić, the new bishop of Mostar, and Cardinal Vinko Puljić, head of Bosnia-Herzegovina's new Episcopal Conference, both shared Žanić's views on the matter. Indeed, Perić's reaction to a 1997 article about the "authentic apparition" in Medjugorje written by retired bishop Franić of Split, one of the most zealous advocates of the Medjugorje miracles, was very polemical. He reminded the retired bishop of the Vatican's instructions and the Zadar Statement. Nevertheless, the church's opinion had changed: In June, 1998, the Vatican's Congregation for the Teachings of the Faith, for which Monsignor Tarsici Bertone serves as secretary, officially approved pilgrimages to Medjugorje.

RENEWAL AND DIVISION OF THE SERBIAN ORTHODOX ECCLESIASTIC STRUCTURE

Unlike Stepinac, Metropolite Josif of the Orthodox Church held a service for the liberators—partisan and Soviet soldiers—when Belgrade was liberated in October, 1944, and Patriarch Gavrilo later thanked "Mother Russia" for rescuing Slavic unity. The Episcopal *sabor*, convened for the first time since April, 1941, ordered Orthodox priests back to their duties and allocated new priests to individual dioceses to fill vacancies. All forced conversions to Catholicism were reversed. Patriarch Gavrilo remained in the West for one and one-half years after his release from a concentration camp. While there, he and Bishop Velimirović met regularly with exiled politicians and, in October 1945, they anointed Prince Aleksander Karađorđević. Church and government leaders anxiously awaited Patriarch Gavrilo's return to Belgrade in November, 1946. The synod expected him to revive the church, and the Socialist authorities, who acknowledged his patriotism and pro-Yugoslav sentiments, were counting on his cooperation.[58] A new ecclesiastic constitution was expected to acclimatize the church with the new situation—its separation from the state.

The problems faced by the Serbian Orthodox Church were similar to those faced by the Catholics: the authorities were nationalizing its schools, property, and presses; persecuting its priests; and shutting down its publications. They accused it of advocating a greater Serbia, and of chauvinism and hostile propaganda. The church was also short on human resources, having lost about 515 clergymen during the war. Several of its senior officials were accused of collaboration, including Bishops Irinej and Velimirović, who spent the duration of the war abroad. What most annoyed the authorities were their anti-Communist attitudes and the fact that they remained in the West after the war and launched attacks on the Yugoslav regime. Velimirović condemned Yugoslavia as "a state without God's blessing, a school without faith, politics without honour, army without patriotism." Moreover, he considered it a slandering of Christ, Saint Sava, the people's past, and all that the people held sacred.[59] Metropolite Josef was also accused of collaboration.

Religious dignitaries who refused to cooperate or who opposed the clerical associations were persecuted or imprisoned, including Metropolite Arsenije of Montenegro, sentenced to eleven years' imprisonment "for opposing the creation of clerical associations," and Bishop Jovan Ilić of Niš, Bishop Emilijan Piperković of Timok, and Bishops Simeon Stanković (Šabac), Arsenije Bradvarović (Montenegrin littoral), Makarije Djordjević (Budimljan-Polimje), Nektarije (Banja Luka), Irinej Ćirić (Bačka), and Varnava Nastić (Dabar-Bosna). The most common charges were "spreading religious and national hatred" and conducting "activities against the Popular Front." Joanikije Lipovac, a pro-Chetnik metropolite from Montenegro who openly collaborated with the Germans and Italians, was killed while fleeing the partisan advance at the end of the war.[60] A number of lower-ranking priests were also under continuous attack and pressure and were continually tormented by the media.

Gavrilo held a meeting with Tito less than a month after his return from the West. From then until his death in May, 1950, he insisted he was loyal to the state and that he believed there were no conflicts between the Serbian Orthodox Church and the regime. Bishop Vikentije, who categorically supported the Yugoslav side in the dispute over Trieste, succeeded him. The regime returned the favor by awarding Vikentije a medal in 1954. The Orthodox Church fared little better than its Catholic counterpart when it came to internal discord: a dispute emerged between the church and an Orthodox clerical association, the Association of Orthodox Priests of Yugoslavia (established in March, 1949),[61] which the regime hoped to use as a weapon against it. The association's title mentions only "Orthodox" priests (as opposed to "Serbian Orthodox"), preempting the hitherto axiomatic likening of Orthodoxy among Yugoslav South Slavs to Serb nationhood ("Serb Orthodoxy"). The UPSJ's goals were harmony, patriotism, enlightenment of the population, cooperation with authorities, and the advancement of literacy and culture in general. Its members, "patriotic" clergymen, were regularly decorated by the state in return for criticizing the church hierarchy and exiled bishops through their publication, the *Vestnik (Gazette)*. In April, 1967, the official journal of the Serbian Orthodox Church, *Pravoslavje (Orthodoxy)*, finally began responding to these attacks.

Such associations first appeared in Serbia in the 1880s and were revived by a reform-minded lower clergy in November, 1942. After the war, an association was established in each republic, disregarding the borders of the existing Orthodox dioceses. The Montenegrin association was established in June, 1945, and the Croatian, Bosnian, Serbian, and Macedonian associations were established between August and December, 1947. According to the newspaper *Borba*, 80 percent of the 1,700 Serbian Orthodox priests were members of the associations by June, 1952. Of those, 81 were elected to organs of the authorities, 527 were active in the Popular Front, 452 in the Red Cross, 201 worked in state agricultural enterprises, and 122 were engaged on various cooperative farms. However, members of the associations, which claimed to represent 83 percent of all Orthodox priests in 1978, were still afraid of church reprisals. Negotiations between the bishops and the UPSJ on the organization of these associations were fruitless.[62] Needless to say, the Holy Synod continued to refuse to recognize the associations, which were also renounced by the patriarchate on the grounds that they contradicted canon law and threatened church unity. The associations were seen as an internal opposition, a Trojan horse, the regime's "religious police."

After Vikentije's death, the *sabor* replaced him in August, 1958, with Bishop German (Hranislav Djorić) of Žiča, the editor of the patriarchate's journal, *Glasnik*, and general secretary of the synod, who was known to have openly collaborated with the UPSJ in the past. He became the "forty-third patriarch since the foundation of the patriarchate under Tsar Dušan, and the fifth in succession of the revived patriarchate." The "traveling Patriarch"—he visited the Soviet Union, the Middle East, and Bulgaria, and traveled widely across Yugoslavia—was the first postwar patriarch to visit Bosnia-Herzegovina and meet with the *reis-ul-ulema*, Sujleman Hadži Kemura. He was decorated several times by both the Soviet Union and Yugoslavia.

The church was particularly affected by the loss of its overseas parishes. In 1963, Bishop Dionisije Milivojević of the North American parish announced that they were seceding. Several Serbian Orthodox parishes in Czechoslovakia (1945, 1948), Hungary (Buda diocese) and Romania (Timisoara diocese) merged with the Orthodox churches in their own countries (the Czechoslovak Orthodox Church, founded in 1951, and the Romanian Orthodox Church). These events were followed by the—as they explained—"arbitrary secession" of the "Macedonian

Orthodox Church" (the dioceses of Skopje, Zletovo-Strumica, Štip, and Ohrid-Bitola). The Macedonians were striving to constitute their own Orthodox Church and revive the historical Ohrid archdiocese in order to defend their national identity from Serbian and Bulgarian appetites and those of the Serbian and Bulgarian Orthodox Churches. The Serbian Orthodox Church's *sabor* refused to recognize the Macedonian Orthodox Church, but the UPSJ did. The ecumenical patriarch in Istanbul also refused to recognize the new church. By the early 1970s, the Serbian Orthodox Church had a total of twenty-one dioceses in Yugoslavia, and the Macedonian Orthodox Church had four.

The church was also concerned that its parishes in Montenegro might secede. Patriarch German's announcement in 1970 that the Montenegrins were merely "Serbs with a different name" was intended as a step toward preventing further ecclesiastic schism and national division.[63] Serb nationalists still use popular idioms in reference to the Montenegrins: "common Serbs," "the elite of the Serbs," "constituent part of the Serb nation," and others. However, many Montenegrins emphasize their individual, non-Serb national identity.

The Serbian Orthodox Church found its modus vivendi with the Communist authorities, although the latter frequently accused it of nationalism: some experts state that it represented a feeble and loyal opposition to the Socialist regime. The Holy Synod and all three postwar patriarchs eagerly cooperated with the authorities during those decades. The church recovered, over a period of several years and with the considerable assistance of the state, both financially and in terms of manpower. By 1971 as many as 181 new churches and eight new monasteries had been built, and 841 churches and forty-eight monasteries had been renovated. The publication of books and journals resumed and began to grow. The state also subsidized the church (social insurance, financial assistance), which in return offered the regime access to eastern European "Orthodox" countries (Romania, Bulgaria, the Soviet Union, and also Greece), which Serbian Orthodox clergy regularly frequented. From around 1955 the Serbian Orthodox Church enjoyed a much higher degree of freedom than other religious organizations under Socialist rule.[64]

As it had throughout its history, the church repeatedly emphasized the strong relationship (because it could not emphasize the identity) between Serb nationhood and Orthodoxy. Among the most outstanding examples are the ritual cremation of Tsar Dušan's mortal remains in the Church of Saint Mark in Belgrade in 1968, the common referral to Macedonians as "southern Serbs," the reaction to Croatia's national euphoria (the Croatian Spring) in the late 1960s and early 1970s, and the appeal to defend the Serbs and their holy sites in Kosovo in 1982.[65] On that occasion, the bulletin *Pravoslavje* used terminology such as "our memories, our heart, the essence of our being," in reference to Kosovo.[66] Some of the clergy began reviving the old myths that the Serbs were "Christ's nation," that as a nation they "suffered more for Christ than other nations," and that the Serb population in Kosovo was being "crucified." An editorial in *Glasnik* criticized attempts to rehabilitate Cardinal Stepinac, holding him responsible for the violence committed against the Serbs during the Catholicization campaign in the NDH. The clergy further demanded that the pope instruct bishops to apologize to the Serbs for the Ustasha's war crimes, and that the pope himself should repent at Jasenovac.[67]

In the 1980s, during the first decade of the Kosovo crisis, the church "saw a chance to pull itself out of the marginal position."[68] In the latter half of the 1980s it began making more demands, seeking, for example, a simpler procedure for acquiring building permits for churches, social benefits for teachers and students at the Faculty of Theology, and the restitution of nationalized property. It had already started to address the issues of religious education in schools and civil marriages. It also demanded that the state stop interfering in its internal affairs. The church was growing in confidence and its relations with the state were improving. Indeed, the wave of rejuvenated Serb nationalism was riding abreast of the church's renaissance. In the April 1, 1986, issue of *Pravoslavje*, Father Žarko Gavrilović mentioned the alleged threats to Serbs in Bosnia-Herzegovina and posed the question, "Is Bosnia and Herzegovina becoming another Kosovo for Orthodox Serbs and Serbian priests?" Similarly, in 1988, Father Dragomir Ubiparipović wrote that the Orthodox Serbs in Bosnia-Herzegovina were being subjected to "cultural and religious genocide." Atanasije Jevtić and Jovan Pavlović, representatives of the church hierarchy, began to contribute "in highlighting the threat from Islam and delegitimizing Islam's very presence as valid."[69]

In 1988, the remains of Prince Lazar, who had recently been canonized by the Serbian Orthodox Church, were taken on a procession through all "Serb" lands, including Bosnia-Herzegovina and Kosovo. The trek began at the monastery in Ravanica and continued through the dioceses of Zvornik-Tuzla, Šabac-Valjevo, Šumadija, and Žiča, to Gračanica in Kosovo. In some places, the remains of Serb soldiers and civilians killed during the Second World War were disinterred and, following a special service, ritually buried in Bileća, Kupres, Fahovići, and Vlasenica in 1990; and in Žitomislić, Prebilovci, Glamoč, Livno, Ljubinje, Trebinje, Majevica, and Banja Luka in 1991. "The grave is the greatest sacred object and the oldest Serbian church," wrote Matija Bećković in 1988. "The grave is our farthest and most persisting faith. We are still swearing solemnly to bones and graves because we are still not having steadiest pillars, better remedies, nor more powerful convictions."[70] The logic of such events—which will be discussed in more detail in the next chapter—helped to set the stage for the carnage that was to eventually follow in Croatia and especially in Bosnia-Herzegovina.

THE JEWISH COMMUNITY

Only one-fifth of Yugoslavia's thriving prewar Jewish community survived the war. Of the 12,495 Jews residing there in 1946, 7,578 emigrated to Israel between 1948 and 1952.[71] According to Jewish sources, 1,292 survived the war in Bosnia-Herzegovina, 1,871 were there in 1948, 1,285 in 1958, and 1,292 in 1965. Their suffering during the war helped reduce the difference between Sephardim and Ashkenazi within the Jewish community. Although formally organized as the Federation of Jewish Communities of Yugoslavia, it never regained the vitality and influence it enjoyed before the war. However, it is difficult to estimate the correct number of Bosnian Jews after the war because official censuses and data provided by the Jewish community differ considerably. Many Jews moved to other parts of Yugoslavia or declared themselves as members of other national groups. So, officially there were only 310 in 1953, 381 in 1961, 708 in 1971, and 343 in 1981. According to data from the Jewish community, about 1,100 Jews lived in Sarajevo in 1984 and 1,200 in 1992.[72] In Sarajevo alone there were 1,413 Jews in 1946 and 1,304 in 1964—all served by a single rabbi.

THE MUSLIM RELIGIOUS COMMUNITY

The Muslim religious community fared little better under Socialist rule than its Orthodox and Catholic counterparts. Muslim schools were mostly closed, religious orders were banned, and *vakuf* property was nationalized. Islamic courts, religious education in public schools, tax collection, and cultural-religious organizations and associations were abolished. The religious press was shut down, and orthodox Muslim women were forbidden to wear the veil. Islam was forced to retreat to the private sphere. Among the associations that were banned was the Young Muslims. Although it at first "succeeded in re-establishing around the same three founding groups a network," it was soon severely attacked and practically disappeared.[73] Many of its members and leaders were arrested and imprisoned. Some were condemned to death. The persecution of this student body, which openly opposed the regime's moves against Muslim religious organizations, took place from March, 1946, to August, 1949. One of its members, Alija Izetbegović, was sentenced to six years' imprisonment in 1946. Three year later, a number of defendants received much harsher sentences, and four of them—Hasan Biber, Nusref Fazlibegović, Halid Katjaz, and Omer Stupac—were executed.

In 1947, the Socialist regime formalized its relations with the Islamic Religious Community *(Islamska zajednica vjernika* [IZV]). Irwin describes it as a passive and patriotic organization, loyal to the regime, and with a politically correct leadership. This enabled it to freely manage its property according to Islamic law. The IZV's 1947 constitution defined its highest body as the "Vakuf Sabor of the Muslim Religious Community in SFRJ" and was chaired by the *reis-ul-ulema.* It included the *sabors* of four administrative provinces in Yugoslavia with headquarters in Sarajevo (for Bosnia-Herzegovina, Croatia, and Slovenia), Skopje, Priština, and Titograd. In 1957, Hadži Sujleman efendi Kemura, known for his loyalty to the state, became the new *reis-ul-ulema.* The IZV was again reorganized by the constitutions of 1957 and 1959, which allowed it to control its own spiritual and secular matters and broadened access to religious education and religious material.[74] It adopted yet another constitution in 1969 and changed its name to simply the Islamic Community *(Islamska zajednica* [IZ]).

There was a high level of trust between the Communist authorities and the Muslim community. This was confirmed by the *reis-ul-ulema,* who stated that the Muslims recognized both secular authority and "Socialist science." The Socialist regime lauded Kemura for preventing "reactionaries" from infiltrating the Islamic Community's leadership. The Muslim religious press in Yugoslavia was not as critical of the authorities as were the Orthodox and Catholic newspapers, and Muslim religious leaders did not figure as prominently in public life as their Orthodox and Catholic counterparts.[75] This benevolent attitude toward Islam later changed considerably. The rise of Muslim national self-awareness contributed to a religious revival as well. The result was that religious institutions became the legitimate representatives of their national identity.

There is scant and inaccurate data on the number of mosques and Muslim religious institutions in Socialist Yugoslavia. In 1945, there were some 1,022 mosques and *mesdžids.* Some 900 mosques were built in the country after the Second World War, bringing the total to 1,985 in the 1970s. Of those, 1,092 were in Sarajevo's province (plus 592 *mesdžids),* 445 were in Priština's, 372 were in Skopje's, and 76 were in Titograd's province. According to some estimates, there were 2,000 to 3,000 mosques in Yugoslavia in the 1980s, most of which were in Bosnia-Herzegovina. Muslim religious publications, periodicals, and schools were also widespread (three regional *madrasahs*). Although the "Faculty of Islamic Theology" was established in Sarajevo in 1977, many Yugoslav Muslim students were educated in Islamic countries, including Egypt, Iraq, Libya, Morocco, Saudi Arabia, Kuwait, and Sudan.[76]

The Yugoslav Islamic community nurtured strong ties with the Islamic world, from Indonesia and Pakistan to Algeria and Morocco. It sent its delegates to the World Islamic Conference, the Soviet Congress of Muslims, Muslim youth congresses, and Islamic scientific seminars. The community also received financial assistance from wealthy Islamic countries and other countries that supported the development of Islam, including Saudi Arabia, Kuwait, Libya, Iraq, and Sudan. In 1977, the *reis-ul-ulema*, Hadži Naim efendi Hadžiabdić, declared that the material position of the Muslim community and clergy "had never been better."[77]

As was the case with Yugoslavia's other religious communities, the Muslim religious community was subjected to internal conflict. A new order of dervishes, which had an especially large following in Kosovo, appeared in Yugoslavia in 1974. The IZV banned the order, which was led by Sheikh Jemali Hadži-Šehu, forcing it to register as an independent organization.[78] On the other hand, the beginning of construction in 1981 on the Zagreb mosque also stirred considerable commotion. Although it suffered several setbacks, including a fire in 1984 and a lot of red tape, the mosque opened in 1987. Muslim authorities also publicly supported the Albanian Muslims in their conflict with Serbian authorities in Kosovo.

THE MUSLIMS AS A NATION

Pointing at the interdependence of Islam and Bosnian Muslims (Bosniaks), sociologist Ibrahim Bakić notes, "Islam was needed by Bosniaks to come into being and to constitute themselves, while Bosniaks secured Islam its subsistence."[79] The secularization of Bosnia's Muslims began under the Austro-Hungarians and continued through both prewar and postwar Yugoslavia. The confusion and differences of opinion regarding the Muslims' identity as a nation and religious community also was evident in the first three postwar population censuses. At first, Yugoslav Communists were convinced that Muslims would opt for either Serb or Croat national identity since only five constitutive nations were recognized.

The table 8-2 shows the results (in absolute figures) for all six censuses conducted in Socialist Yugoslavia. The ensuing paragraphs present the

TABLE 8-2 *Population of Bosnia-Herzegovina by national identities, 1948–91*

Census	Muslims	Serbs	Croats	Yugoslavs	Total in B-H
1948	788,403[a]	1,136,116	614,142	0	2,563,764
1953	0	1,264,372	654,229	891,800[b]	2,847,459
1961	842,248[c]	1,406,057	711,665	275,883	3,277,948
1971	1,482,430[d]	1,393,148	772,491	43,796	3,746,111
1981	1,629,924[e]	1,320,644	758,136	326,280	4,102,783
1991	1,905,829[e]	1,369,258	755,895	239,834	4,364,574

[a] Muslims, undetermined.
[b] Yugoslavs, undetermined.
[c] Muslims in ethnic sense.
[d] Muslims in sense of nationality.
[e] Muslims.

TABLE 8-3 *Self-identification of Bosnian Muslims, 1948*

Muslim Serbs	71,125
Muslim Croats	24,914
Muslims, Undetermined	788,403
Total Muslims in Bosnia-Herzegovina	890,094

chronology of events and the changing status and statistics of Bosnia's Muslim Slavs.[80]

The Muslims, who represented about 34.5 percent of Bosnia-Herzegovina's total population, had three options in the first census of 1948: they could identify themselves as Serbs, Croats, or "nationally undeclared" Muslims. Banac notes that "this was the time of Serb predominance in Bosnia-Herzegovina" and most of the high-level Bosnian Muslim leaders—including Avdo Humo, Hajro Kapetanović, Šefket Maglajlić, and Hakija Pozderac—identified themselves as Serbs, although others, including Džemal Bijedić, Osman Karabegović, and Pašaga Mandžić, identified themselves as Yugoslavs.[81]

Unlike their counterparts in Bosnia-Herzegovina, Muslim Slavs in other republics identified themselves with the predominate nation. Another process must be mentioned at this point: the migration of Yugoslavia's Muslim population—Slavic Muslims, Turks, and Albanians—into Turkey during the first two decades after the war.[82]

By the 1953 census, the category "nationally undeclared Muslim" had been replaced by "nationally undeclared Yugoslav." An estimated 918,500 ethnic Muslims were in Yugoslavia and 891,800 in Bosnia-Herzegovina (32.2 percent of the Bosnian population). By the third census in 1961, there were about 1,118,000 Muslims in Bosnia-Herzegovina (34.1 percent), including those in the new "ethnic Muslim" category (842,248) and the majority of those in the "nationally undeclared Yugoslav" category.[83]

The first postwar politician to emphasize the urgency of recognizing Muslim Slavs as a sixth Yugoslav constitutive nation was Hussein Husaga Čisić, a liberal parliamentarian from Mostar. However, the proposals he made in 1945 and in January, 1946, were largely ignored, partly because of his ambiguous wartime role.[84] The Serb Communists in particular tried to have Bosnia-Herzegovina annexed to Serbia immediately after the war, but were unsuccessful. Although the question was discussed, no final conclusion was reached. Rodoljub Čolaković, a leading Bosnian Serb Communist, told Parliament in 1946 that Bosnia-Herzegovina's Muslims are a "separate—but, for the most part, still nationally undeclared—Slavic ethnic group" and are "equal to Serbs and Croats." In 1953, Moša Pijade declared that the Muslim category "indicates a distinct affiliation to the Muslim faith and is not related to the issue of nationality." He added that Muslims could define themselves as Serbs, Croats, or "nationally undeclared" Yugoslavs. This, he hoped, would "bring an end to the non-scientific and unenlightened habit of confusing religious and national identities."[85]

It was not until later that the League of Communists began nurturing the development of the distinct Muslim national consciousness that was emerging in response to the national and territorial appetites of the neighboring republics. The ruling party's position at the time was that the Muslims "consider themselves as a distinct ethnic and historical group, and even more so as a religious group." By the mid-1960s, however, there was talk about the three "constitutive nations" of Bosnia-Herzegovina—the Serbs, Croats, and Muslims—although the latter had not yet been fully recognized as being constitutive. The Socialist authorities wanted to establish a Muslim national identity that would include Islam merely as part of a wider cultural and political doctrine.[86] They wanted to distinguish between Muslim national identity and religious affiliation, which, they claimed, were related only through cultural tradition, distinct lifestyle, and custom.

Islam did, indeed, represent only one of the many facets of Bosnian Muslim national identity, together with cultural characteristics, traditions, festivities, and personal names. They were more exposed to Western influence than were their eastern counterparts. Individual "secular-ized" laic elements of Muslim culture and religion, such as names, ex-pressions, apparel, customs, and epic traditions, were highlighted. The inappropriate use of the word *Muslim* as a designation for the nation up-set many secularized or atheist Bosnian Muslims.

Two Bosnian Muslim politicians in particular gave vocal support to the cause of establishing a distinct Muslim national identity. Atif Puri-vatra, president of the Socialist Alliance of Bosnia-Herzegovina's Com-mittee for Interethnic Relations, stated that religion was only the first step to Muslim national identity, as was the case with the Serbs and the Croats. Similarly, Avdo Sućeska saw Islam as only the foundation on which socialism enabled the development of national awareness. The campaign for the "capital M," that is, for a Muslim national (rather than religious) identity, inevitably drew the participation of members of the Muslim intelligentsia, such as Prof. Muhamed Filipović. Džemal Bijedić, a confidant of President Tito, played a crucial role in the affirmation of Muslims as a Yugoslav constitutive nation "more than any other single Communist leader of Muslim origin."[87]

The recognition of Muslim national identity is also linked to the dis-missal of Aleksander Ranković and the politics he promoted (and to a certain degree symbolized). Ranković's downfall at the Brioni plenary meeting in July, 1966, heralded a turning point in the Yugoslav political scene: it curbed Serb centralism and pressure for assimilation and boosted the autonomist aspirations of Macedonians (the creation of the Macedonian Orthodox Church in July, 1967), Muslims (now recognized as a nation), and Croats (the liberal *maspok* movement of the early 1970s). The plenary meeting resulted in a new, reformist political orien-tation for the country. It was, however, short-lived: the withdrawal of so-called Liberals within the Communist leadership in Croatia, Serbia, Slovenia, and Macedonia had already occurred in the early 1970s. "Leka"—Ranković's partisan pseudonym—was a popular figure, espe-cially in Serbia. His funeral in 1983 was a unique national manifestation attended by over a hundred thousand mourners.[88]

Following its eighteenth and twentieth sessions—held in February and May, 1968—respectively, the League of Communists of Bosnia-Herzegovina's (LCBiH) Central Committee passed a resolution entitled the "Ideological-Political Tasks of the Communists in the Further Real-ization of the Equal Rights of Nations and Nationalities and the Devel-opment of Inter-Republican Cooperation," which formally recognized Muslims Slavs as Yugoslavia's sixth constitutive nation, and no longer merely an "ethnic group." A similar resolution was passed at the LCBiH's

Fifth Congress in early January, 1969. "Yugoslavism" had finally been jettisoned as a solution to the issue of nationality. Despite a disproportionately high representation of Serbs in the LCBiH, the Central Committee took a unilateral step that required the amendment of the federal constitution by formally recognizing Muslims as a nation—and they did it without discussing the matter outside of Bosnia-Herzegovina.

Shortly thereafter, the Yugoslav leadership also publicly supported a distinct national identity for Muslims and their equal status with other nations. Commenting on the recognition of the "Muslim nation," Todo Kurtović, a senior Bosnian official and president of the Socialist Alliance of Bosnia-Herzegovina at the time, said that the "objective conditions for its recognition and affirmation have been created." Kurtović dismissed any eventual response by Bosnia's neighbors, saying, "it is important what a nation is, and not what others think it is."[89] It is significant to note that the League of Communists in Serbia and Croatia did not fully accept the notion of a Muslim national identity until the early 1970s. Mika Tripalo addressed the issue at the tenth session of Croatia's League of Communists in January, 1970, and Serb Marko Nikezić did the same in Sarajevo in December of that year. Muslim nationhood was opposed by nationalist Serb Communists and conservatives, such as authors Dobrica Ćosić and Josip Potkozorac, but the prevailing political mood of the time was a liberal one and was unburdened with myths of a greater Serbia.[90]

We must also consider the fact that the new situation seemed acceptable to Serbia and Croatia because it neither favored nor discriminated against the Serbs or the Croats. Irwin surmises that this option was most strongly supported by Edvard Kardelj because it corresponded to his notions of decentralized federalism. In his view, Bosnia-Herzegovina was intended to become "an outpost of political and national stability" in the heart of the federation.[91] The new national self-confidence of the Muslims was illustrated in the subsequent population censuses of 1971 and 1981, as shown in tables 8-4 and 8-5.

The number of "ethnic Yugoslavs" increased to 43,796 by 1971 and 326,280 by 1981 (7.9 percent of the Bosnian population). By the next census, however, their number had again decreased to 5.5 percent (239,834). The "Yugoslav" category in Bosnia-Herzegovina was particularly strong because of the increasing number of ethnically mixed marriages, especially in urban areas, where 20–30 percent of marriages were mixed: 28 percent in Mostar, 22 percent in Sarajevo, and 19 percent in Zenica. The Bosnian average was 16 percent.[92]

The last population census (table 8-6) before the outbreak of hostili-

TABLE 8-4 *Bosnia-Herzegovina population census, 1971*

Muslims	39.6%
Serbs	37.2%
Croats	20.6%

TABLE 8-5 *Bosnia-Herzegovina population census, 1981*

Muslims	39.5%
Serbs	32%
Croats	18.4%

TABLE 8-6 *Bosnia-Herzegovina population census, 1991*

Muslims	43.5%
Serbs	31.2%
Croats	17.4%

ties shows a continuation of the trend from previous censuses: decreasing Serb and Croat figures and increasing Muslim figures.

The second-largest serried group of Muslims—numbering about 240,000—lives in neighboring Sandžak Province in Serbia proper.

The national and cultural (as opposed to religious) facets of Muslims as a nation were emphasized by senior Yugoslav Communists, including Bosnian Muslims, who were characterized by their strong pro-Yugoslav inclination and the fact that they did not merely represent their own Muslim interests but always those of the republic as a whole. The process of secularizing Muslims' national identity was accompanied by a coincidental and opposite process: the ascent of Islamic self-confidence and the announcement of the explicit significance of the religious nature of the Muslim nation. Although the laic category of Muslims was favored, Islamic leaders in the 1970s revealed the strong internal bond that existed between their religion and nationality. In an article in the Muslim religious publication *Glasnik,* Imam Hadži Hussein Djozo declared that Islam was the foundation of the Muslim nation. This Islamic revival emerged from Muslims' traditional religiosity and the recognition of a national identity that was considerably marked by their religion.[93]

Until the 1970s, the Socialist regime was much more lenient with secular and religious Muslim nationalism than with other forms of religious nationalism in Yugoslavia. Part of the reason for this lay in Yugoslavia's foreign policy and its role in the Nonaligned Nations Movement, which included many Islamic states. It drew on its loyal domestic Muslim community in matters of state as well. For example, leaders of friendly Muslim countries such as Nasser and Sukarno were introduced to the *reis-ul-ulema* and taken on trips to places where minarets and Islamic architecture in general indelibly infused the landscape with Muslim culture when they made state visits to Yugoslavia.

The worldwide revival of religious consciousness as experienced by Muslim associations in the 1970s helped to spread political Islam. There were attempts to confine secularization with Qu'ranic and Islamic principles (also in response to what was viewed as an excessively pro-Western inclination by some governments), and reorganize society and the state according to Islamic principles. The perils of—as Communist authorities and press called it—"Muslim nationalism and pan-Islamism" were pointed out in a pan-Yugoslav antinationalist campaign in the early 1970s. Two senior Muslim politicians and prewar Communists, Avdo Humo and Osman Karabegović, both members of the Bosnian political leadership during the Second World War, were dismissed in 1972 for alleged "exclusivism" and "nationalism." The *ulema*, the learned clergy of Islam, were permitted to run cultural institutions for ethnic Muslims only and not for Muslims in a religious sense. Moreover, the religious publication *Preporod (Revival*, established in 1970) was accused of exploiting religious sentiments. Nevertheless, public appearances by Islamic leaders were increasing, and the authorities accused them of trying to transform Islam into a political ideology. Bosnian Muslim politicians like Hamdija Pozderac and Fuad Muhić are quoted as saying that religious integrism was weakening Muslims' national identity and emancipation.[94]

The new situation in the country (weakening of internal integration, Tito's death, unrest in Kosovo, and the economic crisis) and outside its borders (the rise of pan-Islamic fundamentalism, the Iranian revolution in 1979) prompted the regime to take tougher measures against Islamic "nationalists and fundamentalists." *Preporod's* editorial board was accused of "pan-Islamism" and its members were partly replaced in 1979. Also accused of trying to transform the Muslim identity from a national attribute to a purely religious one were the imams of Belgrade and Bugojno, Hilmo Niemarlja and Hussein Djozo, respectively (the latter was also accused of threatening "brotherhood and unity"). The new editorial board and the reorganized IZ were more inclined toward the authorities.

An important player in these events was the LCBiH because its leaders had a reputation for being "rigidly conservative" while performing in unity whenever dealing with the federal authorities. Not until the late 1960s and early 1970s did the Muslims begin to exert greater influence in the organization.[95] Branko Mikulić, a member of the Presidium of the LCY, launched a scathing attack on "clero-fascists of all creeds" within a year of Tito's death. Also targeted were Muslims calling for a "jihad," "Khomeini fundamentalism," and a "pan-Islamic conspiracy."

Serb nationalist circles were wary of the autonomous policies of Bosnia's leaders, especially during the Mikulić era. They accused them of undermining the historical links between Bosnia and Serbia. They were also displeased with the 1974 constitution, which rendered Yugoslavia a de facto confederate state, claiming that it victimized the Serb nation. In the summer of 1984, Vojislav Šešelj, a Bosnian Serb and assistant professor at the University of Sarajevo, was tried for an article he submitted to the Komunist that was never published in which he criticized Kardelj's national theories and policies. He wrote of a greater Serbia that, in addition to Serbia proper, included Vojvodina, Kosovo, and parts of Bosnia-Herzegovina. He said that the Muslims were simply Serbs or Croats, and that the Montenegrins were Serbs.[96] Šešelj was sentenced to eight years' imprisonment but was released after serving two.

In August, 1983, a group of thirteen people, including two imams (four of them former Young Muslims), were charged with "hostile and counter-revolutionary acts derived from Muslim nationalism."[97] Eleven were sentenced to prison. The leading defendant, lawyer Alija Izetbegović, subsequently faced charges for writing the text of a short treatise entitled the Islamic Declaration in 1970, that is, during a period of greater tolerance toward Islam. The Islamic Declaration was published for the first time in 1990, immediately before the democratic elections in Bosnia-Herzegovina. Other defendants included Hasan Čengić, who was sentenced to ten years' imprisonment (later commuted to six and one-half years).

In the Islamic Declaration, Izetbegović touches on several abstract but highly suggestive matters that were unsettling to the Socialist authorities and laic readers, and were seen as being potential weapons in the hands of Islamic extremists and integrationists. For example, the treatise begins with two maxims: "Our objective is the Islamization of Muslims" and "Our motto is to have faith and fight."[98] He stresses the need for a peaceful introduction of Muslim authority and social order, which would not only conform to but also be infused with Islamic religious and moral principles. According to Izetbegović, the new authority and social order would unite religion and science, morality and politics, ideals and interests, and so forth. He supported the idea of creating a united Islamic community ranging from Morocco to Indonesia, from sub-Saharan Africa to Central Asia. The Islamic Declaration rejected nationalism, communism, and the modernist secularization of Muslim societies.

Izetbegović made no direct reference to the situation in Bosnia-Herzegovina, nor did he advocate violence, hatred, or ethnic cleansing in Bosnia, as the prosecution contended. He did, however, emphasize the incompatibility of Islam with non-Islamic political systems: "There can be no peace or harmony between the "Muslim religion" and non-Muslim social and political institutions." The following statement was also particularly disturbing to the authorities: "Islamic resurrection cannot begin without an Islamic revolution, and cannot continue and come to fruition without political revolution." All this should be accomplished by a young generation of Muslims "with labour, fight and sacrifices."[99] Indicted for attempting to create an Islamic republic in Yugoslavia, Izetbegović was sentenced to fourteen years' imprisonment.

The trial was clearly a political process: the indictment included several suspected senior exponents of pan-Islamism (supposedly under the patronage of a candidate for the federal presidency, Hamdija Pozderac) and went some way in "placating the Serb lobby within the republic and outside it."[100] It came as no surprise, then, that Pozderac himself ostracized the defendants, whom he accused of pan-Islamism, as did Fuad Muhić, who stated that their objective was "Khomeini-style socialism."[101] Muhić considered Muslim nationalism to be the most dangerous form of nationalism. Dušan Dragosavac, a dogmatic and centralist Serb politician from Croatia and LCY leader, also ostracized the defendants. A similar political trial took place in the summer of 1987 when three Muslims were charged with "pan-Islamism, undermining the Yugoslav political system," and attempting to "create an ethnically clean Islamic republic of Bosnia Herzegovina, Islamizing the Muslims."[102]

A process of national and political homogenization that seized "local" religious and ecclesiastic communities as well began to emerge in individual Yugoslav republics in the late 1980s. Unlike in other republics, where the gap between the interests of the Socialist authorities and the principal church was gradually closing, the Muslim religious community did not have a constructive relationship with Bosnia's political leaders. I believe there are three reasons for this: Bosnia's religious and national heterogeneity, the "orthodoxy" and pro-Yugoslav orientation of the ruling party's leadership, and Muslims' pro-Yugoslav orientation. One of the last public opinion surveys before the war showed that Bosnian Muslim affinity for the collective Yugoslav state was greater (88 percent) than the affinity of the republic's Serbs and Croats (85 and 63 percent, respectively).[103]

THE RELATIONSHIP BETWEEN RELIGIOUS AND NATIONAL IDENTITY BEFORE THE WAR

A poll conducted in 1988 by the Institute for the Study of National Relations involving 3,120 respondents from thirty-seven municipalities in Bosnia-Herzegovina showed some interesting results. Ibrahim Bakić, who compiled the data and presented it six years later, notes that the tendency to liken religious and national issues had always been present in the past, albeit in varying degrees. The basic supposition of the study was that religion is and remains an important factor in identifying national dissimilarities. The events of the next few years made it clear that religion had regained its political role and, moreover, that it was becoming belligerent. I have summed up only those aspects of this comprehensive study that have a bearing on the topic of this book. An indicative piece of information is the relationship between nationality and religiosity in Bosnia-Herzegovina.

Other sources also confirm that religious observance of all Yugoslav nations was very low in 1990. The figures from one other survey show that 34 percent of Serbs, 37 percent of Muslims (34 percent of the youth) and 53 percent of Croats claimed to be religious.[104]

It seems that religion was least important to the Serbs, although Orthodoxy was historically one of the most important factors in their national development. The same can be said for Muslims. On the other hand, religion was taken most seriously by the Croats, whose tradition, disappointment in the regime, and belief that they were being nationally threatened might have driven them to embrace religion and the Roman Catholic Church as a national institution. One of the questions touched on the relationship between nationality and religion.

The data indicate quite a large overlap between religion and nationality for the three largest nationalities, least of all for the Serbs. The exact opposite is true for the "political nationality" of the Yugoslavs. Furthermore, a majority of the respondents considered neither nationality nor religion as important for friendships (from the highest share 83.51 percent for the Yugoslavs and lowest 56.64 percent for the Muslims). The figures were much lower when asked whether nationality and religion

TABLE 8-7 **Relationship between nationality and religiosity in**
Bosnia-Herzegovina, 1988
Question: *Are you religious?*

Nationality	Yes
Croats	55.78%
Muslims	37.32%
Serbs	18.60%
Yugoslavs	2.28%

Source: Ibrahim Bakić, *Nacija i religija* (Sarajevo: Bosna Public, 1994), 72.

TABLE 8-8 **Relationship between nationality and prayer in**
Bosnia-Herzegovina, 1988
Question: *Where, if at all, do you pray: at home or in church/mosque?*

		Croats	Muslims	Serbs	Yugoslavs
Regularly	Home	21.11%	10.63%	4.73%	1.30%
	Church	21.93%	11.97%	14.09%	12.46%
Occasionally	Home	30.24%	27.41%	12.85%	2.28%
	Church	10.98%	16.71%	17.51%	23.61%
Rarely	Home	14.55%	12.05%	15.83%	4.56%
	Church	20.54%	20.02%	18.24%	14.10%
Never	Home	28.53%	42.95%	61.05%	88.27%
	Church	46.56%	51.30%	50.16%	49.84%

Source: Ibrahim Bakić, *Nacija i religija* (Sarajevo: Bosna Public, 1994), 73.

TABLE 8-9 **Religious self-identification by nationality in**
Bosnia-Herzegovina, 1988
Question: *What is your religion?*

	Croats	Muslims	Serbs	Yugoslavs
Orthodox	0.58%	0.09%	76.62%	9.43%
Muslim	0.43%	82.28%	1.67%	10.77%
Roman Catholic	88.87%	0.63%	0.42%	5.72%
None	10.12%	17.00%	25.29%	74.04%

Source: Ibrahim Bakić, *Nacija i religija* (Sarajevo: Bosna Public, 1994), 53, 74.

were important when selecting a spouse: it is not important for 66.9 percent of Yugoslavs, 43.22 percent of Serbs, 32.01 percent of Croats, and 25.91 percent of Muslims.[105]

The next few questions of the study are particularly important to the topic of this book.

TABLE 8-10 *Influence of religion on the development of a nation*
Question: What has been the influence of religion on the evolution and development of the nation?

	Very Positive and Mainly Positive
Croats	32.07%
Serbs	25.56%
Muslims	24.91%
Yugoslavs	18.55%

Source: Ibrahim Bakić, *Nacija i religija* (Sarajevo: Bosna Public, 1994), 104.

TABLE 8-11 *Religion and nationalism*
Question: Is religion the essence of a nation or national sentiments?

	Yes, Primacy of the religion for the nation	*No difference between religious and national affiliation*
Croats	17.55%	22.11%
Serbs	12.64%	15.62%
Muslims	12.14%	17.05%
Yugoslavs	7.49%	12.7%

Source: Ibrahim Bakić, *Nacija i religija* (Sarajevo: Bosna Public, 1994), 105.

TABLE 8-12 *Religion as a surrogate for national affiliation*
Question: Is religious affiliation also a designation for national affiliation?

	Always and Mostly
Serbs	60.22%
Croats	57.63%
Muslims	56.96%
Yugoslavs	42.34%

Source: Ibrahim Bakić, *Nacija i religija* (Sarajevo: Bosna Public, 1994), 107.

The next question deals with the relationship between nationality and the traditional identification of nationality and religion.

TABLE 8-13 *Attitudes toward the relationship between religious and national identity*
Question: Does being a Serb mean being Orthodox, a Croat mean being Catholic, and a Muslim mean being Muslim?

	Basically the Same
Muslims	54.11%
Serbs	50.98%
Croats	49.36%
Yugoslavs	37.73%

Source: Ibrahim Bakić, *Nacija i religija* (Sarajevo: Bosna Public, 1994), 112.

Similar results for the Serbs, Croats, and Muslims and the relatively low result for Yugoslavs reflect the totally different historical backgrounds of their development: whereas religion and descent are the basic elements of identification for Serbs, Croats, and Muslims, the political dimension is far more important to the Yugoslavs.

TABLE 8-14 *Opinions on religious communities as representatives of the nation*
Question: Do religious communities appear to be representatives of their nations?

	Yes and In Most Cases
Yugoslavs	66.67%
Serbs	66.18%
Croats	63.83%
Muslims	59.91%

Source: Ibrahim Bakić, *Nacija i religija* (Sarajevo: Bosna Public, 1994), 113.

The answers to this question indicate that the least religious respondents, the Yugoslavs, realized the importance of religious communities in representing the interests of nationalities. On the other hand, Muslims, whose religious community had weak links with the republican leadership, were least inclined to think so.

Bakić's study offered a number of meaningful conclusions. Firstly, researchers identified a correlation between one's national affiliation and the relationship between nationality and religion: "the stronger the national affiliation, more frequent and intensive the likening between nationality and religion and vice versa." Secondly, "believers felt a stronger sense of national affiliation": they "more readily identified nationality with religion, in global sense and in some individual aspects of national and religious life." Thirdly, Croats and Muslims in Bosnia-Herzegovina displayed a greater sense of religious-national affiliation ("communication and correspondence") than Serbs and Yugoslavs, which corresponds to "a lower level of religious self-identification" among the latter. Fourthly, "the emphasis on the relationship between nationality and religion was greater in day-to-day life than in the public or social sphere" (although even there it is neither omitted nor forgotten). And finally, "the communication and correspondence of national and religious self-identification is more intensive in personal than in public life."[106]

Below are the results of a 1989 study, conducted one year after the first study, for the youth in Bosnia-Herzegovina.

TABLE 8-15 *Religious identification of youth in Bosnia-Herzegovina, 1989*

	Muslims	Croats	Serbs	Yugoslavs
Religious	34%	53%	21%	12%
Nonreligious	56%	38%	68%	79%

Source: Lenard J. Cohen, "Bosnia's Tribal Gods: The Role of Religion in Nationalistic Politics," in *Religion and the War in Bosnia,* ed. Paul Mojzes (Atlanta: American Academy of Religions; Scholars Press, 1998), errata.

The percentage of religious Serb youth in Bosnia-Herzegovina (21 percent) was lower than for Serb youth from Serbia proper (26 percent), Croatia (26 percent), Vojvodina (29 percent) and Kosovo (43 percent). The study showed that church attendance by young people in Bosnia-Herzegovina was: 65 percent for Croats, 39 percent for Muslims, 30 percent for Serbs and 26 percent for Yugoslavs.[107] This is a relatively low level of religiosity for a generation that was, within a few years, to participate in what many religious militants and also nonreligious observers described as a "religious war."

9

A WAR OVER DIFFERENCES
The Religious Dimensions of Conflict in Bosnia-Herzegovina, 1992–95

Less than ten years later, Tito's rapturous words seemed almost forgotten. In Yugoslavia as a whole and in Bosnia-Herzegovina, the catastrophe in

The people of Bosnia-Herzegovina can be proud of their achievements. They have overcome mutual conflict and tension.

—MARSHAL JOSIP BROZ TITO, NOVEMBER 25, 1979

the 1990s was in large part a logical consequence of the processes taking place in the second half of the 1980s: the deterioration of national relations within the federation and the party, growing economic crisis, gradual decomposition of the legitimacy of the Socialist political system, and media wars.[1] It would be wrong to understand the last Bosnian war in terms of a religious, civil, or ethnic war, or as the result of ancient hatreds or some specific Balkan mentality, or even as an internal Bosnian affair. It would also be wrong to adopt the explanation that all sides are equally to blame, as was often publicly proclaimed by some foreign diplomats and some in the international media, who were merely recapitulating the course of events as interpreted by the aggressors' spin doctors and myth-makers. Of course, some dimensions of that sort cannot be neglected, but they "cannot mask the external causes and the dimensions of this conflict, its dimension of the war of aggression and the territorial conquests."[2] In my opinion, the war in Bosnia-Herzegovina was first of all a classical example of expansionist war for a Greater Serbia instigated by the Milošević's régime in Belgrade. But it was also—during the Croat-Muslim clashes from the autumn of 1992 to March, 1994—a war for a Greater Croatia instigated by the Zagreb regime, which seized the opportunity presented by a weak and inefficient Bosnian army and the re-

TABLE 9-1 *National composition of cities in Bosnia-Herzegovina, 1991*

	Muslims	*Serbs*	*Croats*	*Others*
Sarajevo	49.3%	29.9%	6.6%	14.2%
Banja Luka	14.6%	54.8%	14.9%	15.7%
Zenica	55.2%	15.5%	15.6%	13.7%
Tuzla	47.6%	15.5%	15.6%	21.3%
Mostar	34.8%	19%	33.8%	12.4%

luctance of the West to intervene in Bosnia-Herzegovina to carve up a piece of territory for itself.

Discussions on the future of the country began even before the outbreak of hostilities. An analysis of the national composition of Bosnia-Herzegovina's 100 municipalities reveals some interesting facts: the Muslims had an absolute majority in 31 municipalities and a relative majority in 14; the Croats had an absolute majority in 13 municipalities and a relative majority in 6.[3] The national composition of Bosnia-Herzegovina's five largest cities is shown in table 9-1.

Franjo Tudjman and Slobodan Milošević met in Karađorđevo in March, 1991, to discuss plans for partitioning Bosnia-Herzegovina. Their meeting was followed by meetings in Austria involving Bosnian Serb leader Radovan Karadžić, Milošević, and Tudjman in February, 1992, and by Bosnian Croat leader Mate Boban and Karadžić in May, 1992.[4]

The late 1980s saw Yugoslavia's decomposition as a federal state. After the elections in Slovenia and Croatia in the spring of 1990, which clearly pointed toward complete national emancipation, Milošević 's political orientation and actions turned from seeking Yugoslavian unity to promoting a Greater Serbia. Meanwhile, the face of political pluralism in Bosnia-Herzegovina began assuming a national and increasingly religious profile when the first multiparty elections there were held six months after those in Slovenia and Croatia. The Muslim Party for Democratic Action *(Stranka demokratske akcije* [SDA]), which advocated a pluralistic society and was led by Alija Izetbegović, adopted traditional Muslim rhetoric and symbolism. Like their brethren in Croatia, the Bosnian Serbs founded a Serbian Democratic Party *(Srpska demokratska stranka* [SDS]), whose declared objective was to fight for Serb rights. Led by Radovan Karadžić, an immigrant from Montenegro, its first course was one of cooperation. The Croatian Democratic Community (HDZ), the "authentic defender of Croat interests," was originally opposed to any changes to Bosnia's borders. It was headed Stjepan Kljuić, a moderate politician from central Bosnia and an advocate of Bosnia-Herzegovina's integrity and autonomy as an independent state. There was also another but smaller Muslim party, the secularist Muslim Bosniak Organization (*Muslimanska bošnjačka organizacija* [MBO]), founded by Adil Zulfi-karpašić after he fell out with Izetbegović. However, despite warnings about the consequences of nationality profiling, any party that was not nationally based suffered total defeat.

Before concentrating on the religious and mythological dimensions of the Bosnian war, we should first consider the balance of political power in Bosnia's democratically elected parliament, the escalation of tension, and the dramatic events that took place in Bosnia from December, 1990, to April, 6, 1992—the day it achieved its independence and war broke out. I shall also discuss the scenarios drawn up by Western diplomats and op-posing parties during the war for partitioning the country.[5] Of the 240 parliamentary seats being contested in the 1990 general elections, 86 were won by the SDA, 70 by the SDS, 45 by the HDZ, and 8 by the MBO. The winners, therefore, were the three biggest national parties, whereas leftist and pro-Yugoslav parties were the big losers—the reformed Com-munists won 14 seats and Yugoslav prime minister Ante Marković's party took only 12.[6] The assembly's composition roughly corresponded to Bosnia-Herzegovina's national composition (44:33:17). At the begin-ning of 1991—six hundred years after the death of Tvrtko Kotromanić, Bosnia's greatest medieval ruler—Bosnia-Herzegovina replaced its state symbols (coat of arms and flag) with new ones that implied it had ties with that period in Bosnia's history.

Influenced by events in Croatia and supported by Serbia, Bosnian Serb extremists consciously decided to increase tension within Bosnia-Herzegovina. In September, 1991, they established six "Serbian Autono-mous Regions," founded their own Parliament the following month, and SDS delegates and politicians adjourned to attend state functions. They opted in a November plebiscite to form the Serbian Republic (*Republika Srpska* [RS]), a Serb state within Bosnia-Herzegovina, which would re-main in Yugoslavia. In December, the Bosnian Serb Parliament declared that the RS would be annexed to Yugoslavia. In response to the Bosnian Serbs' unilateral policy, the European Union (EU) called on Bosnian au-thorities to seek a referendum on the state's independence. The question asked was: "Are you in favor of a sovereign and independent Bosnia-Herzegovina, a state of equal citizens and nations of Muslims, Serbs, Croats, and others who live in it?" Voters cast their ballots on Febru-ary 29 and March 1, 1992, and, despite a boycott by the Serbian parties, the referendum succeeded with the help of Muslim and Croats. A total of 62.7 percent of the eligible electorate—"including," according to Malcolm, "many thousands of Serbs in the major cities"—voted for Bosnian independence.[7] The newly born state, however, was already marked for death.

The former Yugoslav People's Army (*Jugoslovenska narodna armija* [JNA]), which until recently had considered itself to be the only remaining unifying force, the "last link" between the Yugoslav nations, was driven from Slovenia and most of Croatia. Its ostensible role in Bosnia-Herzegovina was to preserve the peace between national groups, but it gradually took sides with the Serbs, further strengthening the well-equipped illegal Serb paramilitary groups operating on both sides of the Drina River.[8] After several incidents in the second half of 1991, war broke out on April 6, 1992, the same day Bosnia-Herzegovina was officially and internationally recognized. The Serbian Republic, presided over by Radovan Karadžić, was proclaimed on April 7 in Pale, a village above Sarajevo.

The proposal to partition Bosnia-Herzegovina was made at a conference in Lisbon in February, 1992. It was to be divided into three parts: a Muslim canton (in which Muslims would have a 56.5 percent majority), a Serb canton (in which Serbs would have a 61.5 percent majority), and a Croat canton (in which Croats would have a 65.7 percent majority). The cantons would vary in size: the Muslim canton would have a population of about 2.8 million citizens, the Serb canton more than a million, and the Croat canton less than five hundred thousand.[9] The plan was rejected the next month, first by the Serb delegation, while the second draft, which included some Serbian supplements, was also rejected by the Croatians and Muslims.

A second conference convened in London six months later, presided over by UN ambassador Cyrus Vance and EU mediator Lord David Owen. The Serbs already had control of more than two-thirds of Bosnia-Herzegovina's territory by then. In January, 1993, Owen and Thorwald Stoltenberg, who replaced Vance that month, proposed that Bosnia be parceled into nine ethnic cantons (three each), plus the multiethnic canton of Sarajevo. The Bosnian Serbs, who at the time were at their strongest, rejected the proposal in May, and it was finally abandoned in August. According to the proposal, the "three-partite" Muslim canton would have a Muslim majority of 67.6 percent, the Serb canton a Serb majority of 65.2 percent, and the Croat canton a Croat majority of 77.8 percent. The fourth and largest canton (Sarajevo), would include two-fifths of the entire population and have the following composition: Muslims, 42 percent; Serbs, 27.6 percent; Croats, 19.8 percent; and others, 10.6 percent.[10]

The Bosnian peace initiative was taken over by the United States in 1994. An agreement signed in Washington in March of that year ended the conflict between the Bosnian (mostly Muslim) government and Bosnian Croats, and created a Croat-Muslim federation within Bosnia-Herzegovina. A new federal constitution was adopted the same month, and cooperation was further bolstered by a meeting between Izetbegović and Tudjman in July, 1995.

PREPARATION FOR WAR: IDEOLOGIZING ANCIENT SERBIAN MYTHS

One of the most important indicators and dimensions of mythical reasoning is timelessness: the past, present, and future arbitrarily interchange, complement, and supplement each other. The myth abolishes historical, linear time: the future becomes the new past; what is perceived as progression is, in fact, regression; and that which has been is experienced again. The catastrophes that occurred in the former Yugoslavia have in many ways been the result of the extreme ideologizing of ancient mythical stories and the abuse of the people's religious identity. However, even after the painful establishment of a "new order" in the central Balkans, myth and tradition remain an important inspiration for the future. As Tismaneanu presumes, "the post-communist political and intellectual world will remain a battlefield between different, often incompatible myths."[11]

Serb nationalism was articulated in its most obvious form in the notorious "Memorandum" of the Serbian Academy of Sciences and Arts (SANU), written in 1985 and partly published in September, 1986, in which twenty-three authors (leading intellectuals, academicians, artists) strongly attacked—among other things—the "anti-Serb" Yugoslav régime, its "discrimination," and "neo-Fascist aggression" in Kosovo.[12] Their demands were clear: the annulment of the 1974 "confederal" constitution (that is, the subjugation of the autonomous provinces of Vojvodina and Kosovo to Serbia), an end to their "economic subjection" to the northern republics, a renewal of the "complete national and cultural integrity" of the Serbs in all parts of Yugoslavia, and the rejection of "artificially created, new, regional literature" (for example, Bosnian literature). Banac notes that this memorandum is "usually regarded as the intellectual justification of and the prodromus to contemporary Serbian nationalism."[13] It's masterminds were Mihajlo Marković, a Marxist philosopher and former member of the Praxis group, Prof. Kosta Mihajlović, and writers Antonije Isaković and Dobrica Ćosić, who became the Federal Republic of Yugoslavia's first president in May, 1992.

The memorandum's main points were aptly exploited by the new Serb ruler, Slobodan Milošević, who became the leader of the Serbian League of Communists in September, 1987, and later president of Serbia. A sly and unscrupulous politician, he turned the complicated circumstances facing Yugoslavia and Serbia—loss of the legitimacy of the Socialist regime, national tensions (most explicit in Kosovo), growing economic crisis, and social instabilities—to his own benefit. Milošević used time-tested populist methods to portray himself as the only authentic representative of Serb interests and as the invincible leader of all Serbs dispersed across Yugoslavia.[14] In a 1991 interview, Dobrica Ćosić stated that Milošević "has done more for the Serbs in the last four years than any other Serb politician in the last fifty." He made a similar statement for the newspaper *Borba* in November, 1989. The Episcopal Synod of the Serbian Orthodox Church also supported Milošević's maxim that "all Serbs must live in one country."

The spellbound and overheated atmosphere in Serbia in the late 1980s and early 1990s, the obsession with internal and external enemies, the treason syndrome, and the impending danger in the political, national, religious, and cultural fields are best expressed by media headlines. Several Serb historians and representatives of the sciences, culture, sport, and public life were also involved in Serb military endeavors and in forging the impressive Serb national solidarity.[15] Many who had previously had an ardent pro-Yugoslav and Communist orientation slowly or dramatically turned toward Greater Serbian nationalism. In 1993, for example, Bosnian Serb general Ratko Mladić said, "through this war I broke as a Communist and a Yugoslav to become the greatest Serb."[16]

It is disturbing to note that a number of the most respectable literary magazines, authors, and university professors fell to the level of profane political agitation. The new Serbian leadership and the academy "successfully harmonized their activities" from 1988 until the mass anti-Milošević demonstrations in March, 1991. Later, Great Serbian rhetoric and hatred against "the enemies of the Serbs and Serbianism" were common in the public appearances of some Serbian intellectuals. Miroljub Jeftić stated that "Balkan Muslims have the blood of the martyrs of Kosovo on their hands," and advocated the defensive and righteous nature of Serb military endeavors. For him, "international Islamic planners, aided by domestic fellow-thinkers, have as their objective to Islamize all of Serbia, but only as the first step of a breakthrough into Europe." He was convinced that "Islam is an enemy religion today, as it was yesterday." Modern Bosnian Muslim Slavs, according to him, were converted Serbs, and it is because of "this strong awareness that they so despise the Serbs." Aleksandar Popović spoke of Islam's "totalitarianism," and an other prominent Serbian Orientalist, Darko Tanasković, saw the Bosnian war as "a struggle between fundamentalist Muslims on the one hand and Serbs" dedicated to keeping "Church and State separate on the other."[17]

In August, 1991, Vojislav Šešelj, a Chetnik duke and president of the Radical Party, stated that the Bosnian Muslims were "actually Islamized Serbs," and that many of the Croats were "Catholicized Serbs." Radoslav Unković, director of the Institute for the Preservation of the Cultural, Historical, and Natural Heritage of the Republika Srpska, shared this opinion. The Bosnian *balija* (a pejorative name for Muslims) were, according to Unković, descended from the Serbs but seemed to be ashamed of that fact and tried to suppress it. Catholics who had recently become Croats were likewise accused of suppressing their Orthodox and Serb identity. Šešelj's program also included the unification of all Serbian lands, which for them are "Serbia proper, Montenegro, Serbian Bosnia, Serbian Herzegovina, Serbian Dubrovnik, Serbian Dalmatia, Serbian Lika, Serbian Kordun, Serbian Banija, Serbian Slavonia, Serbian Western Srem, Serbian Baranja, and Serbian Macedonia." At the congress of the ruling Serbian Socialist Party, Mihajlo Marković anticipated the creation of a new Yugoslavia consisting of Serbia, Montenegro and the *Serbian parts* of Croatia and Bosnia-Herzegovina.[18] The plan was even acclaimed in songs from the production line of "military-propaganda folklorism," to borrow an expression from the Belgrade ethnologist Ivan Čolović.

Kordun, Lika and Banija,
Orthodox Dalmatia,
Herzeg-Bosnia, Slavonia,
All these are Western Serbia.[19]

Academician Veselin Djuretić also believed that Bosnian Muslims were "Islamized Serbs," and writer Momo Kapor was renowned for his anti-Muslim and anti-Western statements.[20] In the summer of 1998, Radmilo Marojević, dean of the Faculty of Philology at the University of Belgrade, declared that Croatian literature may be considered the "literature of Catholic Serbs." The only true Croatian literature, according to Marojević, was that written in the Chakavian dialect. Belgrade University professor Kosta Čavoški, a member of the RS senate, publicly defended Karadžić's leadership of the Bosnian Serbs during the last war.

Motifs from the Kosovo myths were worn to dilapidation: "Beam, bright sun of Kosovo, we shall not give up great Dušan's land."[21] Newspaper headlines shouted familiar aphorisms about the "battle for Christ and Europe," "holy Serbs," and "Asian despotism." Academician Radomir Lukić stated—and the Belgrade daily *Politika* quoted him—that: "Although the act of choosing the Heavenly Kingdom is religiously toned because Heaven and Earth are connected, that's not the apotheosis of suicide but the indication toward the way of Salvation. Heavenly Kingdom is the soul of the nation." Addressing a crowd of two million celebrating in Kosovo (which was persistently called the "heart of Serb nationhood" and the "cradle of the Serb nation" by the media) on the six hundredth anniversary of the Battle of Kosovo, Milošević declared that Serbia was defending European culture and religion from the advance of Islam. He even foretold future battles (*Politika* alleged that Lazar's words "it is better to die honorable than to live in shame" were repeated).[22]

The celebration included a "secular" and a "religious" ceremony conducted by senior dignitaries of the Serbian Orthodox Church, which was represented by Archbishop Lavrentij (in charge of western Europe), Patriarch German, and all the archbishops. Archbishops Vladislav, Pavle, and Simeon read the sermons. Motifs from the Battle of Kosovo were everywhere: on posters, cartoons, calendars, and badges; in movies and music. Several books on the subject also were published. The six hundredth anniversary celebration—like the demonstrations in front of Parliament in Belgrade on February 28, 1989, when more than a million people protested against the "separatism" of the Albanians and Slovenians (the strike at the Stari Trg colliery and the "Slovenian betrayal" at the rally in the *Cankarjev dom* cultural center in Ljubljana)—represented the culmination of Serb political populism and "happenings of the people," and was a harbinger of the destructive powers the newly ideologized myths from the past were about to unleash.

During the euphoria of the Battle of Kosovo's six hundredth anniversary celebration, several high-profile Serb theologians and church dignitaries—including Jevtić, Radović, and Mijać—wrote and spoke about the Serbs' heavenly nature and revived other similar Christoslavic myths. Bishop Jovan of Šabac-Valjevo stated that Prince Lazar and the Kosovo Serbs "primarily created a heavenly Serbia which by today surely grew into the greatest heavenly state." Serb leaders and Orthodox priests in Bosnia-Herzegovina held a similar celebration at the same time, but were criticized by high-ranking leaders of the Bosnian League of Communists.[23]

Belgrade sociologist Nebojša Popov sees "war as a part of the Serbian way of life and not only as a myth, legend, or epics."[24] It is therefore not surprising that the ensuing war in Bosnia was also often interpreted with pathetic mythological categories: there was "a new Battle of Kosovo" going on, and Serbs loyal to the Sarajevo government were branded "traitors of the Branković kind," and Milošević was proclaimed the "new great leader and military commander." The following poem provides an illustrative example of this:

> *Slobodan, our keenest saber,*
> *Will there be war on Kosovo?*
> *Shall we summon Strahinjić,*
> *Old Jug, the nine Jugovići,*
> *Or should Boško bear our banner*
> *And scythe his saber through Kosovo?*
> *Will red burning blood be shed*
> *Where the peonies bloom blood red?*
> *If there is need, just say the word,*
> *We shall fly, like bullets from guns.*[25]

Old tales about heroic *hajduk* bandits, Chetniks, dukes, and so forth were infused with a spirit of romantic barbarism. Parliament of *Republika Srpska* awarded the Order of Nemanjić to the most deserving, including Montenegro's president, Momir Bulatović. Against such a mythical backdrop, the advent of Murat, the ancient archenemy, was inevitable. Indeed, there were two candidates for the role, Alija Izetbegović and Franjo Tudjman, as illustrated by the following verses:

> *Oh, Alija and Tudjman,*
> *You are to blame for the war,*
> *The fate of Murat*
> *Awaits you both.*[26]

The persecution complex that results in seeking and identifying "local" traitors—from the so-called armchair traitors *(foteljaši)*, bureaucrats, and autonomists to Ustasha or irredentist Croats, separatist Slovenes, and degenerate Muslims—became an important element of the renewed Serbian political mythology and rhetoric. Another important source was undoubtedly the myth of foreign conspiracy. During the war, the religious press published articles claiming that "Serbia is threatened by the entire West," and about the "Pope's lackeys in Italy, Austria, and Germany." Socialist Yugoslavia was said to be "a 'Trojan horse' for the penetration of the Vatican, Germany, Austria to the South, and East and 'Jihad' to the North and West." According to the Orthodox metropolite of Zagreb-Ljubljana, Pope John Paul II, with his alleged anti-Serb stance, was behind the war in Croatia. From the perspective of political myths, therefore, the international conspiracy by "eternal" enemies was one of the essential explanations of local developments. According to Swiss publicist and historian Viktor Meier, "the majority of the Serbs blame the ostensible antipathy of the West, rather than Slobodan Milošević, for their hardships."[27]

The most popular myths were those about local and foreign Muslim conspiracies. Balkanologist Harry T. Norris lists the main elements of the attack by Serb "experts" on Islam and Yugoslav Muslims. First, the rise of Islamic fundamentalism in Yugoslavia is "a result of the firm relations established by Tito with the Arab and the Islamic countries." Second, "Arab Muslims have a strategy to enable them to dominate the world and form a single world-wide state." Third, "by its very nature, Islam allows the extermination of others who are not in agreement with it." Finally, "Bosnian Muslims have betrayed their race."[28]

Ankara's alleged political objective was to create a "Turkish empire that would extend from the Adriatic Sea to the Great Wall of China." Haris Silajdžić was accused of being a triple agent in the employ of the CIA, the Mossad, and Libyan intelligence. "Conspiracies by Islamic fundamentalists" ("the Sarajevo-Istanbul Green Transversal") were "uncovered," as were conspiracies by the Vatican or a "German-Catholic alliance" or a "Catholic and German clique." Jeftić wrote about "the natural anti-Serbian alliance between Turkey and Albania." Some Serbian sources saw "conspiracies by various combinations of Germany, NATO, the Masons, the Vatican, the CIA, 'American Generals,' Saudi Arabia, and even by a 'Bonn-Vienna-Zagreb-Sofia-Tirana-Rome axis,' among others."[29] Dragoš Kalajić, a nationalist journalist, painter, and the "mentor" of the "White Eagles" Serb paramilitary organization, wrote in 1994: "The Muslim assault on western Europe through peaceful means, i.e. mass immigration, which threatens to transform European nations into national minorities in their own countries, only serves to confirm the significance of the Serb struggle to defend the integrity of Europe, its culture and civilization."[30] Equating the Serbian situation with that of Israel, Vuk Drašković in September, 1988, concluded that "Israel and the Serbs live in a hellish siege where the sworn goal is to seize, and then cover with mosques or Vaticanize, the lands of Moses and the people of Saint Sava."[31]

The Bosnian war was, therefore, preceded and accompanied by an unprecedented and aggressive political propaganda campaign targeted at different elements of the Serb population. Much of it was based on adapting ancient myths to current ideology. Laboratories of hate renewed ancient atrocities and evidence about the widespread anti-Serb conspiracies, and fabricated new ones. They claimed that Muslims "were plotting to put Serb women in harems."[32] They reported that the Croats, especially their new leaders, were all Ustasha. They spread rumors of Muslim and Albanian conspiracies ("a demographic atomic bomb for the Serbs"). They accused Tito's regime of promoting anti-Serb policies and referred to Tito as the "Serb Slayer" or "Serb Eater."[33] They trumpeted the invincibility and superhuman strength of Serb warriors, and replayed the horrors of the Ottoman period. The Serbs in Foča were told that Muslims planned to transform their town into a new Mecca. Serb forces eventually occupied the town, ethnically "cleansed" it, and renamed it Srbinje. The radicalization of national sentiments reached its peak during this period, which scholars refer to as the "frenzy of myth" or "furor Serbicus."

It would be difficult to explain the events taking place in Serbia in the late 1980s and 1990s without mentioning the myth of the new leader and his cult. The Serbs looked to the past to find legitimacy for their "anti-bureaucratic revolutions" and "manifestations of the people": the deceased, charismatic, pan-Yugoslav leader Tito was to be replaced by a— as he was initially called by his followers—"new Tito" in the person of Slobodan Milošević.[34] His supporters rearranged old and invented new slogans in his praise, such as "Comrade Slobo, we pledge ourselves to you" and "Serbia keeps on asking: when will Slobo replace Tito?"[35] He was called the "Tsar of Dedinje," the "Savior of the Serbhood," and the "Balkan Napoleon." The new Serb leader was portrayed as a savior, the initiator of a new era who would "finally bring order." These views were reflected in poems dedicated to Milošević, as illustrated by the following excerpts:

Slobodan, majestic name,
Whatever is wrong, change it from the roots.

Or:

Dear brothers, see a new age dawn,
Slobodan Milošević is born![36]

"Sloba" is a man who "works up to twenty hours a day, including Saturdays and Sundays."[37] The political myth portrays him as stalwart, fair, and resolute; a uniter, protector, and savior; a brother, father, and mother ("Help us, Slobo, brother/you are our father and mother"). The following verses are also revealing:

Slobodan, son of Serbian faith,
When your eyes pierce alien aims,
Bright lightning flashes from them,
When you speak, honey flows,
Before your beauty, the springtime
Will conceal the sun and flowers.[38]

Paramilitary units modeled on historical military formations were also created. One example is that of the Chetnik duke Šešelj. The title was bestowed on Šešelj in 1989 by the self-declared Chetnik duke, Father Momčilo Đujić, who emigrated to the United States after the Second World War. Đujić ordered him "to expel all Croats, Albanians, and other foreign elements from holy Serbian soil," adding that he would return to Serbia only when Šešelj succeeded in cleansing "Serbia of the last Jew, Albanian, and Croat."[39]

As was the case in other post-Socialist countries, cults of ambiguous and contestable personalities from recent history began reemerging.[40] In Serbia, for example, that of Draža Mihajlović, Second World War Chetnik commander, of Milan Nedić, Nikolaj Velimirović, and the Karađorđe dynasty. In 1993, Vuk Drašković, a Herzegovina-born Serbian writer and politician, unveiled a monument to Mihajlović, the "holy warrior," at Ravna gora. A poem dedicated to Mihajlović was entitled "Draža Lives, He Has Not Died!"[41] We also find such slogans as:

Dražo, we pledge ourselves to you,
We shall not swerve from your path.

And:

Return, noble Duke,
Once more to the Dinaric mountains.[42]

Anyplace with Serb graves or where Serb soldiers set foot was said to be part of Serbia. Politicians and military commanders alike skillfully built their strategies on the rich tradition of ancient Serb mythopoesis:

Milošević became the *vožd* (leader), "protector of the Serb nation," and "Tsar from Dedinje." General Mladić, the Bosnian Serb military commander, became the "greatest warrior for the liberation of the Serb nation," and the "Liberator-General." There was also Captain Dragan, the "invincible warrior"; the Kninjas (warriors from Knin, analogous to the Japanese Ninja), and the "Serb Sparta." In the ethnically "cleansed" town of Bijeljina, RS vice president Biljana Plavšić emotionally declared the infamous Serb paramilitary commander Arkan a "Serb hero" and a "true Serb who was prepared to give his life for his people," and added: "We need such people!"

Dragoš Kalajić saw in Mladić the "radiance of the unhesitating determination of a fighting spirit," and in Karadžić, "a personality forged of the finest highland material of the Serbian ethos and ethnos" whose strength emanated "holy dread." Plavšić stated that Karadžić was a "great figure of the living legend of the Serb struggle."[43] Plavšić herself has been referred to as the "Iron Lady" and "Tsarina Biljana." Arkan returned her kind words by declaring her the "Serb Empress," and several Serb armored vehicles were christened with her name. In a documentary film, Radovan Karadžić poses in a house in Tršić that belonged to his more famous namesake, Vuk S. Karadžić, to whom he claimed to be related (finding evidence of this in the dimple in his chin), and plays the *gusle*, a traditional musical instrument.[44] A second mythical reference to Radovan Karadžić is military, emancipating, and nationally integrationist, as seen in the following verse: "Oh, Radovan, man of steel/The first leader since Karadjordje."

Against such a backdrop—the obsessive and ethnocentric argumentation of their own superiority—Serb metaphysical myths (Serbs as the "heavenly nation") and myths about Serb military superiority (Serbs as a "warrior nation") were followed by "scientific" myths about the Serbs and their enemies. The mythical discourse becomes "naturalized," according to Roland Barthes. Specific situations or facts are "presumed naturally," "objectively," and are, therefore, "scientifically provable." The situations or facts are thus depoliticized and lose their historicalness. In 1989, Jovan Rašković, a psychiatrist and later leader of the Croatian Serbs, told an interviewer the Muslims were stuck in the anal phase of their psycho-socio development, which, he said, explains their aggressiveness and obsession with precision and morality. Moreover, he said the Croats were suffering from a castration complex.[45] Commenting on his own people, the Serbs, he said that they "have always been a nation characterized by tragic fate, God's chosen people in a sense."

Another example: Biljana Plavšić—a biology professor who defended her doctoral thesis in Zagreb, former Fulbright Scholar, and dean at Sarajevo University—told the newspaper *Borba* in July, 1993, that Bosnian Serbs were not only ethnically and racially superior to Muslims but to Serbs from Serbia proper as well because they had developed special defensive mechanisms in the course of their evolution. "I know as a biologist," she added, "that species that are surrounded and threatened by other species develop a higher level of adaptation and survival." In September of the same year, while arguing in favor of the theory that Muslim Slavs are actually descended from Serbs, she explained that "genetically damaged Serb material passed over to Islam." She said she believed this gene became condensed over the centuries and "continued to degenerate." The two newly created Serb states in Croatia and Bosnia-Herzegovina (Republika Srpska Krajina and Republika Srpska) were seen as the fresh energy or "blood" that would invigorate the existing Serbian states (Serbia and Montenegro), which were showing clear signs of aging. "Beyond the Drina, Serbdom is being tempered and toughened. I do not see that here."[46] For some Orthodox thinkers, the only real Serbian states were those in Croatia and Bosnia-Herzegovina because of the religiosity of their leaders and because they adopted Orthodoxy in their national symbols.

As in many countries, the countryside is the heartland of nationalism and religious and political intolerance. In the case of the Serbs, traditional and conservative parts of rural population joined the nationalist intellectuals. Ramet notes that the modernization and secularization of Serb society under socialism suppressed rural conservatism, which reemerged in the late 1980s. Collective loyalty and so-called traditional values were sacralized by aggressive rural mobilization ("When countrymen take up arms") and religious revival.[47] The simple rural folk were said to posses the "true values," those virtues that preserve national and religious purity. However, it also nurtured other "qualities," such as xenophobia, anti-intellectualism, anti-Western, and antiurban sentiments, belligerent religiousness, and gender discrimination. Ramet therefore concludes that Milošević's rise to power signified the victory of the rural over the urban.

Economic and rural backwardness became in mythical interpretation the proof of messianism, uniqueness, and election. A large proportion of Serbia's population is rural (27.6 percent in 1981, well above the Yugoslav average of 19.9 percent; in comparison, Slovenia's rural population accounted for just 9.4 percent of the population). More than half of all Serbs worked in the agricultural sector.[48] Bosnia-Herzegovina, Kosovo, and Serbia were also the least urbanized republics in Yugoslavia. It therefore came as no surprise that the new Serb nationalist ideas found the most support in the countryside, as they had throughout history. Towns and cities were seen as a thorn in the side of the warlords and as a unique form of degeneration and artificiality: a suspicious coexistence of different cultures, religions, and races; mixed marriages; democracy; cosmopolitanism; and pacifism. An eloquent example comes from an RS parliamentary session in 1994. One of the deputies is quoted as having said that he was for "Serbianizing those who are not Serb enough. I am thinking of the capital city, Belgrade. "[49]

Čolović cites specific examples of such cognizance in his analysis of the poetry of Božidar Vučurović, a folk poet and truck driver from Trebinje who became the political and military leader of the Serbs there during the last war, and finds similar examples in Dragoš Kalajić's and publicist Momčilo Selić's statements.[50] The result is the systematic destruction of towns (regardless of their strategic significance) or "urbicide" as the next characteristic of the Bosnian war, in the spirit of the ancient proverb "God created villages, but people created towns." According to such logic, the path to the future would be to return to the past: the nation will be redeemed of its bygone conceptual and political errors. An illustration of this is the postwar (July, 1998) statement by Draško Radusinović, president of the Montenegrin national community in Croatia: "In the coming century, Montenegrins and their national essence will be liberated from these ideologies [the great ideologies of the twentieth century] and we shall return to our traditions."

The Serb nation, its religion, and culture were ostensibly threatened. Excerpts from Izetbegović's Islamic Declaration were maliciously interpreted. The media, including Belgrade television, announced that Muslims and Croats (a "fundamentalist-Ustasha coalition") were planning to create a unitary Bosnia-Herzegovina. They justified their military preparations as being "defensive" in nature. Historian Kržišnik-Bukić cites an interesting example that contradicts one of the myths about neglecting the Serbs in Bosnia-Herzegovina. In 1992, she says, there were in the center of Sarajevo "over sixty streets and squares that bore names from Serbian medieval history, but none—for example—of the rulers of the independent Bosnian medieval state."[51]

Indeed, there were even proposals for the creation of a so-called Orthodox Creed Circle, an association of countries that once included the Byzantine cultural sphere, as a counterweight to the European Union. Such an association "would comprise the Russian Federation, Ukraine, Byelorussia, Serbia, Montenegro, Greece, Bulgaria, Rumania, and Cyprus."[52] On the other hand, a "Balkan Orthodox Alliance" would unite only the Balkan "Orthodox" countries. The Serbian Orthodox Church, however, never officially supported these initiatives formulated by lay circles.

NEW AND OLD CROATIAN NATIONAL MYTHS

Croatia was also drawing plans for a "permanent solution" to the Croat national issue, as it was called. Franjo Tudjman, in the December 31, 1991, edition of *Slobodna Dalmacija*, called Bosnia-Herzegovina a "colonial formation" and said it would soon be partitioned between Serbia and Croatia, with a small Muslim state in between. He considered Bosnia a "creation of the Ottoman invasion of Europe." In September, 1995, he asserted that "Croatia accepts the task of Europeanizing Bosnian Muslims," who, according to Tudjman, were part of the Croat ethnic body. He also declared "Bosnia was naturally in the Croatian sphere of interest."[53]

During these years, Croatia was going through a phase of "national revival" and reorientation into "thinking in a Croatian way" (an expression coined by retired priest Ante Baković) in the sense of mythic exaggerations, reinterpretations of mythical figures, and the invention of new ones. Myths began to spread about an "uninterrupted thousand-year Croatian statehood," about the "Croatian nation being the oldest," about the affliction of the Croatian nation in "Serboslavia," and about the "eternal Croatian nation." They complained about their servitude under monarchic and socialist Yugoslavia, and the unceasing violence being committed against them (for example, the postwar "Bleiburg victims," "death marches," and the "Way of the Cross" of Croatian collaborators). The sense of self-victimization was particularly strong: books and brochures about Croatian martyrs were published for several decades.[54] The following comment by A. Bakić sheds some light on the policy of arousing a sense of peril and danger from all quarters as a means of homogenizing the population and luring it toward specific goals: "the Croatian individual must be liberated from communist totalitarianism, the fallacy of Yugoslavism, the practice of Serbian pillage, and venality and corruption inherited from an Ottoman way of thinking in the sense of 'don't worry, we'll do it tomorrow,' as well as our new slavery to Western European currency."[55]

The cult of President Tudjman—referred to as the "Croatian Giant," the "Architect of Croatian Defense," and the "Greatest Croatian of All Time"—grew steadily. He stated several times that he drew inspiration from Stjepan Radić. Judging from a statement he made in 1998, his second historical model was Spain's fascist dictator Francisco Franco: "History shall place me abreast of Franco as a savior of Western civilization."[56] Like Milošević, he was panegyrized in lyrics and song, which referred to him as a "prince" and "knight." In 1992, at an exhibition of the work of Croatian sculptor Kruno Bošnjak entitled "People for All Croatian Time," seven bronze busts of prominent figures who helped realize "Croatia's thousand-year dream" were on display: Hans-Dietrich Genscher, Helmut Kohl, Margaret Thatcher, Alois Mock, Pope John Paul II, an unknown Croat soldier holding a child, and—of course—Franjo Tudjman. There was often no distinction between Tudjman's personality, *his* party, and *his* nation and people. Indeed, in an interview for *Hrvatski vojnik* in April, 1992, he said that "the program for Croatia's statehood did not simply emerge overnight but is the result of my practical and theoretical experience, historical thinking, and theological research into the creation of a state, of which the military is one of the primary elements."[57] His speeches are characterized by egocentricity and conceit, littered with phrases like "I knew," "I sent," and "I believed."

I believe the new Croatian state should have more clearly and unambiguously distanced itself from the quisling Second World War Ustasha state, and that it failed to take appropriate and assiduous measures against those groups and individuals who directly associated themselves with and attempted to revive this tragic period in Croatian history. The following example went beyond Croatia's borders: streets in several Croatian cities, including Dubrovnik, Zadar, Knin, Gračac, Benkovac, Udbina, Vinkovci and Korenica, bear the name of Mile Budak, one of the darkest figures of the NDH. When one of the streets in the city of Split, located near Roman emperor Diocletian's palace, was named after him, representatives of Beith Shemesh, Split's associated city from Israel, and the Wiesenthal Center protested. The excuse of the local authorities was that Budak was an important writer before he became a minister in the Ustasha government. The *pravaši* recently staged a march in Vukovar. They carried pictures of the Poglavnik and the black flag of the HOS, their former militia, and made Nazi salutes. The police reaction to the march was tepid at best, and failed to prevent some partisan monuments from being desecrated. On the other hand, a monument to one of the most brutal Ustasha commanders, Jure Francetić, leader of the infamous "Black Legion," was erected on private initiative.

In February, 1992, an extremist Herzegovinian faction led by Mate Boban, whose goal was partitioning the country, seized control of the HDZ in Bosnia-Herzegovina. At first they fought alongside the Muslims against the Serbs and achieved significant successes. The Bosnian Croats had learned a lesson from the clashes in Croatia the previous year and were better prepared for the Serbs than the Muslims. However, in July, 1993, the Croats announced the creation of "Herceg-Bosna" in Grude. The move was expected to unite the Croats, who were the most dispersed ethnic group in Bosnia-Herzegovina, around a center based in Herzegovina. The first clashes with government forces occurred in October, 1992, and lasted for eighteen months. The Croatian media in Croatia and Bosnia-Herzegovina began a merciless anti-Muslim campaign, and leaders like Boban began considering the emigration of Croats from central Bosnia-Herzegovina to Herceg-Bosna. The situation in Herzegovina was very complicated: in addition to the fighting between ethnic groups, there were clashes between various local Croat factions that were trying to monopolize the lucrative religious tourism business in Medjugorje, which continued to thrive despite the war.

The Croatian army in Bosnia-Herzegovina, the so-called Croat Defense Council *(Hrvatsko vijeće obrane* [HVO]), like the Serbian army, was involved not only in military operations, but the persecution of non-Croats, massacres, brutalities of all kinds, and the destruction of religious and national monuments and symbols of other ethnic groups. Military units were often named after infamous Second World War commanders, and military iconography, symbols, and salutes were borrowed from that period. The Ustasha military slogan "For our home, prepared!"[58] was adopted by the Croat paramilitary unit *Hrvatske oružane snage* (HOS). As in Serbia, a new imagery in the form of comic strips and stories began to emerge *(Superhrvoje).* Cults of "new old" heroes from Croatian history were revived, including the cults of Stepinac, Radić ("a martyr," the "Croat Gandhi"), and even Pavelić. Radić is panegyrized in the following verses written in 1989:

> As Stjepan Radić lay dying,
> He called his Croatian brothers:
> Oh, Croats, my dearest brothers,
> Our mother, Croatia, is alive.[59]

A personality cult similar to Karadžić's developed around Mate Boban, the president of Herceg-Bosna, the HVO, and the Bosnian HDZ. Following another unexpected turnaround in Croatian policy—the normalization of relations with the Bosniaks in March, 1994—Krešimir Zubak, a moderate politician, replaced Boban, who died as a political pensioner on

July 7, 1997. The obituaries and condolences on this occasion make interesting reading. This "Croatian knight" was "our light and inspiration on the path to the goal"; he was "the hope"; "the teacher"; "the symbol of resistance and victory"; "the founder and leader of the Croat national entity in Herceg-Bosna"; "the lightning rod that absorbed the destructive energy of anti-Croat assaults"; the "herald and deliverer of the passion for freedom that had been suppressed for centuries"; "the man who liberated us from fear and gave us the right to fight"; "the usherer in of the new age"; "the great uniter of our aspirations and truths"; "our fellow combatant"; "the right man for hard times"; "the resolute and true defender of the right of the Croat nation to Bosnia-Herzegovina and freedom"; "the torchbearer"; "the important son of the Croatian nation"; and "the helm of the national argosy of freedom."

He had far more than the confidence of the people ("The stars shone on his efforts to create Croatian statehood on this soil"), and more than the people mourned for him ("When people like Mate Boban die, all things on Earth weep"). Under his leadership they "defended their hearths against Serb, then Muslim aggression." His life's work is "an eternal inspiration for the perseverance and future of the Croat nation"; "his strength, ideas, and work are our eternal guide"; "he fought, lived, and suffered for the eternal ideals of Croatian freedom." He was buried on "holy Croatian soil." His death is overpowered by his "living soul," for "even in death you assemble and unite all who have Croatia at heart." Finally, there were the pledges of loyalty: people pledged to continue along his "path in the battle for the freedom and independence of the entire Croat nation"; "his departure did not take away his ideals because his followers remain behind."

BOSNIAKS: IN THE VISE AGAIN

The Bosnian Muslim tragedy in the last war lies in the fact that they were too Muslim for the West and not Muslim enough for the Islamic world. Once again caught between the vise of nationalist interests, the Bosniaks strengthened their own Bosniak nationalism "by giving greater emphasis to the most distinctive thing about it, its religious component" on one hand, while emphasizing "that they stood for the preservation of Bosnia's unique character as a multi-national, multi-religious republic" on the other.[60] In general, Bosniaks had no political goals such as "one nation in one state" like the extremists among their adversaries, the Serbs and Croats.[61] Because of an incorrect political evaluation by the leadership, its naïve optimism in respect to reaching an agreement with the Serbs and the Croats, the sanctimonious policy of the superpowers, and the embargo on arms sales to the Balkans, the Bosniaks were isolated and helpless. They were also disappointed by the response and assistance of the Muslim states, which they found insufficient.

However, the support of the Muslim world to the war efforts of the Bosniak side was many-sided. Despite the embargo, Iran and other Muslim states sent arms and military advisers to the Bosniaks. Saudi Arabia and other Persian Gulf states provided financial aid. Finally, nongovernmental organizations and institutions offered everything from humanitarian help to recruiting Muslim volunteers for the fighting in Bosnia.[62]

Radovan Karadžic said that forcing Serbs and non-Serbs to live together would be like doing the same to "cats and dogs" and added that "Bosnia had never existed and it never will exist." In order to prove this, historical recollection had to be erased first. So, the initial targets of Serb (and later other) militant nationalists were historical, cultural, and religious monuments and signs and symbols of coexistence, collective memory, and the hundreds of years of peaceful coexistence of different ethnic groups, religions, and cultures. The first buildings in Sarajevo to be destroyed were the National Library, the Oriental Institute, and the National Museum. Croat forces in Mostar destroyed the famous Mostar bridge. Furthermore, two of the Bosnian towns that were the most ethnically mixed before the war—Sarajevo and Mostar—were among those that suffered the most. In addition to the liquidation of the Muslim elite, the first targets of Serb aggression in Bosnia-Herzegovina were Muslim clergymen: fifty-four had been killed by mid-June, 1992. According to the president of the Bosnian Ilmija, Halil Mehtić, 107 (10.7 percent) of them were killed, including seventy-seven active imams, and about two hundred were interned in Serbian and Croatian camps for prisoners.[63]

At the founding session of the Bosniak Assembly *(Bošnjački sabor)* in late September, 1993, the name of the Bosnian Muslim nation was changed in what Alija Isaković referred to as a "restoration of the name" of the nation: they became the "Bosniak nation," the "Bosniaks" *(Bošnjaci)*. However, internal discord and even conflicts also appeared on the Bosniak side. In the summer of 1991, Zulfikarpašić's MBO Party, hoping to prevent bloodshed, signed the so-called Serbian-Muslim historic agreement with Karadžić's SDS. According to the agreement's terms, Bosnia's territorial integrity would be preserved within the frame of the reduced Yugoslavia. However, the SDA rejected this initiative. In 1994, fighting broke out between government forces and Muslim supporters of Fikret Abdić, the charismatic leader of the "Autonomous Province" or "Republic of Western Bosnia," which had been established in September, 1993.[65] The rebels in Cazin Province were supported by Croatia and the Serb republics in Croatia and Bosnia-Herzegovina. The rebels even fought with Serbs against government forces. Abdić, affectionately known as "Babo," also developed a personality cult. Kržišnik-Bukić refers to him as "possibly the last feudal lord in Europe."[66] Abdić's followers remained fanatically loyal to their leader even after their defeat at the hands of government forces and their mass exodus in August, 1995.

National and religious homogenization was least pronounced in areas under government control. In February, 1993, there were eight Bosniaks, six Serbs, and five Croats in the *Muslim* government (as the Western and Croatian and Serbian nationalist media insisted on calling it). There were also many Serb and Croat soldiers in the government's army (one-third of the defenders of Sarajevo were Serb, including the second in command), although Muslim influence (including the arrival of mujahideen from Islamic countries and creation of exclusively Muslim military units) and the Bosniaks' prevalence gradually began to increase until they nearly monopolized the power. A number of atrocities, ethnic cleansing, and the destruction of churches and monuments committed by the Bosnian army were recorded. However, according to Bougarel, "for strategic and ideological reasons at the same time," they did not act in the systematic manner of Serbian and Croatian forces.[66] The religious aspects of these events on all sides—Serbian, Croatian, and Bosniak—will be discussed in the following pages.

"THAT PART OF THE WORLD" IN THE EYES OF THE WEST

The archaic misunderstanding and generalization that has characterized the West's view of dramatic events in "that part of the world" since the Middle Ages resurfaced during the Bosnian war. These views varied widely and changed over time. They can generally be categorized in two interrelated types. First are those that were based on the ambiguous attitude of the West toward Bosnia-Herzegovina as an independent state: from initial support for its independence and diplomatic recognition of its statehood that was expected to guarantee the integrity of its borders, to thwarting any form of effective military defense by the legally constituted government by banning the sale of arms; from its indifference to the suffering of the population, justified by excuses of equitable equidistance, to a belated and only partially successful threat of military intervention, which resulted in, at best, the limited use of force.

Western diplomats sought to conceal and justify their passivity with the pretext that Bosnia-Herzegovina is an incurable and chaotic part of the world, a land of savage warriors. Centuries-old myths abound about the Balkan lust for blood, which is occasionally interrupted by brief periods of calm followed by even bloodier wars. This was supposed to create the illusion that nothing could be done to solve the situation. British prime minister John Major spoke of the "ancient hatreds that reappeared." President Bill Clinton was convinced that "their hatreds were five hundred years old," while Sen. John Warren said he believed "these people have fought each other for not hundreds of years, but thousands of years for religious, ethnic, cultural differences." Equally ignorant and rooted in the past were statements by Rep. William Goodling of Pennsylvania, who announced that it "all began in the fourth-century split of the Roman Empire," and British politician Sir Crispin Tickell, who claimed that the hatreds among Yugoslav peoples extend back "thousands of years."[67]

The second characteristic of the view of Western media and diplomats regarding the war in Bosnia-Herzegovina was that they uncritically accepted and reproduced previously discussed mainly Serb ideological myths. The most common of these was the allegation that all parties involved in the war were equally to blame for the situation. This moral equalizing was originally Milošević's position. He repeated this allegation several times and—as many examples show—succeeded in convincing the West of its veracity. European Union negotiators Lord Peter Carrington and Carl Bildt insisted that "everybody is to blame" for the events in Bosnia-Herzegovina. Lord D. Owen was sure that "it's become more apparent that there's civil war."[68] Secretary of State Warren Christopher told the U.S. Congress in June, 1993, the "responsibility for the crimes is shared by all three sides."

The Serb army's open aggression—and to a lesser extent the Croat army's—against an independent, internationally recognized state was officially treated as an internal Bosnian affair when the UN secretary-general, Boutros Boutros-Ghali, accepted Milošević's claim that Bosnian Serb forces were totally independent of Belgrade. James Hogue, editor of *Foreign Affairs*, then wrote that the fighting was a "civil war" in which no side was "impartial." British foreign secretary Douglas Hurd called the conflict in Bosnia-Herzegovina a civil war from the very beginning.[69] Proof of the sheer ignorance regarding the situation abounds. In April, 1995, for example, peace negotiator Thorwald Stoltenberg still maintained that the Muslims were descended from the Serbs, and the media were fond of referring to the Sarajevo government as the "Muslim government."

Some of the following statements speak for themselves. One of the commanders of UN peacekeeping forces in Bosnia-Herzegovina, Lt. Gen. Michael Rose, ostracized the defenders of the surrounded and "protected" enclave of Goražde for "not fighting courageously enough." A second commander, Canadian general Mackenzie, stated that the Muslims were killing their own civilians in order to gain the sympathy of the international public. Len Hamilton, the chairman of the House Foreign Affairs Committee, cynically noted that "unfortunately, the Bosnians do not have oil on their land, like Kuwait."

The response of the Orthodox world—Serbia's "traditional" allies (especially Russia, Ukraine, and Greece)—to the war was diverse, ranging from political support for the regimes in Belgrade, Knin, and Pale to the participation of enthusiastic volunteers and trained mercenaries in Serb military units; from supporting to breaching UN Security Council resolutions such as sanctions against the Federal Republic of Yugoslavia (fuel and supplies were smuggled into Serbia by way of the Danube River); from participation in the UN peacekeeping mission to favoring Serb forces (as was the case with Russian colonel Viktor Loginov, who said there was a conspiracy by the Vatican and others against Orthodoxy and used his position to smuggle fuel and supplies to Serb forces);[70] from opposing Western military intervention in Bosnia-Herzegovina to bowing to the will of the international community under U.S. leadership with the signing of a peace treaty in 1995. On the other hand, uncritical support in favor of Croats and Bosniaks appeared in some Western media, neglecting clear evidence of violence against non-Croats and non-Bosniaks, as well as cases of discrimination and persecution.

WARTIME NEWSPEAK

An obsessive paranoia of being surrounded by enemies triumphed. As Eric Hobsbawm wrote, "there is no more effective way of bonding together the disparate sections of restless peoples than to unite them against outsiders."[71] The Bosnian war introduced a whole range of stigmatic labels for entire nations ("Halt, pashas and Ustasha!").[72] Derisive epithets and pejorative colloquial and historical connotations were used in reference to the enemy, including Chetniks, Ustasha, Janissaries, Turks, *balije* and their brothers in fez, the mujahideen, green berets, and Jihad warriors. They would insult each other with names such as foreign mercenaries, Muslim (or Chetnik or Ustasha) hordes or butchers, criminals, fanatics, extremists, and killers of different sorts. The rhetoric of self-victimization—"nation of martyrs"—was changed as circumstances required. Karadžić claimed that the Serbs were a "nation of warriors," and Plavšić emphasized "traditional Serb pride" on several occasions. Soldiers and military units perceived of and called themselves Croatian knights, dukes, Hajduks, and new Obilićes. Units were given the names of ferocious beasts (dragons, tigers, eagles, and wolves) or of historic personalities, such as the Karadjordje unit. Belgrade linguist Ranko Bugarski speaks of the "language of war," in which even the most absurd neologisms are acceptable, as in "Yugounitarist-serbochetnik-bandit groups" or "Vatican-Kominterna conspiracies." In this new rhetoric, "barehanded defenders" merely defend their "eternal firesides" or their "graveyards and churches," or at times "ardently retaliate or liberate."[73] Linguistic archaisms also returned.

The prevalent obsession was that of distinguishing the "true and patriotic" members of the community from the "traitors, nonnational oriented, and uprooted." Opponents to the new authorities in Croatia were labeled as remnants of the previous regime, careerists, social climbers, sycophants, robbers, hypocrites, "Yugobolsheviks," "cryptocommunists," "torpid Yugonostalgics," "fetid Yugoslav offal," informants, *udbaši* (members of the former Yugoslav secret police UDBa), spies for international Bolshevism, false prophets, "Hejsloveni" (from the first words of the Yugoslav anthem, "Hej, Sloveni"), and "Chetnik scum." The word *miraculous* was used frequently, especially in reference to military victories and weapons (Karadžić warned that the Serbs would use a "miraculous weapon" if the West launched air strikes against their positions, and sometimes the "glory of Serbian weapons" was exposed), independence (perceived as a miracle or the "fulfillment of a thousand-year dream") or self-preservation, and economic success (the *superdinar*). Different sides shared similar jargon: "Gather Serbs/Croats together!" (*Srbi/Hrvati na okup!*), "holy or inviolable Serb/Croat borders," "the glorious medieval Serb/Croat/Bosnian state," or "I hate him like a Serb/Croat," "spirit of Branković/Obilić," "Croatian/Serbian Golgotha," and "largest Serbian/Croatian/Bosniak town under the ground" (respectively, Jasenovac, Vukovar, Srebrenica).

Serbian and Croatian literary language and everyday vocabulary were cleansed of Turkish and Arabic derivatives or derivatives from the language of the "enemy." The choice of alphabet, Cyrillic or Latin, became an important issue. For example, Serb textbooks and passports were printed only in the Cyrillic alphabet in the two *western* Serbian states. The same was true of the *ekavski* and *ijekavski* dialects. Journalists in the RS, a traditionally *ijekavski* region, suddenly began speaking in the "Serb" *ekavski* dialect. Both the RSK and RS introduced textbooks from

Serbia in the *ekavski* dialect. In some places, Serb names replaced Bosnian names, which are "associated with evil and where the Serb tradition had been wiped out," to paraphrase Radoslav Unković. Bosanska Krupa was renamed Krupa na Uni, Bosanski Novi became Novi Grad, and Bosanska Dubica became Kozarska Dubica. The prefixes "Bosanski" and "Bosanska" were removed from the names of Bosanski Brod, Bosanska Gradiška, Bosansko Grahovo, Bosanski Petrovac, Bosanski Šamac and Bosanska Kostajnica. Other places were simply renamed: Donji Vakuf (Srbobran), Skender-Vakuf (Kneževo) and Foča (Srbinje).[74] Republika Srpska did indeed become "the most Serb of all Serb lands," as Biljana Plavšić predicted. A similar purge of the prefix "Serbian" *(Srpski/Srpska)* took place in many localities on Croatian territory that had once been settled by Serbs.

BRUTALITIES IN THE NAME OF RELIGION

The collapse of socialist and Yugoslav myths opened room for the deprivatization of religion and various religio-nationalist mythical constructs that were embedded in the minds of the people. The most important were those of the "chosen" people; the suitability of the dominant religion/church for the nation; the mythologizing of important religio-national figures from the past and present; the demonization of the enemy church/nation; the condemnation of the preceding period of history; and visions of the future infused with religious integrism.[75] The following is a discussion of the processes as well as individual examples of them on all three warring sides.

Pope John Paul II in his public appearances in Rome and Prague in 1990 said "God won in the East." Indeed, in the atmosphere of religious triumphalism, churches emerged—as their religious dignitaries were fond of calling it—from the catacombs of the "Socialist antiecclesiastic regime" and returned not only to the social scene but the political scene as well.[76] A number of religious leaders gave their backing to certain political options and even to specific political parties, sacralized their goals, demonized the opponents of the church (hence also of the country and nation), condemned the laity of the social and political life, which was allegedly opposed to the state and majority nation, and even supported military endeavors. Church organizations relied on the fact that the post-Socialist "thaw" would reinstate the former religious structure. On the other hand, politicians and military commanders were well aware of the power of their people's religious identity and exploited it to their own ends.

Sociologist of religion Srdjan Vrcan notes that the result of desecular-izing society was the radical delaicizing of politics, which was accompa-nied with the process of ethnifying the political and politicizing the eth-nic. The return of religious and nationalist militants and integrationists to the social and political quotidian brought with it interreligious ten-sions and intolerance, and the exclusion of the considerable atheistic population within each nation. The three main religious hierarchies in Bosnia-Herzegovina were sending "open or veiled appeals to religious people of their denomination to support the respective party" of their na-tion (that is, to SDS, HDZ, and SDA), and vice-versa: the strongest polit-ical parties of the Bosnian Serbs and Croats, the SDS and HDZ, tried to exploit the Orthodox and Roman Catholic churches as a means of gar-nering support and legitimacy.[77] Program direction, not to mention ral-lies, symbols (green color, crescent, Qur'anic inscriptions), and the rhet-oric of SDA leaders were also strongly influenced by Islam and the Bosnian Muslim heritage (for example, images of Mujo Hrnjica, an epic hero of the seventeenth century).

The three main religions and ecclesiastic organizations were volun-tarily involved in the war, but in different ways and to different degrees. For Michael Sells, what was going on was a "religious genocide in several senses: the people destroyed were chosen on the basis of their religious identity; those carrying out the killings acted with the blessing and sup-port of Christian church leaders; the violence was grounded in a religious mythology that characterized the targeted people as race traitors and the extermination of them as a sacred act; and the perpetrators of the vio-lence were protected by the policy makers of a Western world that is cul-turally dominated by Christianity."[78]

If our faith is "the only right and righteous," then the enemy's (or of re-ligious minorities within their own nations) is scorned as being false, for-eign, heretical, superstitious, and even sacrilegious.[79] According to this logic of symbolic diades, the elimination of other faiths—religious and ethnic cleansing—became a religious duty; killing is no longer consid-ered "homicide," but "malicide," the liquidation of evil. In an atmo-sphere of religious alarmism, fear of the dangers posed by other religious communities and atheists becomes diffused. A common practice was the justification or minimization of war crimes committed by one's own side or their interpretation as excesses, and the exposure or even invention of those committed by the enemy.

The military sees victory as complete when it is accompanied by sym-bolic triumph over the enemy. The buildings that were most often systematically destroyed throughout the wars in Croatia and Bosnia-

Herzegovina—either in military operations or following conquest—were religious objects: mosques, churches, chapels, and monasteries. According to some estimates, between one thousand and fifteen hundred mosques, about two-fifths of all, were destroyed. The most beautiful of them were the Aladža in Foča and the Ferhadija in Banja Luka. Some sources state that 450 Roman Catholic and 154 Orthodox churches were also destroyed during the first two and one-half years of fighting. According to Serbian data, 340 Orthodox churches and monasteries were destroyed in the wars in Croatia and Bosnia-Herzegovina.[80] As has been the case throughout history, the conquerors' religious symbols were built over the ruins of the sanctuaries of the vanquished. Territory must be symbolically appropriated and the sign of victory "engraved in stone." First to raze, first to erect: it is also very symptomatic that sacral buildings were among the first objects to be restored or rebuilt after the war.[81]

Religious nationalists on all three sides often condemned non-integrist political parties and individuals as atheistic, nihilistic, antinational, foreign, modernist, pro-Western, liberal, and left-oriented. Similarly, the Socialist regime was perceived as being responsible for the outbreak of hatred and violence because of its "desertion" of the Bible/Qur'an and because of its "immorality" and "Godless, soulless, secularist, and anti-Serb/Croat/Muslim" orientation.[82] The false and dangerous logic that there exists only one type of conflict, namely, between faith and nihilism, and that extra ecclesiam nulla salus, reappeared.

Next, the sites of dramatic historic and religious events became the destinations and sites of religio-national pilgrimages and rituals: Medjugorje for the Croats, Ajvatovica for the Bosniaks,[83] and the tombs of Ustasha victims for the Serbs. Religious feasts were turned into national holidays—Easter, Assumption, Christmas, St. Vitus's Day, the Bajram, commemoration of the Battle of Badr, and "the night of the Might"[84]—and celebrated in public buildings.

In Bosnia-Herzegovina, the result of such collective politics and activities on a largely secularized population soon became evident. Public opinion polls in Bosnia-Herzegovina in 1988 showed that only 55.8 percent of Croats, 37.3 percent of Muslims, 18.6 percent of Serbs and 2.3 percent of Yugoslavs declared themselves to be believers. The situation completely changed a decade later: 89.5 percent of Croats and 78.3 percent of Bosniaks in the Bosnian Federation declared themselves to be "religious persons." Research in the Doboj region in 2000 showed that 88 percent of Croats, 84.8 percent of Bosniaks, 81.6 percent of Serbs and 16.7 percent of those nationally undefined declared themselves "very religious" or "medium religious."[85]

The wars in Bosnia-Herzegovina and Croatia were, of course, not religious, but the religious factor was influential. In short, religion and ancient myths gradually and intentionally became an important means of national and political mobilization for the three Bosnian national communities, as has been demonstrated in previous chapters. The foreign media, copying the proregime media, soon adopted the habit of referring to the conflicts as interreligious. This helps us understand Spanish diplomat Carlos Westendorph's harsh statement for the *New York Times* in April, 1998, when he said the churches were partly responsible for the war.

THE THREE-FINGER SALUTE: MILITANT SERBIAN RELIGIO-NATIONAL MYTHOLOGY

First, a few words about the renaissance of Serb religious nationalism. The second Yugoslavia's final years were characterized by an Orthodox renaissance and growing nationalism in the Serb community. The views the Serbian Orthodox Church published "in its media were in accord with many of those of [the Serbian] Academy."[86] And, of course, with the new direction in Serbian politics. When Milošević assumed power he broadened and deepened cooperation and improved relations with the Orthodox Church and held meetings with its highest representatives. Its role in establishing Serb national identity was acknowledged, a program for the construction of churches was initiated, the Orthodox press was released into public circulation, and religious feast days became public holidays. During the Croatian and Bosnian wars, the church acted like a background for—and at the same time like the prolongation of—Serb nationalism, supporting it in an ancient manner characteristic to nationalist clericalism and the politicization of religion and the religionization of politics.[87]

Patriarch German noted at that time "the current changes in the attitude of the Serbian leadership to the Serb Church and to its people marks the beginning of cooperation to the benefit of all." Also, the "Proposal for the Serb Ecclesiastic and National Program," published in a 1989 edition of the *Glas Crkve (Voice of the Church)*, contained a number of proposals for improving state-church relations, including the observation: "There is no strong state without a strong Church." The aging and ailing German, who died in August, 1991, had been patriarch since 1958. He was replaced in 1990 by Pavle Stojčević. Many Orthodox worshippers consider Pavle, a former monk and bishop of the Raška-Prizren diocese, "a living saint."[88]

According to Paul Mojzes, an American expert on East European religious dynamics, the leadership of the Serbian Orthodox Church seem to have played "the most harmful role as compared to the other two major religious communities."[89] Their first step was to reject the "unlawful AVNOJ borders" in Yugoslavia (or "an AVNOJ graveyard"). Parts of Croatia and Bosnia-Herzegovina with a Serbian majority were known simply as the "Serbian Western territories." The church's *sabor* then officially sanctioned an "exclusively defensive war of liberation that has been forced on them" and rejected the Vance-Owen plan. Patriarch Pavle visited Knin, Pale, and even the troops laying siege to Goražde. The church's apparent antimodernist stance was reflected in statements made by individual religious dignitaries, including Amfilohije Radović, the nationalist and controversial Montenegrin metropolite (since 1990), and Bishop Atanasije Jevtić. The church also opposed Pope John Paul II's visit to Belgrade in September, 1994.

A number of senior priests started causing alarm and spreading extremist paranoia, claiming that fiendish forces were conspiring against Orthodoxy. They rejected Westernism, European "atheism, anarchism, and nihilism," and denied the existence of Serb concentration camps. In 1992, Jeftić declared that "militant Islam is using the conflicts to establish a foothold in the Balkans." Speaking about the Serbs, against whom the entire world had apparently turned, Orthodox theologian Božidar Mijač stated that it is "possible that a certain nation, at a specific point in history, becomes the carrier of truth and Divine justice against a multitude of the unrighteous attacking the nation." For the Serbs, Kosovo was "not only a physical domicile but also a metaphysical creation," because it "includes heaven and earth." Serbs bound to Kosovo are "becoming the nation of God, Christ's New Testament nation, heavenly Serbia, part of the new chosen nation."[90] But not only did "God protect the Serbs"—he actually *is* a Serb in a song of turbo-folk star Baja-Mali Kninđa, who sings, "God is a Serb, so do not be afraid you Serb."[91]

The popular strategy of victimhood, which was often applied by all religious groups when they found themselves in a difficult situation and which served as a basis of their mobilization, was revived. In 1992, Bishop Amfilohije Radović wrote a book that rekindled the tales about the "martyrdom of the Serb nation," whose historical fate it is to "suffer" and to be "continually assaulted and butchered"—as in this instance— by others. During a funeral for Serb victims in eastern Bosnia in March, 1993, one local religious dignitary reportedly said: "Not the standards of God but the standards of the devil—these are the criteria that the international public applies to the Orthodox Serbs today."[92] In June, 1998, a number of Orthodox martyrs, Serb clerics killed by the Ustasha regime, attained sainthood, including Zagreb metropolite Dositej Vasić, Bishops Petar Zimonjić, Sava Trljajić, and Platon Jovanović, and Fathers Branko Dobrosavljević and Đorđe Bogić.

Oaths made in front of newly opened graves became the guarantee for the "right" path forward. An example of this happened in June, 1996, when a procession carrying the mortal remains of Saint Vasilij (Saint Basil), led by Patriarch Pavle and Bishops Amfilohije and Atanasije, passed through the "Serb" part of Herzegovina. The Bosnian Serb newspaper described the event passionately: "Birds, flowers and animals rejoiced as the procession passed them. We all noticed the delight of the horse following the column of vehicles, as if to display how very happy it was to live to see the day when Herzegovina's greatest Serbian son returned to his biblical homeland." According to Bishop Atanasije, a "divine fragrance" emanated from the saint's bones. Of course, the lesson learned from all this came when Atanasije urged those present to make a pledge to Saint Vasilij to vanquish the enemy and fight to the last man.

An editorial in *Pravoslavje* served as a source of religio-nationalist incitement and supported extremists in other ways as well. It enthusiastically celebrated Serb victories in Croatia and Bosnia-Herzegovina in 1991–92.[93] At the beginning of the war, it stated that the Bosnian Serbs did not want to live in a *jamahiriyah* like the one in Libya, nor as slaves under the authority of the mujahideen.[94] A similar statement was made by D. Ćosić, who added that there was a "near-metaphysical fear" among the Bosnian Serbs that "two-fifths of them would have to live under Muslim domination." Patriarch Pavle openly referred to the Republic of Croatia as the "new Independent State of Croatia," and justified the fighting as a "righteous" Serb war.[95] Some new religious-national slogans also emerged, including "All the way to Serb Banja Luka with three raised fingers of one hand."

The myth of the defensive wall portrays the Serbs and Montenegrins in two ways: as the shield of Christian Europe against the advance of Islam, and as the protectors of the Orthodox world from Western and Vatican appetites. Orthodox "religious apprehension" was not caused only by Muslims and Catholics, but by Western religious missionaries as well. Bishop Atanasije condemned the work of the Adventist sect in eastern Herzegovina because he considered it a "well-known Western aggressive, extremely Protestant, fanaticized and anti-Orthodox and anti-Christian sect."[96]

A number of senior Orthodox dignitaries praised Serb nationalist leaders, ostensibly because they were a fine example of "true St. Sava Serbs."

Metropolite Nikolaj Mrđa of Dabar-Bosnia, who spent the duration of the war on the Serb side, stated that the Serbs, under the leadership of Karadžić and Mladić, were "following the thorny path of Jesus Christ." In an encouraging speech to a Serbian unit, he said: "we have always won the wars. God will not abandon us this time either." The Greek Orthodox Church declared Karadžić "one of the most prominent sons of our Lord Jesus Christ working for peace" and decorated him with the nine-hundred-year-old Knights' Order of the First Rank of Saint Dionysius of Xanthe. Ecumenical patriarch Bartholomew declared, "the Serbian people have been chosen by God to protect the western frontiers of Orthodoxy."[97] Such strong support helps us understand the position of the Serbian Orthodox Church's Episcopal Conference when it condemned the "partiality" of the International War Crimes Tribunal in The Hague.

Another example of the church's blatant support for Serb extremists and war crimes in Croatia and Bosnia-Herzegovina is the relationship between a number of senior dignitaries and the international felon and war criminal Željko Ražnatović Arkan. He met with Patriarch Pavle, who justified his actions and presented him with an autographed icon of Saint Nicholas, and with Metropolite Amfilohije. Atanasije Jevtić, the bishop of "Serb Herzegovina of St. Sava," said that Arkan "defends the Serbs." Indeed, Arkan considered himself a favorite of the patriarchate. He stated that his commander was Patriarch Pavle and that "we are fighting for our religion, the Serbian Orthodox Church." Bishop Lukijan blessed his military units, the notorious Tigers. According to some sources, the church was helping him with "organizing, financing, and arming his militia."[98] Bishop Vasilij personally traveled from his diocese (Tuzla-Zvornik) to Belgrade to attend Arkan's wedding in February, 1995. Incidentally, the bridegroom's chest was festooned with a large and magnificent cross.[99] However, Arkan's criminal activity seems to have gone too far: RS authorities turned against his units because of the theft, violence, and arrogance they directed against the Serb people.

The more militant clerics maintained "close and supportive ties to Bosnian Serb President Karadžić and the leadership of the Republika Srpska." The synod's public statements emphasized that the Serb nation and church were once again threatened, as they had been during the Second World War and by the Ottoman Empire, and that the Serbs were merely protecting what was theirs. Myths about Orthodoxy being the "spiritual refuge of the Serbs" began to reemerge, as did old slogans about the "sacred Serbs," the "heavenly Serbs," about how "God protects the Serbs," that the Serbs are "bearers of the truth and Divine justice," and that "there can be no Serbianism without Orthodox Christianity."[100] Bishop

Artemije repeated the ancient belief that the church is the "mother of the nation." *Vox populi* becomes *Vox Dei*, and the will of the nation— their nation—is portrayed as the will of God. It would seem that anti-clericalism—an important characteristic of modern society—bypassed the Serbs at that moment.

Other clergymen talked about traitors to the religion and allowed soldiers to decorate their uniforms with Christian iconography. They blessed military criminals, spread and justified ancient stereotypes about Muslims and Croats, condemned those who dared protest against the persecution of Muslims, exposed the Serb (or—as circumstances required—Turkish) origin of the Bosniaks, and denied indisputable evidence of Serb crimes, persecution, and concentration camps. There are even reports of forced conversions of Muslims to Orthodoxy: group baptisms took place, for example, in Bijeljina.[101] A number of Orthodox priests took up arms, including Nikodin Čavić, who was to be found "wherever Serbs and Serb nationhood were threatened," and who condemned the religious fanaticism and atrocities of his Muslim adversaries. In September, 1993, Metropolite Nikolaj publicly declared his opposition to mixed marriages.[102]

The nationalist part of the church supported Milošević's expansionist Greater Serbia policy, although it never fully trusted him because of his Communist background. It did, however, find him to be a suitable partner: Patriarch Pavle visited him several times during the war. This evident support began to falter in the first half of 1992. Senior Orthodox clerics began condemning Belgrade's "leftist regime," claiming that the third Yugoslavia apparently was also prejudiced toward the Serbs, and praised those from Knin and Pale. They claimed that the hardships faced by the entire Serb nation originated from the fact that the Milošević regime had renounced Saint Sava's Orthodoxy, that the government was not working with the church, and that its functionaries never made the sign of the cross, consecrated water, or celebrated baptismal feasts.

Patriarch Pavle and Bishop Amfilohije "openly came out in support of the Bosnian Serb leadership's rejection of the Vance-Owen Plan."[103] When Serbia began to feel the weight of international sanctions, which forced Milošević to abandon his expansionist plans, and especially after the Dayton Peace Agreement (DPA) in November, 1995, the church intensified its condemnation of Milošević and his regime as traitors to Serbs living in Croatia and Bosnia-Herzegovina. The DPA allegedly demanded the "surrender" of the Republika Srpska, and that "Mother" Serbia renounce its "daughter" and behave like a "stepmother." In December, 1995, the church synod defected to the side of Bosnian Serb leader Karadžić and

Serb radical Šešelj, who remained loyal to the policy of uniting all Serbs in one country, and emphasized the "Piedmont role of Pale in uniting all Serbs."

However, there was a split at the very top of the church hierarchy. Although Patriarch Pavle initially supported the DPA, a number of bishops (including Amfilohije and Artemije), under the leadership of the militant Herzegovinian bishop Atanasije, rejected the agreement and harshly criticized Pavle. Atanasije went so far as to urge the Serbs not to "capitulate to the world as Milošević has."[104] Patriarch Pavle and the senior church leadership later changed their position and urged the Serbs to resist the "rule of a dismal ideology and a single individual." In his 1995 Christmas letter, Pavle made no attempt to conceal his disappointment with the DPA and its partitioning of Bosnia-Herzegovina.

War criminals and a number of Serb politicians who had severely compromised themselves in the war made similar sanctimonious statements. They often attempted to hide their actions behind a façade of religion. Mirko Jović, one of the most fanatical Serb nationalists and anti-Semites and commander of the "White Eagles," demanded a "Christian, Orthodox Serbia with no mosques or unbelievers."[105] War songs portrayed the clashes as battles for the Orthodox cause. The following are two good examples:

The Serbian army, that is ourselves
All believers in God.

And:

We have lions' hearts,
We defend Orthodoxy.[106]

Karadžić issued a messianic statement in which he declared that the Serbs were the avant-garde of Orthodoxy and that the Slavs were protecting Europe from the "advance of Islam on the West," that is, from the creation of an "Islamic fundamentalist state in Europe." He described himself as the defender "of the Serb tribe and our Church." In May, 1993, he sent a letter to Patriarch Pavle thanking him for his "advice and support" in the Bosnian Serbs' "just battle." According to Karadžić, the church is the "only spiritual force capable of uniting the Serb nation, regardless of borders." The Orthodox magazine *Svetigora* quotes him as saying that the former Communist authorities were discriminating against the Serbs "while elsewhere the national and religious programs of the

Roman Catholic Church and Islam were being promoted," and "that God probably brought us freedom because he taught us what to do."[107]

Karadžić's position regarding the church is best illustrated in the following statements: "I have profited very much from my firm connections with the Church"; "Not a single important decision was made without the Church"; "Our clergy is present in all of our deliberations and decisions"; and "our deaths, suffering, and endurance we accept as God's grace." Church dignitaries made similar statements. According to Bishop Nikolaj, the war "Orthodoxizes" Serbian soldiers in Bosnia, and "General Mladić accepts all the suggestions of the Metropolitan."[108]

On the other hand, many Orthodox clergymen and believers refused to be engulfed by nationalist euphoria. They realized that it was harmful, not advantageous, to the Serb nation—Orthodox Church organizations in Dalmatia, Gornji Karlovac, Slavonia, and Bihać-Petrovac were already experiencing its negative effects. But the condemnations of violence and persecution (for which "godlessness" and even the "devil" were to blame) were too general. In 1992, Orthodox leaders in Istanbul declared, "the leaders of the Roman Catholic Church and all of us must display a particular attentiveness, pastoral duty, and Divine wisdom in order to prevent the exploitation of religious sentiments for political or nationalist ends." Other Orthodox clergymen were more concrete. Bishop Hrizostom in northeastern Bosnia raised his voice against the Bosnian Serb nationalist campaign, rejected the appeal by the Pale regime urging the withdrawal of all Serbs still outside the RS's borders, and sharply criticized its leadership. Others—like Ignatije Midić and Prof. Vladeta Jerotić of the Belgrade Theological Faculty—rejected war as a means of achieving "higher objectives."[109]

Many of those who ignited international and interreligious hatred were fully aware of the consequences of their actions only during the war and attempted to distance themselves from them. The defeat of the Serbs and their withdrawal from western Slavonia in May, 1995, was followed by "retaliatory action" in which extremists torched Catholic churches in Banja Luka in addition to expelling several thousand Muslims and Croats. Patriarch Pavle condemned such persecution, as well as the killing of non-Serbs in Banja Luka. In the winter of 1993, Dobrica Ćosić and Vuk Drašković (the tendentious writings of the latter in the 1980s can be treated as one of the sources for the anti-Muslim and nationalistic climate) condemned the Serb crimes in Trebinje and Gacko, inviting harsh criticism from Bishop Atanasije.[110] The Serbian Orthodox Church's nationalist policy the was strongly condemned by the World Council of

Churches (WCC), of which the Serbian Orthodox Church is a member, and proposed its expulsion from the organization.

However, even such open support by the church for Serb nationalist aspirations failed to satisfy a number of the most extreme circles (for example, Chetnik leader Đujić, residing in the United States). They ostracized Patriarch Pavle for not consecrating Serb weapons and victories, for not taking a stronger position, for not asking for the assistance of "brotherly Orthodox churches," and for making no effort to create an alliance of Orthodox states, which the Serbian regime, because of its atheistic orientation, was incapable of accomplishing.[111]

This section can be summarized by Vrcan's classification of the most important religio-national mythical constructs of Serb Orthodoxy: that Orthodoxy is the essence of the Serb nation; that the church must always be linked to and in harmony with the Serbian state (the "state church"); that the Serbs are inclined toward spiritual values, such as the hallowed Kingdom of God; that they are, because of this, God's chosen nation, suffering and tormented throughout history; that the church is the defender of Orthodoxy from Catholicism and Islam; that Serb Orthodoxy was the main victim of godless Bolshevism; that the Serb nation was the most affected in AVNOJ-Yugoslavia; and the Serbs' latent anti-Western orientation. All these examples show how the Serbian Orthodox Church became "a servant of religious nationalist militancy."[112] At best, it was symptomatically silent and failed to openly condemn the criminals who were involved in ethnic cleansing and destruction in its name.

"GOD AND THE CROATS": THE ROMAN CATHOLIC CHURCH IN THE BOSNIA WAR

Despite Cardinal Kuharić's announcement in December, 1990, that the Roman Catholic Church would "guard its autonomy, and respect the autonomy of 'state' authority," and reject "Cæsaro-papism," renewed Croat nationalism accommodated many of the religious characteristics of the Croats, who were probably the least secularized of all nations in the former Yugoslavia. Church or lay religio-national extremists reestablished the link between Croat national and religious identity. An illustrative example can be found in the autumn, 1992, issue of the Catholic publication *Veritas:* "The cross of Christ stands next to the Croatian flag, [and the] Croatian bishop next to the Croatian minister of state. Croatian priests and teachers are together again in the schools. . . . Guardsmen wear rosaries around their necks. . . . The Church is glad for the return of its people 'from the twofold' slavery: Serbian and Communist."[113] A Croatian march includes the following verses:

May our unified voice be heard,
There is one God for us all.
A Croatian battle is being waged,
Attention, all your criminals![114]

In many ways, the church tried to pursue a path of Roman Catholic integration: demands began to emerge—for the "spiritual revival of the nation," for the necessity of a Roman Catholic identity for the Croats, and for the church's spiritual domination in society. The Croats' rich religious history was emphasized, as was their glagolitic tradition ("proof that they did not release the pen even when they raised the sword") and loyalty to the Vatican. Sister Marija (Ana Petričević), a nun from Split, dedicated one of the poems in her anthology to Franjo Tudjman and admitted in a 1994 interview that she believed him to be "supernatural," that he is the "carrier of all our aspirations, especially our yearning for freedom." At a symposium on spiritual revival in Croatia, Ante Baković, zealous advocate of the policies of Croatia's ruling party, the HDZ, referred to "people without souls" who were "still alive and scheming after the fall of Communism, St. Sava and Yugoslavia," and added: "These weeds must be uprooted from the new Croatia!"[115]

Such speeches support the opinion of Paul Mojzes, who believes that there were close contacts between the leading Croatian political party and the Catholic Church in Croatia at that time. According to him, Cardinal Kuharić (and other Catholic bishops) "massively supported the activities of the HDZ" in the prewar years and thus contributed to interreligious and international tension. Croatian leader Franjo Tudjman admitted in a 1990 interview that the church molded the Croats' national consciousness, and that it was the only organized force in Croatia capable of continually resisting the Socialist regime. He repeated this position two years later when speaking about the need for "spiritual revival" as an essential element for "general national revival." He said one of his successes was the "alliance between Croatian politics and the Croatian Catholic Church, which has played a important historical role in preserving Croat nationhood."[116]

Let us now return to events in Bosnia-Herzegovina. The Bosnian Catholics were divided into three dioceses: Mostar-Duvno, Banja Luka, and the archdiocese of Vrhbosna-Sarajevo. As Petar Anđelović, the superior of the Franciscan province of Bosna Srebrena, admits, the church initially supported the HDZ, but later reversed its politics and became critical of it.[117] Clergy reacted in different ways to the outbreak and course of the war, and to "cleansing" the occupied territory of members of other ethnic groups or religions. On one hand, the church's most senior representatives—Cardinal Puljić, Provincial Andjelović, Bishop Franjo Komarica of Banja Luka, and Croatia's Cardinal Kuhavić—"have specifically and courageously condemned the crimes of Croat religious nationalists" and supported a nationally and religiously pluralist country.[118] In this respect they operated very independently of the dominant Croat policy of the time: they opposed the partitioning of the country, the exploitation of religion for military ends, and the policies of hardliners from western Herzegovina. Mate Boban's and Gojko Šušak's impetuous reply to Kuharić's accusations in the summer of 1993 warned the church leadership to stay out of matters that did not concern them. There are some opinions that "Boban's counterattack was actually prepared by Herzegovinian Catholic clerics who were pursuing their own differences with the Catholic hierarchy in Zagreb." Franciscan superior Andjelović also criticized Boban's extremist policy.[119]

Cardinal Puljić publicly and unambiguously repeated his demands for a multireligious Bosnia-Herzegovina on several occasions and rejected unofficial appeals by Croat political and military leaders of the divided state to seek refuge in territory under their control.[120] Cardinal Kuharić spoke out against nationalism's "pious egotism," stating in May, 1993, that the collective fate of Bosnia-Herzegovina lay in a congenial coexistence between the Muslims, Serbs, and Croats. He also sent an open letter expressing his views to Bosnia-Herzegovina's Croat leaders. Jozo Zovko, by then the superior of the Franciscan monastery in Široki brijeg (which had come to be known as the "spiritual center of Herzegovina") publicly stated that the fighting in Bosnia was a political conflict and not a religious war.

Similar statements were made by Ratko Perić, the new bishop of Mostar, otherwise known for his nationalist stands. It came as no surprise, then, that the Catholic Church in Bosnia-Herzegovina supported the peace agreement and the federation of the Croats and the Bosniaks in 1994, and condemned the Croat nationalists' violence against Bosniaks in Mostar in February, 1997. Indeed, Pope John Paul II personally spoke about the suffering on all threes sides, especially on the Muslim side. He did not, however, explicitly condemn religious nationalists from the ranks of the Roman Catholic Church.

There were many of these on the Croat side, too. If, on one hand, we can establish that most of the Catholic clergy in Croatia and Bosnia-

Herzegovina maintained a relatively neutral position to the fighting, we must also point out that a number of Catholic clergymen saw matters from a different perspective, which consequently led to action. Some junior Catholic clergymen and Franciscans, especially in western Herzegovina, acted on their own, spreading anti-Muslim hatred and advocating a Greater Croatia: they wanted the "Shrine of the Queen of Peace" (Medjugorje) and Marian ideology to become the focal points of the Croat community and national identity. Their tribalist stance and militant nationalist clericalism was criticized by senior church representatives, who viewed Catholicism from a more universal perspective and according to the principles of the Second Vatican Council (1962–65).

Herzegovinian Franciscan provincial Tomislav Pervan from Mostar accused the Bosnian Muslims of planning to create an "Islamic state"; Franciscan Vinko Mikolić from Bobani compared the Bosnian government to the "Turkish occupiers"; and Rev. Ante Marić from the Mostar vicinity accused the Muslims of waging a "holy war" against the Croats.[121] Popular mythic belief, advocated—among others—also by the mid-nineteenth century Franciscan monk Franjo Jukić, that the Muslims were the descendants of "weak Christians, who accepted Islam in order to save their estates," reappeared. Roman Catholic iconography frequently emblazoned Croat military equipment and uniforms (a rosary winding around a knife, for example), often alongside Ustasha and Nazi symbols. The following are some verses from a song from that period:

> *The Yugo army has to know:*
> *Croatia will win the war.*
> *All the saints are on our side,*
> *While the damned are all on theirs.*

The song was accompanied by a video portraying bearded men wearing Chetnik fur caps as the "damned."[122]

The church's position regarding events in Bosnia-Herzegovina was related to events in Croatia. Mojzes is more direct in his condemnation of the Roman Catholic Church in Croatia than other observers, accusing it of being linked to Croat nationalism and contributing to the outbreak of the war while its bishops "initiated the process of national-religious confrontation." The struggle against the previous regime and the Orthodox Serbs was portrayed "as a war between good and evil, Christianity and communism, culture and barbarity, civilization and primitivism, democracy and dictatorship, love and hatred."[123] In a pastoral letter issued shortly before the multiparty elections in 1990, two bishops from Bosnia-

Herzegovina indirectly, but very clearly, instructed their parishioners to vote for the HDZ. In April of the following year, just before the last Yugoslav population census, they instructed their parishioners to register themselves as Croats and Catholics. Finally, in February, 1992, they urged the very same people to vote for an independent Bosnia-Herzegovina.[124] The pro-HDZ stance of the Catholic Church and its media in Croatia was also criticized by representatives of the Serbian Orthodox Church.

Slogans about a "hallowed Croatia," "God and the Croats," and the "Golgotha of the Croat nation" began to reemerge. The Croatian military's triumphant Operation Tempest in August, 1995, was seen as "testimony that this nation is at certain times touched by God."[125] The war with the Bosniaks rekindled Croatian anti-Muslim sentiments among some extremists.[126] Croatian politicians also made anti-Muslim statements. Tudjman repeatedly referred to the threat of "Islamic fundamentalism" and to the prospect of an "Islamic holy war." His defense minister also spoke of "Islamic fundamentalism."[127]

One of the most vocal admirers of Ante Pavelić and the Ustasha era today is Croat priest Luka Prcela, who caused much commotion in Croatia and abroad in 1997 when he held a requiem mass for Pavelić in the Church of Saint Dominic in Split on the thirty-eighth anniversary of his death.[128] The mass was paid for by the pro-Ustasha "Croatian Liberation Movement." The ceremony was transformed into an enthusiastic political vindication of the war criminal and ended with the Croatian national anthem. Vjekoslav Lasić, a Dominican from Zagreb, is also known for his sympathies for the Ustasha and the NDH. Cardinal Kuharić immediately distanced the Catholic Church in Croatia from Lasić in the statement he made in May, 1997.

The Catholic Church was greatly affected by the last warfare. Its human and material losses were particularly severe in areas under Serb control and during clashes with the Bosniaks. The Catholic population was reduced by half, and the number of killed and tortured priests and monks remains unknown. Auxiliary bishop Pero Sudar of Sarajevo claims that ten clergymen were killed, but other sources place the figure at seven. The Franciscan order in Bosnia-Herzegovina alone suffered the destruction of four monasteries, twenty presbyteries, twenty-five parish churches, and a number of smaller ones. The most difficult situation was in Bishop Franjo Komarica's Banja Luka diocese, where 40 percent of the churches were destroyed and 110,000–120,000 Catholics fled their homes in the first year of the war, leaving only five of the original forty-seven parishes functional. Only 35,000 Catholics were left by December, 1994, and 70 percent of the churches had been destroyed by February,

1995, although there were no military operations in the area. In the end, only 5,000 Catholics remained in the Banja Luka area. The bishop, who stubbornly refused to bow to Serb pressure and leave town, spent eight months under house arrest.[129]

The persistent "Herzegovinian syndrome," that is, the long-lasting conflict between the parish clergy and the Franciscans, intensified, as illustrated by the following event, which took place in Čapljina in October, 1997. A mass was to be conducted there by an unnamed dark-skinned bishop who had enjoyed good relations with the local Medjugorje Franciscans for several years. Bishop Perić of Mostar proscribed the mass, and on the day it was to be held the parishioners found the door to the Church of Saint Francis of Assisi had been walled in. Nevertheless, the "visiting" bishop, referred to only as monsignor, went ahead and conducted the mass with the support of a Franciscan association known as "Peace and Good" (Saint Francis's motto). This was a breach of canonical law, which requires that a visiting bishop seek the assent of the local bishop before conducting a mass. The incident caused strong reactions and debates among the Roman Catholic public.

The church's popularity among Catholics increased when the Vatican became one of the first states to recognize Croatia's and Bosnia's independence. Its popularity was further boosted by the pope's visit to Croatia in September, 1994, and October, 1998. He had been invited to Bosnia-Herzegovina as early as in January, 1993, by President Izetbegović and the Roman Catholic bishops. That visit was planned for September, 1994, but it had to be canceled because of Karadžić's warning that the pontiff might be assassinated by Muslims and the blame laid on the Serbs. In November, 1996, members of the Bosnian presidium invited him to visit Bosnia-Herzegovina in the spring of 1997.

A new head of the Roman Catholic Church in Croatia was appointed in September, 1997. In his farewell speech, Cardinal Kuharić praised the HDZ regime and its relationship with the church. The new archbishop was Josip Bozanić. The first question to emerge was whether the pope had selected him because he was less political than his predecessor. In his first Christmas message, Bozanić made it clear that the church in Croatia was distancing itself from politics by criticizing the Croatian authorities. He talked about the "sins of the [political] structures" and warned against the pauperization of the population, the amassing of wealth by the privileged, and uncontrolled capitalism.

In his Easter address in 1998, he "humbled" the boasts about military, political, and economic success, saying: "It seems to us that the spiritual vacuum is a consequence of aspirations that ascribe religious dimensions to some worldly phenomena, as well as of irresponsible promises and un-warranted trust." In May, 1998, he emphasized the difference between "political and ecclesiastic Catholicism." The latter, he said, "has been blinded by ideology and, as such, has no place in our Church and reli-gion." Such positions were strongly criticized by progovernment circles and right-wing intellectuals from the Croatian Forum association (under the leadership of lawyer Željko Olujić, a Tudjman sympathizer), who ac-cused Bozanić of "anationality," of "spreading teachings that were perni-cious to the Church and the state," and of unfairly criticizing the gov-ernment. He urged believers to ignore the archbishop's example.[130]

A number of other clergymen were also critical of the exploitation of religious sentiments for nationalist or political ends. In interviews and newspaper articles, Father Luka Vincentić, for example, relentlessly at-tacked contemporary clericalism and the undemocratic Croatian gov-ernment. He compared "Tudjman, the nation, and the HDZ" to the myths of the previous regime, namely "Tito, the Working Class, and the Communist Party." Father Tomislav Luka, a member of the Croatian Par-liament, became known for advocating Croatian-Muslim cooperation in Bosnia-Herzegovina. Critics of the relationship between religion and pol-itics were particularly strong in Bosnia-Herzegovina because of the iniq-uitous actions of political and religious extremists in recent years. In statements made to the public in the spring of 1998, Bishop Komarica and Archbishop Puljić cautioned the clergy and the church to avoid party politics. The archbishop mentioned the "false promises" and bad moves made by the authorities during and after the war. In an interview for the *Novi list* in July, 1998, the auxiliary bishop of Sarajevo, Pero Sudar, indi-rectly criticized the HDZ as the strongest Bosnian Croat party and said that he was not sorry to see it break up. Franciscan Bono Zvonimir Šagi, a renowned theologian, admitted that "the Church is presently [January, 2001] more severe toward the state authorities" because before it was "loaded with 'patriotic blockade,' respected the great idea of creation of the state, and did not expose mistakes in this process."[131] In short, there were signs of a distancing between Great Croatian nationalist policies and the stands and behavior of the majority of Croatian and Bosnian Ro-man Catholic clergy.

Recent years have witnessed a revival of Stepinac's martyr cult, *fama martyrii*. Cardinal Kuharić held a special mass every February 10, the an-niversary of Stepinac's death in 1960. The 1946 sentence was repealed in 1992. The Croats, like the Serbs, exhumed their "religious hero" at a crit-ical period in their history. The ceremony took place on June 21, 1993, and an autopsy was conducted the next day. The findings revealed that

Stepinac had posthumously been desecrated. His "martyr's death" has been emphasized in recent times, although there is no official proof that the Communists poisoned him, then wrenched his heart from his chest and burned it. Nevertheless, some of his mortal remains (relics with his blood, made by Carmelite nuns, for example) have become "our priceless relic."[132] To complete the procedure of his beatification, a miracle allegedly "performed" by Stepinac had to be identified. One was found in the healing of a young disabled girl from Dubrovnik. The healing was ostensibly related to her pilgrimage to his tomb in the Zagreb Cathedral.

Pope John Paul II beatified Stepinac on October 3, 1998, in—what is now referred to as the national Marian center, Marija Bistrica. According to Cardinal Bozanić, Stepinac's beatification was an "acknowledgment of the Croat nation." Stepinac has formally become that which the Croatian Catholic clergy and religious nationalists have long been aspiring for: "a national saint"; "a great martyr"; "he proved his saintliness through his heroic virtues, martyr's death, exemplary saintly life, his charitable and pastoral activities, his concern for the material and spiritual well-being of his nation and state"; "a modern-age Saint Paul"; "a slave because of the Gospel"; "a shackled apostle"; and "a just man, a heroic victim of Communist persecution," to quote but a few of the most popular slogans from the Croatian religious press and the statements of senior religious figures. According to this logic, Stepinac becomes an actual "victor," as implicated by his second name (Alojzije *Viktor* Stepinac). On the other hand, Strossmayer is not as fondly remembered in Croatia because of his pro-Yugoslav position and his attitude toward the Vatican. The new authorities changed the name of the institute he founded from the Yugoslav to the Croatian Academy of Sciences and Arts.

SHADES OF GREEN: MUSLIM RELIGIOUS NATIONALISM

Vrcan refers to the Muslim religion in Bosnia-Herzegovina as "peaceful Islam," far removed from the Islamic fundamentalism portrayed by the Serbian and Croatian nationalistic media. Data show that only 37.3 percent of Bosnian Muslims in 1988 declared themselves to be believers: the secularized majority was Muslim only in terms of culture and tradition. These cultural and traditional characteristics included Muslim names, circumcision, characteristic food, the celebration of feast days, and a number of other traditional practices. Both Austria-Hungary and Yugoslavia had supported the nonreligious dimensions of Bosnia-Herzegovina's Muslim Slavs. Yet while the Catholic Church in Croatia and Bosnia-Herzegovina slowly distanced itself from Croatian nationalism in the last Bosnian war and became increasingly critical toward it, developments on the Bosniak side were exactly the opposite. The fact remains that the religious component of Bosniak national identity was strengthened during the Bosnian war. There were also some clear signs and excesses of pan-Islamic fundamentalism and extremism—a phenomenon less known to Bosnia-Herzegovina before.[133] The invigorated religiousness of the Bosniaks was, therefore, more a consequence and than a cause of the war.

Indeed, the SDA itself was accused of gradually transforming into a religio-nationalist party as its founders and leaders included advocates of all the pan-Muslim options found in the Muslim community's religious structure.[134] At least eight out of forty members of its initiating committee once belonged to the Young Muslims group. As Bougarel points out, "*lay* militants of this party have been tempted to use Islam to promote a policy of national homogeneity" while "the *religious* ones expected that an aggravation of tension would favor the re-Islamization of a largely secularized population."[135] In other words, several religious dignitaries and laymen openly pressed for the Bosniaks' "re-Islamization through the war."[136] Just as national affiliation was equated with religious affiliation in the case of the Serbs and Croats, advocates of the Bosniak religio-national integration mythology believed all Bosniaks were inevitably Muslims and the oldest population of the country.[137]

Džemaludin Latić, editor of the journal *Preporod* in the 1980s and later editor of the *Muslimanski glas (Muslim Voice)*, warned against secularized Muslim intellectuals who, he said, were "more dangerous to the Muslim believers than the Chetniks. We must change people," say in the organization Active Islamic Youth (*Aktiv Islamske Omladine* [AIO]). A group of people who rallied around Salih efendi Čolaković also advocated gradual Islamization. Some considered Izetbegović the "father of the homeland," "fighter for Islam," and "our only leader." Others believed he was the hidden thirteenth imam sent by God to lead the Bosniaks along the true path.[138] The following verse illustrates the manner in which he was revered:

> *The Green Flag is fluttering,*
> *long live SDA,*
> *Herceg-Bosna is joyful,*
> *our leader is Alija.*[139]

Local mythmakers distorted the original Shiah messianic prophesy (the Bosnian Muslims belong to the Sunni version of Islam) about the reappearance of the twelfth imam (the so-called hidden imam, Muhammad al-Mahdi al-Hujjah), who has been concealed by God since the third century of the Islamic calendar. The imam reveals himself only to the select, such as the ayatollahs in Iran. The Bosniaks were said to be making sacrifices to save Islam by pointing out its enemies. A number of local imams spread rumors that "Izetbegović is the next after Muhammad, who will tell and realise final truth." These claims were ostensibly confirmed when Saudi Arabia's King Fahd awarded Izetbegović with a medal for his contribution to the spread of Islam.[140] These stands and practices of SDA, its leadership, and the Muslim religious community was criticized and rejected by some of Izetbegović's former close collaborators, including Adil Zulfikarpašić; Sefer Halilović, former commander of the Bosnian army; and another Bosnian army high commander, Jovan Divjak, a Bosnian Serb.

Such inflammatory statements and activities prompted Bosniak religious extremists to raise some fundamentalist notions, including the undesirability of mixed marriages (although they approved marriages between Muslim men and Christian women), the re-Islamization of previously secular elements of Bosniak society, the introduction of Islamic sacred law *(sharia)*, Arabic as the first foreign language in schools (rather than English, French, or German), polygamy, Islamic missionizing, and the legal prohibition of pork and alcohol. Several monuments erected by the former regime in Sarajevo disappeared during the war. However, the monuments were not only those dedicated to Communist heroes such as Čolaković or Masleša, but to writers Skender Kulenović, Mak Dizdar, Meša Selimović, Branko Ćopić, and Ivo Andrić as well. Bosniak deputies at the assembly of the Sarajevo canton held their Friday midday prayers—the *juma* (which, as a rule, should be held in a mosque)—on the assembly grounds.

Some extremists—such as Adnan Jahić in September, 1993—advocated the creation of a "Muslim state as a national state of the Bosniaks or the Muslims" in the area controlled by the Bosnian army, whose leaders would be Izetbegović (secular) and Cerić (religious). It would have "Muslim ideology, based on Islam, its religious-legal and ethical-social principles, but also with those contents of West European provenance that are not in contradiction with the abovementioned" and that would "strive for a gradual abolishment of the duality between sacred and profane, religious and political," and so forth. A similar initiative was suggested by a group of SDA deputies in February, 1994: the "Bosniak Republic" would be the Bosniak national state in which Serbs and Croats would have the status of national minorities.[141]

One source of such ideas was Islamic students studying abroad in

Muslim countries. Another was military units composed exclusively of Muslims, including foreign Islamic soldiers, who openly declared that they were fighting a jihad. Friedman estimates that there could not have been more than 1,000 such mujahedeen fighters, Mojzes reports there were at least 3,000, and Bellion-Jordan cites a figure of from 4,000–6,000. They came from different countries with Muslim populations: from the Arab states, Iran, Afghanistan, and Pakistan to Sudan, Algeria, Egypt, and Turkey. There were also some Albanians from Albania, Kosovo, or from the diaspora. An example of such exclusivist units was the so-called Black Swans, based near Sarajevo. This elite fighting force of from 600–800 men followed Islamic customs and prayer, avoided alcohol and contact with women, and had its own Muslim chaplains. According to Bosniak sources, 420 Muslim clergymen were included in the army.[142]

Other exclusively Muslim military units—including the Green Berets, El Mujahid, the Muslim Forces, the Green Legion, and the Patriotic League, which was a paramilitary organization of the SDA[143]—also borrowed Muslim religious iconography: the color green; Qur'anic inscriptions in Arabic script on badges; bands tied around the forehead, on military equipment and weapons, and flags; beards; salutes; and war cries such as "*Allahu Akbar!* God is great!" There also were posters bearing the slogan "By our faith and on our land" in green at the 1996 general elections. Rasim Delić, a senior Bosniak officer in the Bosnian army, made this revealing statement: "In time of war religion always attracts more followers. . . . It is very important for us to motivate the people in this way."[144] Other commanders pointed out the importance of the spread and respect of Bosnian Islamic culture and religion within Bosnian army units. Many Muslim obituaries included fundamentalist phrases, for example that the deceased fell in "battle against the infidel," or that the deceased had automatically earned "a place in heaven." Bosniak soldiers killed in action are celebrated as *šehids*, which means "witnesses of the faith" or "martyrs sacrificed for their faith."[145] The inscription on the memorial tombstone in Mostar—in the Bosniak part of town on right side of Neretva River (which is otherwise almost entirely under authority of Herzegovian Croats)—is eloquent enough:

In the name of merciful and compassionate Allah!
Believers who are not fighting
—except those who are unfit for the fight—
are not the same as those who are
fighting on Allah's way
with their belongings and their lives.

Those who will fight putting in
their belongings and their lives
Allah will reward with a whole grade
higher over those who will not fight,
and He promises to all fine recompense.
Allah will award fighters, and not to those who are not fighting,
a great recompense.

To martyrs who succeeded in defending Mostar.

Some Bosniaks/Muslim forces committed atrocities against the non-Muslim population. There is evidence that the Bosnian army "had eliminated thirty-three Catholic parishes in Central Bosnia." Muslim extremists killed a number of Franciscan priests. Such events and attitudes justifiably caused alarm among the Bosnian Serbs and Croats and the majority of secularized Muslims. One of the most outstanding critics of this policy was Cardinal Puljić, who warned about the dangers of Islamizing Sarajevo and the territory under government control, and expressed his apprehension of theocracy.[146] Franciscan superior Anđelović also criticized policies that discriminated against other believers.

Alarmist and self-victimizing discourses appeared in some Bosniak circles. They identified evil-minded plots, spoke of "Crusades" launched by both sides and by a "Christian Europe," and suggested that an effort aimed at "the damnation of the Muslims" had been launched.[147] Others persistently repeated the historiographic myth that Bosnian Muslims are the only descendants of the medieval adherents of the Bosnian Church (wrongly named *bogomili*), who converted to Islam en masse after the Ottoman conquest and, for this reason, are the only indigenous nation in Bosnia-Herzegovina (in contrast to the "latecomer" Serbs and Croats). They also glorify the thousand-year continuity of Bosnian statehood and idealize the Ottoman era of Bosnian history.[148] President Iztebegović stated that the Bosniaks were in favor of a multinational and multireligious and pluralist Bosnia-Herzegovina, in which "we Bosniaks, the Muslim nation of Bosnia, are predestined as the leaders of the new integration of Bosnia."[149]

At the same time, the Bosniaks, more than the other two national groups, most strongly emphasized the need for the cooperation of all three Bosnian national groups. A year before the war began, Izetbegović announced that "no one here has any intention of creating an Islamic Bosnia" and advocated "a secular state."[150] However, there are different opinions about Izetbegović's maximal political and religious ambitions in this regard.[151] He was also quoted in a 1990 interview as saying that the Bosnian Muslims were a "religious nation." Haris Silajdžić, the Bosnian prime minister and minister for foreign affairs, said: "We are not Muslims, nor are we Serbs or Croats, but Bosnians."[152] Senior Muslim religious dignitaries like Yugoslav *reis-ul-ulema* Hadži Jakub efendi Selimovski, a Macedonian, opposed the partitioning of Bosnia-Herzegovina and supported its secular status from the very beginning of the war. In the spring of 1992 he stated: "any advancement of one nation above the others, with the goal of domination and subjection, is alien to Islam because the Qur'an teaches us that we are only divided into nations and tribes in order that we may get to know each other better."[153]

There was a change in the leadership of the Bosnian Islamic community during the war. On April 28, 1993, Mustafa Cerić replaced the moderate Selimovski as *reis-ul-ulema*. Cerić had been the imam of the Zagreb mosque and was a known critic of Serb and Croat policies toward and within Bosnia-Herzegovina. Selimovski, who was outside the country, refused to recognize the changes, claiming that he had been appointed in 1990 with an eight-year mandate. Cerić 's closest adviser and deputy is Ismet efendi Spahić, the imam of the Begova džamija mosque in Sarajevo. Salih Čolaković, the president of the Bosnian *mesihad*, was also replaced. Bougarel, French expert on Bosnian Islam, believes that this allowed the radical political trend within Bosnian Islam—represented by the El-Hidaje Association and supported by the SDA—to dominate "over less political trends, both progressive (J. Selimovski) and traditionalist (S. Čolaković)."[154]

In short, there are four main options in contemporary Bosnian Islam. First, the secular option: religion is an intimate affair; the moral values of Islam are emphasized; religion is not the foundation of society, politics, or law. Second, the traditional option: Islam is the religion and the law; Islam should become the state religion; Islamic sacred law should be introduced and religious customs and symbols respected. Third, the modernist option: the modernization of Islamic values and the principle of Islamic sacred law. And fourth, the radical revivalist option: Islam infuses every aspect of life; early Muslim history and the primary sources of Islamic teaching are the basis of everything. Bougarel notes that this inter-Muslim pluralism is "too fragmented for it to be possible to assign individuals, let alone institutions, an exact place" within it. It is more reflected "in several of the debates which have disturbed the Muslim community of Bosnia Herzegovina."[155]

ANOTHER JEWISH EXODUS

About 1,200 Jews lived in Sarajevo at the beginning of the war. Many later left Bosnia-Herzegovina and sought refuge abroad: about 400 in Israel and about 300 elsewhere.[156] Jakob Finci, the leader of the Jewish community, estimates that only about 600 Jews remain in Sarajevo (Bakić believes the figure to be 500).

RELIGIOUS COMMUNITIES STRIVE FOR PEACE

Ethnic cleansing and military clashes are estimated to have claimed some 279,000 lives (killed and missing, out of which 180,000 are Bosniaks, 115,000 Serbs, 38,000 Croats, and 19,000 others).[157] About 2 million refugees fled their homes; captured women—mostly Bosniak—were systematically raped. The Dayton Peace Agreement—signed by Izetbegović, Tudjman, and Milošević in Paris in December, 1995—introduced a fragile peace to the partitioned country (51 percent going to the Bosnia-Herzegovina federation, and 49 percent to the Serbian Republic). The peace is based on complicated and scarcely feasible rules written down in the constitution, legislation, refugee repatriation plans, human rights guarantees, and in other documents. Bosnia-Herzegovina's jurisdiction is very limited.

Refugees are hesitant to return, especially to areas controlled by the "other" side. Only a handful of the 20,000 refugees from minority ethnic groups expected to return to Sarajevo in 1998—as was optimistically announced in the so-called Sarajevo Declaration, signed on February 3, 1998—had returned to the city by the middle of the year: 477 Serbs, 365 Croats, and 47 "others." Serbs attacked a group of Catholics that included Cardinal Puljić in Derventa; Croats assaulted Serbs in Drvar; Croat authorities in Stolac and Čapljina are resisting the return of Bosniak refugees; the tense situation in ethnically divided towns like Mostar needs no comment.

There has been conflict within the leadership of Bosnian Serb and Croat nationalist parties. The new prime minister of the RS was the reconciliatory Milorad Dodik of the Independent Social-Democratic Party. The Croats also have an alternative to the HDZ, which is now headed by Ante Jelavić, an HVO general and defense minister for the Bosnia-Herzegovina federation (and fervent advocate of Croatian Herceg-Bosna as a separate, third entity), in Krešimir Zubak's new party, the New Croatian Initiative. There is much wrangling and mutual accusation between parties on both sides.

Regarding religion, Mojzes notes that "the positive contributions of the religious communities were few, and the negative were many."[158] On the horns of a dilemma between "universalist rhetoric in favor of peace and practice sustaining a political strategy having provoked the war," their most useful contributions were their humanitarian and charity work, as well as care for refugees and for the wounded—regardless of religious or national identity.[159] The volte-face by all three religious communities in recent years is an interesting change: from vocal support for and passive connivance with the nationalist policies of these nations in the late 1980s, to eventual criticism and distancing. Belated and uncommon as they were, individual religious organizations made a number of ecumenical contacts and reconciliatory statements. The following is a brief discussion of the more important meetings held between religious leaders during this period.

The dialogue between the Catholic Church in Croatia and the Serbian Orthodox Church ended in 1989 because of historical and recent contradictions between them.[160] However, Cardinal Kuharić and Patriarch Pavle held several meetings: in Sremski Karlovci in May, 1991; in Slavonski Brod in August, 1991; in Saint Gall, Switzerland, in the spring of 1992; and in Geneva in September, 1992. They invited the Muslim religious leader to the last meeting, but he was unable to leave Sarajevo because of the siege. Both religious leaders condemned the war, war crimes, and ethnic cleansing, and demanded the release of all prisoners.[161] Patriarch Pavle and a Muslim delegation led by the mufti of Belgrade, Hadži Hamdija efendi Jusufspahić, met in the summer of 1991 and appealed "for peace and against the misuse of religious faith for national-political purposes."[162]

In January, 1993, Cardinal Puljić and the Bosnian Roman Catholic bishops, who were accompanied by *Reis-ul-ulema* Selimovski visited Pope John Paul II. Puljić and Patriarch Pavle met again in May of the same year at the Sarajevo airport, but *Reis-ul-ulema* Cerić canceled his participation because the Serbian Orthodox Church refused to condemn Serb war crimes. Catholic and Orthodox bishops, the mufti of Belgrade, and representatives of the Protestant and Jewish communities met in Hungary in December, 1993, but, Muslim representatives from Sarajevo were unable to attend. They condemned the manipulation of religious symbols for military purposes. The following month, six Catholic bishops from the former Yugoslavia announced that Bosnia-Herzegovina must remain the homeland of Muslims, Serbs, and Croats. Furthermore, Muslim and Catholic dignitaries in Bosnia-Herzegovina condemned the Bosniak-Croat clashes and declared the SDA and HDZ were responsible."[163]

A meeting between the pope, Patriarch Alexei II of Russia, and *Reis-ul-ulema* Cerić of Bosnia was planned for November, 1994, but had to be canceled. Puljić, Cerić, and Jevtić (representing the patriarchate of Belgrade) met in Geneva in January, 1995. Puljić also held a meeting with Orthodox metropolite Nikolaj from central Bosnia in April, 1996. The pope met with the *reis-ul-ulema* during his visit to Sarajevo in 1997. Senior representatives of all four religions in Bosnia-Herzegovina signed a declaration on a joint moral endeavor in June, 1997. In it, Cerić, Puljić, Bosnian metropolite Nikolaj Mrđa (representing Serb patriarch Pavle) and Jakob Finci, the leader of the Jewish community, expressed their concern about the sluggish implementation of parts of the DPA and emphasized mutual respect. They supported the return of all refugees and condemned violence; ethnic and religious hatred; the destruction of houses, religious buildings, and cemeteries; and the exploitation of the media for inciting and encouraging retribution.

Senior figures from all religious communities held meetings before, during, and after the war. For the most part, they were in agreement in respect to condemning the war and the persecution of civilians. Their joint statements called for peace, tolerance, mutual respect, and cooperation. It is interesting to note that many of these dignitaries were the original firebrands who tried to justify violence, religio-national homogeniza-tion, ethnic cleansing and *just* wars. Despite their calls for peace—mostly expressed abroad—their actions and statements spoke differ-ently. Moreover, if they did not personally breach their own promises of reconciliation, subordinates within their church hierarchies did so. It is my opinion that the apparent duplicity of such "church diplomacy" and practices deeply compromised the hypocrites who advocated them, and places them abreast other accomplices of the recent tragic events in the Balkans.

The vast majority of the Orthodox clergy fled from territory not under Serb control. Their repatriation to areas not under "their" control there-fore poses a difficult problem. Metropolite Nikolaj of Sarajevo conducted his first mass in "government-controlled" Sarajevo on February 8, 1996. The Orthodox Church did not allow Orthodox bishops and clergy to re-turn until after the meeting in December, 1995. The final details regard-ing the repatriation of about two hundred Orthodox priests to Croatia were agreed on at a meeting of senior Serbian Orthodox Church leaders in June, 1998.

10
FINAL DELIBERATIONS
Maximum Diversity in Minimal Space

If we limit our-
selves to the reli-
gious aspects of the
last war in Bosnia-
Hezegovina, we are

See now, how men lay blame upon us Gods for

what is after all nothing but their own folly.

— HOMER, *THE ODYSSEY*, FIRST BOOK

faced with a fundamental dilemma. Were religions and religious communities and symbols used by nationalist politics/policies in their grand
nationalist schemes? Or, conversely, did they exploit nationalist euphoria and policies to achieve their own religious goals? In short, did they
play an active or passive role in the most recent Balkan history? I think
both. My answer to these questions might seem paradoxical at first. To
certain religious integrationists, political developments in the late 1980s
and early 1990s presented an excellent opportunity for the long-awaited
reconversion of their nations' national, political, and cultural identity
and the reaffirmation of their dominant position in society. The already
belated modernist differentiation and pluralizing of these societies
seemed to have lost to radical premodernist dedifferentiation.[1] Religious
institutions rapidly became an important part of the dominant national/
political/religious/cultural metaplatform and strategy.

This total—and totalitarian—alliance between nationalist policies
and religious communities and institutions was one of mutual benefit:
national, political, and, ultimately, military mobilization of these societies could not be achieved without religious legitimation, while, on the
other hand, religious communities were unable to achieve their goals
without the active support of nationalist parties and politics in general.
Religious elements became an important part of the process of "the eth-
nification of politics and the politicization of ethnicity."[2] In other words,
in this integrationist process of religio-national retraditionalizing com-

bined with religio-national exclusivity, the one needed and strengthened the other: religious institutions lent legitimacy to and opened perspectives for chauvinist politics, and vice versa.

However, recent events in Bosnia-Herzegovina are not an isolated anomaly in the modern world; they are not a kind of local specificity. Similar events are still taking place in other regions. The religious veil of politics and even of war is quite apparent: it can be found in the raving frenzy of Muslim fanatics in North Africa and the Near and Middle East; in the burning churches and prevailing violence between Protestant and Catholic extremists in Northern Ireland; in the suicidal and homicidal tendencies of members of obscure and fanatical sects in places such as Japan and Switzerland; in the appeals for "spiritual restoration" or even terrorist acts by religious fundamentalists in developed societies; and, finally, in the frail attempts at re-Christianizing and religio-national integration in post-Socialist countries.

The twentieth-century history of Bosnia-Herzegovina is, to a considerable extent, the history of its religions and religio-national mythologies. The curse of incessant conflict and the two wars that devastated the region—which have had a destructive effect on the population and included the religio-national dimensions—represent a novelty and precedent in the history of this land of "maximum diversity in minimal space," to borrow a syntagma from Milan Kundera. Far from idealizing or romanticizing Bosnian premodern history, it can be firmly said that never before the twentieth century—with the exceptions I pointed out in the narrative, such as rebellions, riots, uprisings, and revenge—had its citizenry been subjected to such systematic persecution, mass slaughter, dispossession, and forceful proselytizing. Never before had they been forced to seek refuge from the destructive logic of religio-national exclusivity outside their own borders in such vast numbers. It is for these reasons alone that different religious communities—Orthodox and Roman Catholic Christian, Muslim and Jewish—and nations—Muslims/Bosniaks, Serbs, Croats, Jews, and others—have survived to the present day.

The national identities of Bosnia and Herzegovina have been cast from a primarily religio-cultural mold. The linguistic principle, which was a determining factor in the nation-building process in central Europe (the entire population of Bosnia-Herzegovina speaks almost the same language, which is richly embellished with Turkish and Arabic derivatives), and the political-territorial principle, which was a determining factor in the West, were missing in Bosnia and Herzegovina. Religious affiliation had, since the Middle Ages, been the primary source of collective identity. Religious and cultural differences eventually transformed into or blended with national differences.[3] But they lost their erstwhile qualities in doing so. Whereas religions had long been relatively tolerant, their exclusivist "nationalization" served as the basis for preclusion and, eventually, hatred. As Stavrianos points out, "It was not until the later centuries of the Ottoman weakness and Western aggression that both Muslims and Christians became fanatical and intolerant.[4]

The two twentieth-century apocalypses of the Bosnian nations were, therefore, preceded by relative religious tolerance and cooperation between isolated syncretistic idiosyncrasies to various degrees. The Bosnian religious mosaics were both external and internal—religious differences existed outside and also inside the country. Ecclesiastic and religious groups in Bosnia-Herzegovina neither were internally monolithic nor particularly austere. They also were doctrinally weak until the twentieth century and shared doctrines, myths, feasts, and magical practices. This was something foreign observers coming from distant centers of political power and religious orthodoxy were unable to fathom. They chided the laxity of faith and religious organization and attempted to change it by condemnation and military intervention.

Despite the importance people ascribe to traditional group identity and the tenacity and protracted endurance of such identity in different social phenomena, I wrote this book under the conviction that the study of the socio-historical dynamics of a phenomenon cannot espouse any form of determinism or premature exclusion, not even with the most superlative options and conclusions. In other words, nothing is impossible, and future events cannot be predicted. The inertia of the past is not a guarantee for impending development. Bosnia-Herzegovina's religious history is a classical and, unfortunately, tragic example of this.

Few regions and countries in premodern Europe knew so high a level of religious diversity and tolerance as Bosnia, which is peculiar in that that it has never been homogenous (or homogenized).[5] However, we must suppress the urge to idealize this tolerance and instead attempt to illuminate it from various perspectives and expose also its complexity, its mutable alliances and antipathies, its periods of proximity and remoteness, its friendships and preclusion, and the historical basis for subsequent conflicts. Much has been written on religious and national tolerance and intolerance in the history of Bosnia-Herzegovina. I hope my narrative has made clear the degree to which tolerance varied from sincere to cold, almost alienated; from institutionally respected to systematically ruined; from mutual respect to stifled hatred; from syncretism to "living apart together"; with plenty of different contacts to almost none; from mere cohabitation and coexistence to mutual understanding, cooperation, and symbiosis. Even the periods of violence did not batter down the prevailing pluralism. To be sure, it was never an oasis of peace, toleration, and comprehension between different groups as some have idealized it. On the other hand, it has never been the oasis of persistent hatred and violence as some others have portrayed it to be. For this reason, one thing is incontestable: four religious denominations and communities survived centuries of common history as part of different multiethnic states in a small geographic region. This is a remarkable fact that makes Bosnia-Herzegovina stand out not only in a regional, but also in a wider European context.

The situation during the last few decades has been quite different. The West has become more religiously tolerant and pluralistic, whereas Bosnia-Herzegovina, once distinguished by religious tolerance, has been literally transformed into the battleground of a war between different political and great-national options that have been heavily influenced by religion. The most recent Bosnian war has shown that Bosnia-Herzegovina's religious communities are more inclined toward alienation, incitement, and confrontation than peace and reconciliation.[6]

The blame for this lies more in external than internal factors. In other words, autochthonous differences and divisions were, to a lesser degree, the cause of conflicts between religious and national communities than were impositions by neighboring pretenders. An analogy to the Bosnian situation is that of twelfth-century Spain, once a hub of multireligious cultural, scientific, ideological, and philosophical exchange and *convivencia*, where the Bible, Qur'an, and Talmud, and ancient and contemporary philosophers and scientists were all cherished. Spain was later violently "cleansed" of Muslims, Jews, and their offspring, and the kingdom was rendered ethnically and religiously homogeneous by strong-arm methods.

Religio-national exclusivity and carnage were introduced into the kaleidoscope of Bosnian religious and national relations mainly from abroad, but its promoters could always rely upon the assistance if not the initiative of local followers. Belligerent groups and individual pan-nationalist extremists and their henchmen who tried to enforce their hegemonic concepts—which local supporters not only facilitated but also implemented—were brought face-to-face then broken on the backs of the Bosnians. In my opinion, however, the beat of this death dance was dictated for the most part from abroad: Bosnian nations were pushed into conflict by the policies of foreign powers and by their Bosnian executors (in many cases, victims knew the hangmen, who were their neighbors).[7]

In other words, Bosnia-Herzegovina was more the stage than the origin of religious and national conflict and warfare. I thus prefer not to speak about war *in* Bosnia, but rather *upon* it.

In this regard, the fundamental duality of Bosnia-Herzegovina's religious institutions must be emphasized. They played a dual role: as the self-declared defenders of "their" nations, and as the inventors of inter-religious and international dissimilarities. Thus, on one hand, they always nurtured and supported a sense of religious, cultural, and, consequently, ethnic/national identity in the face of other groups and of foreign domination. On the other hand, by usurping national and political attributes, they were equally responsible for the promotion of hegemonic religio-national mythologies and expansionist politics (derived mostly from neighboring political centers) that targeted other religions and nations within Bosnia-Herzegovina.

The greatest dangers to ecclesiastic organizations and religions in Bosnia-Herzegovina are, in my opinion, not other religions or religious communities, or the considerable atheist population within "their" nations, but the excessive relationship between politics, religions, and exclusivist national mythologies still alive at the beginning of the new millennium. The problem, therefore, exists at several different levels. First, in the collectivization of religion, which attaches greater importance to ethnic identity than to bonds of faith and worship, subordinates individual accountability to collective responsibility, and encourages mass action, thus absolving the individual from the consequences of his or her own actions. Second, in the concept of "nationalized" or "boundless" religion (in a sense of "religion without borders" or "all-embracing religion"), which usurps and celebrates nationality and politics, and is occasionally subordinated by them. The myth that the church is the strongest, and sometimes the only, bastion of national and political identity gradually develops, based on the logic that "there can be no nation without a church." Third, in the lack of self-criticism and by condemning "internal" nonconformists or "external" critics as "enemies of the church and the people," "traitors," and "false" members of the church or the nation.

Finally, the problem also lies in the triumphalism and belligerence of post-Socialist ecclesiastic organizations; from *pietas* to *triumphans*, from *ecclesia peregrinans* to *ecclesia militans*.[8] From this perspective, the church can and should govern rather than serve. In short, the problem is in overcoming the extrareligious and nonreligious elements of these religions. They must shake off their self-declared holy or protective roles and the categorical imperative that theirs is the only path to salvation, and they must ultimately desist from representing, or becoming the means of, political and national objectives.

I reiterate, the most recent war in Bosnia-Herzegovina was more a classical war of aggression with clear geopolitical goals rather than a civil or religious war. Nor was it a war between civilizations, as some would have us believe. Many wars have been fought between adherents of different religious denominations or nations, but they were not perceived as "religious wars" or "wars between national groups," but rather as wars between states. If we accept the interpretations provided by inciters and advocates of war, we would obscure the real sources, ambitions, and objectives—which were clearly political—and their protagonists. The wars in Croatia and Bosnia-Herzegovina were—in the words Norman Cigar employs when explaining ethnic cleansing—"a rational policy, the direct and planned consequence of conscious policy decisions."[9]

We cannot overlook the powerful religious and cultural factors or their conspicuous presence. Nevertheless, we find a paradox here: many of those who declared the war was religious or between nations did not care at all for the faith or the fate of their own nation. Among new leaders and "fighters for the faith and homeland" in the last war we find many converted fervent ex-advocates of Socialism and Yugoslavism or people who held high positions in the previous regime. Becoming literally "more Catholic than the pope," they realized how efficient it was to interpret their political and genocidal goals as such and began to speak the same language with other inciters—rigid religious fundamentalists and nationalists within and outside the country.

History repeated itself: Warlords reaped that which was sown by nationalistic and religious militants. The cross and the crescent are easily transformed into the sword, and the brilliance of faith, as comprehended by believers, into the glare of the blade. The step from mythomaniacal theory to bloodthirsty terror is a small one; any creed can be transformed into a ruthless beast. Constantine's *In hoc signo vinces* could very well represent a universal call to arms for the domination of the "true" faith by belligerents of all faiths. Then, after the hostilities cease—when the simpletons among the agitators are horrified and the cunning ones satisfied—there is suddenly a denial of individual involvement, a distancing from the crimes, denial of responsibility, or haughty arrogance. The atrocities are often attributed to a "lack of faith," the "absence of God," an "atheistic lack of scruples," or the "consequence of a Godless regime," to use the words of religious leaders. But the "godlessness" in such events is often the consequence of the indifference and apathy of, and occasionally incitement by, "men of God" who have often been too zealous in the battle for their faith (and nation). To borrow a metaphor from the Bible, germination can be injured by too little as well as too much "salt of the earth."

Religious leaders and individuals with a strong sway over their flock, these "meritorious interpreters of the Word of God and religious doctrine," as they sometimes refer to themselves, often speak in such vague terms that each person can interpret what they say differently. Political or military events, for example, are portrayed as metaphysical categories, that is, as myths, as the result of "divine retribution," "His will," "Providence." I have included in this book several examples of politicians, warlords, intellectuals, and clergymen using mythical explanations for historical political and national events, as well as their realizations, including artillery fire and machine guns. The only aspect of the interpretation of the atrocities that all religious communities agree about—and with which, like Pilate, they wash their hands—is that the blame lies with the "opposite side" or with the "former regime."

Of all those responsible for the carnage in Bosnia-Herzegovina, the most accountable are those among the clergy who directly incited violence and intolerance: we can, like French philosopher Pierre Bayle (1647–1706), call them "religionaries." However, in such situations, that which is not uttered is as important as that which is: silence can be more eloquent than words. Not only explicit, but also another—indirect—policy, and symbolic acts of religious institutions must be pointed out here: namely, their sinister silence regarding the obvious and systematic persecution and liquidation of believers of other faiths, and the destruction of their religious infrastructure. In other words, "hate silence" can be as significant as "hate speech." Rarely do moderate representatives of religious hierarchies condemn acts committed by their compatriots or coreligionists, distance themselves from the blatant manipulation of religious justification, rhetoric, and symbols, and explicitly reject religious nationalists of "their own" faith or nation. They lack directness, initiative, and a clear expression of their position. Religious hierarchies should have spoken out unequivocally against what they believed to be wrong and in favor of what they believed to be right, and clearly identified the offenders and criminals. They failed to condemn incidents that they themselves sometimes incited—intentionally or not—and to criticize their own monumental and mythological national history, which is infused with religion. Extremists usually commit the greatest evils, but an inert majority that fails to react in time or that hypocritically waits for others to do the dirty work silently condones them. A Latin proverb sums it up well: *"Qui tacet, consentit.* He who remains silent, agrees."

The prewar Bosnia-Herzegovina no longer exists. This, however, does not mean that cohabitation is not possible in the future. National and religious pluralism is and remains a necessity, not merely an opportunity. Despite destruction, liquidation, and persecution, this country is still inhabited by members of different nations and religious communities. The solution will not be found in a religious moral campaign, national exclusion, political radicalism, "final solutions" of all sorts, national or religious conversion, or by ignoring or overstating the significance of the religious factor. All this was attempted in the twentieth century. The wheel of history cannot be turned back, but it can provide us with valuable lessons for the future. Needless to say, extremists in post-Dayton Bosnia-Herzegovina will continue to do everything to maintain—here I invert Clausewitz—"peace as the continuation of war by other means."[10]

Historical examples show that political and national hatred within or between the states can be overcome. The French and Germans, or the French and British, or the Poles and Germans have lived for more that fifty years in peace and mutual coexistence despite warfare in previous decades and centuries. The process of conciliation after civil wars in the United States and Spain lasted for decades but finally succeeded. Even closer to home: Slovenes, after many bitter years of war, have had decades of normal and reciprocally cooperative relations with Italians, Austrians, and Germans that have tended to improve. The Bosnian nations must overcome on one hand the mythic imperatives of "supranational brotherhood" promoted by the Socialist regime, and on the other those of "religio-national exclusivity" imposed by religious nationalists, with a common goal that would justify their cohabitation, such as economic progress, social development in general, or approaching the European Union. This process would, of course, take time and, only seven years after the DPA, it is definitely too soon to predict the course of future events.

I think—optimistically, someone would surely argue—that a multinational and multireligious Bosnia-Herzegovina is possible because of its predominately tolerant and plural history. However, the episodes of violence, persecution, and, above all, traumatic experiences in the 1940s and 1990s must be considered. In the past, extremists have used these disasters to justify their radical and destructive actions. It is time now for the primarily tolerant Bosnian tradition to become more exposed. In other words, the solution to the present situation must be based on the understanding that Bosnia-Herzegovina's religious and national history is a unique, rich, and independent entity, and that is intimately related to Bosnia's neighbors and the wider region.

The condition for reestablishing the cohabitation of Bosnia's religious and national communities is the complete and permanent separation of religious institutions from the state and religion from politics. The future can only be guaranteed by bridging extremes and obsessions with the mythically interpreted past to momentarily justify politics: by separating religious communities from politics and nationalism, and by desacralizing politics and the nation. Only in this way can we preclude the recurrence of the fateful integration of various collective identities into a single one that is externally exclusive and internally uniform. Only in this way can there be a promising future for all of Bosnia-Herzegovina's inhabitants, for all its nations and religious communities.

NOTES

INTRODUCTION: A LAND OF DREAMS AND NIGHTMARES

1. Dubravko Lovrenović, "Bosanski mitovi," *Erasmus* 18 (1996): 27.

2. I use the term *national* rather than *ethnic* when speaking of different nations within Bosnia-Herzegovina and, of course, beyond (Bosniaks-Muslims, Serbs, Croats, Montenegrins, etc.). I consider the latter to be a more lax, less self-conscious phase of the formation of the nation (therefore the sense of cultural and linguistic unity). So, the term *nation* is used to indicate politically organized national groups (e.g., Bosniaks, Serbs, Croats) and not their states (Bosnia-Herzegovina, Serbia, Croatia). For Pedro Ramet, an "ethnic group" is "a group of people who believe that they constitute a primary cultural unity and who believe that they have common cultural interests"; while a "nation" is "an 'ethnic group' which seeks to advance its interests through organized political action" ("Primordial Ethnicity of Modern Nationalism: The Case of Yugoslavia's Muslims." *Nationalities Papers* 13, no. 2 [1985]: 168).

3. Robert N. Bellah, "Civil Religion in America," in *Culture and Society: Contemporary Debates*, ed. Jeffrey C. Alexander and Steven Seidman, 263.

4. For an excellent study of the ethnogenetic myths and rhetoric of the Spanish, French, English, Italians, Germans, and Russians, see Leon Poliakov, *Il mito ariano: Le radici del razzismo e dei nazionalismi*. For religious nationalism and religious references in politics in general, see Adrian Hastings, *The Construction of Nationhood: Ethnicity, Religion, and Nationalism*. For Russian, German, Nazi-Fascist, and Anglo-American national messianism in general, as well as French, Austro-Hungarian, Croatian, and Serbian messianism concerning Bosnia-Herzegovina, see Esad Zgodić, *Ideologija nacionalnog mesijanstva*. For an analysis of the American perception and evaluation of the Vietnam War and the construction of warrior values, see Sanimir Resic, *American Warriors in Vietnam: Warrior Values and the Myth of the War Experience during the Vietnam War, 1965–1973*. For the relations and rhetoric of the Roman Catholic Church and extreme right political parties in Europe before and during World War II (Italy, France,

Slovakia, Croatia, etc.), see Richard J. Wolf and Jorg K. Hoensch, eds., *Catholics, the State, and the European Radical Right, 1919–1945*. For renewed political mythologies in post-socialist societies, see Vladimir Tismaneanu, *Fantasies of Salvation: Democracy, Nationalism, and Myth in Post-Communist Europe.*

5. The present analysis of contemporary religious and national mythologies in Bosnia-Herzegovina is based on analytical techniques I developed and presented in my first book (Mitja Velikonja, *Masade duha: Razpotja sodobnih mitologij*, 19–30).

6. George Schöpflin, "The Functions of Myth and a Taxonomy of Myths," in *Myths and Nationhood*, ed. Geoffrey Hosking and George Schöpflin, 20.

7. Tismaneanu, *Fantasies of Salvation*, 13. For Schöpflin, "myth is vital in the establishment of coherence, in the making of thought-worlds that appear clear and logical, in the maintenance of discourses and generally in making cosmos out of chaos" ("Functions of Myth," 20).

8. Claude Lévi-Strauss, *The Raw and the Cooked: Introduction to a Science of Mythology*, 6.

9. Claudio Magris, *Il Mito Absburgico Vella Letteratura Austriaca Moderna*, 4.

10. Tismaneanu, *Fantasies of Salvation*, 15.

CHAPTER I. BOSNIA'S RELIGIOUS
AND MYTHOLOGICAL WATERSHED

1. Miklos Tomka, "Coping with Persecution: Religious Change in Communism and in Post-Communist Reconstruction in Central Europe," *International Sociology* 13, no. 2 (1998): 239, 240.

2. As Bellah points out, at that time "there was an implicit but quite clear division of function between the civil religion and Christianity" ("Civil Religion in America," 267).

3. Adrian Hastings, *The Construction of Nationhood: Ethnicity, Religion, and Nationalism*, 18. He continues: "Perhaps it was an almost terrifyingly monolithic ideal, productive ever after all sorts of dangerous fantasies, but it was there, an all to obvious exemplar for Bible readers of what every other nation too might be, a mirror for national self-imagining" (ibid.).

4. Pedro Ramet, "Religion and Nationalism in Yugoslavia," in *Religion and Nationalism in Soviet and East European Politics*, ed. idem., 299.

5. Ivo Banac, "Separating History from Myth," in *Why Bosnia? Writings on the Balkan War*, ed. Rabia Ali and Lawrence Lifschultz, 138. See also John V. A. Fine Jr., "The Medieval and Ottoman Roots of Modern Bosnian Society," in *The Muslims of Bosnia Herzegovina: The Historic Development from the Middle Ages to the Dissolution of Yugoslavia*, ed. Mark Pinson, 2.

6. Banac, "Separating History from Myth," 138.

7. Ibrahim Bakić, *Nacija i religija*, 110, 111. Of course, politics also continuously intervened in religious and ecclesiastical matters.

8. Tonči Kuzmanić, "Iugoslavia: Una guerra di religione?" *Religioni e societa* 14 (1992): 117.

9. Examples include the *reconquista* in Spain and Portugal, the crusades against the Cathari and Albigensians, the Hussite wars of the fifteenth century, the massacre on Saint Bartholomew's Day, and other religious wars in sixteenth- and seventeenth-century Europe.

10. Bellah, "Civil Religion in America," 269.

11. Francine Friedman, *The Bosnian Muslims: Denial of a Nation*, 68. Similarly, Tone Bringa states: "In Bosnia religious practices and symbols are the constitutive factor in the construction of parallel and competing collective cultural and political entities or *nacije* (Muslim, Croat, or Serb)" (*Being Muslim: The Bosnian Was [Identity and Community in a Central Bosnian Village]*, 197).

12. Harry Thirlwall Norris, *Islam in the Balkans: Religion and Society Between Europe and the Arab World*, 264.

13. See also Radmila Radić, "Crkva i 'srpsko pitanje'," in *Srpska strana rata: Trauma i katarza u istorijskom pamćenju*, ed. Nebojša Popov, 268, 269.

14. See also Paul Mojzes, *Church and State in Postwar Eastern Europe*, 6, 7.

15. Richard Clogg, "The Greek Millet in the Ottoman Empire," in *Christians and Jews in the Ottoman Empire: The Functioning of a Plural Society*, ed. Benjamin Braude and Bernard Lewis, 1:191.

16. Paul Mojzes, *Religious Liberty in Eastern Europe and the USSR Before and After the Great Transformation*, 7, 8.

17. Radić, "Crkva i 'srpsko pitanje'," 267.

18. Pedro Ramet, "Autocephaly and National Identity in Church-State Relations in Eastern Christianity: An Introduction," in *Eastern Christianity and Politics*, ed. idem., 4.

19. *Samo sloga Srbina spasava.* Actually, it is an old Byzantine symbol that, according to some interpretations, signifies the invocation of God. For others, it is a modification and stylization of the symbol of the supreme power of Byzantine emperors, which was seized by the self-proclaimed "Emperor of the Serbs and the Greeks," Dušan the Strong (1331–55).

20. Manojlo Bročić, "The Position and Activities of the Religious Communities in Yugoslavia with Special Attention to the Orthodox Church," in *Religion and Atheism in the USSR and Eastern Europe*, ed. Bohdan R. Bociurkiw and John W. Strong, 359.

21. For an excellent condensed presentation of this relation, see Srdjan Vrcan, "Orthodoxy in Balkan Political Conflicts," in *Identities and Conflicts: Mediterranean*, ed. Furio Cerutti and Rodolfo Ragionieri, 135–60.

22. Ivo Banac, *Nacionalno pitanje u Jugoslaviji: Porijeklo, povijest, politika*, 72, 73.

23. Bakić, *Nacija i religija*, 97.

24. Dinko Tomašić, *Politički razvitak Hrvata*, 137.

25. Bakić, *Nacija i religija*, 98, 99.

26. Aleš Debeljak, *Oblike religiozne imaginacije*, 50.

27. Zachary T. Irwin, "The Islamic Revival and the Muslims of Bosnia Herzegovina," *East European Quarterly* 4 (1983): 438; Pedro Ramet, "Primordial Ethnicity," 184.

28. Halil Mehtić, *Uloga Ilmije u odbrani bića Bosne*, 16.

29. Bringa, *Being Muslim*, 231.

30. See also Bakić, *Nacija i religija*, 93.

CHAPTER 2. ONE GOD, THREE RELIGIONS

1. Francis Conte, *Sloveni*, 431.

2. Mustafa Imamović, *Historija Bošnjaka*, 27.

3. Conte, *Sloveni*, 419.

4. I cite two examples: the old Serbian saying, "It'll do you no good if a wooden God judges you *(Ne valja k'd ti drven bog sudi)*; and a fifteenth century glagolitic religious document from Dalmatia cautioning that it is a mortal sin to worship the sun, moon, or anything already created (Norris, *Islam in the Balkans*, 15–17). See Damjan J. Ovsec, *Slovanska mitologija in verovanje*. Some are described by John V. A. Fine Jr., *The Bosnian Church: A New Interpretation (A Study of the Bosnian Church and Its Place and Society from the 13th to the 15th Centuries)*, 16,17.

5. Byzantine emperor Leo III Isaurian formally took ecclesiastical-administrative jurisdiction over most of the East Balkans and subdued it to the Patriarch of Constantinople in 732. However, Rome never acknowledged this action.

6. Franjo Šanjek, *Kršćanstvo na hrvatskom prostoru*, 138.

7. Vera Kržišnik-Bukić, *Bosanska identiteta med preteklostjo in prihodnostjo*, 13; Muhamed Hadžijahić, *Islam i Musliman u Bosni i Hercegovini*, 20; D. Lovrenović, "Bosanski mitovi," 28, 29.

8. D. Lovrenović, "Bosanski mitovi," 31, 32.

9. Noel Malcolm, *Bosnia: A Short History*, 15.

10. Fine, *Bosnian Church*, 11–13, 22.

11. Šanjek, *Kršćanstvo na hrvatskom prostoru*, 125, 126, 127; Imamović, *Historija Bošnjaka*, 32–35.

12. Fine, *Bosnian Church*, 129–31.

13. Šanjek, *Kršćanstvo na hrvatskom prostoru*, 129.

14. See ibid., 161, 163, 208–10, 298.

15. Ibid., 129; Imamović, *Historija Bošnjaka*, 40–42.

16. Arthur J. Evans, *Pješke kroz Bosnu i Hercegovinu tokom ustanka augusta i septembra 1875*, 33. In general, Crusaders referred to themselves as *crucesegnati*, or Christ's warriors "marked by the cross," while the preachers accompanying them were called "new apostles" or "prophets." The war cry of these Christian belligerents—"God wills it!"—shows they sought to legitimize their actions by claiming a higher cause with universal interests. In an address to crusaders sent to deal with the Albigensians in southern France, Pope Innocent III said:

"Soldiers of Christ, drive out the unclean in all ways that God shall reveal to you. Fight bravely and do not spare those wo spread heresy; slaughter them more brutally than you would the Saracens, for they are worse than them!" Arnold, a monk from Cytax, added, "Kill them all. God will know his own" (Dragan Tashkovski, *Bogomilism in Macedonia*, 102).

17. Šanjek, *Kršćanstvo na hrvatskom prostoru*, 129, 148. See also Srećko M. Džaja, "Od bana Kulina do Austro-Ugarske okupacije," in *Katoličanstvo u Bosni i Hercegovini*, 49.

18. Jaroslav Šidak, *Studije o "Crkvi Bosanskoj" i bogomilstvu*, 87.

19. Stella Alexander, "Religion and National Identity in Yugoslavia," *Occasional Papers on Religion in Eastern Europe (OPREE)* 1 (1983): 8; Irwin, "Islamic Revival," 438; Adem Handžić, *Population of Bosnia in the Ottoman Period: A Historical Overview*, 4; Norman Cigar, *Genocide in Bosnia: The Policy of "Ethnic Cleansing,"* 14; Nijaz Duraković, *Prokletstvo Muslimana*, 15–25; Ignacij Voje, *Nemirni Balkan: Zgodovinski pregled od 6. do 18. stoletja*, 145, 146; Hadžijahić, *Islam i Musliman*. Norris refers to them as Patarins (*Islam in the Balkans*, 18). For the late-nineteenth-century interpretation, see Evans, who calls them "Bosnian Puritans" (*Pješke kroz Bosnu*, 25–40).

20. Šanjek, *Kršćanstvo na hrvatskom prostoru*, 137. See also Srećko M. Džaja, *Konfesionalnost i nacionalnost Bosne i Hercegovine*, 103; and Imamović, *Historija Bošnjaka*, 87, 88.

21. Friedman, *Bosnian Muslims*, 20.

22. Muhamed Hadžijahić, Mahmud Traljić, and Nijaz Šukrić, *Islam i Muslimani u Bosni i Hercegovini: El-Kalem*, 81–89. See also Duraković, *Prokletstvo Muslimana*, 29.

23. See Fine, *Bosnian Church*, 116.

24. Šidak, *Studije*, 55, 95; Šanjek, *Kršćanstvo na hrvatskom prostoru*, 121, 131; Fine, *Bosnian Church*, v, vi, 131, 132, 304.

25. See, e.g., Imamović, *Historija Bošnjaka*, 89, 90.

26. In Latin, *krstjani* were constantly addressed as Patarins (e.g., the Society of Bjelosav in Podbiograd as *societate Biellosavi Pathareni in Neretba*, or the House of Milorad in Bradina as *ad Goysavum gost Patarinum*). See Muhamed Hadžijahić, *Porijeklo bosanskih Muslimana*, 45–46.

27. Šidak, *Studije*, 56, 97, 98.

28. Fine, *Bosnian Church*, 267.

29. Ibid., 16.

30. Šidak, *Studije*, 96.

31. Fine, *Bosnian Church*, 131, 275, 276.

32. Šidak, *Studije*, 96.

33. Fine, *Bosnian Church*, 151, 152. It is common for a native culture or political class, when encircled by an aggressive foreign culture, to react by accentuating the specific aspects of their local culture and bringing them to the fore. Distinction, native peculiarities, and local comprehension of general doctrine thus gain importance.

34. See also Imamović, *Historija Bošnjaka*, 48; Kržišnik-Bukić, *Bosanska identiteta*, 16–18; and Fine, *Bosnian Church*, 228–43, 255–75.

35. Voje, *Nemirni Balkan*, 148.

36. Kržišnik-Bukić, *Bosanska identiteta*, 18.

37. Serbian nationalist historiography insists that he was crowned in Saint Sava's final resting place, the Orthodox monastery of Mileševo, to prove Serbian claims on those territories. See Džaja, *Konfesionalnost*, 23; and D. Lourenović, "Bosanski mitovi," 30–32.

38. Šanjek, *Kršćanstvo na hrvatskom prostoru*, 136; Robert T. Donia and John V. A. Fine Jr., *Bosnia Herzegovina: A Tradition Betrayed*, 7, 25.

39. Voje, *Nemirni Balkan*, 155.

40. Šanjek, *Kršćanstvo na hrvatskom prostoru*, 130.

41. Fine, *Bosnian Church*, 173–78; Dominik Mandić, *Franjevačka Bosna: razvoj i uprava Bosanske vikarije i provincije, 1340–1735*, 41; Šanjek, *Kršćanstvo na hrvatskom prostoru*, 130, 148.

42. Mandić, *Franjevačka Bosna*, 39–41.

43. Šanjek, *Kršćanstvo na hrvatskom prostoru*, 436.

44. Mandić, *Franjevačka Bosna*, 53.

45. For a list of Franciscan monasteries, see Džaja, "Od bana Kulina," 51–53.

46. Fine, *Bosnian Church*, 244–47.

47. Mandić, *Franjevačka Bosna*, 119.

48. Fine, *Bosnian Church*, 328–29.

49. An example from that period: In 1461, three representatives of the Bosnian and Hum *krstjani* abjured their "Manichaean heresy" before Pope Pius II in Rome (Šanjek, *Kršćanstvo na hrvatskom prostoru*, 447, 448).

50. Fine, *Bosnian Church*, 144, 324–27.

51. Heywood, 44n. 16; Fine, *Bosnian Church*, 316–20, 363–75; Šidak, *Studije*, 101, 105.

52. Evans, *Pješke kroz Bosnu*, 51, 52; Ali and Lifschultz, eds., *Why Bosnia?* 133.

53. Nada Klaić, *Povijest Hrvata u ranom srednjem vijeku*, 139; Trpimir Macan, *Povijest hrvatskoga naroda*, 16–18.

54. Stephen Gazi, *A History of Croatia*, 16; Ferdo Šišić, *Pregled povijesti hrvatskoga naroda*, 75; Nada Klaić, *Izvori za hrvatsku povijest do 1526. godine*, 2.

55. Voje, *Nemirni Balkan*, 28.

56. So, according to Croatian religio-national mythology, the Croats were the first Slavs to accept Christianity, the first Slavs to "speak the name of Christ."

57. Šanjek, *Kršćanstvo na hrvatskom prostoru*, 13.

58. Voje, *Nemirni Balkan*, 50, 51.

59. Šanjek, *Kršćanstvo na hrvatskom prostoru*, 64, 65, 67; Voje, *Nemirni Balkan*, 53.

60. Vjekoslav Klaić, *Povijest Hrvata (First Book)*, 105–107.

61. Richard Pattee, *The Case of Cardinal Aloysius Stepinac*, 5; Šanjek, *Kršćanstvo na hrvatskom prostoru*, 28.

62. Voje, *Nemirni Balkan*, 55, 56.

63. Pattee, *Case of Cardinal Aloysius Stepinac*, 5; Voje, *Nemirni Balkan*, 62.

64. Šanjek, *Kršćanstvo na hrvatskom prostoru*, 29.

65. N. Klaić, *Povijest Hrvata*, 31, 32, among others.

66. Voje, *Nemirni Balkan*, 63; N. Klaić, *Povijest Hrvata*, 33.

67. Voje, *Nemirni Balkan*, 83.

68. Conte, *Sloveni*, 529; Fine, *Bosnian Church*, 213, 214, 380. See also Šidak, *Studije*, 93.

69. Imamović, *Historija Bošnjaka*, 52.

70. Šanjek, *Kršćanstvo na hrvatskom prostoru*, 111.

71. George Vid Tomashevich, "The Battle of Kosovo and the Serbian Church," in *Kosovo: Legacy of a Medieval Battle*, ed. Wayne S. Vucinich and Thomas A. Emmert, 204, 205, 214.

72. Ibid., 217, 218.

73. *Hrista Boga blagoverni car Srba i Grka*, in the original.

74. Voje, *Nemirni Balkan*, 103.

75. See, e.g., Rade Mihaljčić, *The Battle of Kosovo in History and in Popular Tradition*, 32, 33.

76. G. V. Tomashevich, "Battle of Kosovo," 212.

77. Mihaljčić, *Battle of Kosovo*, 57.

78. Bellah, "Civil Religion in America," 263.

79. Norris, *Islam in the Balkans*, 260. According to the Book of Genesis, the Hagarites were descendants of Abraham and his Egyptian concubine Hagar. Their first son and founder of the numerous clan was named Ishmael, who "will be a wild man; his hand will be against every man, and every man's hand against him; and he shall dwell in the presence of all his brethren" (Genesis, 16:12).

80. Mihaljčić, *Battle of Kosovo*, 70. See also Olga Zirojević, "Kosovo u kolektivnom pamćenju," in *Srpska strana rata: Trauma i katarza u istorijskom pamćenju*, ed. Nebojša Popov, 209.

81. Conte, *Sloveni*, 508, supplement for the Serbian edition.

82. Mihaljčić, *Battle of Kosovo*, 116–19, 158, 159, 187.

83. Ibid., 125; G. V. Tomashevich, "Battle of Kosovo," 213.

84. Mihaljčić, *Battle of Kosovo*, 103–106.

85. Edward W. Said, *Orientalizem-Zahodnjaški pogledi na Orient*, 82.

86. Tomaž Mastnak, *Evropa: med evolucijo in evtanazijo*, 93–95; review of similar anti-Turkish and Islamophobic sentiments, e.g., Francis Bacon, Liebniz, and Voltaire, 101–102.

87. Debeljak, *Oblike religiozne imaginacije*, 46; Mastnak, *Evropa*, 57–72, among others.

88. Mastnak, *Evropa*, 67, 68; Voje, *Nemirni Balkan*, 166, 167.

89. Šanjek, *Kršćanstvo na hrvatskom prostoru*, 241–43, 290.

90. Donia and Fine, *Bosnia Herzegovina*, 25. This name "most probably reflected either a shared geographical identity or participation in a state or regional enterprise . . . and not something akin to modern ethnicity" (ibid., 71).

CHAPTER 3. *PAX OTTOMANICA*

1. *Šaptom pade* in the original.

2. Hadžijahić, *Islam i Musliman*, 100.

3. Fine, "Medieval and Ottoman Roots," 17; Hadžijahić, *Porijeklo bosanskih Muslimana*, 151–70.

4. Tomašić, *Politički razvitak Hrvata*, 32. Sarajevo's Jewish intellectual, Moritz Levy, had a similar opinion on this issue (*Sefardi u Bosni*, 105). Croatian historian Franjo Šanjek called it "partial toleration" (*Kršćanstvo na hrvatskom prostoru*, 278). L. S. Stavrianos writes about the "unequaled degree of religious tolerance" toward the non-Muslims under the Ottoman Empire, and continues: "In a period when Catholics and Protestants were massacring each other and when Jews were being hounded from one Christian state to another, the subjects of the sultan were free to worship as they wished with comparatively minor disabilities" (*The Balkans since 1953*, 89).

5. Srećko M. Džaja, *Konfesionalnost i nacionalnost Bosne i Hercegovine*, 151.

6. Handžić, *Population of Bosnia*, 30; Imamović, *Historija Bošnjaka*, 181–225; Wayne S. Vucinich, "The Nature of Balkan Society Under Ottoman Rule." *Slavic Review* 4 (1962): 614.

7. See also Vucinich, "Nature of Balkan Society," 607, 608.

8. Mirjana Popović Radović, *Srpska mitska priča*, 22.

9. Stanford J. Shaw, "The Aims and Achievements of Ottoman Rule in the Balkans." *Slavic Review* 4 (1962): 622.

10. This should not, however, be confounded with the national groups that emerged later. As mentioned in footnote 2 in the introduction, I consider "ethnic identity" to be the historical precursor of "national identity."

11. Kemal H Karpat, "Millets and Nationality: The Roots of the Incongruity of Nation and State in the Post-Ottoman Era," in *Christians and Jews in the Ottoman Empire: The Functioning of a Plural Society*, ed. Benjamin Braude and Bernard Lewis, 1:141, 142.

12. Divisions within these communities over the ensuing centuries resulted in the coexistence of fourteen such communities at the beginning of the twentieth century (Harry Luke, *The Making of Modern Turkey: From Byzantium to Angora*, 96–102).

13. Zachary T. Irwin, "The Fate of Islam in the Balkans: A Comparison of Four State Policies," in *Religion and Nationalism*, ed. Ramet, 380; Lopasic, "Bosnian Muslims," 115; Robert T. Donia, *Islam under the Double Eagle: The Muslims of Bosnia Herzegovina, 1878–1914*, 4; G. V. Tomashevich, "Battle of Kosovo," 203; Vucinich, "Nature of Balkan Society," 606.

14. Franjo Šanjek, *Kršćanstvo na hrvatskom prostoru*, 278. The term *pillarization* (derived from the Latin word *pila*, pillar) signifies division into individual, mutually segregated, but neighboring sections of society: the "pillars." The concluding slogan reads, "*Rod svakoji svoju vjeru ima*" in the original.

15. Vucinich, "Nature of Balkan Society," 602. The second title comes from an early-nineteenth-century Greek satire. See Clogg, "Greek Millet," 1:192.

16. Karpat, "Millets and Nationality," 1:142.

17. P. Ramet, "Autocephaly," 7; Malcolm, *Bosnia*, 71; Vucinich, "Nature of Balkan Society," 602, 603, 609.

18. Marcus Tanner, *Croatia: A Nation Forged in War*, 42, 48.

19. Malcolm, *Bosnia*, 55; Voje, *Nemirni Balkan*, 215.

20. Moritz Levy, *Sefardi u Bosni*, 79; Mark A. Epstein, "The Leadership of the Ottoman Jews in the Fifteenth and Sixteenth Centuries," in *Christians and Jews in the Ottoman Empire: The Functioning of a Plural Society*, ed. Benjamin Braude and Bernard Lewis, 1:101–12.

21. Enver Redžić, "Društveno-istorijski aspekt 'nacionalnog opredjeljivanja' Muslimana Bosne i Hercegovine." *Socializam* 5, no. 3 (1961): 43. See, e.g., Harriet Pass Freidenreich, *The Jews of Yugoslavia: A Quest for Community*, 14.

22. See, e.g., Imamović, *Historija Bošnjaka*, 155–63; and Duraković, *Prokletstvo Muslimana*, 42.

23. Colin Heywood, "Bosnia under Ottoman rule," in *The Muslims of Bosnia Herzegovina: The Historic Development from the Middle Ages to the Dissolution of Yugoslavia*, ed. Mark Pinson, 33, 34, 47n. 33; Dominik Mandić, *Etnička povijest Bosne i Hercegovine*, 404, 405; Murvar, *Nation and Religion*, 27, 28.

24. Heywood, "Bosnia under Ottoman rule," 37, 38.

25. Malcolm, *Bosnia*, 94; Friedman, *Bosnian Muslims*, 46.

26. Kržišnik-Bukić, *Bosanska identiteta*, 22. For the precise data, see Džaja, *Konfesionalnost i nacionalnost*, 60–66.

27. For more on this, see Hadžijahić, Traljić, and Šukrić, *Islam i Muslimani*, 35; Imamović, *Historija Bošnjaka*, 10–11.

28. Voje, *Nemirni Balkan*, 213.

29. See, e.g., Džaja, *Konfesionalnost i nacionalnost*, 79, 80.

30. Stavrianos, *Balkans since 1953*, 107.

31. Džaja, *Konfesionalnost i nacionalnost*, 77, 79. See also Šanjek, *Kršćanstvo na hrvatskom prostoru*, 280. For a review of the history of the earliest contacts between Islam and the Slavs, see Hadžijahić, *Islam i Musliman*, 19–28.

32. M. Hadžijahić, *Porijeklo bosanskih Muslimana*, 94–105; Friedman, *Bosnian Muslims*, 18; Handžić, *Population of Bosnia*, 20; Malcolm, *Bosnia*, 54; Tomašić, *Politički razvitak Hrvata*, 31.

33. Donia, *Islam under the Double Eagle*, 3; Hadžijahić, *Islam i Musliman*, 39–52; Malcolm, *Bosnia*, 57; Michael A. Sells, *The Bridge Betrayed: Religion and Genocide in Bosnia*, 36; Fine, *Bosnian Church*, 344, 345; Šanjek, *Kršćanstvo na hrvatskom prostoru*, 131.

34. Mandić, *Etnička povijest Bosne i Hercegovine*, 281; Džaja, *Konfesionalnost i nacionalnost*, 54.

35. Duraković, *Prokletstvo Muslimana*, 41; M. Hadžijahić, *Porijeklo bosanskih Muslimana*, 133–35. There were about six hundred Ottomans in Sarajevo in the 1850s, roughly 2% of the city's population (ibid., 136).

36. Džaja, *Konfesionalnost i nacionalnost*, 49.

37. *"Do podne Ilija, od podne Alija,"* in the original.

38. Džaja, *Konfesionalnost i nacionalnost*, 79; Norris, *Islam in the Balkans*, 264, 265.

39. Xavier Bougarel, *Bosnie: Anatomie d'un conflit*, 14.

40. David A. Dyker, "The Ethnic Muslims of Bosnia: Some Basic Socio-Economic Data," *The Slavonic and East European Review* 119 (1972): 239–41.

41. Mustafa Imamović, "Integracijske ideologije i Bosna." *Erasmus* 18 (1996): 39; Kržišnik-Bukić, *Bosanska identiteta*, 24. See, e.g., Dyker, "Ethnic Muslims of Bosnia," 239.

42. This is similar to the Albanians up to 1912, when all Orthodox were recognized as Greeks because of Greek religious practices and culture, all Muslims as Turks because of Arab religious practices and culture, and all Catholics as Latins because of their Latin rites, or Germans because they had Austrian priests.

43. Redžić, "Društveno-istorijski aspekt," 44, 45. See, e.g., Bogdan Denitch, "Religion and Social Change in Yugoslavia," in *Religion and Atheism in the USSR and Eastern Europe*, ed. Bohdan R. Bociurkiw and John W. Strong, 370, 371.

44. Imamović, "Integracijske ideologije i Bosna," 40; Malcolm, *Bosnia*, 148; Friedman, *Bosnian Muslims*, 43; Kržišnik-Bukić, *Bosanska identiteta*, 58; Lopasic, "Bosnian Muslims," 116; and Ivo Banac, "Bosnian Muslims: From Religious Community to Socialist Nationhood and Postcommunist Statehood, 1918–1992," in *The Muslims of Bosnia Herzegovina: The Historic Development from the Middle Ages to the Dissolution of Yugoslavia*, ed. Mark Pinson, 133.

45. Heywood, "Bosnia under Ottoman rule," 34.

46. Fine, *Bosnian Church*, 19.

47. For examples and anecdotes see Hadžijahić, *Islam i Musliman*, 82–88; idem., *Porijeklo bosanskih Muslimana*, 80–94; idem., Traljić, and Šukrić, *Islam i Muslimani*, 55–66; Norris, *Islam in the Balkans*, 17; Fine, *Bosnian Church*, 310, 311; Lopasic, "Bosnian Muslims," 117; Jezernik, "Oči, da ne vidijo," 207–10; Friedman, *Bosnian Muslims*, 19; Vucinich, "Nature of Balkan Society," 614–16.

48. Malcolm, *Bosnia*, 105; Xavier Bougarel, "From Young Muslims to Party of Democratic Action: The Emergence of a Pan-Islamist Trend in Bosna-Herzegovina," *Islamic Studies* 36 (1997): 533.

49. Norris, *Islam in the Balkans*, 102, 109–17.

50. Hadžijahić, *Islam i Musliman*, 91–98; idem., Traljić, and Šukrić, *Islam i Muslimani*, 91–98.

51. Vatro Murvar, *Nation and Religion in Central Europe and the Western Balkans: The Muslims in Bosnia, Herzegovina, and Sandžak: A Sociological Analysis*, 85.

52. Voje, *Nemirni Balkan*, 207, 208.

53. Ibid., 208.

54. *Dokle Turska dotle Srbija* in the original.

55. Voje, *Nemirni Balkan*, 208; Imamović, *Historija Bošnjaka*, 144, 145; G. V. Tomashevich, "Battle of Kosovo," 216; Cigar, *Genocide in Bosnia*, 15.

56. Banac, *Nacionalno pitanje u Jugoslaviji*, 71, 72.

57. Voje, *Nemirni Balkan*, 209.

58. Hadžijahić, *Islam i Musliman*, 100.

59. Veselin Ilić, *Mitologija i kultura*, 254–57.

60. Malcolm, *Bosnia*, 55; Banac, *Nacionalno pitanje u Jugoslaviji*, 70, 71; Džaja, *Konfesionalnost i nacionalnost*, 94, 109.

61. Fine, *Bosnian Church*, 11.

62. G. V. Tomashevich, "Battle of Kosovo," 217–19.

63. Ibid., 217. See also Voje, *Nemirni Balkan*, 258.

64. G. V. Tomashevich mentions approximately forty thousand families (ibid., 219, 220). Šanjek mentions thirty-seven thousand families (*Kršćanstvo na hrvatskom prostoru*, 297). Džaja says both these estimates are exaggerated (*Konfesionalnost i nacionalnost*, 90).

65. See, e.g., Božidar Jezernik, "Oči, da ne vidijo," *Nova revija* 9 (1990): 208.

66. Radoman Kordić, *Nasilje svakidašnjice*, 132, 133; Damjan J. Ovsec, *Slovanska mitologija in verovanje*, 453, 454.

67. *Gde je slava, tu je Srbin* in the original.

68. Their patron saint was Saint Sava.

69. An example of this can be found in the early nineteenth century, when a banner sent as a gift from the Metropolitan See of Karlovac to the Hilandrian monks bore the motive of the resurrection on one side and the portraits of Serbian rulers King Milutin and Prince Lazar on the other.

70. Pattee, *Case of Cardinal Aloysius Stepinac*, 6.

71. Šanjek, *Kršćanstvo na hrvatskom prostoru*, 272; V. Klaić, *Povijest Hrvata*, 669; Tomašić, *Politički razvitak Hrvata*, 34, 35.

72. Džaja, *Konfesionalnost i nacionalnost*, 152–55; Šanjek, *Kršćanstvo na hrvatskom prostoru*, 278; Mandić, *Etnička povijest Bosne i Hercegovine*, 189, 190. See, e.g., Dominik Mandić, *Franjevačka Bosna: razvoj i uprava Bosanske vikarije i provincije, 1340–1735*, 130–37; Džaja, "Od bana Kulina," 59.

73. Voje, *Nemirni Balkan*, 215.

74. Fine, *Bosnian Church*, 380. See the list in Džaja, *Konfesionalnost i nacionalnost*, 134, 135. See also Imamović, *Historija Bošnjaka*, 143.

75. Mandić, *Franjevačka Bosna*, 142, 171, 176, 184, 205, 206; Imamović, *Historija Bošnjaka*, 149; Voje, *Nemirni Balkan*, 216; Džaja, *Konfesionalnost i nacionalnost*, 186.

76. Džaja, *Konfesionalnost i nacionalnost*, 90.

77. Šanjek, *Kršćanstvo na hrvatskom prostoru*, 446; Džaja, *Konfesionalnost i nacionalnost*, 174, 175; Mandić, *Franjevačka Bosna*, 206, 209.

78. Mart Bax, *Medjugorje: Religion, Politics, and Violence in Rural Bosnia*, 53–57, 64–65n. 5.

79. Imamović, *Historija Bošnjaka*, 282, 283. See, e.g., Džaja, *Konfesionalnost i nacionalnost*, 85.

80. The Uniates, whose name is derived from the Brest-Litovsk Union of 1595, are descended from Orthodox Christians who were pressured into canonical com-

munion with the Roman Apostolic See, which appoints their bishops, and are required to include a prayer for the pope in their liturgy. They are, in other words, Catholics of the Eastern (Orthodox) rite.

81. Šanjek, *Kršćanstvo na hrvatskom prostoru*, 462, 294, 295.

82. Avram Pinto, *Jevreji Sarajeva i Bosne i Hercegovine*, 12; Levy, *Sefardi u Bosni*, 10, 11.

83. For a review of the organization, customs, culture, and everyday activities of the Bosnian Sephardic community, see Pinto, *Jevreji Sarajeva*, 23–64; and Levy, *Sefardi u Bosni*, 32–40, 69–87.

84. Levy, *Sefardi u Bosni*, 27; Malcolm, *Bosnia*, 111; Pinto, *Jevreji Sarajeva*, 13.

85. Hadžijahić, *Islam i Musliman*, 111; Džaja, *Konfesionalnost i nacionalnost*, 84.

86. Justin McCarthy, "Ottoman Bosnia," in *The Muslims of Bosnia Herzegovina: The Historic Development from the Middle Ages to the Dissolution of Yugoslavia*, ed. Mark Pinson, 74, 75.

87. Imamović, *Historija Bošnjaka*, 333–36; Friedman, *Bosnian Muslims*, 50n. 30; also Hadžijahić, *Islam i Musliman*, 113.

88. Imamović, *Historija Bošnjaka*, 338–40; Friedenreich, 1977, 15.

89. Friedman, *Bosnian Muslims*, 37.

90. Mihaljčić, *Battle of Kosovo*, 218, 219; Norris, *Islam in the Balkans*, 262; Olga Zirojević, "Kosovo u kolektivnom pamćenju," in *Srpska strana rata*, ed. Popov, 204.

91. Norris, *Islam in the Balkans*, 146–56.

92. Hadžijahić, *Islam i Musliman*, 61, 62, 100. See also Norris, *Islam in the Balkans*, 157–60. See an anthology of Bosnian Muslim epics, Đenana *Buturović*, ed., *Od Đerzelez Alije do Tale Ličanina*.

93. Malcolm, *Bosnia*, xxi, 129, 234.

94. Kržišnik-Bukić, *Bosanska identiteta*, 24, 26.

95. Cigar, *Genocide in Bosnia*, 13.

96. See also Friedman, *Bosnian Muslims*, 165.

97. Karpat, "Millets and Nationality," 1:162, 163; Friedman, *Bosnian Muslims*, 43.

98. McCarthy, "Ottoman Bosnia," 58.

99. See also Hadžijahić, *Islam i Musliman*, 107–10.

100. Vucinich, "Nature of Balkan Society," 638; Friedman, *Bosnian Muslims*, 31, 32.

CHAPTER 4. HONED MINDS

1. D. Lovrenović, "Bosanski mitovi," 26.

2. Sells, *Bridge Betrayed*, 36, 51.

3. Zirojević, "Kosovo u kolektivnom pamćenju," 202–209; Sells, *Bridge Be-*

trayed, 37; Dimitrije Djordjević, "The Tradition of Kosovo in the Formation of Modern Serbian Statehood in the Nineteenth Century," in *Kosovo: Legacy of a Medieval Battle*, ed. Wayne S. Vucinich and Thomas A. Emmert, 322, 323.

4. Dimitrise Djordjević, "Tradition of Kosovo," 310; Kordić, *Nasilje svakidašnjice*, 123; Dragoljub Djordjević, "The Serbian Orthodox Church, the Disintegration of the Second Yugoslavia, and the War in Bosnia Herzegovina," in *Religion and the War in Bosnia*, ed. Paul Mojzes, 320. The entire Serbian brigade reportedly "saw" him leading the attack on Prilep (Zirojević, "Kosovo u kolektivnom pamćenju," 225).

5. The phrase reads *"Kosovska truba zvoni u nama od toga dana svaki dan""* in the original.

6. Geert Van Dartel, "Towards a Culture of Peace: Remarks on the Religious Aspects of the War in Bosnia and Croatia," *Religion, State and Society* 23, no. 2 (1995): 204.

7. Mihaljčić, *Battle of Kosovo*, 188, 189.

8. The quoted phrase reads *"Srbstvo gaji Obiliće"* in the original text.

9. Wayne S. Vucinich, "Introduction," in *Kosovo: Legacy of a Medieval Battle*, ed. Wayne S. Vucinich and Thomas A. Emmert, ix.

10. Mihaljčić, *Battle of Kosovo*, 75; Sells, *Bridge Betrayed*, 39, 40.

11. *"Srpsko biće"* in the original.

12. Drinka Gojković, "Trauma bez katarze," in *Srpska strana rata*, ed. Popov, 386, 387; Kordić, *Nasilje svakidašnjice*, 75; Zirojević, "Kosovo u kolektivnom pamćenju," 211–15.

13. Žika R. Prvulovich, *Religious Philosophy of Prince-Bishop Njegosh of Montenegro, 1813–1851*, 209, 210; Zirojević, "Kosovo u kolektivnom pamćenju," 214.

14. Djordjević, "Tradition of Kosovo," 311; Voje, *Nemirni Balkan*, 260. See also Imamović, *Historija Bošnjaka*, 292–93.

15. *"Ne slozi se Bajram s Božićem!"* in the original.

16. See the selected list of authors in Zirojević, "Kosovo u kolektivnom pamćenju," 226–28.

17. Among the two hundred writers, politicians, and priests attending the festivities were Dobrica Ćosić, Radovan Karadžić, and Nikolaj Mrđa, the bishop of central Bosnia. On the fiftieth anniversary of the publication of *Bridge on the Drina River* and the twentieth anniversary of the writer's death, Ćosić made a speech in which he referred to Bosnia-Herzegovina as the "land of hate," representing the "international battleground against the Muslim advance on Europe", and of the "righteous defensive war of liberation" of the Bosnian Serbs (Žanić, "Pisac na osami," 56).

18. Milorad Ekmečić, "The Emergence of St. Vitus Day as the Principal National Holiday of the Serbs," in *Kosovo: Legacy of a Medieval Battle*, ed. Wayne S. Vucinich and Thomas A. Emmert, 334–36.

19. Mihaljčić, *Battle of Kosovo*, 231.

20. Djordjević, "Tradition of Kosovo," 318, 319.

21. Banac, *Nacionalno pitanje u Jugoslaviji*, 274.

22. Djordjević, "Tradition of Kosovo," 322; Danac, 140.

23. Zirojević, "Kosovo u kolektivnom pamćenju," 210.

24. Smail Balić, "Culture Under Fire," in *Why Bosnia?* ed. Ali and Lifschultz, 79; McCarthy, "Ottoman Bosnia," 73; Heywood, "Bosnia under Ottoman rule," 41. See also Imamović, *Historija Bošnjaka*, 291–92, 329–32; and Cigar, *Genocide in Bosnia*, 16, 17.

25. Voje, *Nemirni Balkan*, 218. Under the old Serbian and Montenegrin administrative order, a *knežina* was a district with a considerable level of autonomy.

26. Prvulovich, *Religious Philosophy*, ix.

27. Djordjević, "Tradition of Kosovo," 314, 315.

28. Popović Radović, *Srpska mitska priča*, 42, 54–78.

29. *"Za Krst časni i Slobodu Zlatnu!"* in the original.

30. Ekmečić, "Emergence of St. Vitus Day," 331, 338–41; Zirojević, "Kosovo u kolektivnom pamćenju," 215–19.

31. Djordjević, "Tradition of Kosovo," 319; Zirojević, "Kosovo u kolektivnom pamćenju," 222–24.

32. See, e.g., Banac, *Nacionalno pitanje u Jugoslaviji*, 276–78.

33. Stella Alexander, *Trostruki mit: Život zagrebačkog nadbiskupa Alojzija Stepinca*, 23.

34. Geert Van Dartel, "The Nations and Churches in Yugoslavia," *Religion, State and Society* 20, nos. 3–4 (1992): 281, 282.

35. Djordjević, "Serbian Orthodox Church," 153.

36. Mihaljčić, *Battle of Kosovo*, 60.

37. Banac, *Nacionalno pitanje u Jugoslaviji*, 72.

38. See also Djordjević, "Tradition of Kosovo," 317, 318.

39. Janko Pleterski, "Religija i crkva nemaju narodotvornu funkciju," *Kulturni radnik* 1 (1984): 45.

40. See, e.g., Djordjević, "Tradition of Kosovo," 312.

41. Philip J. Cohen, *Serbia's Secret War: Propaganda and the Deceit of History*, 3, 4.

42. Redžić, "Društveno-istorijski aspekt," 70; Banac, *Nacionalno pitanje u Jugoslaviji*, 87; Djordjević, "Tradition of Kosovo," 315, 316.

43. Vrcan notes: "since 1918 the history of Serbian Orthodoxy ceased to be fused and identified with the political history of the Serbian nation . . . but was reduced to only one component of this history" ("Orthodoxy in Balkan Political Conflicts," 138).

44. *"Srbi svi i svuda"* in the original.

45. See also Aleksandar Pavković, "The Serb National Idea: A Revival 1986–1992," *Slavonic and East European Review* 3 (1994): 442, 443; Ekmečić, "Sudbina jugoslovenske ideje do 1914," in *Sveske Trećeg programa*, 44; Redžić, "Društveno-istorijski aspekt," 70. The last phrase reads *"Najstarije srpsko stanovništvo ovih oblasti"* in the original.

46. D. Lovrenović, "Bosanski mitovi," 26, 27.

47. Philip J. Cohen, *Drugi svetski rat i suvremeni četnici*, 30; Stavrianos, *Balkans since 1953*, 550.

48. Vasilije Đ. Krestić, *Srpsko-hrvatski odnosi i jugoslovenska ideja u drugoj polovini XIX, Veka*, 296.

49. Dugandžija, *Jugoslavenstvo*, 19, 20.

50. A. Pavković, "Serb National Idea," 447–52.

51. See also Pleterski, "Religija i crkva nemaju," 46.

52. Ibid., 46–48.

53. Šanjek, *Kršćanstvo na hrvatskom prostoru*, 299, 300; Conte, 1989, 552, 553. See also Tomašić, *Politički razvitak Hrvata*, 41.

54. Alexander, *Trostruki mit*, 23.

55. Imamović, *Historija Bošnjaka*, 152; Kržišnik-Bukić, *Bosanska identiteta*, 26, 27.

56. Friedman, *Bosnian Muslims*, 40.

57. Nikola Dugandžija, *Jugoslavenstvo*, 52.

58. Šanjek, *Kršćanstvo na hrvatskom prostoru*, 336.

59. See also Alexander, *Trostruki mit*, 15.

60. Stella Alexander, *Church and State in Yugoslavia Since 1945*, 58n. 14; Šanjek, *Kršćanstvo na hrvatskom prostoru*, 333.

61. See Banac, *Nacionalno pitanje u Jugoslaviji*, 94; and Šanjek, *Kršćanstvo na hrvatskom prostoru*, 338.

62. Ekmečić, "Sudbina jugoslovenske," 42, 43.

63. Dugandžija, *Jugoslavenstvo*, 161.

64. Bogdan Krizman, "Hrvatske stranke prema ujedinjenju i stvaranju jugoslovenske države," in *Sveske Trećeg programa*, 117.

65. Tomašić, *Politički razvitak Hrvata*, 23. This author views the efforts for equating Croatism and Catholicism as "pernicious for the Croatian national interests" because that concept of Croatism would exclude Croat Muslims and Croats of other religious denominations (ibid., 137). Martin Tomičić expressed a similar opinion in 1940 ("Narodnost bosanskih Muslimana," in *Hrvatsko podrijetlo bosansko-hercegovačkih Muslimana*, ed. Petar Šarac and Miljenko Primorac, 29, 30).

66. Banac, *Nacionalno pitanje u Jugoslaviji*, 75; George Schöpflin, "The Ideology of Croatian Nationalism," *Survey* 19, no. 4 (1973): 141.

67. Ekmečić, "Sudbina jugoslovenske," 33.

68. Also known as the "Katholischer Verein" in Germany, the "Ligue catholique" in France, the "Catholic Union" in Great Britain, and the "Associazione cattolica per la liberta della Chiesa" in Italy (Šanjek, *Kršćanstvo na hrvatskom prostoru*, 345, 346).

69. Tomašić, *Politički razvitak Hrvata*, 23. See, e.g., Banac, *Nacionalno pitanje u Jugoslaviji*, 110.

70. Krizman, "Hrvatske stranke prema," 110, 126.

71. See also Banac, *Nacionalno pitanje u Jugoslaviji*, 106–108, 110.

72. Friedman, *Bosnian Muslims*, 41.

CHAPTER 5. BENEATH THE TWO-HEADED EAGLE

1. See, e.g., Denitch, "Religion and Social Change," 368; Jezernik, "Oči, da ne vidijo," 202. In an appeal for defense against the Austrian occupation in 1878, the inhabitants of Bosnia-Herzegovina were still addressed as "Islams, Hristians [Orthodox] and Latins" (Duraković, *Prokletstvo Muslimana*, 60).

2. Malcolm, *Bosnia*, 132. See also Imamović, *Historija Bošnjaka*, 370–72. For a travelogue of that period, see Evans, *Pješke kroz Bosnu*, 117–267.

3. Djordjević, "Tradition of Kosovo," 317.

4. Imamović, *Historija Bošnjaka*, 352; Duraković, *Prokletstvo Muslimana*, 60; Friedman, *Bosnian Muslims*, 60; Ekmečić, "Sudbina jugoslovenske," 37.

5. Donia, *Islam under the Double Eagle*, 14, 15.

6. Hadžijahić, *Islam i Musliman*, 119. Compare with the statistics for the neighboring principality (and later kingdom) of Serbia: in 1866, 4.2% of the population was literate (1.6% of rural), increasing to 11% (6.4% of rural) by 1884, and 21% (14.5% of rural and 55% of urban) by 1910 (Ekmečić, " Emergence of St. Vitus Day," 333).

7. Duraković, *Prokletstvo Muslimana*, 106.

8. Heywood, "Bosnia under Ottoman rule," 45–46n. 25; Malcolm, *Bosnia*, 96, 97. According to Tomašić, the population of Zagreb was 16,000 in 1848 (*Politički razvitak Hrvata*, 64). In the late 1860s, the number reached 20,000; in 1890, 40,000; and in 1910, 80,000 (Tanner, *Croatia*, 109).

9. Donia, *Islam under the Double Eagle*, 42; Freidenreich, *Jews of Yugoslavia*, 213.

10. McCarthy, "Ottoman Bosnia," 60, 61.

11. Donia, *Islam under the Double Eagle*, 69. The figures for the 1885 census have again been omitted.

12. McCarthy, "Ottoman Bosnia," 61.

13. Karpat, "Millets and Nationality," 1:141; Imamović, "Integracijske ideologije i Bosna," 41. See also Karpat, "Millets and Nationality," 1:143.

14. See, e.g., Malcolm, *Bosnia*, 149; Kržišnik-Bukić, *Bosanska identiteta*, 27; Donia and Fine, *Bosnia Herzegovina*, 10.

15. Donia, *Islam under the Double Eagle*, 4, 5.

16. Ibid., 6, 7; Banac, *Nacionalno pitanje u Jugoslaviji*, 343; Arif Purivatra, *Nacionalni i politički razvitak Muslimana*, 142.

17. *Vakufs* were property owning religious-charitable foundations. The *shariat* are sacred Islamic laws.

18. Friedman, *Bosnian Muslims*, 64, 72–74; Kržišnik-Bukić, *Bosanska identiteta*, 34.

19. Charles Jelavich, "The Revolt in Bosnia Herzegovina, 1881–1882," *Slavonic and East European Review* 31 (1953): 422; Donia, *Islam under the Double Eagle*, 18.

20. M. Hadžijahić, Traljić, and Šukrić, *Islam i Muslimani*, 146–48.

21. Ibid., 148–49; Friedman, *Bosnian Muslims*, 63; Donia, *Islam under the Double Eagle*, 27, 28, 187; Malcolm, *Bosnia*, 145, 146; Mark Pinson, "The Muslims of Bosnia Herzegovina under Austro-Hungarian rule," in *The Muslims of Bosnia Herzegovina: The Historic Development from the Middle Ages to the Dissolution of Yugoslavia*, ed. idem., 100–102.

22. See, e.g., M. Hadžijahić, Traljić, and Šukrić, *Islam i Muslimani*, 122–26; P. Ramet, "Primordial Ethnicity," 180, 181.

23. Hadžijahić, *Islam i Musliman*, 36; McCarthy, "Ottoman Bosnia," 81; Imamović, *Historija Bošnjaka*, 371, 439; Donia and Fine, *Bosnia Herzegovina*, 87.

24. Duraković, *Prokletstvo Muslimana*, 87. According to Austro-Hungarian data, 61,114 (ibid.).

25. Alexander Lopasic, "Bosnian Muslims: A Search for Identity," *Brismes Bulletin* 2 (1981): 121; Malcolm, *Bosnia*, 139; Hadžijahić, *Islam i Musliman*, 36; Pinson, "Muslims of Bosnia Herzegovina," 94.

26. Šanjek, *Kršćanstvo na hrvatskom prostoru*, 479.

27. Bax, *Medjugorje*, 89.

28. Marko Karamatić, "U doba Austro-Ugarske (1878–1918)," in *Katoličanstvo u Bosni i Hercegovini*, 88.

29. Hamdija Kapidžić, *Bosna i Hercegovina u vrijeme austrougarske vladavine*, 200; Friedman, *Bosnian Muslims*, 65.

30. Malcolm, *Bosnia*, 126, 130. See also Imamović, "Integracijske ideologije i Bosna," 41, 42.

31. See Banac, *Nacionalno pitanje u Jugoslaviji*, 50–52; Džaja, *Konfesionalnost i nacionalnost*, 40–48, 92; and Voje, *Nemirni Balkan*, 265, 266.

32. Kržišnik-Bukić, *Bosanska identiteta*, 70. Tomašić notes that a minority of Vlachs converted to Catholicism and later assumed Croatian national identity (*Politički razvitak Hrvata*, 20, 21, 135, 136).

33. Ashkenazi means "west" in Hebrew (Pinto, *Jevreji Sarajeva*, 13).

34. Ibid. For more about the Jewish people and their activities and organizations in different towns in Bosnia-Herzegovina, see ibid., 16–18.

35. Freidenreich, *Jews of Yugoslavia*, 18, 19; Pinto, *Jevreji Sarajeva*, 14–16.

36. See also P. Ramet, "Religion and Nationalism," 311; Donia, *Islam under the Double Eagle*, 187; Pleterski, "Religija i crkva nemaju," 48, 49; Friedman, *Bosnian Muslims*, 32, 33.

37. P. Ramet, "Primordial Ethnicity," 179.

38. Redžić, "Društveno-istorijski aspekt," 86, 87.

39. Banac, *Nacionalno pitanje u Jugoslaviji*, 341.

40. Irwin, "Fate of Islam," 405; Donia, *Islam under the Double Eagle*, 182–190; Pinson, "Muslims of Bosnia Herzegovina," 89, 90, 91.

41. See also Banac, *Nacionalno pitanje u Jugoslaviji*, 337.

42. See also Šarac and Primorac, *Hrvatsko podrijetlo*, 7.

43. Munir Šahinović-Ekremov, "Muslimani u prošlosti i budućnosti hrvat-

stva," in *Hrvatsko podrijetlo,* ed. Šarac and Primorac, 24. A number of other Croatian and pro-Croatian Bosnian Muslim intellectuals advocated this theory. See ibid.

44. Tomičić, "Narodnost bosanskih Muslimana," 28; Abdulatif Dizdarević, "Bosansko-hercegovački Muslimani Hrvati," in *Hrvatsko podrijetlo,* ed. Šarac and Primorac, 48; Ivo Pilar, *Usud hrvatskih zemalja,* 43n. 5.

45. Malcolm, *Bosnia,* 28.

46. P. Ramet, "Primordial Ethnicity," 174, 175.

47. Imamović, "Integracijske ideologije i Bosna," 42, 43; Redžić, "Društveno-istorijski aspekt," 48.

48. Friedman, *Bosnian Muslims,* 62.

49. Peter F. Sugar, "The Historical Role of Religious Institutions in Eastern Europe and Their Place in the Communist Party-State," in *Religion and Nationalism,* ed. Ramet, 57, 58; Friedman, *Bosnian Muslims,* 71.

50. Donia, *Islam under the Double Eagle,* xii.

51. P. Ramet, "Primordial Ethnicity," 182. See also Imamović, *Historija Bošnjaka,* 397–417.

52. P. Ramet, "Primordial Ethnicity," 180, 181.

53. Donia, *Islam under the Double Eagle,* 171.

54. Donia and Fine, *Bosnia Herzegovina,* 103.

55. Banac, *Nacionalno pitanje u Jugoslaviji,* 340.

56. Friedman, *Bosnian Muslims,* 67.

57. Malcolm, *Bosnia,* 153–55.

58. P. Ramet, "Primordial Ethnicity," 180.

59. For the development of Muslim education and cultural and economic associations in Bosnia-Herzegovina, see Hadžijahić, *Islam i Musliman,* 124–27, 134–36; and Duraković, *Prokletstvo Muslimana,* 88–94.

60. M. Hadžijahić, Traljić, and Šukrić, *Islam i Muslimani,* 132–34; Imamović, *Historija Bošnjaka,* 377–83.

61. P. Ramet, "Primordial Ethnicity," 182; Redžić, "Društveno-istorijski aspekt," 64, 65.

62. See also Redžić, "Društveno-istorijski aspekt," 65, 66.

63. Hadžijahić, *Islam i Musliman,* 131.

64. Duraković, *Prokletstvo Muslimana,* 65.

65. See, e.g., Imamović, *Historija Bošnjaka,* 458, 459 (describing the violence of Montenegrin troops); and Friedman, *Bosnian Muslims,* 78.

66. Kapidžić, *Bosna i Hercegovina,* 237. See also Duraković, *Prokletstvo Muslimana,* 98.

67. Mihaljčić, *Battle of Kosovo,* 105.

68. See, e.g., Banac, *Nacionalno pitanje u Jugoslaviji,* 342n. 18; Malcolm, *Bosnia,* 158.

CHAPTER 6. BETWEEN THE SERBS AND THE CROATS

1. Banac, *Nacionalno pitanje u Jugoslaviji*, 378.

2. Jože Pirjevec, *Jugoslavija, 1918–1992: Nastanek, razvoj in razpad Karadjordjevićeve in Titove Jugoslavije*, 60.

3. On the other hand, some advocated only the expansion of the Serbian Kingdom. In the early stages of war, prominent Serbian Radical Ljubomir Jovanović declared that their goal was "to annex Bosnia Herzegovina, Boka [Kotorska] and Dubrovnik, [the] rest of the littoral will get the Italians, while Croatia will remain under Hungarians" (Ivan Meštrović, *Spomini*, 67).

4. Djordjević, "Tradition of Kosovo," 309.

5. Meštrović, *Spomini*, 89; Banac, "Bosnian Muslims," 136; Pirjevec, *Jugoslavija*, 15, 16; Imamović, *Historija Bošnjaka*, 490, 491. See also Duraković, *Prokletstvo Muslimana*, 105, 106, 146.

6. Banac, *Nacionalno pitanje u Jugoslaviji*, 347. See also Duraković, *Prokletstvo Muslimana*, 114, 115.

7. Imamović, *Historija Bošnjaka*, 490; Friedman, *Bosnian Muslims*, 99.

8. Banac, "Bosnian Muslims," 135, 136.

9. Alexander, *Trostruki mit*, 48n. 8.

10. Banac, "Bosnian Muslims," 140, 141. See also Imamović, *Historija Bošnjaka*, 520, 521.

11. Banac, *Nacionalno pitanje u Jugoslaviji*, 58; Pirjevec, *Jugoslavija*, 13.

12. P. Ramet, "Primordial Ethnicity," 183. See also Duraković, *Prokletstvo Muslimana*, 110, 111.

13. Banac, *Nacionalno pitanje u Jugoslaviji*, 347, 348. See also Kržišnik-Bukić, *Bosanska identiteta*, 36.

14. Irwin, "Islamic Revival," 453.

15. Bougarel, "From Young Muslims," 537.

16. Friedman, *Bosnian Muslims*, 122.

17. Imamović, *Historija Bošnjaka*, 492; Vladimir Žerjavić, *Gubici stanovništva Jugoslavije u drugom svjetskom ratu*, 140; Friedman, *Bosnian Muslims*, 96.

18. Edvard Kardelj, *Razvoj slovenskega narodnega vprašanja*, 26, 347, 369, 391.

19. Purivatra, *Nacionalni i politički*, 57, 117; Banac, "Bosnian Muslims," 144; Irwin, "Islamic Revival," 455 n.

20. Žerjavić, *Gubici stanovništva*, 127, 128.

21. Pirjevec, *Jugoslavija*, 60.

22. Banac, *Nacionalno pitanje u Jugoslaviji*, 381.

23. Van Dartel, "Nations and Churches in Yugoslavia," 282. A mystical version of Orthodoxy was also used as the basis for Dimitrij Ljotić's pan-Slav and Serbo-centric nationalist and anti-Semitic movement "Zbor," which was openly sympathetic to the Nazis.

24. Pirjevec, *Jugoslavija*, 21, 25; Stella Alexander, "Croatia: The Catholic Church and the Clergy, 1919–1945," in *Catholics*, ed. Wolf and Hoensch, 20.

25. Hadžijahić, *Islam i Musliman*, 130; Bax, *Medjugorje*, 11. Šarić remained bishop until he fled from advancing partisan forces in 1945.

26. Alexander, *Trostruki mit*, 30; Kuzmanić, "Iugoslavia," 114; Šanjek, *Kršćanstvo na hrvatskom prostoru*, 357–59.

27. For example, 95% of all generals were Serbs in 1938 (Friedman, *Bosnian Muslims*, 111n. 30). Of two hundred generals, only two were Croats (Glavina, 1998). For more on the large number of Serbs holding high rank in the kingdom of Yugoslavia, see P. J. Cohen, *Serbia's Secret War*, 8, 9.

28. Pirjevec, *Jugoslavija*, 411; Friedman, *Bosnian Muslims*, 110n. 17.

29. Alexander, *Trostruki mit*, 30.

30. In the speeches, oaths, and poems dedicated to him we are faced with a motivating spirit similar to that of the Kosovo myths: The temporal and eternal spheres not only complement each other, they blend with and overlap each other as well; suffering today will be replaced by ultimate salvation tomorrow; the immortality of a more consequential thing—the exaltation of a leader—is raised above the mortality of man; the revival of contradictory mythical narratives such as holy and damned, and so forth. Radić was thus exalted as, among other things, the "mentor of the Croatian people," the "greatest of Croats," the posthumous "leader" of his nation—a reference that many Croat politicians have used in recent years. For an epic interpretation of his death, see Nikola J. Kordić, *Hrvatski mučenici Pavao Radić i Đuro Basariček*.

31. The full name was Ustashe-Croatian Revolutionary Organization (*Ustaše-Hrvatska revolucionarna organizacija* [HRO]).

32. Ivan Mužić, *Katolička crkva: Stepinac i Pavelić*, 269.

33. Trpimir Macan, *Povijest hrvatskoga naroda*, 461–63. The educational structure of Pavelić's early followers was low: 95% of them were "peasants, laborers, or sailors" (P. J. Cohen, *Serbia's Secret War*, 87).

34. Alexander, *Church and State*, 19; idem., *Trostruki mit*, 26.

35. Alexander, *Trostruki mit*, 26, 27, 45, 149.

36. Alexander, *Church and State*, 150.

37. Alexander, *Trostruki mit*, 30–32.

38. The document's contents are in Mužić, *Katolička crkva*.

39. M. Landercy, *Le cardinal Stepinac: martyr des droits de l'homme*, 45, 63.

40. Alexander, *Trostruki mit*, 30.

41. Ibid., 29; Landercy, *Le cardinal Stepinac*, 57.

42. *"Kriste, Euharistijski Kralju, štiti hrvatski narod!"* in the original text.

43. Šanjek, *Kršćanstvo na hrvatskom prostoru*, 348, 350–53; Alexander, "Croatia," 41, 42.

44. See also M. Hadžijahić, Traljić, and Šukrić, *Islam i Muslimani*, 129; Imamović, *Historija Bošnjaka*, 522.

45. Malcolm, *Bosnia*, 170.

46. Hadžijahić, *Islam i Musliman*, 128, 138.

47. Pinto, *Jevreji Sarajeva*, 16, 81–154, 162.

48. See R. J. Crampton, *Eastern Europe in the Twentieth Century*, 168–76.

49. Bročić, "Position and Activities," 352. See also Malcolm, *Bosnia*, 168.

50. Mužić, *Katolička crkva*, 134.

51. Srdjan Vrcan, *Vjera u vrtlozima tranzicije*, 32.

CHAPTER 7. *Bellum Omnium in Omnes*

1. *Vladimir Dedijer, Vatikan i Jasenovac*, 142. Croatian Franciscan historian Dominik Mandić also misinterpreted the Vlach element of national identity of Croatian and Bosnian Serbs in 1963. See Mandić, "Herceg-Bosna i Hrvatska," in *Hrvatsko podrijetlo*, ed. Šarac and Primorac, 122, 123.

2. Alexander, *Church and State*, 22; idem., *Trostruki mit*, 57, 67n. 2. See also Pirjevec, *Jugoslavija*, 114; Dedijer, *Vatikan i Jasenovac*, 185. A similar statement was made by Milovan Žanić, president of the Ustasha Legislative Council, in the same month in Nova Gradiška. He said there was no room in the NDH for these "settlers" from the east, and announced a policy of ethnic cleansing of the Serbs "who have endangered us for centuries" (Tanner, *Croatia*, 150, 151).

3. Bogdan Krizman, "Pitanje priznanja ustaške države 1941. godine," *Posebni otisak Jugoslovenskog istorijskog časopisa*, special issue, 1970, 104.

4. See, e.g., P. J. Cohen, *Serbia's Secret War*, 12–21.

5. Dedijer, *Vatikan i Jasenovac*, 143; P. J. Cohen, *Serbia's Secret War*, 32, 33, 53, and the list on pages 137–52.

6. P. J. Cohen, *Drugi svetski rat*, 26.

7. Like Kosta Pećanac's, Momčilo Đujić's or Pavle Đurišić's Montenegrin Chetniks, Dimitrije Ljotić's Serbian Volunteers, and others.

8. P. J. Cohen, *Drugi svetski rat*, 26; Banac, "Bosnian Muslims," 143.

9. Cigar, *Genocide in Bosnia*, 18, 19; Duraković, *Prokletstvo Muslimana*, 138–42. Soviet leader Joseph Stalin maintained ties with Draža Mihajlović's headquarters through Vasić until the Teheran Conference in November-December, 1943.

10. Malcolm, *Bosnia*, 188.

11. Jozo Tomashevich, *The Chetniks*, 218.

12. Ibid., 233, 234, 247.

13. P. J. Cohen, *Drugi svetski rat*, 34; J. Tomashevich, *The Chetniks*, 162.

14. Alexander, *Trostruki mit*, 51; idem., *Church and State*, 34n. 133.

15. Juraj Batelja, *Sluga Božji Alojzije Stepinac*, 29; Alexander, *Church and State*, 19.

16. Batelja, *Sluga Božji Alojzije Stepinac*, 25. This is a quotation from the Bible (Psalm 118:23): *A Domino factum est istud hoc est mirabile in oculis nostris*. For the whole letter, see Dedijer, *Vatikan i Jasenovac*, 109–11. See also Fiorello Cavalli, *Il processo dell'arcivescovo di Zagabria*, 74, 75.

17. Richard West, *Tito and the Rise and Fall of Yugoslavia*, 384.

18. In his memoirs, Ivan Meštrović writes that, regarding the fate of Serbs in NDH, Poglavnik told him during the war: "I do not care about the Catholic Church," and that he would be contented if the Serbs "would declare themselves as Croats. Then, we'll create Croatian Orthodox Church and settle the disagreement." (*Spomini*, 438).

19. Alexander, *Church and State*, 22. See, e.g., Petar Požar, *Hrvatska pravoslavna crkva u prošlosti i budućnosti*, 88–91.

20. Alexander, *Church and State*, 25, 156; Pedro Ramet, "The Serbian Orthodox Church," in *Eastern Christianity and Politics*, ed. idem., 237, 238.

21. See also P. Ramet, "Serbian Orthodox Church," 237; Alexander, 1979, 11, 24, 25.

22. Cavalli, *Il processo*, 225. See also Alexander, *Church and State*, 27, 33.

23. Alexander, *Church and State*, 26, 27, 28.

24. For its contents, see Cavalli, *Il processo*, 205–208.

25. Ibid., 122–25, 210–29; Dedijer, *Vatikan i Jasenovac*, 470, 471. However, he believed that these "acts" were "the reaction to a politics mostly in the past twenty years and to crimes of the Chetniks and Communist" (Cavalli, *Il processo*, 215, 216, 220, 221, 228).

26. Požar, *Hrvatska pravoslavna*, 215.

27. Ibid., 240–55. For further discussion, documents, and data, see ibid., 103–370.

28. Alexander, *Church and State*, 28; idem., *Trostruki mit*, 55n. 4. For his condemnation of such politics, see Cavalli, *Il processo*, 121, 122. Ustasha authorities sent a parish priest, Father Franjo Rihar, to Jasenovac. Father Rihar did not want that "Te Deum" sung in his church in honor of independence day on April 10, 1942. He was killed there some months later.

29. Ćiril Petešić, *Katoličko svećeništvo u NOB-u, 1941–1945*, 95–97. Mišić added that if the right methods were not applied, "we will lose the chance to contribute in favor of the Croatian cause and of the Holy Catholic cause by becoming the majority in Bosnia Herzegovina" (letter to Stepinac, August 18, 1941 in Cavalli, *Il processo*, 217, 218).

30. Alexander, *Trostruki mit*, 72.

31. For Muslims, the Qur'an replaces the crucifix. However, the Episcopal Conference of the Roman Catholic Church in Croatia officially prohibited them on October 15, 1943 (Cavalli, *Il processo*, 201n. 1).

32. Dedijer, *Vatikan i Jasenovac*, 61.

33. Ibid., 111–15.

34. Alexander, *Church and State*, 29.

35. For a list of pro-Ustasha Catholic priests and friars, see Pattee, *Case of Cardinal Aloysius Stepinac*, 131; Dedijer, *Vatikan i Jasenovac*, 169–82; and Alexander, *Church and State*, 28.

36. Alexander, *Trostruki mit*, 70.

37. Šanjek, *Kršćanstvo na hrvatskom prostoru*, 373–76; Tanner, *Croatia*, 155.

38. See, e.g., Alexander, *Church and State*, 34.

39. Cavalli, *Il processo*, 278, 279.

40. Ibid., 253–56. For his protests and letters to the Ustasha regime regarding the persecutions, see ibid., 82–84, 176–86.

41. Alexander, *Trostruki mit*, 79. Estimates are available in ibid., 73, and P. J. Cohen, *Serbia's Secret War*, 93. In private, he called the Ustasha "bandits and madmen, just like Hitler." For him, Pavelić was a "traitor" (Meštrović, *Spomini*, 442).

42. Alexander, *Trostruki mit*, 71, 72. For example, there are reports that he succeeded in rescuing "7,000 children, belonging to Partisan [and Serbian] families, from camps and putting them into private families" (idem., *Church and State*, 36, 75; idem., *Trostruki mit*, 72).

43. Alexander, *Trostruki mit*, 74; Meštrović, *Spomini*, 442; Anthony Henry O'Brien, *Archbishop Stepinac: The Man and His Case*, 23; Cavalli, *Il processo*, 94; Pattee, *Case of Cardinal Aloysius Stepinac*, 55–65; Šanjek, *Kršćanstvo na hrvatskom prostoru*, 370; and Alexander, *Church and State*, 21, 34n. 132.

44. For studies of relations between the Roman Catholic Church and right-wing and fascist movements during the interwar period, see Wolf and Hoensch, eds., *Catholics*.

45. For his post–World War II years, see Bogdan Krizman, *Pavelić u bjekstvu*.

46. Zirojević, "Kosovo u kolektivnom pamćenju," 210.

47. Alexander, *Church and State*, 14, 15.

48. P. J. Cohen, *Serbia's Secret War*, 45.

49. Alexander, *Church and State*, 16, 18n. 54.

50. Friedman, *Bosnian Muslims*, 125.

51. Banac, "Bosnian Muslims," 141. See also Duraković, *Prokletstvo Muslimana*, 130, 131.

52. Friedman, *Bosnian Muslims*, 122.

53. Duraković, *Prokletstvo Muslimana*, 132; Imamović, *Historija Bošnjaka*, 536; Friedman, *Bosnian Muslims*, 123.

54. Friedman, *Bosnian Muslims*, 122, 123; Atif Hadžikadić, "Potomci hrvatskog plemstva," in *Hrvatsko podrijetlo*, ed. Šarac and Primorac; Kasim Gujić, "Hrvatstvo Muslimana u Bosni i Hercegovini," in *Hrvatsko podrijetlo*, ed. Šarac and Primorac, 73; Banac, "Bosnian Muslims," 141. See also Duraković, *Prokletstvo Muslimana*, 132n. 56.

55. See data in Imamović, *Historija Bošnjaka*, 530–32.

56. A unit from this division was involved in an interesting incident in Villefranche-du-Rouergue in France's Department of Aveyron, where it had been sent for military training. Instead of sending the Muslims back to the Balkans to fight the Chetniks after they completed their training, the Germans decided to send them to the Russian front. On September 17, 1943, led by Ferid Džanić (a former partisan officer), the soldiers mutinied and killed a number of German officers. They were eventually encircled by German troops and severely punished. A monument was erected in Villefranche to commemorate the "Croat mutiny," as it came to be known.

57. Imamović, *Historija Bošnjaka*, 535; Mehtić, *Uloga Ilmije*, 8; Duraković, *Prokletstvo Muslimana*, 134, 135; Hadžijahić, *Islam i Musliman*, 136; idem., Traljić, and Šukrić, *Islam i Muslimani*, 136–37.

58. See, e.g., Duraković, *Prokletstvo Muslimana*, 150–52.

59. Malcolm, *Bosnia*, 190, 191.

60. Žerjavić, *Gubici stanovništva*, 71. The total number of war victims for all of postwar Yugoslavia was 1,027,000, including 530,000 Serbs, 192,000 Croats, and 103,000 Muslims (ibid., 70, 73).

61. See, e.g., P. J. Cohen, *Serbia's Secret War*, 63, 64, 73–84. Žerjavić, *Gubici stanovništva*, 73. See also Freidenreich, *Jews of Yugoslavia*, 192. P. J. Cohen estimates that only fifteen thousand of Yugoslavia's 82,500 Jews survived (*Serbia's Secret War*, 93).

62. Malcolm, *Bosnia*, 176. Žerjavić says there were nine thousand (*Gubici stanovništva*, 73).

63. Dedijer, *Vatikan i Jasenovac*, 294n. 2.

64. See documents in ibid., 151–53, 155–58.

65. P. J. Cohen, *Serbia's Secret War*, 93; Pinto, *Jevreji Sarajeva*, 182–93. For a review of the annihilation of Jews in different towns in Bosnia-Herzegovina, see ibid., 165–81. Thirteen Bosnian Jews also fought on the Republican side in the Spanish Civil War.

66. Alexander, *Church and State*, 49, 50.

67. Owen Chadwick, *The Christian Church in the Cold War*, 36–39; Alexander, *Church and State*, 49, 49n. 188, 49n. 189.

68. For a list, see Jakov Blažević, "Predgovor reprintu," in *Magnum Crimen: Pola vijeka klerikalizma u Hrvatskoj*, by Viktor Novak, xix.

69. Alexander, *Church and State*, 49, 50.

70. Some Slovenian Catholic clergymen also joined the National Liberation Army. For a review and comments on the cooperation of the Catholic clergy with the partisans, see Petešić, *Katoličko svećeništvo*.

71. Imamović, *Historija Bošnjaka*, 536; Mehtić, *Uloga Ilmije*, 14.

72. Bougarel, "From Young Muslims," 538.

73. Purivatra, *Nacionalni i politički*, 62. On that occasion, one of the leading communist leaders, Rodoljub Čolaković, stated that "our Muslims brothers" were equal with Serbs and Croats and that they would not be "forced to declare themselves as Serbs and Croats." He guaranteed them "full freedom in their national determination" (Duraković, *Prokletstvo Muslimana*, 165).

CHAPTER 8. *M* OR *m*?

1. See Požar, *Hrvatska pravoslavna*, 339–62.

2. A group of seven U.S. Protestant clergymen invited by the Yugoslav government in mid-1947 to document religious freedom came to a number of interesting conclusions. The group met with representatives from all religious com-

munities. In their report, "Religion in Yugoslavia: A Report on Conferences with Roman Catholic, Orthodox, Muslim, Jewish and Protestant Leaders and Investigations Through the Medium of Religious Institutions and Documents," they stated that although some tension did exist, the door to religious harmony and cooperation was open. Persecution was limited to individual clergymen who had collaborated with the enemy and not the church as a whole (Pattee, *Case of Cardinal Aloysius Stepinac*, 51). However, state authorities carefully managed the visit, maintaining pressure on members of the clergy who met with the Americans during their stay.

3. Alexander, *Church and State*, 166.

4. Ibid., 213–19.

5. Ibid., 131, 132, 251.

6. Lenard J. Cohen, "Bosnia's Tribal Gods: The Role of Religion in Nationalistic Politics," in *Religion and the War*, ed. Mojzes, 45, 46.

7. Esad Ćimić, "Bosnian Crossroads," in *Religion and the War*, ed. Mojzes, 138; L. Cohen, "Bosnia's Tribal Gods," 48 errata.

8. Chadwick, *Christian Church*, 181. See also L. Cohen, "Bosnia's Tribal Gods," 50–54.

9. Rusinow, 1977, 106; Pedro Ramet, *Nationalism and Federalism in Yugoslavia, 1963–1983*, 54, 55. This model differed from the Soviet one in its objective: The Soviets' goal was to gradually blend the various peoples living within their borders into one Soviet nation.

10. *"Bratstvo i jedinstvo,"* in the original text.

11. Friedman, *Bosnian Muslims*, 145, 146; P. Ramet, *Nationalism and Federalism*, 55, 146, 147; idem., "Serbian Orthodox Church," 243.

12. Mitja Hafner-Fink, "Jugoslovanska družba ali "jugoslovanske" družbekomparativna analiza socialne stratifikacije" (Ph.D. diss. University of Ljubljana, 1993), 178–81.

13. Milovan Djilas, *Članki, 1941–1946*, 59, 77; Stevan K. Pavlowitch, *The Improbable Survivor: Yugoslavia and Its Problems, 1918–1988*, 41.

14. Ivan Čolović, *Bordel ratnika: folklor, politika I rat*, 32.

15. Djilas, *Članki*, 134; Franjo Tudjman, *Stvaranje socialističke Jugoslavije*, 33–37; Alenka Puhar, "Genij in nekaj gnusnih klevet," *Delo*, August 23, 1997, 31.

16. For a typical review of Tito's life, see Kurtović, *Komunisti i nacionalne slobode*, 574.

17. Puhar, "Genij in nekaj," 31.

18. Pirjevec, *Jugoslavija*, 366.

19. Viktor Meier, *Zakaj je razpadla Jugoslavija*, 37; Malcolm, *Bosnia*, 216. Similar data can be found in Tanner, *Croatia*, 191.

20. George Schöpflin, "Nationality in the Fabric of Yugoslav Politics," *Survey* 25, no. 3 (1980): 15. See also Pirjevec, *Jugoslavija*, 366. Meier states that 60% of the officer corps was from Serbia and Montenegro (*Zakaj je razpadla Jugoslavija*, 20). Bougarel, on the other hand, estimates that they represented 65–70% in the late 1980s (*Bosnie*, 119n. 8).

21. Tanner, *Croatia*, 197.

22. Donia and Fine, *Bosnia Herzegovina*, 183; Schöpflin, "Nationality in the Fabric," 8, 9.

23. Nora Beloff, *Tito's Flawed Legacy: Yugoslavia and the West, 1939–1984*, 33; Alexander, *Trostruki mit*, 87, 100n. 3.

24. Pirjevec, *Jugoslavija*, 162 Alexander, *Church and State*, 69–73.

25. Sabrina Petra Ramet, *Balkan Babel: Politics, Culture, and Religion in Yugoslavia*, 126; Alexander, *Trostruki mit*, 12, 128.

26. For the most important parts of his speech, see Batelja, *Sluga Božji Alojzije Stepinac*, 53–60; Cavalli, *Il processo*, 147–58; and Dedijer, *Vatikan i Jasenovac*, 691–95.

27. Robert F. Miller, "Church and State in Yugoslavia: Exorcising the Spectre of 'Clerico-Nationalism'," in *Religion and Politics in Communist States*, ed. idem. and T. H. Rigby, 81, 82.

28. Cavalli, *Il processo*, 7.

29. Alexander, *Trostruki mit*, 133, 134.

30. Ibid., 11, 12.

31. Batelja, *Sluga Božji Alojzije Stepinac*, 67, 68–78; Tanner, *Croatia*, 187.

32. Alexander, *Trostruki mit*, 93. See, e.g., Chadwick, *Christian Church*, 14, 15.

33. O'Brien, *Archbishop Stepinac*, 36; Pattee, *Case of Cardinal Aloysius Stepinac*, 149.

34. Tomo Vukšić, "Od 1918 do naših dana," in *Katoličanstvo u Bosni i Hercegovini*, 113.

35. West, *Tito*, 391; Sells, *Bridge Betrayed*, 197n. 35.

36. Pirjevec, *Jugoslavija*, 168.

37. Alexander, *Church and State*, 69. For an analytical review of mutual relations between the state, the League of Communists, and the Roman Catholic Church, see Zdenko Roter, *Katoliška cerkev in država v Jugoslaviji, 1945–1973*, 173–240.

38. S. Ramet, *Balkan Babel*, 129, 130; Alexander, *Church and State*, 229.

39. S. Ramet, *Balkan Babel*, 131, 132.

40. Chadwick, *Christian Church*, 17–19.

41. Roter, *Katoliška cerkev*, 276–83. See also S. Ramet, *Balkan Babel*, 133.

42. Pirjevec, *Jugoslavija*, 324.

43. See ibid., 167, 168, 402; P. Ramet, *Nationalism and Federalism*, 97; and Meier, *Zakaj je razpadla Jugoslavija*, 38–40, 190.

44. See Pedro Ramet, *Cross and Commissar: The Politics of Religion in Eastern Europe and the USSR*, 109–11; S. Ramet, *Balkan Babel*, 122, 138, 139. See also Šanjek, *Kršćanstvo na hrvatskom prostoru*, 387, 390.

45. Kuharić, like Stepinac, hails from the hamlet of Krašić, which has been dubbed the "Valley of the Cardinals."

46. Mandić, "Herceg-Bosna i Hrvatska," 142; Franjo Tudjman, *Nationalism in Contemporary Europe*, 115. Or that the "majority of the population of Bosnia Herzegovina is Croatian" (ibid., 114).

47. Bax, *Medjugorje*, 12, 13.

48. Ibid., 13–15.

49. Ibid., 68–73; Mary Craig, *Spark from Heaven: The Mystery of the Madonna of Medjugorje*, 17.

50. Bax, *Medjugorje*, 13–15, 25.

51. Christopher Cviic, "A Fatima in a Communist Land?" *Religion in Communist Lands* 10, no. 1 (1982): 4.

52. See, e.g., Chadwick, *Christian Church*, 17.

53. S. Ramet, *Balkan Babel*, 139; Bax, *Medjugorje*, 9, 24, 25.

54. Chadwick, *Christian Church*, 76; Kenny, 1991, 7; Cviic, "Fatima," 5.

55. Cviic, "Fatima," 5, 6.

56. Ibid., 7.

57. See also Chadwick, *Christian Church*, 197.

58. Alexander, *Church and State*, 165, 166.

59. J. Tomashevich, *Chetniks*, 177, 178; Radmila Radić, "Serbian Orthodox Church and the War in Bosnia Herzegovina," in *Religion and the War*, ed. Mojzes, 177n. 50.

60. Pirjevec, *Jugoslavija*, 240; J. Tomashevich, *Chetniks*, 176, 177. See also Alexander, 1979, 174. Nastić's fate is especially interesting. He was one of the few Serbian Orthodox priests to survive the war in the NDH, he turned down Pavelić's offer to lead the Croatian Orthodox Church, and he was even associated with the partisans for a while. In February, 1947, the authorities tried him for hostile propaganda, assisting terrorists, and undermining Yugoslavia's military and economic might. He was sentenced to eleven years' imprisonment, but was pardoned after serving three. He spent the rest of his life in various monasteries (Alexander, *Church and State*, 174–78).

61. *Udruženje pravoslavnih svećenika Jugoslavije* (UPSJ).

62. Alexander, *Church and State*, 188, 189–91; S. Ramet, *Balkan Babel*, 153–59.

63. This concern was justified: there are calls today for Montenegro's ecclesiastical autonomy. An example of this occurred during Christmas, 1995, when two *badnjaks* (Christmas clogs) were lit instead of the customary one. Serbian Orthodox bishop Amfilohije of Montenegro lit one, and the second was lit by proponents of an autocephalous Montenegrin Orthodox Church.

64. Bročić, "Position and Activities," 359; P. Ramet, "Religion and Nationalism," 312; idem., "Autocephaly," 14; idem., "Serbian Orthodox Church," 240; Chadwick, *Christian Church*, 32, 33, 100.

65. Most prominent Serbian Orthodox dignitaries and theologians—including Jevtić, Bulović, and Radović—also signed it.

66. The truth of the matter is that some Orthodox churches were, indeed, attacked in this autonomous province, and part of the Peć monastery was damaged.

67. Beloff, *Tito's Flawed Legacy*, 202.

68. Vesna Pešić, "Rat za nacionalne države," in *Srpska strana rata*, ed. Popov, 33n. 48.

69. Friedman, *Bosnian Muslims*, 192; Radić, "Serbian Orthodox Church,"

168; Cigar, *Genocide in Bosnia*, 30. See also Duraković, *Prokletstvo Muslimana*, 195. In the 1980s, when Serbs represented about 32% of Bosnia-Herzegovina's population, their share was 46% in the League of Communists, 54% in the Administration of Justice, 56% in the universities, almost 50% in the police forces, and 57% in high positions in economics. The situation was similar in the spheres of culture and the media (Duraković, *Prokletstvo Muslimana*, 195).

70. Dubravka Stojanović, "Traumatični krug srpske opozicije," in *Srpska strana rata*, ed. Popov, 511.

71. There were 6,853 in 1948, according to the first postwar census (Žerjavić, *Gubici stanovništva*, 136).

72. Pinto, *Jevreji Sarajeva*, 16; Freidenreich, *Jews of Yugoslavia*, 193–210; Bakić, *Nacija i religija*, 204n. 85.

73. Bougarel, "From Young Muslims," 538.

74. Irwin, "Islamic Revival," 440, 441. See M. Hadžijahić, Traljić, and Šukrić, *Islam i Muslimani*, 156–58.

75. Kurtović, *Komunisti i nacionalne slobode*, 92. See, e.g., Sabrina Petra Ramet, "Islam in Yugoslavia Today," *Religion in Communist Lands* 18, no. 3 (1990): 230, 231.

76. M. Hadžijahić, Traljić, and Šukrić, *Islam i Muslimani*, 159. See also Mohammad Bin Nasir Al-Aboudi, "Muslim Experiences in Eastern Europe: A Firsthand Report," *Journal of Muslim Minority Affairs* 1 (1986): 91–99; Alexandre Popovic, "La communaute Musulmane de Yougoslavie sous le regime communiste: Coup d'oeil sur son histoire et sur les principales institutions," in *Les religions a l'est*, ed. Patrick Michel, 176–81.

77. Friedman, *Bosnian Muslims*, 189.

78. S. Ramet, "Islam in Yugoslavia," 232–35.

79. Bakić, *Nacija i religija*, 194.

80. In different sources these numbers slightly differ (for some ten persons).

81. Banac, "Bosnian Muslims," 144, 145.

82. Duraković, *Prokletstvo Muslimana*, 47.

83. All estimates are taken from Dyker, "Ethnic Muslims of Bosnia," 241, 242; and Friedman, *Bosnian Muslims*, 155, 156.

84. See also Kržišnik-Bukić, *Bosanska identiteta*, 40, 42; Imamović, *Historija Bošnjaka*, 555.

85. Pirjevec, *Jugoslavija*, 164; Banac, "Bosnian Muslims," 144; Moša Pijade, *Izbrani spisi: I. tom, 5. knjiga*, 947–49.

86. See, e.g., Schöpflin, "Nationality in the Fabric," 9; Irwin, "Islamic Revival," 438; P. Ramet, "Primordial Ethnicity," 176.

87. Banac, "Bosnian Muslims," 145. See also Irwin, "Islamic Revival," 445, 446. In the Serbian, Croatian, and Bosniak languages, *Muslim* in the sense of religious identity is written *musliman. Musliman* is used when referring to national identity.

88. See also Pešić, "Rat za nacionalne države," 35n. 53.

89. Todo Kurtović, *Komunisti i nacionalne slobode*, 37.

90. See, e.g., Malcolm, *Bosnia*, 199, 204; Pirjevec, *Jugoslavija*, 286; and P. Ramet, *Nationalism and Federalism*, 147.

91. Irwin, "Islamic Revival," 444; Pirjevec, *Jugoslavija*, 285, 286.

92. Duraković, *Prokletstvo Muslimana*, 208n. 116.

93. See also Popovic, "La communaute Musulmane," 174.

94. Friedman, *Bosnian Muslims*, 159; P. Ramet, *Nationalism and Federalism*, 153. See Irwin, "Islamic Revival," 449, 450.

95. Tanner, *Croatia*, 193; Friedman, *Bosnian Muslims*, 158, 159.

96. See also Pirjevec, *Jugoslavija*, 373; and Meier, *Zakaj je razpadla Jugoslavija*, 41.

97. Bougarel, "From Young Muslims," 546.

98. Alija Izetbegović, *Islamska deklaracija*, 1.

99. Ibid, 22, 32, 38, 57.

100. Pirjevec, *Jugoslavija*, 371.

101. This reproof was quite inappropriate and contradictory, if for no other reason than that the revolution in Iran was not a socialist one. Unlike the Sunni majority (including Bosnian Muslims), most Iranians are Shiites.

102. See P. Ramet, "Religion and Nationalism," 323–26.

103. S. Ramet, "Islam in Yugoslavia," 232; L. Cohen, "Bosnia's Tribal Gods," 53, 54.

104. Xavier Bougarel, "Ramadan During a Civil War (As Reflected in a Series of Sermons)," *Islam and Christian Muslim Relations* 1 (1995): 80.

105. Data for both is in Bakić, *Nacija i religija*, 75.

106. Ibid., 67, 68.

107. L. Cohen, "Bosnia's Tribal Gods," 52, 53, errata; Xavier Bougarel, "L'Islam bosniaque, entre identité culturelle et idéologie politique," in *Le Nouvel Islam balqanique: Les musulmans, acteurs du post-communisme, 1990–2000*, ed. Xavier Bougarel and Nathalie Clayer, 83.

CHAPTER 9. A WAR OVER DIFFERENCES

1. See, e.g., Zoran N. Marković, "Nacija-žrtva i osveta," in *Srpska strana rata*, ed. Popov, 640–52. For an analysis of political rhetoric in the later Socialist years in Yugoslavia, see Ivo Žanić, *Mitologija inflacije: Govor kriznog doba*. One of the most disreputable scandals involved the agro combine "Agrokomerc" in Velika Kladuša in northwestern Bosnia in the autumn of 1987. Fikret Abdić, who later became leader of Muslims in the region, headed the organization.

2. Bougarel, *Bosnie*, 58.

3. Stjepko Golubic, Susan Campbell, and Thomas Golubic, "How Not to Divide the Indivisible," in *Why Bosnia?* ed. Ali and Lifschultz, 211, 212, 230, 231.

4. See, e.g., Xavier Bougarel, "Bosnia and Herzegovina: State and Communitarianism," in *Yugoslavia and After: A Study in Fragmentation, Despair, and Rebirth*, ed. David A. Dyker and Ivan Vejvoda, 102.

5. For the chronology, see Branka Magaš and Ivo Žanić, eds., *Rat u Hrvatskoj i Bosni i Hercegovini*, 371–99, and added maps.

6. As Bougarel points out, "the non-nationalist or 'civic' parties were supported rather by the urban intellectual elites and the working-class social strata created by the economic development of the postwar period" ("Bosnia and Herzegovina," 97)

7. Malcolm, *Bosnia*, 231.

8. For the JNA's plans and those of Milošević's League of Communists of Serbia and later the Socialistic Party of Serbia on how to reunite pro-Serb parts of Yugoslavia during the years of its disintegration, see Marija Obradović, "Vladajuća stranka," in *Srpska strana rata*, ed. Popov, 491–93.

9. Golubic, Campbell, and Golubic, "How Not to Divide," 211, 212.

10. Ibid., 213–17.

11. Tismaneanu, *Fantasies of Salvation*, 15.

12. See Olivera Milosavljević, "Zloupotreba autoriteta nauke," in *Srpska strana rata*, ed. Popov, 306–16.

13. Banac, "Bosnian Muslims," 146. Similary, Cigar points out that it "crystallized the revival among Serbian intellectuals of earlier nationalist goals" (*Genocide in Bosnia*, 23).

14. See Olivera Milosavljević, "Jugoslavija kao zabluda," in *Srpska strana rata*, ed. Popov, 76–82. With the help of staged political rallies described as "manifestations of the people" and "antibureaucratic revolutions," the Milošević government abolished the autonomy of the provinces of Kosovo and Vojvodina in all but name, subdued Montenegro, and instigated and supported the armed resistance of Croatian and Bosnian Serbs. In 1988, attendance at pro-Milošević " Meetings of Truth" reached 3,360,000 (Milosavljević, "Zloupotreba autoriteta nauke," 337).

15. See examples in Gojković, "Trauma bez katarze." For expressions and slogans most frequently used at Serb rallies in the late 1980s, see Ivan Čolović, *Pucanje od zdravlja*, 23–39; Milosavljević, "Jugoslavija kao zabluda," 80; Zirojević, "Kosovo u kolektivnom pamćenju," 228n. 66. For the evolution of football fan rhetoric into nationalistic and militant, see Ivan Čolović, "Fudbal, huligani i rat," in *Srpska strana rata*, ed. Popov.

16. Sreten Vujović, "Nelagoda od grada," in *Srpska strana rata*, ed. Popov, 151. Mladić was born in the same Bosnian village, Bradina, as Ante Pavelić (Tanner, *Croatia*, 231).

17. Milosavljević, "Zloupotreba autoriteta nauke," 316–22; Sells, *Bridge Betrayed*, 121, 122; Cigar, *Genocide in Bosnia*, 69, 70, 77, 78; Čolović, *Pucanje od zdravlja*, 70; Branislav Milinković, "Propaganda and the Structure of the Public in Serbia," in *Propaganda in War*, ed. Marjan Malešić, 171, 172.

18. Čolović, *Pucanje od zdravlja*, 66, 68; Stojanović, "Traumatični krug srpske opozicije," 514; Malcolm, *Bosnia*, 228, 229.

19. Čolović, *Bordel ratnika*, 110.

20. Čolović, *Pucanje od zdravlja*, 37, Milinković, "Propaganda," 170, 171.

21. *"Sini jarko sunce sa Kosova, ne damo te zemljo Dušanova,"* in the original.

22. Aleksandar Nenadović, "'Politika' u nacionalističkoj oluji," in *Srpska strana rata*, ed. Popov, 604n. 12; Zirojević, "Kosovo u kolektivnom pamćenju," 230.

23. Radić, "Serbian Orthodox Church," 167, 168; L. Cohen, "Bosnia's Tribal Gods," 57.

24. Nebojša Popov, "Traumatologija partijske države," in *Srpska strana rata*, ed. Popov, 89.

25. Čolović, *Bordel ratnika*, 34.

26. Ibid., 159.

27. Radić, "Serbian Orthodox Church," 178; idem., "Crkva i 'srpsko pitanje'," 291; Meier, *Zakaj je razpadla Jugoslavija*, 71.

28. Norris, *Islam in the Balkans*, 295, 296.

29. Marjan Malešić, "Printed Media Empirics," in *Propaganda in War*, ed. idem., 121; Milinković, "Propaganda," 172; Cigar, *Genocide in Bosnia*, 77.

30. For more of his statements and opinions, see Cigar, *Genocide in Bosnia*, 26, 27.

31. Ibid., 76. The fate of Serbs and Jews was also compared by D. Ćosić.

32. Sells, *Bridge Betrayed*, 23.

33. *Srbosjek* or *Srbožder*.

34. He comes from interesting family background: his father taught religious education at the local school and his mother was a Communist.

35. Čolović, *Bordel ratnika*, 30, 31.

36. Ibid., 102, 103.

37. Čolović, *Pucanje od zdravlja*, 23.

38. Ibid., 25, 83.

39. P. J. Cohen, *Drugi svetski rat*, 10.

40. If I may use Adam Michnik's synthagma, "old demons."

41. P. J. Cohen, *Drugi svetski rat*, 11–15.

42. Čolović, *Bordel ratnika*, 105, 118.

43. Čolović, *Pucanje od zdravlja*, 36, 37.

44. Ibid., 112, 113.

45. S. Ramet, "Islam in Yugoslavia," 226.

46. Čolović, *Pucanje od zdravlja*, 65, 69, 70, 117; Sreten Vujović, *Grad u senci rata*, 96. For Radovan Karadžić's arguments for Croatian Serb and Bosnian Serb national messianism, see Popov, "Traumatologija partijske države," 114, 115.

47. Sabrina Petra Ramet, "Nationalism and the 'Idiocy' of the Countryside: The Case of Serbia," *Ethnic and Racial Studies* 19, no. 1 (1996): 70.

48. Ibid., 74–76.

49. For more examples of similar statements see Vujović, "Nelagoda od grada," 136–52.

50. Čolović, *Pucanje od zdravlja*, 28–32, 116. Vučurović's nickname, "Kamijondžija," means the lorry driver.

51. Kržišnik-Bukić, *Bosanska identiteta*, 48.

52. Marjan Malešić, "Television Empirics (Serbian Television, Croatian Television)," in *Propaganda in War*, ed. Malešić, 75.

53. Magaš and Žanić, eds., *Rat u Hrvatskoj*, 119n. 1, 120n. 1. See also Zgodić, *Ideologija nacionalnog mesijanstva*, 191–200; Tanner, *Croatia*, 242; Sells, *Bridge Betrayed*, 95. See also L. Cohen, "Bosnia's Tribal Gods," 56.

54. For more on works about Croatian martyrs, see, e.g., Kordić, *Hrvatski mučenici Pavao Radić i Đuro Basariček*; Rudolf Švagel-Resić, *Hrvatski mučenici*; and Mladen Pavković, *Hrvatski mučenici*.

55. Nikica Mihaljević, "Hrvaška v duhovno-kulturnih razvalinah," *Delo (Ljubljana)*, August-September, 1994, 6.

56. Quoted in the Slovenian daily *Delo*, April 25, 1998.

57. Dubravka Ugrešić, *Kultura laži: Antipolitički eseji*, 174; Mihaljević, "Hrvaška v duhovno-kulturnih razvalinah."

58. *"Za dom, spremni!"*

59. Čolović, *Bordel ratnika*, 126, 127.

60. Malcolm, *Bosnia*, 218, 219.

61. Srdjan Vrcan, "La guerra nell'ex Jugoslavia: il coinvolgimento delle religioni," in *Mare di guerra, mare di religioni*, ed. Luciano Martini, 166.

62. See, e.g., Bougarel, "L'Islam bosniaque," 103, 104; and Alireza Bagherzadeh, "L'ingérence iranienne en Bosnie-Herzégovine," in *Le Nouvel Islam balqanique*, ed. Bougarel and Clayer, 402–406. See also Jérôme Bellion-Jordan, "Les réseaux transnationaux islamiques en Bosnie-Herzegovine," in *Le Nouvel Islam balqanique*, ed. Bougarel and Clayer. According to CIA estimates, almost half of the arms supplied to the Bosniak side throughout the war came from Iran (Bagherzadeh, "L'ingérence iranienne," 399), and, according to some American estimates, no more than five hundred advisers were dispatched. (ibid.," 400).

63. Mehtić, *Uloga Ilmije*, 14.

64. At the same time, some Serbian troops mutinied in Banja Luka.

65. Kržišnik-Bukić, *Bosanska identiteta*, 65.

66. Fine, "Medieval and Ottoman Roots," 1. The Bosnian army consisted predominately of Bosniaks. About 20% were Croats, and 15% were Serbs (Jovan Divjak, "Prva faza rata, 1992–1993: borba za opstanak i nastanak Armije BiH," in *Rat u Hrvatskoj*, ed. Magaš and Žanić, 201); Bougarel, *Bosnie*, 13, 14.

67. Cigar, *Genocide in Bosnia*, 12; Murad, "Death of Muslim Bosnia," 8; Sells, *Bridge Betrayed*, 128.

68. Cigar, *Genocide in Bosnia*, 120.

69. For a more detailed account and more examples, see Sells, *Bridge Betrayed*, 126, 127, 133–36; Malcolm, *Bosnia*, 239, 242, 245, 246; and Cigar, *Genocide in Bosnia*, 11, 12.

70. See also Sells, *Bridge Betrayed*, 195n. 18. For similar statements and the anti-Islamic attitude of Russian nationalist Zhirinovski, see Cigar, *Genocide in Bosnia*, 79, 113.

71. Eric J. Hobsbawm, *Nations and Nationalism since 1780*, 91.

72. *"Stan'te, paše i ustaše!"*

73. Ranko Bugarski, *Jezik od mira do rata*, 80–82. See also Igor Kotnik, "The Use of Language in Propaganda," in *Propaganda in War*, ed. Marjan Malešić, 144–

55. For an excellent cultural-anthropological comparative study of the politicization and militarization of folk heritage, oral tradition and epics, legends, mythic motives, heroic characters and the language itself, propaganda terminology, its syntax, and *"guslar* estrade," see Ivo Žanić, *Prevarena povijest: Guslarska estrada, kult hajduka i rat u Hrvatskoj i Bosni i Hercegovini, 1990–1995. godine.*

74. Bugarski, *Jezik od mira do rata,* 113, 114, 115–26; Čolović, *Pucanje od zdravlja,* 54n. 1.

75. For more detailed classification, see Mitja Velikonja, "Religija in cerkev: dejavnika oblikovanja nacionalnih mitologij v postsocialističnih družbah," *Družboslovne razprave* 12 (1996).

76. Vrcan, *Vjera u vrtlozima tranzicije,* 43. For an analysis of fundamental changes in the field of religion in postsocialist countries, see Smrke, *Religija in politika: Spremembe v deželah prehoda,* 143–80, 181–89.

77. Vrcan, "La guerra nell'ex Jugoslavia," 160; idem., *Vjera u vrtlozima tranzicije,* 21–25, 59, 60; idem., "Orthodoxy in Balkan Political Conflicts," 139; Paul Mojzes, "The Camouflaged Role of Religion in the War in Bosnia Herzegovina," in *Religion and the War,* ed. idem., 81; L. Cohen, "Bosnia's Tribal Gods," 61.

78. Sells, *Bridge Betrayed,* 144. However, it seems that Sells's list completely disregards the actions of Bosniak religious nationalists (although to a lesser degree).

79. According to research conducted in the Bosnian Federation in 1999, 53.7% of Bosniaks and 41.2% of Croats think that either Islam or Christianity is the sole true religion (Vrcan, *Vjera u vrtlozima tranzicije,* 175). Unfortunately, no data are available for the Serbian Republic.

80. Handžić, *Population of Bosnia,* 33–37; Gerard Powers, "Religion, Conflict, and Prospects for Peace in Bosnia, Croatia, and Yugoslavia," in *Religion and the War,* ed. Mojzes, 240n. 68.

81. For example, Croatian forces erected a huge concrete cross in place of a destroyed mosque in Počitelj (Vrcan, *Vjera u vrtlozima tranzicije,* 22). Foreign countries or their religious communities often sponsored reconstruction. The first synagogue to be built in Bosnia-Herzegovina since 1945 is expected to be completed in Mostar by the end of 2002. The cornerstone was laid in early May, 2001.

82. As Petar Anđelović points out, by driving God out of schools, universities, homes, and, finally, out of human souls, the Communists "made room for Evil" (*Vjerni Bogu vjerni Bosni,* 176).

83. Known also as the "Bosnian Mecca," "small hajji," or "hajji for the impoverished" (see M. Hadžijahić, Traljić, and Šukrić, *Islam i Muslimani,* 87; Ivan Lovrenović, "Bosna," *Erasmus* 18 [1996]: 55, 56)

84. *"Laiat at-kadr,"* the night when the Qur'an was revealed to Mohammed.

85. Bakić, *Nacija i religija,* 72; Vrcan, *Vjera u vrtlozima tranzicije,* 167; Dijana Krajina, "Povojni trendi hiperreligioznosti in religijsko-nacionalnega ekskluzivizma (Študija primera Doboja in okolice)," *Časopis za kritiko znanosti* 29 (2001): 248.

86. Latinka Perović, "Beg od modernizacije," in *Srpska strana rata,* ed. Popov, 122. See also Bougarel, *Bosnie,* 42.

87. As Vrcan notes, this "reawakening of the sacred" was "in terms of a return to the faith of the forefathers and of a reaffirmation of religion, but basically as the religion-patrimony which was accompanied by a reaggregation around the traditional ecclesiastical institution" (*Vjera u vrtlozima tranzicije*, 167).

88. Radić, "Crkva i 'srpsko pitanje'," 282; Djordjević, " Serbian Orthodox Church," 157.

89. Mojzes, "Camouflaged Role of Religion," 84. It "gave total and unconditional legitimacy to this re-born and re-awakened Serbian nationalism" and, after the break with Milošević, "full and unconditional legitimacy to the radical nationalist politics of Karadžić in Bosnia and Martić in Croatia" (Vrcan, "Orthodoxy in Balkan Political Conflicts," 150).

90. Khurram Murad, "The Death of Muslim Bosnia: A Tale of Two Cities." *Muslim World Book Review* 1 (1996): 9, 10; Mislav Kukoć, "Konfesije i postkomunistički sukob civilizacija," *Društvena istraživanja* 4, no. 6 (1995): 944. See also Vrcan, "Orthodoxy in Balkan Political Conflicts," 145, for similar constructs of Nikolaj Velimirović and Atanasije Jevtić; Radić, "Serbian Orthodox Church," 165; idem., "Crkva i 'srpsko pitanje'," 278n. 8.

91. *"Bog je Srbin, ne boji se Srbine."* The song is titled, "There will not be a border on the Drina River" (MC, "The Truth will Win," 1994).

92. Žabkar, "Neutrudni kovači stereotipov," 28; Malešić, "Television Empirics," 68.

93. S. Ramet, "Nationalism," 84–86.

94. See, e.g., Radić, "Crkva i 'srpsko pitanje'," 294.

95. Malešić, "Television Empirics," 71; Van Dartel, "Nations and Churches in Yugoslavia," 284. For examples of Patriarch Pavle's anti-Muslim statements, see Cigar, *Genocide in Bosnia*, 67, 68.

96. Radić, "Serbian Orthodox Church," 177, 178.

97. Cigar, *Genocide in Bosnia*, 68; Sells, *Bridge Betrayed*, 85; Vrcan, "Orthodoxy in Balkan Political Conflicts," 145.

98. Cigar, *Genocide in Bosnia*, 36.

99. See also Radić, "Serbian Orthodox Church," 172n. 31; Sells, *Bridge Betrayed*, 82; idem., "Serbian Religious Nationalism, Christoslavism, and the Genocide in Bosnia, 1992–1995," in *Religion*, ed. Mojzes, 206.

100. L. Cohen, "Bosnia's Tribal Gods," 71; Radić, "Crkva i 'srpsko pitanje'," 296.

101. Cigar, *Genocide in Bosnia*, 111.

102. Malešić, "Printed Media Empirics," 102, 103; Čolović, *Pucanje od zdravlja*, 68.

103. Cigar, *Genocide in Bosnia*, 66, 67.

104. Sells, *Bridge Betrayed*, 84, 85. He had already severely attacked Milošević in March, 1992.

105. P. J. Cohen, *Drugi svetski rat*, 12.

106. Čolović, *Bordel ratnika*, 123.

107. Murad, "Death of Muslim Bosnia," 4–10; L. Cohen, "Bosnia's Tribal

Gods," 71, 72; Mojzes, "Camouflaged Role of Religion," 87, 88, 89. For more of Karadžić's and Mladić's statements, see Cigar, *Genocide in Bosnia*, 99–101.

108. L. Cohen, "Bosnia's Tribal Gods," 43, 89; Popov, "Traumatologija partijske države," 115; Radić, "Serbian Orthodox Church," 177; Powers, "Religion," 236; Radić, "Serbian Orthodox Church," 176.

109. Vrcan, "La guerra nell'ex Jugoslavia," 173n; Radić, "Crkva i 'srpsko pitanje'," 294, 295. See also Powers, "Religion," 235.

110. Sells, *Bridge Betrayed*, 189n. 35; Radić, "Serbian Orthodox Church," 175. For Drašković's prewar Greater Serbia political rhetoric and party program, see Stojanović, "Traumatični krug srpske opozicije," 515, 516. For the two-faced Drašković's interwar attitude—from his condemnation of the siege of Dubrovnik, criticism of the Vukovar tragedy, and acceptance of peace proposals from the international community to his enthusiastic support for the military efforts of Serbian units—see ibid., 526–28; and Cigar, *Genocide in Bosnia*, 105, 106.

111. Anton Žabkar, "Neutrudni kovači stereotipov," *Delo*, March 19, 1994, 28.

112. Vrcan, "La guerra nell'ex Jugoslavia," 160–63; Sells, *Bridge Betrayed*, 79. Vrcan distinguishes four main currents within the Serbian Orthodoxy of this period (the last two are less important). The first is radical (militant) to the extreme; the second is more realistic (oriented toward accommodating the present unfavorable situation); the third is more open to the modern world, to the West and democracy; and the last is defined primarily in terms of support and spiritual comfort for those who are traumatized by developments in the last decade (Vrcan, "Orthodoxy in Balkan Political Conflicts," 153, 154).

113. L. Cohen, "Bosnia's Tribal Gods," 63, 64; Paul Mojzes, *Yugoslavian Inferno: Ethnoreligious Warfare in the Balkans*, 130.

114. Igor Antič, "Poletni zapiski iz dežele vitezov," *Delo*, September 21, 1996, 36.

115. Mihaljević, "Hrvaška v duhovno-kulturnih razvalinah."

116. Mojzes, "Camouflaged Role of Religion," 90; S. Ramet, *Balkan Babel*, 121; Mihaljević, "Hrvaška v duhovno-kulturnih razvalinah."

117. Anđelović, *Vjerni Bogu vjerni Bosni*, 207, 208.

118. Sells, *Bridge Betrayed*, 105.

119. L. Cohen, "Bosnia's Tribal Gods," 67; Cigar, *Genocide in Bosnia*, 130.

120. See also Mato Zovkić, "War Wounds in Croatian Catholic Population in Bosnia Herzegovina," in *Religion*, ed. Mojzes, 211, 212; and Cigar, *Genocide in Bosnia*, 131, 132.

121. Sells, *Bridge Betrayed*, 106; Powers, "Religion," 222; Mojzes, "Camouflaged Role of Religion," 91n. 34.

122. Čolović, "Fudbal, huligani i rat," 124.

123. Paul Mojzes, "The Roman Catholic Church in Croatia and Its Contribution to National Sentiment." *Religion, State, and Society* 21, nos. 3–4 (1993): 391, 392.

124. Zovkić, "War Wounds," 208, 209.

125. Vrcan, *Vjera u vrtlozima tranzicije*, 207n. 11. Boris Buden provides an-

other example of Croatian Catholic exclusivity: "Someone said that Europe is ill. That's right. Europe is ill in its wealth. The Croatian nation has preserved its morality and its Christianity" ("'Europe is a Whore,'" in *Media & War*, ed. Brunner Skopljanac, Gredelj Nena, Stjepan Hodžić, Krištofić Alija, and Branimir, 59).

126. As late as the summer of 1998 "religious" passion was aroused by a proposal to build a mosque at Zamet near Rijeka. Three former Croatian soldiers threatened to burn themselves in front of the townhall; a letter of protest was addressed to the "stinking Islamic-Gipsy-Albanian manure" and signed, "The people of Zamet—locals ready for gunpowder and slaughter." Minarets, they claimed, would announce that "Europe had been uprooted from this region."

127. Cigar, *Genocide in Bosnia*, 124.

128. A similar mass, held in Zagreb in 1996, was condemned by Cardinal Kuharić.

129. Anđelović, *Vjerni Bogu vjerni Bosni*, 162, 163, 167; Zovkić, "War Wounds," 210; Powers, "Religion," 245n. 78.

130. Reported in the Slovenian daily *Delo*, April 9, 1998; ibid., May 13, 1998; ibid., May 14, 1998.

131. Bono Zvonimir Šagi, interview with author, "Sveti ratovi ne postoje," *Feral Tribune (Split)*, January 6, 2001, 11.

132. See Batelja, *Sluga Božji Alojzije Stepinac*, 93.

133. Bakić, *Nacija i religija*, 72. See also Vrcan, "La guerra nell'ex Jugoslavia," 171.

134. See Adil Zulfikarpašić, *Okovana Bosna*. Discussion with Vlado Gotovac, Mika Tripalo, and Ivo Banac; and *Bošnjak Adil Zulfikarpašić*. Dialogue with Nadežda Gaće and Milovan Đilas. For Bougarel, "the role of religious structures in the nationalist mobilization is flagrant in the case of Muslim community" (*Bosnie*, 44). See also Bougarel, "Bošnjaci pod kontrolom panislamista," *Dani (Sarajevo)*, June 18, 1999, 46–49; June 25, 1999, 46–49; and July 2, 1999, 48–50.

135. Bougarel, "From Young Muslims," 546; idem., "Ramadan During a Civil War," 99. See also idem., "L'Islam bosniaque," 109, 110.

136. Bougarel, "Bošnjaci pod kontrolom panislamista," *Dani (Sarajevo)*, June 25, 1999, 49. Anthropologist Bringa also states: "As a reaction to and part of the process of the war and the politics behind it, many Bosnian Muslims are redefining both the content and the function of their collective identities, and identifying with a wider world community of Muslims more than before" (*Being Muslim*, 197, 198).

137. For *Reis-ul-Ulema* Mustafa Cerić, without Islam, Islamic civilization, and Islamic culture, "we are nothing." For him, the Bosniak national identity, language, and the army can focus around Islam (Xavier Bougarel, "Le ramadan, révélateur des évolutions de l'islam en Bosnie-Herzégovine," in *Ramadan et politique*, ed. Fariba Adelkhah and François Georgeon, 92, 93).

138. Bougarel, "Ramadan During a Civil War," 98, 99; idem., "Le ramadan," 90; Dženana Karup, "Kur'an je naš ustav," *Dani (Sarajevo)*, March 30, 1998, 16; Zulfikarpašić, *Bošnjak Adil Zulfikarpašić*, 144, 172.

139. Žanić, *Prevarena povijest*, 255.

140. Zulfikarpašić, *Bošnjak Adil Zulfikarpašić*, 172; Mojzes, "Camouflaged

Role of Religion," 94. The Serbian press quickly declared Izetbegović to be the "world's foremost soldier of jihad," just another of his many epithets, such as "leader of the Muslim terrorists," "moderator from Baščaršija," "self-declared president" and "war criminal."

141. Jahić, "Krijeposna muslimanska država," 249–51; Bougarel, "L'Islam bosniaque," 99.

142. Friedman, *Bosnian Muslims*, 223; Mojzes, "Camouflaged Role of Religion," 95; Bellion-Jordan, "Les réseaux transnationaux," 444; L. Cohen, "Bosnia's Tribal Gods," 68; Mehtić, *Uloga Ilmije*, 14.

143. *Zelene beretke, El Mudžahid, Muslimanske snage, Zelena legija, Patriotska liga.* According to Bosniak sources, the El Mujahid military unit consisted of "500–600 Bosniaks and at most 200 Arabs" (Karup, "Kur'an je naš ustav," 15); according to other estimates, from 2,000–3,000 (Bagherzadeh, "L'ingérence iranienne," 401).

144. L. Cohen, "Bosnia's Tribal Gods," 43, 69.

145. For the theological explanation of the significance of *šehids*, see Omerdić, 1997.

146. Cigar, *Genocide in Bosnia*, 137; L. Cohen, "Bosnia's Tribal Gods," 66. In an interview for the Italian Catholic periodical *Jesus* in the winter of 1998, Puljić declared that it was difficult for Catholics to live in Sarajevo because they have serious problems "finding a house or an apartment, job, walk safely on the streets" and that "for all these reasons many of them decide to leave the city" (quoted in *Dani*, March 30, 1998).

147. In 1992, a handbill signed by anonymous "Muslim Brothers" and addressed to the "Children of Allah" explains that "our fatherland Bosnia-Herzegovina is attacked and enslaved by pagans. Chetniks slaughter us, while Latins [traditional name for Catholics] deceive us, they are taking and abducting our land" (Srećko M. Džaja, "Bosna i Bošnjaci u hrvatskom političkom diskursu." *Erazmus* 9 [1994]: 34). According to Latić, "brutal European encirclement would destroy such a state [Islamic] with the atomic bomb if necessary" (Bougarel, "Bošnjaci pod kontrolom panislamista," *Dani* [Sarajevo], June 18, 1999, 47). Meanwhile, Duraković calls Muslims an "exhausted and peaceful nation" and mentions the "old 'damnation' of the Bogomils" and "new Golgothas of the Muslims" (*Prokletstvo Muslimana*, 9, 75, 180).

148. See Mahmed Handžić, *Islamizacija Bosne i Hercegovine i porijeklo bosansko-hercegovačkih Muslimana;* A. Handžić, *Population of Bosnia;* Divjak, "Prva faza rata," 202; and to some degree also Hadžijahić, *Porijeklo bosanskih Muslimana;* and idem., Traljić, and Šukrić, *Islam i Muslimani.*

149. Kržišnik-Bukić, *Bosanska identiteta,* 98.

150. Cigar, *Genocide in Bosnia,* 178.

151. According to Izetbegović critic Muhamed Filipović, "he wanted to return Muslims/Bosniaks to Islam [which was one of the mottos in his 1970 *Islamic Declaration*] and, after many centuries, to create a Muslim state in Europe," interview, "Moški plačani za brado, ženske za feredžo," *Delo,* Saturday supplement, August 5, 2000, 14, 15). Mustafa Cerić also thinks that his "eternal

dream" was the creation of the Muslim state in Bosnia (Adnan Jahić, "Krijeposna muslimanska država," in *Krv boje benzina,* ed. Fatmir Alispahić, 249). On the other hand, Džemaludin Latić, one of the main Bosnian Islamic ideologues, firmly rejects that Izetbegović had such plans (Bougarel, "Bošnjaci pod kontrolom panislamista," *Dani [Sarajevo],* June 18, 1999, 47. See also Vrcan, *Vjera u vrtlozima tranzicije,* 197n. 4).

152. L. Cohen, "Bosnia's Tribal Gods," 60; Malešić, "Printed Media Empirics," 114.

153. Bougarel, "Ramadan During a Civil War," 95.

154. Ibid., 102. See also L. Cohen, "Bosnia's Tribal Gods," 69, 70.

155. Bougarel, "Ramadan During a Civil War," 93, 94; idem., "Le ramadan," 88.

156. Bakić, *Nacija i religija,* 205n. 85.

157. Bougarel, *Bosnie,* 11.

158. Mojzes, "Camouflaged Role of Religion," 96.

159. Vrcan, "Orthodoxy in Balkan Political Conflicts," 151.

160. Radić, "Crkva i 'srpsko pitanje'," 284.

161. The most important part of this joint statement is quoted by Paul Mojzes in *Yugoslavian Inferno,* 147, 148, and "Camouflaged Role of Religion," 96, 97.

162. Radić, "Serbian Orthodox Church," 171.

163. Bougarel, *Bosnie,* 64.

CHAPTER 10. FINAL DELIBERATIONS

1. This process can be called "conservative revolution."

2. As discussed by Vrcan in *Vjera u vrtlozima tranzicije.*

3. See, e.g., Imamović, *Historija Bošnjaka,* 22; Džaja, *Konfesionalnost i nacionalnost,* 14.

4. Stavrianos, *Balkans since 1953,* 85.

5. Others include Poland, Transylvania, and the Iberian Peninsula before the *reconquista.*

6. See also Vrcan, "La guerra nell'ex Jugoslavia," 171.

7. For more on the Bosnian war, see Bougarel, *Bosnie,* 81–96. He points out that "the invariable initiators of ethnic cleansing were militias coming from outside," but they "always sought the participation of local people" (Bougarel, "Bosnia and Herzegovina," 104).

8. Vrcan, "La guerra nell'ex Jugoslavia," 170.

9. Cigar, *Genocide in Bosnia,* 4. Or "premediated strategy, rather than being an improvisation arising from unfolding events" (ibid., 47).

10. Among many clear examples are the events in Trebinje on May 5, 2001, and Banja Luka on May 7, 2001, when Serbian extremists held violent protests against the ceremonies at which foundations were to be laid for new mosques intended to replace the destroyed ones.

BIBLIOGRAPHY

Al-Aboudi, Mohammad Bin Nasir. "Muslim Experiences in Eastern Europe: A Firsthand Report." *Journal of Muslim Minority Affairs* 1 (1986): 88–99.

Anđelović, Petar. *Vjerni Bogu vjerni Bosni*. Sarajevo: Rabic, 2000.

Alexander, Stella: *Report on a Visit to Yugoslavia: Autumn 1968*. Oxford: Keston Institute Archive, 1969.

———. *Church and State in Yugoslavia Since 1945*. Cambridge University Press, 1979.

———. *Trostruki mit: Život zagrebačkog nadbiskupa Alojzija Stepinca*. Zagreb: Golia, 1990.

———. "Religion and National Identity in Yugoslavia." *Occasional Papers on Religion in Eastern Europe (OPREE)* 1 (1983): 1–19.

———. "Croatia: The Catholic Church and the Clergy, 1919–1945." In *Catholics, the State, and the European Radical Right, 1919–1945*, ed. Richard J. Wolff and Jorg K. Hoensch. New York: East European Monographs, 1987.

Ali, Rabia, and Lawrence Lifschultz, eds. *Why Bosnia? Writings on the Balkan War*. Stony Creek, Conn.: Pamphleteer's Press, 1993.

Antič, Igor. "Poletni zapiski iz dežele vitezov." *Delo,* September 21, 1996, 36.

Bagherzadeh, Alireza. "L'ingérence iranienne en Bosnie-Herzégovine." In *Le Nouvel Islam balqanique: Les musulmans, acteurs du post-communisme, 1990–2000*, ed. Xavier Bougarel and Nathalie Clayer. Paris: Maison and Larose, 2001.

Bakić, Ibrahim. *Nacija i religija*. Sarajevo: Bosna Public, 1994.

Balić, Smail. "Culture Under Fire." In *Why Bosnia? Writings on the Balkan War,* ed. Rabia Ali and Lawrence Lifschultz. Stony Creek, Conn.: Pamphleteer's Press, 1993.

Banac, Ivo. *Nacionalno pitanje u Jugoslaviji: Porijeklo, povijest, politika*. Zagreb: Globus, 1988

———. *Protiv straha*. Zagreb: Slon, 1992.

———. "Separating History from Myth." In *Why Bosnia? Writings on the Balkan War,* ed. Rabia Ali and Lawrence Lifschultz. Stony Creek, Conn.: Pamphleteer's Press, 1993.

———. "Multikulturalni identitet Bosne i Hercegovine." *Erazmus* 7 (1994): 4–7.
———. "Bosnian Muslims: From Religious Community to Socialist Nationhood and Postcommunist Statehood, 1918–1992." In *The Muslims of Bosnia Herzegovina: The Historic Development from the Middle Ages to the Dissolution of Yugoslavia*, ed. Mark Pinson. Harvard Middle Eastern Monographs 28. Cambridge, Mass.: Harvard University Press, 1996.

Batelja, Juraj. *Sluga Božji Alojzije Stepinac.* Zagreb: Nadbiskupijski Duhovni Stol, 1995.

Bax, Mart. *Medjugorje: Religion, Politics, and Violence in Rural Bosnia.* Amsterdam: V. U. Uitgeverij, 1995.

Bellah, Robert N. "Civil Religion in America." In *Culture and Society: Contemporary Debates*, ed. Jeffrey C. Alexander and Steven Seidman. Cambridge: Cambridge University Press, 1998.

Bellion-Jourdan, Jérôme. "Les réseaux transnationaux islamiques en Bosnie-Herzegovine." In *Le Nouvel Islam balqanique: Les musulmans, acteurs du post-communisme, 1990–2000*, ed. Xavier Bougarel and Nathalie Clayer. Paris: Maison and Larose, 2001.

Beloff, Nora. *Tito's Flawed Legacy: Yugoslavia and the West, 1939–1984.* London: Victor Gollancz, 1985.

Blažević, Jakov. "Predgovor reprintu." In *Magnum Crimen: Pola vijeka klerikalizma u Hrvatskoj*, by Viktor Novak. Belgrade: BIGZ, 1989.

Bogosavljević, Srđan. "Nerasvetljeni genocid." In *Srpska strana rata: Trauma i katarza u istorijskom pamćenju*, ed. Nebojša Popov. Belgrade: Republika, 1996.

Bougarel, Xavier. *Bosnie: Anatomie d'un conflit.* Paris: Éditions La Découverte, 1996.
———. "Ramadan During a Civil War (As Reflected in a Series of Sermons)." *Islam and Christian Muslim Relations* 1 (1995): 79–103.
———. "Bosnia and Herzegovina: State and Communitarianism." In *Yugoslavia and After: A Study in Fragmentation, Despair, and Rebirth*, ed. David A. Dyker and Ivan Vejvoda. London and New York: Longman, 1996.
———. "From Young Muslims to Party of Democratic Action: The Emergence of a Pan-Islamist Trend in Bosna-Herzegovina." *Islamic Studies* 36 (1997): 533–49.
———. "Bošnjaci pod kontrolom panislamista." *Dani (Sarajevo)*, June 18, 1999, 46–49; June 25, 1999, 46–49; and July 2, 1999, 48–50.
———. "Le ramadan, révélateur des évolutions de l'islam en Bosnie-Herzégovine." In *Ramadan et politique*, ed. Fariba Adelkhah and François Georgeon. Paris: CNRS, 2000.
———. "L'Islam bosniaque, entre identité culturelle et idéologie politique." In *Le Nouvel Islam balqanique: Les musulmans, acteurs du post-communisme, 1990–2000*, ed. Xavier Bougarel and Nathalie Clayer. Paris: Maison and Larose, 2001.

Branimirova Hrvatska u pismima pape Ivana VIII. Foreword by Mate Zekan. Split: Književni krug, 1990.

Bringa, Tone. *Being Muslim: The Bosnian Way (Identity and Community in a Central Bosnian Village)*. Princeton, N.J.: Princeton University Press, 1995.

Braude, Benjamin, and Bernard Lewis. "Introduction." In *Christians and Jews in the Ottoman Empire: The Functioning of a Plural Society*. Vol. 1, ed. Benjamin Braude and Bernard Lewis. New York and London: Holmes and Meier, 1988.

Bročić, Manojlo. "The Position and Activities of the Religious Communities in Yugoslavia with Special Attention to the Orthodox Church." In *Religion and Atheism in the USSR and Eastern Europe*, ed. Bohdan R. Bociurkiw and John W. Strong. London: Macmillan, 1975.

Buden, Boris. "'Europe is a Whore.'" In *Media & War*, ed. Nena Skopljanac Brunner, Alija Hodžić, and Branimir Krištofić. Belgrade: Agency Argument; Zagreb: Center for Transition and Civil Society Research, 2000.

Bugarski, Ranko. *Jezik od mira do rata*. Belgrade: Beogradski krug, 1994.

Buturović, Đenana, ed. *Od Đerđelez Alije do Tale Ličanina: Izbor iz usmene epike Bošnjaka*. Sarajevo: Svjetlost, 1996.

Cavalli, Fiorello. *Il processo dell'arcivescovo di Zagabria*. Rome: Edizioni La Civilta Cattolica, 1947.

Chadwick, Owen. *The Christian Church in the Cold War*. New York and London: Allen Lane, 1992.

Cigar, Norman. *Genocide in Bosnia: The Policy of "Ethnic Cleansing."* College Station: Texas A&M University Press, 1995.

———. *The Role of Serbian Orientalists in Justification of Genocide Against Muslims of the Balkans*. Sarajevo: Institute for the Research of Crimes Against Humanity and International Law; Bosnian Cultural Centre, 2000.

Ćimić, Esad. "Bosnian Crossroads." In *Religion and the War in Bosnia*, ed. Paul Mojzes. Atlanta: American Academy of Religions, Scholars Press, 1998.

Clogg, Richard. "The Greek Millet in the Ottoman Empire." In *Christians and Jews in the Ottoman Empire: The Functioning of a Plural Society*. Vol. 1, ed. Benjamin Braude and Bernard Lewis. New York and London: Holmes and Meier, 1988.

Cohen, Lenard J. "Bosnia's Tribal Gods: The Role of Religion in Nationalistic Politics." In *Religion and the War in Bosnia*, ed. Paul Mojzes. Atlanta: American Academy of Religions; Scholars Press, 1998.

Cohen, Philip J. *Serbia's Secret War: Propaganda and the Deceit of History*. College Station: Texas A&M University Press, 1996.

———. *Drugi svetski rat i suvremeni četnici*. Zagreb: Ceres, 1997.

Conte, Francis. *Sloveni*. Belgrade: Zavod za izdavačku djelatnost Filip Višnjić, 1989.

Craig, Mary. *Spark from Heaven: The Mystery of the Madonna of Medjugorje*. Toronto, London, Sydney, and Auckland: Hodder and Stoughton, 1988.

Crampton, R. J. *Eastern Europe in the Twentieth Century*. London, New York: Routledge, 1995.

Cviic, Christopher. "A Fatima in a Communist Land?" *Religion in Communist Lands* 10, no. 1 (1982): 4–9

Cvitković, Ivan. "Katolička crkva i nacija." *Pogledi* 4 (1983): 32–45.

Čolović, Ivan. *Pucanje od zdravlja*. Belgrade: Beogradski krug, 1994.

———. *Bordel ratnika: folklor, politika i rat*. Belgrade: Biblioteka XX. vek, 1994.

———. "Fudbal, huligani i rat." In *Srpska strana rata: Trauma i katarza u istorijskom pamćenju*, ed. Nebojša Popov. Belgrade: Republika, 1996.

Dartel, Geert Van. "The Nations and Churches in Yugoslavia." *Religion, State and Society* 20, nos. 3-4 (1992): 275–88.

———. "Towards a Culture of Peace: Remarks on the Religious Aspects of the War in Bosnia and Croatia." *Religion, State and Society* 23, no. 2 (1995): 199–206.

Davis, Scott, ed. *Religion and Justice in the War Over Bosnia*. New York and London: Routledge, 1996.

Debeljak, Aleš. *Somrak idolov*. Celovec-Salzburg: Založba Weiser, 1994.

———. *Oblike religiozne imaginacije*. Ljubljana: Znanstveno in publicistično središče, 1995.

Dedijer, Vladimir. *Vatikan i Jasenovac*. Belgrade: Rad, 1987.

Denitch, Bogdan. "Religion and Social Change in Yugoslavia." In *Religion and Atheism in the USSR and Eastern Europe*, ed. Bohdan R. Bociurkiw and John W. Strong. London: Macmillan, 1975.

Divjak, Jovan. "Prva faza rata, 1992–1993: borba za opstanak i nastanak Armije BiH." In *Rat u Hrvatskoj i Bosni i Hercegovini*, ed. Branka Magaš and Ivo Žanić. Zagreb-Sarajevo: Dani, 1999.

Dizdarević, Abdulatif. "Bosansko-hercegovački Muslimani Hrvati." In *Hrvatsko podrijetlo bosansko-hercegovačkih Muslimana*, ed. Petar Šarac and Miljenko Primorac. Zagreb: Hrvatska Hercegovačka zajednica "Herceg Stjepan," Vjesnik, 1992.

Djilas, Milovan. *Članci, 1941–1946*. Ljubljana: Cankarjeva založba, 1948.

Djordjević, Dimitrije. "The Tradition of Kosovo in the Formation of Modern Serbian Statehood in the Nineteenth Century." In *Kosovo: Legacy of a Medieval Battle*, ed. Wayne S. Vucinich and Thomas A. Emmert. Minneapolis: University of Minnesota Mediterranean and East European Monographs, 1991.

Djordjević, Dragoljub. "The Serbian Orthodox Church, the Disintegration of the Second Yugoslavia, and the War in Bosnia Herzegovina." In *Religion and the War in Bosnia*, ed. Paul Mojzes. Atlanta: American Academy of Religions, Scholars Press, 1998.

Donia, Robert T. *Islam under the Double Eagle: The Muslims of Bosnia Herzegovina, 1878–1914*. New York: East European Monographs, 1981.

———, and John V. A. Fine, Jr. *Bosnia Herzegovina: A Tradition Betrayed*. London: Hurst, 1994.

Dragojlović, Dragoljub. *Krstjani i heretička crkva bosanska*. (Summary in French) Belgrade: SANU, 1987.

Dugandžija, Nikola. *Jugoslavenstvo*. Belgrade: Mladost, n.d.

Duijzings, Ger. "The Kosovo Epic: Religion and Nationalism in Serbia." Ph.D. diss., School of Slavonic and East European Studies, University of London, 1999.

Duraković, Nijaz. *Prokletstvo Muslimana.* Sarajevo: Oslobođenje, 1993.

Dyker, David A. "The Ethnic Muslims of Bosnia: Some Basic Socio-Economic Data." *The Slavonic and East European Review* 119 (1972): London: 238–256

Džaja, Srećko M. *Konfesionalnost i nacionalnost Bosne i Hercegovine.* Sarajevo: Svjetlost, 1992.

———. "Bosna i Bošnjaci u hrvatskom političkom diskursu." *Erazmus* 9 (1994): 33–41.

———. "Od bana Kulina do Austro-Ugarske okupacije." In *Katoličanstvo u Bosni i Hercegovini.* Sarajevo: Napredak, 1997.

Ekmečić, Milorad. "Sudbina jugoslovenske ideje do 1914." In *Sveske Trećeg programa.* Belgrade: Radio Belgrade, 1973.

———. "The Emergence of St. Vitus Day as the Principal National Holiday of the Serbs." In *Kosovo: Legacy of a Medieval Battle,* ed. Wayne S. Vucinich and Thomas A. Emmert. Minneapolis: University of Minnesota Mediterranean and East European Monographs, 1991.

Epstein, Mark A. "The Leadership of the Ottoman Jews in the Fifteenth and Sixteenth Centuries." In *Christians and Jews in the Ottoman Empire: The Functioning of a Plural Society.* Vol. 1, ed. Benjamin Braude and Bernard Lewis. New York and London: Holmes and Meier, 1988.

Étienne, Bruno. *Radikalni islamizem.* Ljubljana: Cankarjeva založba, 2000.

Evans, Arthur J. *Pješke kroz Bosnu i Hercegovinu tokom ustanka augusta i septembra 1875.* Sarajevo: Veselin Masleša, 1973.

Filipović, Muhamed. Interview with author. "Moški plačani za brado, ženske za feredžo." *Delo,* Saturday supplement, August 5, 2000, 14–16.

Fine, John V. A., Jr. *The Bosnian Church: A New Interpretation (A Study of the Bosnian Church and Its Place and Society from the 13th to the 15th Centuries).* New York and London: East European Monographs, 1975.

———. "The Medieval and Ottoman Roots of Modern Bosnian Society." In *The Muslims of Bosnia Herzegovina: The Historic Development from the Middle Ages to the Dissolution of Yugoslavia,* ed. Mark Pinson. Harvard Middle Eastern Monographs 28. Cambridge, Mass.: Harvard University Press, 1996.

Freidenreich, Harriet Pass. *The Jews of Yugoslavia: A Quest for Community.* Philadelphia: Jewish Publication Society of America, 1979.

Friedman, Francine. *The Bosnian Muslims: Denial of a Nation.* Boulder, Colo.: Westview Press, 1996.

———. "The Bosnian Muslim National Question." In *Religion and the War in Bosnia,* ed. Paul Mojzes. Atlanta: American Academy of Religions; Scholars Press, 1998.

French, R. M. *Serbian Church Life.* New York: MacMillan, 1942.

Gazi, Stephen. *A History of Croatia.* New York: Philosophical Library, 1973.

Glavina, Frano. "Hrvati u travanjskom ratu 1941." *Vjesnik,* July, 1998.

Gojković, Drinka. "Trauma bez katarze." In *Srpska strana rata: Trauma i katarza u istorijskom pamćenju,* ed. Nebojša Popov. Belgrade: Republika, 1996.

Golubic, Stjepko, Susan Campbell, and Thomas Golubic. "How Not to Divide the Indivisible." In *Why Bosnia? Writings on the Balkan War*, ed. Rabia Ali and Lawrence Lifschultz. Stony Creek, Conn.: Pamphleteer's Press, 1993.

Gujić, Kasim. "Hrvatstvo Muslimana u Bosni i Hercegovini." In *Hrvatsko podrijetlo bosansko-hercegovačkih Muslimana*, ed. Petar Šarac and Miljenko Primorac. Zagreb: Hrvatska Hercegovačka zajednica "Herceg Stjepan," Vjesnik, 1992.

Hadžijahić, Muhamed. *Islam i Musliman u Bosni i Hercegovini.* Sarajevo: Svjetlost, 1977.

———. *Porijeklo bosanskih Muslimana.* Sarajevo: Bosna, (1990).

———, Mahmud Traljić, and Nijaz Šukrić. *Islam i Muslimani u Bosni i Hercegovini: El-Kalem.* Sarajevo: El Kalem, 1991.

Hadžikadić, Atif. "Potomci hrvatskog plemstva." In *Hrvatsko podrijetlo bosansko-hercegovačkih Muslimana*, ed. Petar Šarac and Miljenko Primorac. Zagreb: Hrvatska Hercegovačka zajednica "Herceg Stjepan," Vjesnik, 1992.

Hafner-Fink, Mitja. *Sociološka razsežja razpada Jugoslavije.* Ljubljana: Znanstvena knjižnica FDV, 1995.

———. "Jugoslovanska družba ali 'jugoslovanske' družbe-komparativna analiza socialne stratifikacije." Ph.D. diss. University of Ljubljana, 1993.

Handžić, Adem. *Population of Bosnia in the Ottoman Period: A Historical Overview.* Istanbul: IRCICA, 1994.

Handžić, Mehmed. *Islamizacija Bosne i Hercegovine i porijeklo bosansko-hercegovačkih Muslimana.* Sarajevo: Islamska dionička štamparija, 1940.

Hastings, Adrian. *The Construction of Nationhood: Ethnicity, Religion, and Nationalism.* Cambridge and New York: Cambridge University Press, 1997.

Heywood, Colin. "Bosnia under Ottoman rule." In *The Muslims of Bosnia Herzegovina: The Historic Development from the Middle Ages to the Dissolution of Yugoslavia*, ed. Mark Pinson. Harvard Middle Eastern Monographs 28. Cambridge, Mass.: Harvard University Press, 1996.

Hobsbawm, Eric J. *Nations and Nationalism since 1780.* Cambridge, New York, and Melbourne: Cambridge University Press, 1995.

Hosking, Geoffrey, and George Schöpflin, eds. *Myths and Nationhood.* London: Hurst and SSEES, University of London, 1997.

Huizinga, Johan. *Jesen srednjeg vijeka.* Zagreb: Naprijed, 1991.

Ilić, Veselin. *Mitologija i kultura.* Belgrade: Svet kulture, 1988.

Imamović, Mustafa. *Historija Bošnjaka.* Sarajevo: Bošnjačka zajednica kulture Preporod, 1998.

———. "Integracijske ideologije i Bosna." *Erasmus* 18 (1996): 38–47.

Irwin, Zachary T. "The Islamic Revival and the Muslims of Bosnia Herzegovina." *East European Quarterly* 4 (1983): 437–58.

———. "The Fate of Islam in the Balkans: A Comparison of Four State Policies." In *Religion and Nationalism in Soviet and East European Politics*, ed. Pedro Ramet. Durham, N.C., and London: Duke University Press, 1989.

Izetbegović, Alija. *Islamska deklaracija.* Sarajevo: Bosna, 1990.

Jahić, Adnan. "Krijeposna muslimanska država." In *Krv boje benzina*, ed. Fatmir Alispahić. Tuzla: Radio Kameleon, 1996.

Janković, Dragoslav. "Srbija i stvaranje Jugoslavije." In *Sveske Trećeg programa.* Belgrade: Radio Belgrade, 1973.

Jelavich, Charles. "The Revolt in Bosnia Herzegovina, 1881–1882." *Slavonic and East European Review* 31 (1953): 420–36.

Jezernik, Božidar. "Oči, da ne vidijo." *Nova revija* 9, nos. 3–4 (1990): 199–217.

Južnič, Stane. "Zgodovinske determinante jugoslovanske družbe." *Teorija in praksa* 27, 5 (1990): 552–66, and 6 (1990): 812–20.

Kapidžić, Hamdija. *Bosna i Hercegovina u vrijeme austrougarske vladavine.* Sarajevo: Svijetlost, 1968.

Karamatić, Marko. "U doba Austro-Ugarske (1878–1918)." In *Katoličanstvo u Bosni i Hercegovini.* Sarajevo: Napredak, 1997.

Kardelj, Edvard. *Razvoj slovenskega narodnega vprašanja.* Ljubljana: DZS, 1957.

Karpat, Kemal H. "Millets and Nationality: The Roots of the Incongruity of Nation and State in the Post-Ottoman Era." In *Christians and Jews in the Ottoman Empire: The Functioning of a Plural Society.* Vol. 1, ed. Benjamin Braude and Bernard Lewis. New York and London: Holmes and Meier, 1988.

Karup, Dženana. "Kur'an je naš ustav." *Dani (Sarajevo),* March 30, 1998, 14–19.

Kenny, Mary. "The Jury Is Still Out on Medjugorje 10 Years on." *Catholic Herald (London),* June 28, 1991, 7.

Kerševan, Marko. "Religija i (dez)integracijski procesi u Jugoslaviji." *Pogledi* 13, no. 4 (1983): 23–32.

———. "Nacionalna identiteta in religija v Jugoslaviji." *Teorija in praksa* 24, no. 7 (1987): 810–20.

——— "L'ambivalence dans la revitalisation religieuse dans les societes post-socialistes." *Social Compas* 1 (1993): 123–33.

Klaić, Nada. *Povijest Hrvata u ranom srednjem vijeku.* Zagreb: Školska knjiga, 1971.

———. *Izvori za hrvatsku povijest do 1526. godine.* Zagreb: Školska knjiga, 1972.

Klaić, Vjekoslav. *Povijest Hrvata: First Book.* Zagreb: Nakladni zavod Matice Hrvatske, 1980.

Kocbek, Edvard. *Dnevnik, 1945.* Ljubljana: Cankarjeva založba, 1991.

Kordić, Nikola J. *Hrvatski mučenici Pavao Radić i Đuro Basariček.* Mostar: Naklada N. Kordića, 1928.

Kordić, Radoman. *Nasilje svakidašnjice.* Belgrade: Slovo Ljubve, 1980.

Kotnik, Igor. "The Use of Language in Propaganda." In *Propaganda in War,* ed. Marjan Malešič. Stockholm: Styrelsen for Psykologiskt forsvar, 1998.

Krajina, Dijana. "Povojni trendi hiperreligioznosti in religijsko-nacionalnega ekskluzivizma (Študija primera Doboja in okolice)." *Časopis za kritiko znanosti* 29 (2001): 243–65.

Kraljević, Svetozar. *The Apparitions of Our Lady at Medjugorje.* Chicago: Franciscan Herald Press, 1984.

Krestić, Vasilije D. *Srpsko-hrvatski odnosi i jugoslovenska ideja u drugoj polovini XIX. Veka.* Belgrade: Nova knjiga, 1988.

Krizman, Bogdan. *Ustaše i Treći Reich.* Zagreb: Globus, 1986.

———. *Ante Pavelić i ustaše.* Zagreb: Globus, 1986.

————. *Pavelić u bjekstvu*. Zagreb: Globus, 1986.

————. "Pitanje priznanja ustaške države 1941. godine." *Posebni otisak Jugoslovenskog istorijskog časopisa.* Special issue, 1970.

————. "Hrvatske stranke prema ujedinjenju i stvaranju jugoslovenske države." In *Sveske Trećeg programa.* Belgrade: Radio Belgrade, 1973.

Kržišnik-Bukić, Vera. *Bosanska identiteta med preteklostjo in prihodnostjo.* Ljubljana: Inštitut za narodnostna vprašanja, 1996.

Kukoč, Mislav. "Konfesije i postkomunistički sukob civilizacija." *Društvena istraživanja* 4, no. 6 (1995): 937–47.

Kurtović, Todo. *Komunisti i nacionalne slobode.* Sarajevo: NIŠP Oslobođenje, 1975.

Kuzmanić, Tonči. "Iugoslavia: Una guerra di religione?" *Religioni e societa* 14 (1992): 107–22.

Landercy, M. *Le cardinal Stepinac: martyr des droits de l'homme.* Paris: Apostolat des Editions, 1981.

Lauer, Reinhard. "4C." *Razgledi,* June 11, 1993, 19–21.

Laurentin, Rene, and Henri Joyeux. *Scientific and Medical Studies on the Apparitions at Medjugorje.* Dublin: Veritas; Paris: OEIL, 1987.

———— and Ljudevit Rupčić. *La vierge apparait elle a Medjugorje.* Paris: OEIL, 1984. (English version: *Is the Virgin Mary Appearing at Medjugorje?* Washington: The Word Among Us Press, 1984.)

Lederer, Ivo J. "Nationalism and the Jugoslavs." In *Nationalism in Eastern Europe,* ed. Peter F. Sugar and Ivo John Lederer. Seattle and London: University of Washington Press, 1994.

Leger, Louis. *Slovenska mitologija.* Belgrade: Grafos, 1984.

Le Goff, Jacques. *Srednjovjekovna civilizacija zapadne Evrope.* Belgrade: Jugoslavija, 1974.

Lévi-Strauss, Claude. *The Raw and the Cooked: Introduction to a Science of Mythology.* London, Sydney, Auckland, and Bergvlei: Pimlico, 1994.

Levy, Moritz. *Sefardi u Bosni.* Sarajevo: Bosanska biblioteka, 1996.

Lockwood, William G. *European Muslims: Economy and Ethnicity in Western Bosnia.* New York: Academic Press, 1975.

Lopasic, Alexander. "Bosnian Muslims: A Search for Identity." *Brismes Bulletin* 2 (1981): 115–25.

Lovrenović, Dubravko. "Bosanski mitovi." *Erasmus* 18 (1996): 26–37.

Lovrenović, Ivan. "Bosna." *Erasmus* 18 (1996): 2–13.

————. "Bosanski Hrvati." *Feral Tribune (Split),* December 30, 2000, 56, 57.

Luke, Harry. *The Making of Modern Turkey: From Byzantium to Angora.* London: Macmillan, 1936.

Lukić, Reneo. "Greater Serbia. A New Reality in the Balkan." *Nationalities Papers* 1 (1994): 49–70.

Macan, Trpimir. *Povijest hrvatskoga naroda.* Zagreb: Nakladni zavod Matice Hrvatske; Školska knjiga, 1992.

Magaš, Branka, and Ivo Žanić, eds. *Rat u Hrvatskoj i Bosni i Hercegovini, 1991–1995.* Zagreb, Sarajevo, and London: Dani, 1999.

Magris, Claudio. *Il Mito Absburgico Nella Letteratura Austriaca Moderna.* Torino: Einaudi Editore, 1996.

Malcolm, Noel. *Bosnia: A Short History.* London: Papermac, 1996.

Malešič, Marjan. "Television Empirics (Serbian Television, Croatian Television)." In *Propaganda in War,* ed. Marjan Malešič. Stockholm: Styrelsen for Psykologiskt forsvar, 1998.

———. "Printed Media Empirics." In *Propaganda in War,* ed. Marjan Malešič. Stockholm: Styrelsen for Psykologiskt forsvar, 1998.

Mandić, Dominik. *Etnička povijest Bosne i Hercegovine.* Toronto, Zürich, Rome, and Chicago: Ziral, 1967.

———. *Franjevačka Bosna: razvoj i uprava Bosanske vikarije i provincije, 1340–1735.* Rome: Hrvatski povijesni institut, 1968.

———. "Herceg-Bosna i Hrvatska." In *Hrvatsko podrijetlo bosansko-hercegovačkih Muslimana,* ed. Petar Šarac and Miljenko Primorac. Zagreb: Hrvatska Hercegovačka zajednica "Herceg Stjepan," Vjesnik, 1992.

Markotich, Stan. "Serbian Orthodox Church Regains a Limited Political Role." *Transition* 2 (1996): 30–32.

Marković, Zoran N. "Nacija-žrtva i osveta." In *Srpska strana rata: Trauma i katarza u istorijskom pamćenju,* ed. Nebojša Popov. Belgrade: Republika, 1996.

Mastnak, Tomaž. *Kristjanstvo in muslimani.* Ljubljana: Znanstveno in publicistično središče, 1996

———. *Evropa: med evolucijo in evtanazijo.* Ljubljana: Studia humanitatis, Apes, 1998.

McCarthy, Justin. "Ottoman Bosnia." In *The Muslims of Bosnia Herzegovina: The Historic Development from the Middle Ages to the Dissolution of Yugoslavia,* ed. Mark Pinson. Harvard Middle Eastern Monographs 28. Cambridge, Mass.: Harvard University Press, 1996.

Mehtić, Halil. *Uloga Ilmije u odbrani bića Bosne.* Sarajevo: Vijeće Kongresa bošnjačkih intelektualaca, 1998.

Meier, Viktor. *Zakaj je razpadla Jugoslavija.* Ljubljana: Znanstveno in publicistično središče, 1996.

Meštrović, Ivan. *Spomini.* Ljubljana: Državna založba Slovenije, 1971.

Mihaljčić, Rade. *The Battle of Kosovo in History and in Popular Tradition.* Belgrade: BIGZ, 1989.

Mihaljević, Nikica. "Hrvaška v duhovno-kulturnih razvalinah." *Delo,* August-September, 1994.

Milinković, Branislav. "Propaganda and the Structure of the Public in Serbia." In *Propaganda in War,* ed. Marjan Malešič. Stockholm: Styrelsen for Psykologiskt forsvar, 1998.

Miller, Nicolai. "Two Strategies in Serbian Politics in Croatia and Hungary before the First World War." *Nationalities Papers* 23, no. 2 (1995): 327–51.

Miller, Robert F. "Church and State in Yugoslavia: Exorcising the Spectre of 'Clerico-Nationalism'." In *Religion and Politics in Communist States,* ed. Robert F. Miller and T. H. Rigby. Canberra: Australian National University, 1986.

Milosavljević, Olivera. "Jugoslavija kao zabluda." In *Srpska strana rata: Trauma i katarza u istorijskom pamćenju,* ed. Nebojša Popov. Belgrade: Republika, 1996.

———. "Zloupotreba autoriteta nauke." In *Srpska strana rata: Trauma i katarza u istorijskom pamćenju,* ed. Nebojša Popov. Belgrade: Republika, 1996.

Mirković, Mirko. "Versko pitanje u borbi za stvaranje jugoslovenske države." In *Sveske Trećeg programa.* Belgrade: Radio Belgrade, 1973.

Mojzes, Paul. *Church and State in Postwar Eastern Europe.* Westport, Conn.: Greenwood Press, 1987.

———. *Religious Liberty in Eastern Europe and the USSR Before and After the Great Transformation.* New York: East European Monographs, 1992.

———. *Yugoslavian Inferno: Ethnoreligious Warfare in the Balkans.* New York: Continuum, 1994.

———. "The Roman Catholic Church in Croatia and Its Contribution to National Sentiment." *Religion, State, and Society* 21, nos. 3–4 (1993): 391–93.

———. "The Camouflaged Role of Religion in the War in Bosnia Herzegovina." In *Religion and the War in Bosnia,* ed. Paul Mojzes. Atlanta: American Academy of Religions; Scholars Press, 1998.

Murad, Khurram. "The Death of Muslim Bosnia: A Tale of Two Cities." *Muslim World Book Review* 1 (1996): 3–15.

Murvar, Vatro. *Nation and Religion in Central Europe and the Western Balkans: The Muslims in Bosnia, Herzegovina and Sandžak: A Sociological Analysis.* Brookfield: University of Wisconsin, 1989.

Mužić, Ivan. *Pavelić i Stepinac.* Split: Logos, 1991.

———. *Katolička crkva: Stepinac i Pavelić.* Zagreb: Dominović, 1997.

Nenadović, Aleksandar. "'Politika' u nacionalističkoj oluji." In *Srpska strana rata: Trauma i katarza u istorijskom pamćenju,* ed. Nebojša Popov. Belgrade: Republika, 1996.

Norris, Harry Thirlwall. *Islam in the Balkans: Religion and Society Between Europe and the Arab World.* London: Hurst, 1993.

Obradović, Marija. "Vladajuća stranka." In *Srpska strana rata: Trauma i katarza u istorijskom pamćenju,* ed. Nebojša Popov. Belgrade: Republika, 1996.

O'Brien, Anthony Henry. *Archbishop Stepinac: The Man and His Case.* Westminster: Newman Bookshop, 1947.

Omerdić, Muharem. *Šehidi-svjedoci Vjere.* Sarajevo: Vijeće Kongresa bošnjačkih intelektualaca, 1997.

Opći šematizam katoličke crkve u Jugoslaviji (Cerkev v Jugoslaviji). Zagreb: Biskupska konferencija Jugoslavije, 1975.

Ovsec, Damjan J. *Slovanska mitologija in verovanje.* Ljubljana: Domus, 1991.

Pattee, Richard. *The Case of Cardinal Aloysius Stepinac.* Milwaukee: Bruce, 1953.

Pavković, Mladen. *Hrvatski mučenici.* Koprivnica: Glas Podravine, 1991.

Pavković, Aleksandar. "The Serb National Idea: A Revival 1986–1992." *Slavonic and East European Review* 3 (1994): 440–55.

Pavlowitch, Stevan K. *The Improbable Survivor: Yugoslavia and Its Problems, 1918–1988*. London: Hurst, 1988.

———. "En Yougoslavie: la religion totem du clan." *L'Autre Europe*, nos. 21–22 (1989): 245–62.

Perović, Latinka. "Beg od modernizacije." In *Srpska strana rata: Trauma i katarza u istorijskom pamćenju*, ed. Nebojša Popov. Belgrade: Republika, 1996.

Pešić, Vesna. "Rat za nacionalne države." In *Srpska strana rata: Trauma i katarza u istorijskom pamćenju*, ed. Nebojša Popov. Belgrade: Republika, 1996.

Petešić, Ćiril. *Katoličko svećeništvo u NOB-u, 1941–1945*. Zagreb: VPA-Vjesnik, 1982.

Pijade, Moša. *Izbrani spisi: I. tom, 5. knjiga*. Belgrade: Institut za izučavanje radničkog pokreta, 1966.

Pilar, Ivo. *Usud hrvatskih zemalja*. Zagreb: Consilium, 1997.

Pinson, Mark. "The Muslims of Bosnia Herzegovina under Austro-Hungarian rule." In *The Muslims of Bosnia Herzegovina: The Historic Development from the Middle Ages to the Dissolution of Yugoslavia*, ed. Mark Pinson. Harvard Middle Eastern Monographs 28. Cambridge, Mass.: Harvard University Press, 1996.

Pinto, Avram. *Jevreji Sarajeva i Bosne i Hercegovine*. Sarajevo: Veselin Masleša, 1987.

Pirjevec, Jože. *Jugoslavija, 1918–1992: Nastanek, razvoj in razpad Karadjordjevićeve in Titove Jugoslavije*. Koper: Lipa, 1995.

"Pismo bosanskega kralja Štefana Tomaševića papežu Piju II." In *Why Bosnia? Writings on the Balkan War*, ed. Rabia Ali and Lawrence Lifschultz. Stony Creek, Conn.: Pamphleteer's Press, 1993.

Pleterski, Janko. "Religija i crkva nemaju narodotvornu funkciju." *Kulturni radnik* 1 (1984): 40–50.

Poliakov, Leon. *Il mito ariano: Le radici del razzismo e dei nazionalismi*. Rome: Editori Riuniti, 1999.

Popov, Nebojša. "Traumatologija partijske države." In *Srpska strana rata: Trauma i katarza u istorijskom pamćenju*, ed. Nebojša Popov. Belgrade: Republika, 1996.

Popovic, Alexandre. "La communaute Musulmane de Yougoslavie sous le regime communiste: Coup d'oeil sur son histoire et sur les principales institutions." In *Les religions a l'est*, ed. Patrick Michel. Paris: Cerf, 1992.

Popović Radović, Mirjana. *Srpska mitska priča*. Belgrade: Pečat, 1989.

Powers, Gerard. "Religion, Conflict, and Prospects for Peace in Bosnia, Croatia, and Yugoslavia." In *Religion and the War in Bosnia*, ed. Paul Mojzes. Atlanta: American Academy of Religions; Scholars Press, 1998.

Požar, Petar. *Hrvatska pravoslavna crkva u prošlosti i budućnosti*. Zagreb: PIP, 1996.

Prvulovich, Žika R. *Religious Philosophy of Prince-Bishop Njegosh of Montenegro, 1813–1851*. Birmingham, UK: n.p., 1984.

Puhar, Alenka. "Genij in nekaj gnusnih klevet." *Delo*, August 23, 1997, 31

Purivatra, Arif. *Nacionalni i politički razvitak Muslimana.* Sarajevo: Svjetlost, 1969.

Radić, Radmila. "Crkva i 'srpsko pitanje'." In *Srpska strana rata: Trauma i katarza u istorijskom pamćenju,* ed. Nebojša Popov. Belgrade: Republika, 1996.

———. "Serbian Orthodox Church and the War in Bosnia Herzegovina." In *Religion and the War in Bosnia,* ed. Paul Mojzes. Atlanta: American Academy of Religions; Scholars Press, 1998.

Ramet, Pedro. *Nationalism and Federalism in Yugoslavia, 1963–1983.* Bloomington: Indiana University Press, 1984.

———. *Cross and Commissar: The Politics of Religion in Eastern Europe and the USSR.* Bloomington and Indianapolis: Indiana University Press, 1987.

———. "Religious Ferment in Eastern Europe." *Survey* 29, no. 4 (1984): 87–116.

———. "Primordial Ethnicity of Modern Nationalism: The Case of Yugoslavia's Muslims." *Nationalities Papers* 13, no. 2 (1985): 165–87.

———. "Autocephaly and National Identity in Church-State Relations in Eastern Christianity: An Introduction." In *Eastern Christianity and Politics in the Twentieth Century,* ed. Pedro Ramet. Durham, N.C., and London: Duke University Press, 1988.

———. "The Serbian Orthodox Church." In *Eastern Christianity and Politics in the Twentieth Century,* ed. Pedro Ramet. Durham, N.C., and London: Duke University Press, 1988.

———. "The Interplay of Religious Policy and Nationalities Policy in the Soviet Union and Eastern Europe." In *Religion and Nationalism in Soviet and East European Politics,* ed. Pedro Ramet. Durham, N.C., and London: Duke University Press, 1989.

———. "Religion and Nationalism in Yugoslavia." In *Religion and Nationalism in Soviet and East European Politics,* ed. Pedro Ramet. Durham, N.C., and London: Duke University Press, 1989.

Ramet, Sabrina Petra. *Balkan Babel: The Disintegration of Yugoslavia from the Death of Tito to the War for Kosovo.* 3d ed. Boulder, Colo.: Westview Press, 1992.

———. "Islam in Yugoslavia Today." *Religion in Communist Lands* 18, no. 3 (1990): 226–35.

———. "Nationalism and the 'Idiocy' of the Countryside: The Case of Serbia." *Ethnic and Racial Studies* 19, no. 1 (1996): 70–87.

Redžić, Enver. "Društveno-istorijski aspekt 'nacionalnog opredjeljivanja' Muslimana Bosne i Hercegovine." *Socializam* 5, no. 3 (1961): 31–89.

Resic, Sanimir. *American Warriors in Vietnam: Warrior Values and the Myth of the War Experience during the Vietnam War, 1965–1973.* Malmö, Sweden: Nordic Press, 1999.

Rooney, Lucy, and Robert Faricy. *Medjugorje Unfolds.* Herefordshire: Fowler Wright Books; Cork: Mercier Press, 1985.

———. *Mary, Queen of Peace.* Herefordshire: Fowler Wright Books, 1994.

Roter, Zdenko. *Katoliška cerkev in država v Jugoslaviji, 1945–1973.* Ljubljana: Cankarjeva založba, 1976.

Rusinow, Dennison I. *The Yugoslav Experiment, 1948–1974.* London: Hurst, 1977.

Šagi, Bono Zvonimir. Interview with author. "Sveti ratovi ne postoje." *Feral Tribune (Split),* January 6, 2001, 10, 11.

Šahinović-Ekremov, Munir. "Muslimani u prošlosti i budućnosti hrvatstva." In *Hrvatsko podrijetlo bosansko-hercegovačkih Muslimana,* ed. Petar Šarac and Miljenko Primorac. Zagreb: Hrvatska Hercegovačka zajednica "Herceg Stjepan," Vjesnik, 1992.

Said, Edward W. *Orientalizem-Zahodnjaški pogledi na Orient.* Ljubljana: ISH, Studia humanitatis, 1996.

Sarajevska Hagada. Sarajevo: Svjetlost, 1988.

Šanjek, Franjo. *Kršćanstvo na hrvatskom prostoru.* Zagreb: Kršćanska sadašnjost, 1991.

Schöpflin, George. "The Ideology of Croatian Nationalism." *Survey* 19, no. 4 (1973): 123–46.

———. "Nationality in the Fabric of Yugoslav Politics." *Survey* 25, no. 3 (1980): 1–19.

———. "Konservativna politika in konservativni dejavniki v postkomunističnih družbah." *Nova revija* 13, no. 3 (1993): 515–24.

———. "The Functions of Myth and a Taxonomy of Myths." In *Myths and Nationhood,* ed. Geoffrey Hosking and George Schöpflin. London: Hurst and SSEES (1997).

Shaw, Stanford J. "The Aims and Achievements of Ottoman Rule in the Balkans." *Slavic Review* 4 (1962): 617–22.

Selimović, Meša. *Derviš in smrt.* Ljubljana: Cankarjeva založba, 1978.

Sells, Michael A. *The Bridge Betrayed: Religion and Genocide in Bosnia.* Berkeley: University of California Press, 1996.

———. "Serbian Religious Nationalism, Christoslavism, and the Genocide in Bosnia, 1992–1995." In *Religion and the War in Bosnia,* ed. Paul Mojzes. Atlanta: American Academy of Religions; Scholars Press, 1998.

Šidak, Jaroslav. *Studije o "Crkvi Bosanskoj" i bogomilstvu.* Zagreb: Liber, 1975.

Šišić, Ferdo. *Pregled povijesti hrvatskoga naroda.* Zagreb: Nakladni zavod Matice Hrvatske, 1975.

Smrke, Marjan. *Religija in politika: Spremembe v deželah prehoda.* Ljubljana: Znanstveno in publicistično središče, 1996.

Špegelj, Martin. *Sjećanja vojnika.* Zagreb: Znanje, 2001.

Stavrianos, L. S. *The Balkans since 1953.* London: Hurst, 2001.

Stoianovich, Traian. "Factors in the Decline of Ottoman Society in the Balkans." *Slavic Review* 4 (1962): 623–32.

Stojanović, Dubravka. "Traumatični krug srpske opozicije." In *Srpska strana rata: Trauma i katarza u istorijskom pamćenju,* ed. Nebojša Popov. Belgrade: Republika, 1996.

Stojić, Mile. "Mrtvi." *Erasmus* 18 (1996): 62–67.

Sugar, Peter F. "The Historical Role of Religious Institutions in Eastern Europe and Their Place in the Communist Party-State." In *Religion and Nationalism in Soviet and East European Politics*, ed. Pedro Ramet. Durham, N.C., and London: Duke University Press, 1989.

———. "External and Domestic Roots of Eastern European Nationalism." In *Nationalism in Eastern Europe*, ed. Peter F. Sugar and Ivo John Lederer. Seattle and London: University of Washington Press, 1994.

Švagel-Resić, Rudolf. *Hrvatski mučenici.* Županja: n.p., 1941.

Tanner, Marcus. *Croatia: A Nation Forged in War.* New Haven, Conn., and London; Yale University Press, 1997.

Tashkovski, Dragan. *Bogomilism in Macedonia.* Skopje: Macedonian Review Editors, 1975.

Tismaneanu, Vladimir. *Fantasies of Salvation: Democracy, Nationalism, and Myth in Post-Communist Europe.* Princeton, N.J.: Princeton University Press, 1998.

Todorova, Maria. *Imaginarij Balkana.* Ljubljana: Inštitut za civilizacijo in kulturo, 2001.

Tomashevich, George Vid. "The Battle of Kosovo and the Serbian Church." In *Kosovo: Legacy of a Medieval Battle*, ed. Wayne S. Vucinich and Thomas A. Emmert. Minneapolis: University of Minnesota Mediterranean and East European Monographs, (1991).

Tomashevich, Jozo. *The Chetniks.* Stanford, Calif.: Stanford University Press, 1975.

Tomašić, Dinko. *Politički razvitak Hrvata.* Zagreb: Hrvatska književna naklada, 1938.

———. "Osebnost in kultura v vzhodnoevropski politiki." *Nova revija* 9, nos. 3–4 (1990): 176–99.

Tomičić, Martin. "Narodnost bosanskih Muslimana." In *Hrvatsko podrijetlo bosansko-hercegovačkih Muslimana*, ed. Petar Šarac and Miljenko Primorac. Zagreb: Hrvatska Hercegovačka zajednica "Herceg Stjepan," Vjesnik, 1992.

Tomka, Miklos. "Coping with Persecution: Religious Change in Communism and in Post-Communist Reconstruction in Central Europe." *International Sociology* 13, no. 2 (1998): 229–48.

Tudjman, Franjo. *Stvaranje socialističke Jugoslavije.* Zagreb: Naprijed, 1960.

———. *Nationalism in Contemporary Europe.* New York: East European Monographs, 1981.

Ugrešić, Dubravka. *Kultura laži: Antipolitički eseji.* Zagreb: Biblioteka Bastard, Arkzin, 1996.

Vasilj, Snježana. "Od rimskog osvajanja do bana Kulina." In *Katoličanstvo u Bosni i Hercegovini.* Sarajevo: Napredak, 1997.

Velikonja, Mitja. *Masade duha: Razpotja sodobnih mitologij.* Ljubljana: Znanstveno in publicistično središče, 1996.

———. "Religija in cerkev: dejavnika oblikovanja nacionalnih mitologij v post-socialističnih družbah." *Družboslovne razprave* 12 (1996): 57–67.

———. "Liberation Mythology: The Role of Mythology in Fanning War in the Balkans." In *Religion and the War in Bosnia*, ed. Paul Mojzes. Atlanta: American Academy of Religions; Scholars Press, 1998.

———. "Historical Roots of Slovenian Christoslavic Mythology." *Religion in Eastern Europe* 19, no. 6 (1999): 15–32.

———. "Sharpened Minds: Religious and Mythological Factors in the Creation of the National Identities in Bosnia-Herzegovina." In *Religious Quest and National Identity in the Balkans*, ed. Celia Hawkesworth, Muriel Heppell and Harry Norris. London: Palgrave in association with the School of Slavonic and East European Studies, University College, 2001.

———. "*In hoc signo vinces:* Religious Symbolism in the Balkan Wars 1991–1995." Paper presented at the Conference for International Convergence, "Nationality and Citizenship in post-Communist Europe," Paris, July 9 and 10, 2001.

Vodopivec, Peter. "Srednja Evropa, nekdanja Jugoslavija in Balkan: novi ali stari nacionalizmi?" *Glasnik Slovenske matice* 17, nos. 1-2 (1993): 1–14.

Voje, Ignacij. *Nemirni Balkan: Zgodovinski pregled od 6. do 18. stoletja.* Ljubljana: DZS, 1994.

Vrcan, Srdjan. *Vjera u vrtlozima tranzicije.* Split: Glas Dalmacije, 2001.

———. "The War in Former Yugoslavia and Religion." *Religion, State and Society* 22, no. 4 (1994): 367–78.

———. "La guerra nell'ex Jugoslavia: il coinvolgimento delle religioni." In *Mare di guerra, mare di religioni*, ed. Luciano Martini. Florence: ECP, 1994.

———. "Orthodoxy in Balkan Political Conflicts." In *Identities and Conflicts: Mediterranean*, ed. Furio Cerutti and Rodolfo Ragionieri. London: Palgrave, 2001.

Vucinich, Wayne S. "The Nature of Balkan Society Under Ottoman Rule." *Slavic Review* 4 (1962): 597–616, 633–38.

———. "Introduction." In *Kosovo: Legacy of a Medieval Battle*, ed. Wayne S. Vucinich and Thomas A. Emmert. Minneapolis: University of Minnesota Mediterranean and East European Monographs, 1991.

Vujović, Sreten. *Grad u senci rata.* Novi Sad: Prometej, 1997.

———. "Nelagoda od grada." In *Srpska strana rata: Trauma i katarza u istorijskom pamćenju*, ed. Nebojša Popov. Belgrade: Republika, 1996.

Vukšić, Tomo. "Od 1918 do naših dana." In *Katoličanstvo u Bosni i Hercegovini.* Sarajevo: Napredak, 1997.

West, Richard. *Tito and the Rise and Fall of Yugoslavia.* London: Sinclair-Stevenson, 1994.

Wolf, Richard J., and Hoensch, Jorg K., eds. *Catholics, the State, and the European Radical Right, 1919–1945.* New York: Social Science Monographs, 1987.

Žabkar, Anton. "Neutrudni kovači stereotipov." *Delo*, March 19, 1994, 28, 29.

Žanić, Ivo. *Mitologija inflacije: Govor kriznog doba.* Zagreb: Globus, 1987.

———. "Pisac na osami." *Erasmus* 18 (1996): 48–54.

———. *Prevarena povijest: Guslarska estrada, kult hajduka i rat u Hrvatskoj i Bosni i Hercegovini, 1990–1995. godine.* Zagreb: Durieux, 1998.

Žerjavić, Vladimir. *Gubici stanovništva Jugoslavije u drugom svjetskom ratu.* Zagreb: Jugoslovensko viktimološko društvo, 1989.

Zgodić, Esad. *Ideologija nacionalnog mesijanstva.* Sarajevo: Vijeće Kongresa bošnjačkih intelektualaca, 1999.

Zirojević, Olga. "Kosovo u kolektivnom pamćenju." In *Srpska strana rata: Trauma i katarza u istorijskom pamćenju,* ed. Nebojša Popov. Belgrade: Republika, 1996.

Zovkić, Mato. "War Wounds in Croatian Catholic Population in Bosnia Herzegovina." In *Religion and the War in Bosnia,* ed. Paul Mojzes. Atlanta: American Academy of Religions; Scholars Press, 1998.

Zulfikarpašić, Adil. *Okovana Bosna: Discussion with Vlado Gotovac, Mika Tripalo, and Ivo Banac.* Zürich: Bošnjački institut, 1995.

———. *Bošnjak Adil Zulfikarpašić: Dialogue with Nadežda Gaće and Milovan Đilas.* Zürich: Bošnjački institut; Zagreb: Globus, 1995.

INDEX

Abdić, Fikret, 254–55, 325n1
Acontius (papal legate), 25
Adrian IV (Pope), 53
Aehrenthal, Alois, 140
Akšamović, Antun, 172, 318n29
Albania, during World War II, 163, 177
Albanians and Serbian mythmaking, 100
Alcalay, Isaak, 160
Alexander, Stella, 157, 187, 199
Alexander I (king), 154
Alexander II (Pope), 43
alphabets. *See* languages/alphabets
Amfilohije, Bishop, 266, 323n63
ancestor cult, 58, 74, 101, 128, 217–18. *See also* myths/mythmaking
Anđelović, Petar, 270–71, 280, 329n82
Andrassy, Julius, 117, 118
Andrić, Ivo, 96
Arkan, Željko Ražnatović, 247, 265
Armenian millet, defined/described, 59, 62
Arnautović, Šerif, 138
Arsenije, Metropolite, 214
Arsenije III Crnojević (patriarch), 76
Arsenije IV Šakabenta (patriarch), 76
Artemije, Bishop, 266
Ashkenazi Jews, 129–30, 160
Association of Contemporary Christian Theologians (TDKS), 205–206

associations, clerical (post-World War II): Roman Catholic, 202–206; Serbian Orthodox, 214–16
Atanasije, Bishop, 264, 267, 268
Austria, 58, 81–82
Austro-Hungarian empire: Balkan aspirations, 117–21, 140–41; and nationalization processes, 122–23, 130–40; religious communities described, 121–30

Baba, Hasan Quaimi, 71
Babukić, Vjekoslav, 109
Bajazit (Ottoman sultan), 48, 51
Bakarić, Vladimir, 196, 199
Bakić, Ibrahim, 14, 220, 221, 229
Baković, Ante, 250, 270
Banac, Ivo, 18, 73, 101, 113, 131, 239–40
Barbucci, Nicholas, 37
Barthes, Roland, 247
Bašeskija, Mula Mustafa Ševki, 71
Basilij, Bishop, 98
Batrić, Duke, 95
Battle of Kosovo. *See* Kosovo battle/mythmaking
Bauer, Anton, 151–53, 154, 158
Bauerlein, Stjepan, 200
Bax, Mart, 208, 209
Bećković, Matija, 95, 217–18

Croat mutiny, 319*n*56

Croats, Bosnian: under Austro-
Hungarian protectorate, 123, 124,
134–41; post-World War II, 194,
195, 229–33; during World War II,
165, 181; during Yugoslavia's disintegration, 236–39, 252, 270–72. *See
also* Croatia

Crusaders, 300–301*n*16

Čule, Petar, 152, 200, 203–204, 207

Cvijić, Jovan, 104

Cvijović, Josif, 177

Cyril (Byzantine missionary), 22, 40

Cyrillic alphabet, 169, 258

Dalmatia, during Middle Ages, 24, 33,
40, 42–43

Danilo, Patriarch, 49

Dayton Peace Agreement, 266–67, 282

Dećanski, Stephen, 46

Dedijer, Vladimir, 165

Delić, Rasim, 279

dervish orders, 70, 220

devşireme practice, 62, 65

Đikić, Osman, 139

Dizdarević, Abdulatif, 132

djed (Bosnia Church bishop), 30

Djilas, Milovan, 150, 157, 192, 198

Djordjević, Dimitrije, 95, 97

Djozo, Imam Hadži Hussein, 225, 226

Djuretić, Veselin, 241

Dobri pastir (Good Shepard), 202–203

Domagoj movement, 158

Dominican clergy (Middle Ages), 25,
26, 35

Donia, Robert T., 131

Dorotić, Andrija, 106

Draganović, Krunoslav, 170–71

Dragojlović, Dragoljub, 28

Dragonja, Bishop, 25

dragon myths. *See* myths/mythmaking

Dragosavac, Dušan, 228

Drašković, Vuk, 244–45, 268

Đujić, Momčilo, 178, 246

Dušan the Strong, 38, 46–47

Džabić, Ali Fehmi efendi, 135

Džaja, Srećko, 57, 66, 67

Džanić, Ferid, 319*n*56

Džemijet Party, 147

Ekmečić, Milorad, 113–14

elections/referendums: in early *1990*s,
236–38; between World Wars, 147

Eljas, Gerz, 86

El Mujahid military unit, 332*n*143

Emeric (king), 24

emigrations. *See* migrations/emigra-
tions

Erasmus, 52

ethnic cleansings: during Bosnian war,
254, 255; and Serbian mythmaking, 97–99; during World War I,
141; during World War II, 164–67,
169–71, 173–74, 177, 201–202, 209

ethnic group, defined, 297*n*2

ethno-origin theories/myths: under
Austro-Hungarian protectorate,
98–99, 131–33; during Bosnian war,
240–42, 247–48, 250, 256; during
Middle Ages, 39–40; and nationalistic mythmaking, 103–104, 106–
107, 108–109, 111, 112; post-World
War II, 206–207, 216, 222; during
World War II, 165, 179, 180; between World Wars, 149. *See also*
myths/mythmaking

Eugene IV (Pope), 34, 37

European Union, 237

Fazilibegović, Nusref, 219

Filipović, Miroslav, 173

Filipović, Muhamed, 333*n*151

Finci, Jakob, 282, 284

Fine, John, 23, 30, 31, 32

Firdus, Osman Nuribeg, 148

ISBN 1-58544-226-7

90000